From Puerto Rico to Philadelphia

From Puerto Rico to Philadelphia

Puerto Rican Workers and Postwar Economies

Carmen Teresa Whalen

TEMPLE UNIVERSITY PRESS

PHILADELPHIA

Temple University Press, Philadelphia 19122
Copyright © 2001 by Temple University
All rights reserved
Published 2001
Printed in the United States of America

Library of Congress Cataloging-in-Publication Data

Whalen, Carmen Teresa, 1964–
  From Puerto Rico to Philadelphia : Puerto Rican workers and postwar economies /
Carmen Teresa Whalen.
    p. cm.
  Includes bibliographical references (p.) and index.
  ISBN 1-56639-835-5 (cloth : alk. paper) — ISBN 1-56639-836-3 (pbk. : alk. paper)
    1. Puerto Ricans—Pennsylvania—Philadelphia—Economic conditions—20th century.
2. Puerto Ricans—Migrations—History—20th century. 3. Puerto Ricans—Pennsylva-
nia—Philadelphia—Social conditions—20th century. 4. Puerto Rico—Emigration and
immigration—History—20th century. 5. Philadelphia (Pa.)—Emigration and immigration—History—20th century. 6. Philadelphia (Pa.)—Economic conditions—20th
century. 7. Philadelphia (Pa.)—Social conditions—20th century. 8. Puerto Rico—
Economic conditions—1952- . 9. Puerto Rico—Social conditions—20th century.
I. Title.

F158.9.P85 W53 2001
305.868'72950748—dc21   00-034349

ISBN 13: 978-1-56639-836-7 (paper : alk. paper)

110807P

Dedicado a la memoria de mi abuelito,
José Francisco Beauchamp Pagán (1913–1993)

Contents

Photographs follow pages 82 and 174

Maps, Figures, and Tables

Acknowledgments

This project has been a long and rewarding journey, made possible by the generous support of many people along the way. My deepest appreciation goes to the people whose stories fill the pages of this book. As the director and as a migrant, Carmen Aponte first welcomed me to the Norris Square Senior Citizens' Center in North Philadelphia in 1991. I spent countless hours there, visiting, conversing, and interviewing. When I returned to the Center after completing my dissertation, the new director, Carmen Constable, and the activities director, Sister Noelita Rodríguez, welcomed me again. I thank everyone at the Center for their warm hospitality and for sharing their wealth of knowledge with me. Ana Benítez and Israel Colón introduced me to others in Philadelphia's Puerto Rican community. I've been deeply touched by the many people who have welcomed me in their homes, introduced me to their families, and shared their histories with me. I hope that I have done justice to their stories and have given them in return something they can share with their families.

Approaching churches in Philadelphia and Puerto Rico, I was again welcomed warmly, as people provided me with access to their records, space to work, and conversations that were enjoyable and informative. I started at La Milagrosa, where Sister John Judith D'Alessandro opened their doors to me, permitting me to return again and again. Pastor Jaime Rodríguez made the records of La Primera Iglesia Bautista Hispana available to me, shared his knowledge of the church's history and its mission, and introduced me to members of the church. Reverend Frank Kensill at the Methodist Memorial Temple told me the history of the church and its work with the Puerto Rican community, while helping me locate available records. At St. Peter the Apostle Church, Father John McGowen and everyone else were just as kind and helpful. In San Lorenzo, Padre William Spillane and Padre Marco Wise welcomed me at Parroquia Nuestra Señora de las Mercedes. In Salinas, Padre Angel M. Sánchez Párroco and Padre Edwin Vázquez Vega at Nuestra Señora de Monserrate assisted me in every way they could, and our many conversations over lunch taught me a great deal about Salinas.

At all the archives I visited, I found staff who were extremely talented and dedicated. My special thanks go to those who helped me delve into materials that had not yet been inventoried, with skill and patience beyond the call of duty. Pedro Juan Hernández helped me unearth materials in the documents of Puerto Rico's Migration Division, first at the Department of Puerto Rican Community Affairs in the United States and later, when the collection was transferred, at the Centro de Estudios Puertorriqueños. Margaret Jerrido and the entire staff at Temple University's Urban Archives helped me discover materials on Puerto Ricans in the Archive's Collections, while making my time there a pleasant experience. At Philadelphia's City Hall, the staff of the Court of Orphans Pleas and the Court of Common Pleas took the time to help me locate what I needed. Everyone at the Archivo General de Puerto Rico, especially Milagros Pepín, made the extraordinary effort that enabled me to locate important documents in the very large and not yet organized collections of the Department of Labor. The sheer number of boxes I examined created a tremendous amount of work for all involved, and I appreciate their willingness to do it.

The book has benefited immeasurably from the insightful comments, queries, and suggestions of the many people who were kind enough to take time from their busy schedules to read all or portions of the manuscript. My colleagues Pedro Cabán, Paul Clemens, and Virginia Yans-McLaughlin have been vital throughout the process of transforming the project from a dissertation into the book it has become. Their willingness to discuss issues and strategies, to ask the difficult questions, to read and read again, and to share their keen insights have enriched the book tremendously. Sam Baily, Alice Kessler-Harris, and David Levering Lewis offered invaluable suggestions on the directions in which to move from the dissertation to the book. In the early stages of the project, Jackson Lears encouraged me to explore possible connections between the street fighting in Philadelphia and the "culture of poverty," and Regina Kunzel encouraged me to foreground the competing agendas of policy makers and migrants. Graciously agreeing to read chapters, sometimes on very short notice, Jerma Jackson and Félix Matos Rodríguez lent their ideas, skills, and support, improving the book and giving me the courage to finish it. Although too numerous to name, I appreciate the commentators, co-panelists, and audiences at the various forums where I have presented my work, as well as my students over the years, who have asked challenging questions and probed the issues I've presented while adding many of their own.

In a profession where so much is learned by trial and error, I have found that the occasional kind word or bit of guidance has had a tremendous impact on my ability to complete this book and on the quality of my everyday work life. In addition to those mentioned above, I thank all of my colleagues at Rutgers University, faculty and staff, in the Puerto Rican and Hispanic Caribbean Studies Department, the History Department, and Women's Studies for helping me to find my way and for lightening my load at critical moments. My sincere appreciation goes to my former colleague, José Morales, for his crucial support in my first years as a faculty member at Rutgers, and to Monica Licourt, for her amazing skills as a departmental administrator and for keeping me and the department afloat every day, too often without the recognition she deserves. From the very beginning, Pedro Cabán has been a dedicated mentor and friend. For inspiration, helpful conversations, and encouraging words, I thank Rudy Bell, Frank Bonilla, Roger Daniels, Linda

Delgado, Antonio Díaz Royo, Kenneth Kusmer, George Lipsitz, Clara Rodríguez, Vicki Ruiz, Virginia Sánchez Korrol, Neil Smith, Andrés Torres, and Olga Jiménez Wagenheim.

Several fellowships provided the time and resources to complete this book. In 1996–1997, I received a postdoctoral research fellowship from the International Migration Program of the Social Science Research Council with funds provided by the Andrew W. Mellon Foundation, enabling me to continue my research in Puerto Rico. The following year, I had a residency fellowship with the Sweatshop Project, a Rockefeller Foundation Humanities Institute sponsored by the Lower East Side Tenement Museum in collaboration with UNITE. I strengthened my treatment of the garment industry in this project, while beginning new research on New York City's garment industry. Rutgers University's generous support enabled me to take advantage of these fellowships through its Competitive Fellowship Leave program. A faculty fellowship from Rutgers's Center for the Critical Analysis of Contemporary Cultures in 1998–1999 offered an intellectually stimulating environment to pursue issues, develop comparisons, and keep writing.

In bringing the book to fruition, I was again fortunate. Several dedicated and skilled research assistants provided indispensable aid, with my special thanks to Isai Acevedo, Sally Fuentez, Manuel Rodríguez, and Víctor Vázquez. María Ocasio and Maritza Raimundi transcribed oral histories and helped with translations with sensitivity, enthusiasm, and a willingness to discuss them with me for hours on end. In reproducing photographs, I relied on the skills of Axel Santana and Kevin Martin. Going beyond the basics, Mike Siegel took a sincere interest in my materials and taught me a great deal about maps, as he produced the maps for this book. I thank Doris Braendel for her support of this project and for her tireless efforts to publish the emerging scholarship on Puerto Ricans in the States.

My heartfelt thanks go to my many families for nurturing me over the years, encouraging me in this work, and never losing faith in me. The book is dedicated to the memory of my grandfather, José Francisco Beauchamp Pagán, who along with my grandmother, Carmen María González de Beauchamp, and my mother, Carmen Beauchamp DaCosta, taught me to love learning and to respect my family, my elders, and who I am and where I come from. My thanks to all of the Beauchamps, Whalens, and DaCostas for trusting that I was doing something worthwhile even when it was hard to tell exactly what I was doing or why. Your support and our family reunions have nourished my spirit and kept me going. To Jerma Jackson, Kay Hagemann, Stephanie Westnedge, laurie prendergast, and Peggy Hunter and family, I could not have done this without your encouragement through the years and your reminders that no matter how important the work may be, the life beyond it beckons. I thank Janice Loux, for coming to know me at such a challenging point in my life and for believing in me always.

From Puerto Rico to Philadelphia

Chapter One

Looking for Work in the Global Economy: An Introduction

Sitting in the Norris Square Senior Citizen's Center in North Philadelphia, Doña Epifania reminisced about her decision to leave Coamo, Puerto Rico:

> You didn't earn money. I am from a family of twelve children and my parents were poor, but we never lacked everyday things, because it was a parcel of 89 *cuerdas,* and with that we lived, from the crops and the animals. . . . We were poor but we had what we needed. [My father] worked with four daughters and just one son, and no one outside the family worked there. You harvested a lot and it lasted the year. The only thing we sold were the *gandules.*

Born in 1911, Doña Epifania came to the Philadelphia area in 1954 as a single mother, when someone she knew in Coamo told her about a job. "The man who brought me had worked in the Greenhouse. He went to Puerto Rico . . . and told me there were beans to cook. I came here and cooked for fourteen workers." Although it was men who were recruited for agricultural work, such as that at the Greenhouse, some women found jobs as well. Doña Epifania worked for wages and free housing. With her first paycheck, she sent for her eleven-year-old son, who had stayed with her parents. Telling her, "I'm going to help you with this boy," her boss gave him a job. Her son earned $7.50 a week watering plants and then worked in the farm's market, giving half of what he made to his mother.[1]

After two years at the Greenhouse, Doña Epifania moved to Philadelphia, lived with a friend, and found another job:

> Another friend of mine told me, "Let's go to the factory, I'm going to take you and they are going to give you work right away." Right away they chose me, took me to the office, asked me my name and social security. They gave me the job even though I didn't know English, but I could learn it.

For seventeen years Doña Epifania worked, with many other Puerto Ricans, mostly women, as a sewing machine operator. She explained, "At first they gave me, I think, for two or three weeks a small check for two hundred dollars. . . . You didn't know the laws well," but she considered it "a good union and a good job, the only thing was they moved to Florida." In the early 1970s her company relocated. Doña Epifania, however, had made Philadelphia her home; she had bought a house and married in 1960. While visiting a senior citizens center in Coamo, she was offered another job. "They offered me a job right away," she recounted. "I asked what they were going to give me and they told me the kitchen and I said, 'Oh my God, the worst, no I'm not going to work.'" With the closing of her garment factory, Doña Epifania had retired at the age of sixty-one.

Doña Epifania's narrative reveals important contours of Puerto Rican migration to Philadelphia. Like Doña Epifania, most migrants came to Philadelphia from rural areas. In the post–World War II era, Puerto Rico shifted from an agricultural economy with a predominantly rural population to an industrialized society with a largely urban population. According to economic historian James Dietz, Puerto Rico's "transformation from an agricultural economy was compressed into less than twenty-five years, from the late 1940s to 1970—one of the more rapid industrial revolutions." Economic change and government policies prompted massive emigration from Puerto Rico's rural areas to urban areas, both in Puerto Rico and in the States. Describing it as "one of the greatest population exoduses registered in contemporary history," demographer José Vázquez Calzada calculates that more than a million people left the rural areas of Puerto Rico between 1940 and 1970, with 700,000 moving to Puerto Rico's urban areas and 388,000 to the continental United States. As a result, the rural population decreased from 70 to 42 percent of the total in that thirty-year period.[2]

Coinciding with these dramatic shifts, the growth of Philadelphia's Puerto Rican population illustrates the causes of migration and of Puerto Ricans' increasingly dispersed settlement in the States. The postwar era was the peak period of Puerto Rican migration, as the population grew from fewer than 70,000 in 1940 to 1,391,463 in 1970. Although scholarly and public attention has focused on New York City, the history of Puerto Rican migration has been defined by dispersion. Whereas 88 percent of U.S. Puerto Ricans lived in New York City in 1940, only 58 percent made the city their home in 1970. This trend continued, and by 1990 only one-third of Puerto Ricans lived in New York City. As migrants settled beyond the barrios of New York, the Puerto Rican population in Philadelphia grew rapidly—from fewer than 2,000 to more than 14,000 during the 1950s. The city soon had the third largest Puerto Rican community in the country, behind New York and Chicago. By 1970, close to 27,000 Puerto Ricans lived in Philadelphia, and in 1990, with a Puerto Rican population of almost 68,000, Philadelphia remained the third largest Puerto Rican community in the States.[3]

This history of Puerto Rican migration to Philadelphia in the postwar era also helps to remedy the invisibility of Puerto Ricans in U.S. history. This is the first full-length historical work on the peak period of Puerto Rican migration since 1959, when Oscar Handlin's *The Newcomers* addressed Puerto Ricans and African Americans in New York City.[4] U.S. immigration history, defined largely by the study of European immigrants at the turn of the century, has ignored Puerto Ricans, who are U.S. citizens and post–World War II migrants. Puerto Ricans have also been omitted from most U.S. labor, social, and women's histories of the postwar era.[5] Meanwhile, Puerto Rican Studies, which emerged as an interdisciplinary field in the 1970s, has been dominated by disciplines that focus on contemporary issues. While early works provided important overviews, detailed historical studies relying on historical methodologies have emerged slowly, and tend to focus on New York City between the World Wars. Although works on the Puerto Rican diaspora are increasing, Philadelphia has so far received very little attention.[6]

As a product primarily of the postwar migration, Philadelphia's Puerto Rican community illuminates the causes of migration, its regional and gendered dimensions, and the economic changes that affected Puerto Rican migrants in the States. While some rural households, like Doña Epifania's, relied primarily on subsistence economic activities, most also depended on commercial agriculture in the declining sugar, tobacco, and coffee industries. Confronting the rural economic crisis in their local communities, people migrated in search of work and came to Philadelphia through government-sponsored contract labor programs or *por su cuenta,* on their own. Philadelphia's economy sustained the migration by providing jobs. As Doña Epifania's work history suggests, men found agricultural work surrounding the city and women found work in the city's garment industry. Social networks increased the migration, as migrants helped each other to finance the airfare and to find housing and jobs. Doña Epifania got both of her jobs through friends, and after settling in the city she reciprocated. When she visited Puerto Rico, her nieces and nephews wanted to come to Philadelphia, so she paid their airfare:

> They all came to my house and worked and gave me money. After work, I cooked for nine people. If I tell you the story, I'll never finish! They were all my nephews and nieces and on Fridays I collected money from each of them. Then they got married.

Once in Philadelphia, "They started working right away because my husband found them work." Yet, as migrants struggled to recreate their household economies, Philadelphia shifted from a manufacturing to a service economy. Puerto Ricans, who had made the city their home, became displaced labor migrants. Doña Epifania was not the only one to lose her job as factories relocated or closed.[7]

Redefining Labor Migration

In the post–World War II era, Puerto Rican men and women came to Philadelphia as labor migrants. Highlighting the interplay of structural factors and of human agency in shaping migration, my definition of labor migration bridges Puerto Rican Studies with immigration, labor, and women's history. First, Puerto Ricans became labor migrants because they were displaced from Puerto Rico's rural economies. Second, Puerto Ricans were recruited as a source of cheap labor through both formal, government-sponsored contract labor programs and less formal employer recruitment. Third, although recruited as laborers, Puerto Ricans were not always welcomed as community members. Finally, Puerto Rican migrants were individuals and household members seeking work and a better life. They were looking for work in a global economy.

Economic change in the postwar era displaced Puerto Rico's rural peoples. Agriculture, agricultural processing, and the home needlework industry declined, while the economic development strategy based on export-oriented industrialization failed to replace lost jobs. Employment decreased during the 1950s. The colonial relationship between the United States and Puerto Rico defined Puerto Rico's niche in the global economy, and made Puerto Ricans U.S. citizens. State policies in the United States and Puerto Rico affected economies and directly promoted migration, assuring that the economic and political causes of migration were thoroughly intertwined. The regional dimensions of economic change and government policies affected local communities, and it was from within their local communities and their households that people perceived and responded to changing conditions and developed strategies for economic survival. Migrating in search of work, with or without government-sponsored labor contracts, was one of those strategies. Residents of rural areas became part of Puerto Rico's massive internal migration and of the migration to the States.

Although labor migrants are still often portrayed as men, Puerto Rican women's narratives reveal the complexities of women's "work" and provide the basis for a redefinition of labor migration that includes women. Women as well as men were displaced by economic change, they were recruited as a source of cheap labor, and they migrated in search of work. Women like Doña Epifania considered themselves "workers." Reflecting on her life, Doña Epifania remarked, "I've spent my life working since I was six years old," and "I don't complain because I was a worker." She noted that in Coamo she contributed to her household's economy, and that among her brothers and sisters she was "the one that helped my father the most." She also considered her mother's domestic tasks as work: "My mother worked a lot in the kitchen." In addition to reproductive and subsistence work, she and her mother took in home sewing, getting materials on Mondays and delivering shirts on Fridays. Earning $18 a week, she gave half of what she made to her mother and still saved $80 before migrating. In Puerto Rico and in the States, her definition of "work" included her mother's reproductive work, subsistence labor on the family farm, home sewing, and paid employment outside the home.[8]

Arguing that women are labor migrants requires greater attention to gender divisions of labor in the countries of origin and destination, as well as a broader definition of "labor." Here I take "labor" to include reproductive and subsistence work, paid employment within and beyond the household, informal economic activities, and community work both paid and unpaid. This approach draws extensively on the scholarship on women and development, which examines women's productive labor, gender divisions of labor, and the impact of economic development policies. This literature has not, however, fully included reproductive labor, nor connected the impact of economic development with women's migration.[9] While immigration historians have focused more on women's reproductive roles within their families and communities, scholars of Puerto Rican migration have treated women as labor migrants, emphasizing their paid employment, especially in New York's garment industry.[10] Still, the intersections of productive and reproductive work require fuller exploration, supported here by my broad definitions of "labor" and the "household economy." I define the household economy as what its self-defined members do in order for the household to survive and prosper. The household can be nuclear, extended, or alternative, and its economy can include reproductive and subsistence labor, paid employment, the financial contributions of migrant laborers, informal economic activities, and/or transfer payments, such as welfare, food stamps, or social security.[11]

Puerto Rican women contributed to their household economies in a variety of ways both in Puerto Rico and in the States. In their oral history narratives Puerto Rican women emphasized the continuities in their contributions to their household economies even though the contexts changed considerably, from Puerto Rico's rural areas to an urban area in the States. While balancing productive and reproductive work was challenging and assumed different forms at various points in their lives, these women did not understand paid employment outside the home as a conflict in gender roles. By redefining labor migration and by connecting women's displacement from Puerto Rico's rural economies with their search for paid employment in the States, this book challenges the persisting notion that "work" is something migrating women discover in the host society. In addition, attention to women's labor migrations is pivotal in understanding the increased migration of the postwar era, migrants' destinations, their economic strategies, and their efforts to recreate their household economies. Likewise, economic changes affecting urban areas in the States displaced Puerto Rican women from the labor force. As Puerto Rican women became displaced labor migrants, the poverty of Puerto Rican communities in the inner cities increased.[12]

While Puerto Ricans came to Philadelphia *buscando mejor ambiente,* in search of a better life, they were recruited for jobs that traditionally relied on the cheap labor of immigrants or African Americans: farm and railroad work for men, domestic and garment work for women. The post–World War II era is often portrayed in immigration history as a hiatus between European immigrations at the turn of the century and renewed immigration after 1965. Despite Puerto Ricans' absence from U.S. historiography, this era is a hiatus only if migrants are separated from immigrants and if im/migration and labor history are treated as separate and unrelated endeavors. Instead, during the postwar era, U.S. labor needs were met by Puerto Ricans, southern African Americans, and Mexicans, as well as by increasing numbers of women. Like southern African Americans, Puerto Ricans have been recruited most heavily precisely when European immigration has been restricted, especially after the first and second World Wars. Labor migration, then, is not best understood only as the crossing of national boundaries. Puerto Rican migration demonstrates that labor migration includes internal and transnational elements and is best understood as a global process. In this sense, Puerto Rican migration has been a missing link in im/migration and labor history.[13]

Highlighting a central paradox of labor migration, Puerto Ricans arrived as unwanted community members, despite their recruitment as cheap labor. In his assessment of U.S. immigration policies, Aristide Zolberg contends, "The very characteristics that made them desirable as *workers* made them undesirable as *members* of the receiving society." As a result, U.S. immigration policy created a "'back door' through which American employers imported successive groups of temporary workers," who were then "confined to a prescribed economic role and excluded from membership in the national society." Similarly, economist Michael Piore argues that migrant workers solved the problem of filling jobs at the bottom of the occupational hierarchy precisely "because they come from outside and remain apart from the social structure in which the jobs are located." As long as workers were viewed as temporary, few problems arose; however, the transition to permanent settlement sparked "problems" and became "a focal point of clashes between native and foreign populations" that were "aggravated by latent racial and national prejudices." The benefit to U.S. employers, who recruited low-wage laborers, stemmed from the fact that these workers were "marginal," especially where "ethnic and racial traits provide a convenient criteria for limiting entry and justifying the distinctions among the work force that such limitations maintain."[14]

Puerto Ricans' U.S. citizenship meant that, unlike foreign workers, they could not be deported when their labor was no longer needed. During World War II, U.S. policy makers were reluctant to recruit Puerto Ricans precisely because their status as U.S. citizens meant that they could stay in the States. The limited recruitment of Puerto Ricans and more extensive recruitment of southern African Americans was accompanied by policy makers' efforts to ensure that their migrations would be "seasonal" and therefore temporary. Of course, since Puerto Ricans and African Americans are U.S. citizens, policy makers had no enforcement authority. Mexicans, however, also recruited for agricultural work, were brutally deported when their labor was no longer needed, graphically depicting the tension between wanting laborers and not wanting community members. In helping growers secure a vulnerable group of foreign agricultural workers, historian Cindy Hahavamovitch concludes, "the federal government intervened on behalf of growers, undermining farmworkers' bargaining power and relieving growers of the need to recruit labor by improving wages and conditions."[15]

As U.S. citizens, not undocumented workers or illegal aliens, Puerto Ricans were theoretically entitled to all the rights and privileges accorded other citizens. Yet they still had characteristics deemed undesirable by the receiving society. They were, after all, both a racially heterogeneous and racially mixed group, and a Spanish-speaking group with a distinctive culture. The U.S. Commission on Civil Rights observed in 1976, "The United States has never before had a large migration of citizens from offshore, distinct in culture and language and also facing the problem of color prejudice." In the postwar era, U.S. policy makers officially classified Puerto Ricans as mostly "white" and as "citizens," while many people in the States defined Puerto Ricans as "colored" and as "foreigners." Even arriving as U.S. citizens in a largely state-organized migration did not render Puerto Rican migrants acceptable in public sentiment. In Philadelphia new neighbors, social service workers, and policy makers reacted with alarm, and sometimes with open hostility, to Puerto Rican settlement in the city.[16]

At the same time, academic discourses characterized Puerto Ricans as having a "culture of poverty." Rather than an accurate assessment of Puerto Ricans, the "culture of poverty" was a historically specific national discourse that evolved into a racial ideology. Anthropologist Oscar Lewis was not the sole architect of this racial ideology, but he articulated the concept clearly, applying it to Puerto Ricans. In a 1965 work, Lewis considered "poverty and its associated traits as a culture . . . with its own structure and rationale, as a way of life which is passed down from generation to generation along family lines." For Lewis this "relatively thin" culture was characterized by minimal integration into the larger society, minimal organization within the ethnic community, families that verbally emphasized unity but rarely achieved it, and individuals with a high tolerance for pathology. He also saw "fatalism and a low level of aspiration as one of the key traits for the subculture of poverty." Lewis severed the "culture of poverty" from the conditions of poverty as the former became self-perpetuating and equated with the "national culture" of Puerto Rico. Migrating Puerto Ricans carried this culture of poverty with them, so that "many of the problems of Puerto Ricans in New York have their origin in the slums of Puerto Rico."[17]

This ahistorical perspective is fundamentally at odds with an interpretation of Puerto Ricans as labor migrants responding to changes in a global economy. Instead of an economic displacement motivated by a search for work, Puerto Rican migration was attributed to personal problems, to "overpopulation," and to a desire for welfare dependency. For example, Lewis wrote, "Although economic factors, such as low income and unemployment, created an atmosphere conducive to migration, we found that noneconomic factors were actually more important . . . the precipitating factor for leaving Puerto Rico was most often a personal social-psychological crisis." Writing in the postwar era, C. Wright Mills, Clarence Senior, and Rose Kohn Goldsen emphasized overpopulation: "The population pressures upon the island are so acute and the need for adjustment so grave that these movements can be expected to continue." Historian Oscar Handlin agreed: "Puerto Rico's central problem since its annexation to the United States has been overpopulation." Similarly, Nathan Glazer and Daniel Patrick Moynihan commented that "the economic pinch on the individual grew tighter because, just as his demands and desires were rising, his family was growing, too, and to sizes that were exceptional even for Puerto Rico." They included welfare among the causes of migration: "One must not underestimate another set of material advantages: the schools, hospitals, and welfare services." Once in New York City, welfare supplanted Puerto Ricans' national culture: "The culture of welfare . . . is as relevant for the future of Puerto Ricans in the city as the culture of Puerto Rico." As Puerto Ricans won the dubious distinction of being among the first to be cast as migrating in search of welfare benefits, the tension between wanting them as workers and rejecting them as community members dissipated—Puerto Ricans were portrayed as welfare dependent.[18]

Meanwhile, the new immigration history was reclaiming European immigrants' culture. Challenging Oscar Handlin's portrayal of "uprooted peasants," the new immigration history argued that European immigrants' culture was resilient and dynamic and mediated their confrontation with their new environment. The resultant scholarship was rich with attention to cultural adaptations and immigrant agency, with nuanced community studies, and with explorations of the connections between home towns and new areas of settlement. Yet even as they stressed immigrants' agency, scholars devoted little attention to economic exploitation, nativism, or the anti-Catholicism and anti-Semitism that confronted the immigrants. Since John Higham's *Strangers in the Land* first appeared in 1955, immigration and nativism have remained separate areas of study. Although southern and eastern European immigrants were unwelcome in their own time, in retrospect they have appeared as an "immigrant success story," largely as a result of this emphasis on agency, cultural resiliency, and ethnic communities, and of an expanding economy that enabled upward mobility. Even as they have sought to connect immigrant agency with the global economy, immigration historians often portray the global economy as a neutral and inevitable process with little attention to the unequal relations between countries. Continuing an earlier emphasis on southern and eastern European immigrants, immigration historians addressed neither Puerto Ricans nor the post–World War II era, instead citing uncritically and often works written during the peak period of Puerto Rican migration that were imbued with the "culture of poverty."[19]

Puerto Rican Studies, on the other hand, challenged the "culture of poverty" thesis by providing structural analyses of the causes of migration and poverty in the States. In contrast to immigration history, Puerto Rican Studies scholars focused on colonialism and economic exploitation, linking colonialism and global capitalism to explain the displacement of Puerto Ricans. In their assessments of the economic conditions of Puerto Ricans in the States, they turned to dual labor market theories or internal colonialism. This was not the immigrant success story. Nor was it the culture of poverty, since scholars treated Puerto Ricans as labor migrants. While this scholarship proliferates, providing an alternative to the culture of poverty perspectives in the dominant scholarly and public discourses, few of the works have used historical methodologies. This lack of historical work has mitigated against fully linking structure to human agency, or historical roots to contemporary issues.[20]

My treatment of Puerto Ricans as labor migrants and of the "culture of poverty" as a historically specific racial ideology provides a fundamental critique of the "culture of poverty" perspectives still embedded in the mainstream literature on Puerto Ricans. In defining Puerto Ricans as labor migrants, I draw on Puerto Rican Studies' attention to structural factors, to unequal relations between countries and within national borders, and to the gender dimensions of economic development, labor migration, and economic incorporation. At the same time, I provide a historical perspective, employing methodologies from immigration history that foreground migrants' agency, community studies, and the connections between sending and receiving societies. As a result, my work provides the first micro-level analysis of Puerto Rican migration, detailing migrants' origins and their destinations and including the ways gender has shaped migration and settlement patterns. I rely extensively on church records, archival materials that have been largely unused and are not yet inventoried, published and unpublished government documents, and oral histories. By bridging these fields, this full-length historical work on Puerto Rican migration in the postwar era seeks to link structure and agency, revealing the complexity of Puerto Rican migration and its human dimensions.

From the Global to the Local

Levels of analysis from the global to the local explain the causes of Puerto Rican migration and the contemporary poverty affecting Puerto Rican communities in the inner cities. Therefore, the causes of Puerto Rican migration emerged from the global econ-

omy, the colonial relationship between the United States and Puerto Rico, state policies, regional and local economies, social networks, and the decisions migrants made.
Similarly, the causes of contemporary inner-city poverty are rooted in the postwar
globalization of the economy, state policies, and the local economy. In the case of
Puerto Rico, colonial ties set the unequal power dynamics of the global economy in
sharp relief. Globalization in the postwar era brought U.S. corporations to Puerto
Rico, dislocating the economy and the people. By the 1960s, the relocation of manufacturing industries from the inner cities of the States to other regions and overseas was
displacing Puerto Ricans. The role of the state, in both Puerto Rico and the United
States, is also crucial to understanding the causes of migration and of contemporary
conditions in the inner cities. In addition to economic development programs, Puerto
Rico's government directly promoted emigration. While the lack of immigration
restrictions may seem to limit the role of the U.S. government, the United States was
an active participant in the contract labor programs that brought migrants to the
States. In addition, U.S. economic development and housing policies affected Puerto
Ricans in the inner cities. Nor does the state constitute a solely structural component
of migration and its consequences; ideological perspectives and assumptions shape policy makers' attitudes and the decisions they make. In other words, policy makers had
human agency, too.[21]

Attention to the global economy, colonial ties, and the state, however, does not
diminish the significance of the local, of social networks, and of human agency. Instead,
I use local communities—San Lorenzo, Salinas, and Philadelphia—as loci for examining the impact of the global, the colonial, and the state on communities and on people's
lives. Such an approach does not isolate these communities from larger trends and
dynamics, but it does allow for local differences and varying responses. It was, after all,
from within their local communities that Puerto Ricans perceived and responded to economic change and government policies. Their economic strategies were derived from
their local communities and their households in Puerto Rico and in Philadelphia. Social
networks of family and friends shaped migration and settlement, as Puerto Ricans
helped each other finance migration or signed up for labor contracts together, and then
helped each other find jobs and housing in Philadelphia. The question then is not
whether formal contract labor programs or informal networks brought people to
Philadelphia but rather how they interacted with each other and with changing economic conditions. Likewise, the concern is how the global economy and social networks
were connected. Chapters 2 through 6 cover the period roughly between 1945 and
1970, addressing and connecting these various levels of analysis to provide a historical
perspective on the causes and consequences of Puerto Rican migration to Philadelphia
in the postwar era. The last chapter brings the discussion from the postwar era to 1990,
and the Epilogue revisits the postwar era, as well as the comparative dimensions of the
Puerto Rican experience.

The colonial relationship set the parameters for Puerto Rican migration to the continental United States. The United States acquired Puerto Rico in 1898 at the end of the
Spanish-Cuban-American War and has retained sovereignty over the island ever since.

In 1917, the U.S. Congress passed the Jones Act, which made Puerto Ricans citizens of the United States. Both the legal and economic aspects of the colonial relationship were solidified in the post–World War II period. The U.S. military presence in Puerto Rico increased dramatically as the United States acquired more territory for bases, and as Puerto Ricans continued to serve in the armed services.

Economic policies fostered industrialization with U.S. capital and increased migration. Puerto Rico's political ties to the United States were formalized as Puerto Rico became the *Estado Libre Asociado* or the Commonwealth of Puerto Rico in 1952. The U.S. Congress, concerned with the decolonization mandate of the United Nations Charter and with U.S. relations with Latin America, passed a bill specifying the process in 1950, and two years later Puerto Rico's new constitution was accepted by a referendum in Puerto Rico and by the U.S. Congress. Although debated in Puerto Rico, the United States, and the United Nations, this political status has remained unchanged to this day. This colonial relationship increased Puerto Rican migration in the postwar era via its effects on Puerto Rico's economy and its fostering of both contract labor programs and the unfettered functioning of informal networks.[22]

The colonial relationship defined Puerto Rico's insertion into the expanding global economy, and U.S. government policies and U.S. investors had a direct impact on Puerto Rico's economy. In 1950, economist Harvey Perloff noted that "the most striking fact about the character of Puerto Rico's external trade is its close tie to the United States." Puerto Rico sent only 4 percent of its exports to other countries and received only 8 percent of its imports from outside the United States. U.S. tariff policy, as Perloff contended, "reflects changing economic and political situations on the mainland and requires adjustment of the Puerto Rican economy to mainland influences." According to economist Richard Weisskoff, Puerto Rico's economy is "subject to two sets of economic laws"—one set determined by U.S. policies and the U.S. labor market, and the other by "Puerto Rico's own rules and logic." The colonial relationship continued to affect Puerto Rico's agricultural economies in the postwar era, and as Puerto Rico's strategy for economic development shifted to industrialization the United States continued to play a defining role. For Weisskoff, Puerto Rico's model for industrial development was "a return to the familiar colonial plantation model of the nineteenth and early twentieth centuries, in which the foreigner owns and operates the factory while the local elite oversees the workers and overlooks the foreigner." Puerto Rico became an investment site for U.S. capital and a market for U.S. goods.[23]

The massive displacement of Puerto Rico's rural peoples was shaped by a particular kind of economic development based on export-oriented, labor-intensive industrialization. Political economists Frank Bonilla and Ricardo Campos demonstrate that the "larger the increment of capital, the higher the rate of unemployment," and that this unemployment and subsequent migration "are a result of swift industrialization, not a problem of backwardness." The model of industrialization was based on private, foreign investment (in this case from the United States) and export-oriented, labor-intensive industries that relied on tax incentives and cheap labor, especially of women. Export-oriented industrialization creates few linkages in the economy and few additional jobs, as marketing and support services remain based in the investor's country of origin. Puerto Rico's industrialization program, known as Operation Bootstrap or *Operación Manos a la Obra*, failed to generate sufficient employment. As agriculture declined, total employment decreased during the 1950s, and between 1940 and 1970 labor force participation declined substantially. While many policy makers and scholars measure the success of industrialization by the Gross National Product, with employment levels a secondary concern, Dietz emphasizes the contradictions: "Just when the most rapid growth of GNP was occurring, unemployment levels were rising and a growing number of people were migrating to the mainland in search of work."[24]

The architects of Puerto Rico's economic development were the politicians and policy makers of the Partido Popular Democrático (PPD). Under the leadership of Luis Muñoz Marín, the PPD dominated Puerto Rico's politics from their landslide victory in 1944 to the election of a pro-statehood governor in 1968. Founded in 1938, the PPD stepped into the political vacuum created during the Depression, when the traditional political dominance of U.S. sugar corporations and local sugar growers was undermined and a short-lived Nationalist and workers' alliance collapsed under political repression and internal ideological differences. Elements of their political program were outlined in the "Chardón Plan" for the restructuring of Puerto Rico's economy in light of the economic crisis in the sugar industry. The plan called for reduced sugar production, state-controlled sugar mills, more diversified agriculture, an industrialization program, and emigration. Although the Chardón Plan was not implemented, President Franklin D. Roosevelt established New Deal programs in Puerto Rico by executive order, and the resultant patronage was used to build a political machine that became the PPD. The party's rapid ascendancy was characterized by its close relationship with U.S. political leaders. Electoral victories in 1940 foreshadowed their landslide victory in the 1944 elections. The PPD worked closely with appointed Governor Rexford G. Tugwell, and when he resigned in 1946 the PPD was in a position to influence the appointment of the first Puerto Rican governor, Jesús T. Piñero. In 1947, the U.S. Congress passed the elective governor's law, and Luis Muñoz Marín became the first elected governor of Puerto Rico.[25]

Given the colonial relationship, scholars debate the extent to which the PPD operated autonomously or as "mere puppets used by the metropolis at will." There is no question that the politicians and policy makers of the PPD developed strategies and made decisions within the confines of the colonial relationship. Political sociologist Emilio Pantojas-García contends that "development strategies within the colonial context represent particular modes of accumulation of imperialist capitalism that assume the subordination of wage labor to capital as well as the political subordination of the colony to the United States." Rather than threatening U.S. economic or political interests, the "development strategies in Puerto Rico are the ideological representation of the political project of a class coalition that represents the interests of metropolitan and local dominant sectors." At the same time, PPD and U.S. policy makers shared ideologies that shaped Puerto Rico's economic development strategy. As political economist Pedro Cabán notes, a "vision of state-society relations evolved gradually and reflected the thinking of the most powerful and politically sophisticated sectors in Puerto Rico and

Washington." PPD leaders, many of whom had studied and worked in the States, were "influenced by their exposure to American liberal thought" and "technocratic ideology," according to historian Michael Lapp, and their New Deal experiences in Puerto Rico merged "a liberal technocratic strain of American social science" with "populist politics in Puerto Rico."[26]

As a result, the colonial context forged an economic development strategy based on the decline of agriculture, increasing industrialization, and the reduction of Puerto Rico's population through population control and emigration. Policy makers in Puerto Rico and the United States perceived Puerto Rico's "problems" in similar ways and proposed similar solutions. They defined Puerto Rico's continuing "problem" as "overpopulation," industrialization as the only possible economic solution, and emigration and population control as crucial corollaries to economic development. Women were at the nexus of this strategy, as industrialization relied on the cheap labor of Puerto Rican women, and as population control promoted the sterilization and emigration of women. Through Puerto Rico's industrialization, U.S. investors reaped tax-free profits. Industrialization did not, however, offset the loss of agricultural jobs or increase employment in Puerto Rico. In addition, the "solutions" crafted in the post–World War II period—tax exemptions, U.S. investment, migration, and the later food stamp program—were dependent on closer and more permanent ties between Puerto Rico and the United States.[27]

Building on the scholarship in Puerto Rican Studies, which has emphasized the colonial relationship, industrialization, and island-wide trends, in Chapter 2 I explore the regional and gender dimensions of economic change, government policies, and migration, as well as how these dimensions shaped the towns of origin of Puerto Rican migrants in Philadelphia. Although the colonial relationship set the parameters for Puerto Rican migration, there were important regional and gender dimensions to economic change, government policies, and emigration that have not been fully explored in the existing literature.[28] In 1950, Puerto Rico was a largely agricultural society with three main commercial crops—sugar, tobacco, and coffee—that were grown in different geographical regions. While all regions were characterized by commercial agriculture combined with subsistence economic activities, the production of these crops created regional variations in landholding patterns, household structures, and the gender division of labor. Most manufacturing work was in agricultural processing and the home needlework industry. Agricultural decline affected Puerto Rico's crops and regions differently, while the industrialization program concentrated new manufacturing jobs in the metropolitan area and employed mostly women. These regional and gender dimensions in turn fostered internal migration and migration to the States, creating a Puerto Rican community in Philadelphia that reflected the economic crisis in Puerto Rico's rural areas.

In addition to economic development, the state shaped migration through government-sponsored contract labor programs. In Chapter 3 I examine the competing agendas of Puerto Rico's policy makers, U.S. policy makers, and Puerto Rican migrants. For Puerto Rico's policy makers, contract labor programs were a key component of efforts to reduce the population. Despite their initial reluctance to recruit Puerto Ricans because of their status as U.S. citizens, U.S. policy makers turned to contract labor and Puerto Ricans to meet the needs of U.S. capital for cheap labor in the States in the post-war era. These were gender-based programs that recruited Puerto Ricans for areas of work that had traditionally relied on the labor of immigrants and African Americans. Puerto Rican women were contracted as domestics, and the men for seasonal food processing, seasonal agricultural work, and the railroads. While the government of Puerto Rico promoted permanent settlement in the States, U.S. policy makers remained ambivalent about accepting Puerto Ricans as permanent community members. Meanwhile, Puerto Rican migrants used labor contracts as their own economic strategy, some for seasonal income and others as a vehicle for permanent settlement. Contract labor programs contributed to the growth of the Puerto Rican community in Philadelphia and revealed the ways in which migrants' actions could complement or contradict policy makers' objectives.

In Chapter 4 I look more closely at the impact of economic changes and government policies in two *municipios* in different regions, San Lorenzo and Salinas, and at the choices migrants faced and the decisions they made to leave their local communities.[29] Both municipios sent a significant number of migrants to Philadelphia. San Lorenzo, a tobacco-producing municipio, and Salinas, a sugar-producing municipio, had different modes of production, gender divisions of labor, and household economies. Yet both had economies based on agriculture and agricultural processing, and both comprised households that combined work in commercial agriculture with subsistence activities. As both tobacco and sugar production declined, neither municipio benefited from Puerto Rico's industrialization program. Employment decreased and people migrated in search of work. Within these local contexts, Puerto Ricans developed economic strategies that included the difficult decision to leave their homes. Both municipios experienced significant emigration as residents joined the massive migration within Puerto Rico and to the States. Individuals left on their own or using labor contracts; significant numbers of men from both municipios signed on for farm labor contracts. Their destinations reflected the regional and gendered dimensions of economic change in Puerto Rico, the impact of the contract labor program, and economic opportunities in the States. Migrants from San Lorenzo and Salinas settled in Philadelphia and elsewhere, responding to the availability of unskilled jobs in the States.

Shaping contract labor programs, Puerto Ricans' status as U.S. citizens also enabled them to migrate to the States free from immigration restrictions. Extolling the virtues of combining industrialization with emigration, in a 1965 work economist Stanley Friedlander recognized the role of the colonial relationship: "The unique relationship was responsible for the absence of immigration barriers and allowed for the large-scale movement of the Puerto Rican population." U.S. citizenship facilitated migration and influenced migrants' destinations, as a 1947 study found that less than two percent of Puerto Ricans went to other countries. Migrants could respond to the availability of jobs in the States, and those who settled in the city could send for family and friends, without regard for the restrictive national origins provisions of U.S. immigration policy before 1965, or for the family reunification categories instituted in the 1965 Immigration Act.[30]

The postwar reconversion left gaps in Philadelphia's labor market, and for a time Puerto Rican migrants found particular jobs readily available, which is the subject of Chapter 5. In addition to those who came to the area with labor contracts, other migrants came directly to the city without contracts. The jobs available to Puerto Rican men and women, however, were determined within a labor market divided along racial and gender lines. Puerto Ricans found work in the secondary labor market, in low-paying jobs that required few skills and offered poor working conditions, little job security, and few avenues for economic mobility. As they struggled to recreate their household economies, migrants became concentrated in specific sectors of the city's economy, with men in the service industries, especially restaurants and hotels, and women in the garment and food processing industries.

Despite labor recruitment and U.S. citizenship, Puerto Ricans were not always welcomed in the city as community members or neighbors. In Chapter 6 I explore the reception of Puerto Ricans in the City of Brotherly Love. Puerto Ricans arrived in the city during an era of racial change and tension, as southern African Americans came to the city and whites left for the suburbs, and as civil rights activism continued. As recent scholarship suggests, racial change and civil rights activism played out not just as national phenomena, but also as a series of intense local confrontations.[31] Like African Americans, Puerto Ricans confronted the hostilities that accompanied racial change in the postwar era. In July 1953 street fighting broke out between whites and Puerto Ricans in one Philadelphia neighborhood. Social service workers and policy makers transformed this incident from a racially motivated attack against Puerto Ricans into an indication of Puerto Ricans' "problems of adjustment." In defining the "problem" as Puerto Ricans and their culture, social service workers and policy makers began formulating "the culture of poverty" ideology in Philadelphia. With its emphasis on culture, family, and generations, the "culture of poverty" implied that women, traditionally held responsible for these domains, were to blame for many of the "problems" affecting their families and communities. Examination of how this ideology developed in a local context provides new insights, allowing a concrete exploration of how the "culture of poverty" dismissed racism and racial discrimination and rendered invisible labor recruitment, state policies, and economic displacement, as well as migrants' struggles to recreate their household economies and their communities.

Chapter 7 brings these discussions from the postwar era to the early 1990s, by examining Puerto Ricans' efforts to recreate their communities, the impact of economic restructuring and residential segregation, and "underclass" interpretations of Puerto Rican poverty. In addition to the attitudes of neighbors, policy makers, and social service workers, Puerto Ricans confronted the city's shift to a postindustrial economy. Although they came as labor migrants when low-wage, unskilled jobs were available, economic restructuring meant the relocation of industry, the loss of jobs within the city limits, and the growth of a service economy. Within this changing context, Puerto Ricans strove to recreate their communities, challenging existing social service agencies, developing their own agencies and organizations, and entering city politics. Economic shifts, combined with residential segregation and government policies, nevertheless created conditions of concentrated poverty for many of the Puerto Ricans who had made the city their home. Puerto Ricans in Philadelphia became displaced labor migrants.

By the 1990s economic conditions, government policies, and racial ideologies had transformed Puerto Rican labor migrants into the "underclass." A national discourse emerged defining Puerto Ricans as the "other underclass." For proponents of the "underclass," as historian Michael Katz notes, "a new social stratum, identified by a set of interlocking behaviors, not primarily by poverty, dominated the wastelands that were all that remained of America's urban-industrial heartland."[32] For Puerto Ricans, the "underclass" was a continuation of earlier "culture of poverty" interpretations that pointed to particular groups of people, emphasized their "pathological" behaviors, and blamed them for their poverty. In this interpretation, the obstacles that confronted Puerto Ricans stemmed not from a new urban environment, a tight job market, or racism and discrimination, but from their own cultural deficiencies. The "culture of poverty" and "underclass" paradigms ignore labor recruitment, the impact of structural changes, and migrants' motivations in seeking work and a better life. As economic conditions changed, racialist ideologies proved resilient.

While sharing much with other postwar im/migrations, Puerto Rican migration also highlights important dimensions of the post-1965 immigrations. Like African Americans and Mexicans, Puerto Ricans were recruited for low-wage jobs and confronted the racial ideologies and discrimination that characterized the postwar era, as well as the subsequent economic restructuring that affected many of the cities where these im/migrants had settled. At the same time, the colonial relationship between the United States and Puerto Rico illustrates dramatically the impact of U.S. political and economic interventions in shaping immigrations. The post-1965 immigrants have come overwhelmingly from countries in the Caribbean, Latin America, and Asia, where the U.S. presence has been felt via military intervention, political ties, and economic investment, especially the proliferation of export processing zones. Coming in search of a better life, many of these immigrants then face the changed urban environments inhabited by the Puerto Ricans, African Americans, and Mexicans who came before. These issues are addressed in the Epilogue.

Chapter Two

From the Country to the Cities: Internal Migration and Migration to the States

Although Santurce is part of the San Juan metropolitan area, Doña Margarita remembered helping her mother care for chickens and gather eggs. "A lot of people built the house on the land, but left a part of the land and grew some things there," she recalled. Her stepfather worked on the docks in San Juan, loading and unloading ships, and also grew sugar cane, lemons, peppers, tomatoes, and other vegetables. Their chicken coop was underneath the elevated house. In addition to raising four children and tending chickens, her mother did laundry for wealthier families. In 1940, when Doña Margarita was eight years old, her mother died. After four years of living with several different relatives and being mistreated, Doña Margarita left home and got her first paid job, as a live-in domestic. A couple of years later she was having her first child and living with the child's father, Don Marcelino, a plumber. "There was work, but very little. And the salary—my husband at that time, when he was working, the most he earned was 75 cents an hour." Doña Margarita explained:

> Mostly what there was, was agriculture, in the country. But the people, well, they didn't want to go to the country anymore. Already, by this time, they were losing the coffee, they were losing the vegetables. . . . People wanted to work in the factories, and at that time there were very few factories.

Considering her domestic responsibilities as "work," she described her days:

> But at home, I had more than enough work because there was the house—the obligations of the house, getting [the kids] that were already going to school ready, doing the laundry, going to the public spigot to get on line. It wasn't like everyone had their own plumbing. . . . Then you had to wash diapers, there were no Pampers. . . . Nothing by machine, nothing, nothing of convenience or anything, all of this was by hand.

She also took in ironing. "I didn't work outside, but yeah, there were people who . . . brought me the clothes, and at home, I earned a few dollars, too." By 1954 the couple

had four children, and Don Marcelino decided to get a government-sponsored labor contract for seasonal agricultural work in the States because "the children were already growing up and everything was getting more expensive." Finding conditions in the farm labor
camp harsh, he left for Philadelphia and, with the help of his brother who was already living in the city, got an apartment and a job in a metal factory. Doña Margarita and the
children soon joined him. In her narrative, Doña Margarita revealed both the continuities
in efforts to maintain the household and the changes wrought by migration.[1]

In 1950, most Puerto Ricans (60 percent) lived in rural areas. Even the San Juan metropolitan area had a significant rural population, and like Doña Margarita, many of those
who lived in the city were not very far removed from more rural ways of life. Puerto Rico's
economy was based on agriculture, agricultural processing, and the home needlework
industry. The production of three principal commercial crops—coffee, tobacco, and
sugar—created regional variations in land ownership, wage labor, subsistence activities,
and gender divisions of labor. Most rural households depended on commercial agriculture for wages or income, and also relied on a variety of subsistence and informal economic activities. Women were important contributors to their households, performing the
labor-intensive reproductive tasks of raising children and meeting the household's domestic needs; providing food by growing crops and tending animals; and earning wages
through home needlework, employment in certain phases of agricultural production and
processing, or other informal economic activities, like taking in laundry.[2]

In the post–World War II era, sweeping economic changes sparked massive migration
from Puerto Rico's rural areas to urban areas in Puerto Rico and the States, including
Philadelphia. Puerto Rico's rural peoples were displaced by the decline of agriculture, agricultural processing, and the home needlework industry; by a particular model of economic
development based on export-oriented industrialization; and by government policies that
promoted population control through emigration. These economic changes are best
understood within the global, colonial, and state contexts. As economist Richard Weisskoff suggests, agricultural regions, even those that combined "self-sufficiency" farming
with "supplemental" farming for market, had only "some measure of independence from
the national and world markets." At the same time, state policies shaped economic development and fostered migration. The regional and gender dimensions of economic change
and government policies were pronounced. While the decline of agriculture, agricultural
processing, and home needlework affected rural areas, the industrialization program
failed to replace all of the lost jobs, concentrated what new jobs there were in the metropolitan areas, and attracted labor-intensive industries, such as the garment industry, that
employed mostly women. Though the government's industrialization program centered
on urban areas, its contract labor program for seasonal agricultural workers came to rural
areas, enabling even poor rural men to migrate directly to the States.[3]

As economic change threatened the viability of the household economy, migrants left
in search of work. Reflecting the regional and gender dimensions of economic change
and government policies, migrants to Philadelphia were mostly rural people. Over a
twenty-year period, Philadelphia marriage records indicate that very few migrants came
from the San Juan metropolitan area. Instead, most came from the tobacco region, especially San Lorenzo, and the southeastern sugar region, especially Salinas—areas that

fared poorly during this period of rapid agricultural decline and urban industrialization. Yet even those living in the metropolitan area, like Doña Margarita and her family, faced declining economic opportunities and turned to labor contracts and migration. This chapter explores the island-wide context of economic change and emigration and the rural origins of migrants to Philadelphia, while Chapter 4 looks more closely at San Lorenzo and Salinas.

Puerto Rico's Rural Economies

During the 1950s, Puerto Rico's policy makers portrayed migrants as coming from urban areas, a view incorporated into the scholarship on Puerto Rican migration. Writing in 1950, C. Wright Mills, Clarence Senior, and Rose Kohn Goldsen described New York City's migrants as "urban," "more privileged," and "better fitted than stationary islanders for struggle on the continent." Similarly, anthropologist Oscar Lewis minimized the rural-to-urban transition in his study of a migrant family in San Juan and New York, arguing that "the culture of poverty" transcends "rural-urban" differences and "can best be studied in urban or rural slums." In the absence of new research on the origins of New York's Puerto Rican population, most scholarship still suggests urban origins for migrants until the 1960s. Yet the nature of economic change and the government's farm labor program assured that a significant proportion of migrants came from rural areas. Hence, Puerto Rico's rural economies reveal the impact of economic change and government policies, as well as the premigration characteristics of Philadelphia's Puerto Rican community.[4]

Puerto Rico during the postwar era of heavy emigration can be divided into six loosely defined regions based on geography and the principal cash crop produced—the west central coffee-producing area, the east central tobacco-producing area, the southeastern sugar-producing area, the southwestern sugar-producing area, the northern sugar-producing area, and the San Juan metropolitan area (see Map 2.1).[5] Shaped by history and Puerto Rico's diverse terrain, with its coastal lowlands, mountainous interior, and wide variety of land forms, the regional production of these crops fostered different land ownership patterns and social relations, ranging from large sugar plantations owned by absentee U.S. corporations to small, family-owned and operated tobacco farms that also grew food for home consumption. Writing in 1956, anthropologist Julian Steward suggested that "regional subcultures" emerged as a "response to the distinctive technological, financial, and social arrangements under which these crops were produced." Because of the seasonal nature of cash crops and low wages for agricultural work, subsistence and informal economic activities were important for household survival. Household economies reflected the production of commercial crops, the availability of paid employment, and subsistence activities. Economic change and government policies affected these regions differently, and it was within these varying regional contexts that Puerto Ricans responded to changing conditions, sometimes by migrating in search of paid employment.[6]

MAP 2.1.   Puerto Rico's Regions, ca. 1950–1970

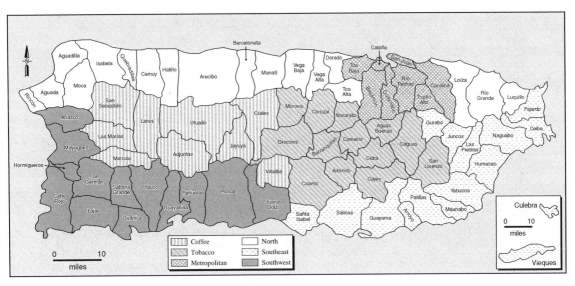

Sources: See Chapter 2, note 5.

The United States' occupation of Puerto Rico in 1898 sparked changes in the island's regional economies. Under Spanish colonialism, coffee was the leading export and was grown throughout the mountainous interior. With the change in sovereignty, Puerto Rico's coffee industry lost its primary market, as protections were removed and import taxes were raised. A U.S. market did not develop, and since coffee was not grown in the States, the U.S. government did not protect Puerto Rico's coffee with a tariff. Instead, Puerto Rico's coffee competed unsuccessfully with less expensive imports from South America, especially Brazil, to which U.S. consumers had grown accustomed. This loss of markets was immediately followed by a hurricane in 1899 that devastated coffee crops. Coffee production continued in the western highlands, but was replaced by tobacco in the eastern highlands. Tobacco found a ready market in the States, its growth was encouraged, and production increased. It was sugar, however, that came to dominate the economy. The most profitable of Puerto Rico's cash crops, sugar was planted anywhere it would grow. U.S. sugar corporations brought sugar plantations to the southern coast, irrigating the land and absorbing smaller farms and subsistence plots. Sugar production also increased along the northern coast, where local families invested more heavily in sugar.[7]

In the post–World War II era, coffee production still defined the municipios of the west central highlands. As economist Harvey Perloff concluded in 1950, "Even though coffee exports have dwindled almost to the vanishing point, the industry is still of great economic significance. A sizable proportion of the population lives in the coffee regions and is economically dependent upon coffee and related enterprises." The dominant crop in terms of cultivated land, employment, and income, the coffee industry remained an important component of household economies. The industry's decline continued, however, as hurricanes in 1899, 1928, and 1932 damaged crops and decreased production.

European markets dissipated, while the United States continued to import coffee from elsewhere. Coffee producers were unwilling or unable to invest in improvements, techniques of cultivation and processing changed very little, and crop yields decreased. Although the Cooperativa de Cafeteros de Puerto Rico, founded in 1925 with government support, sought to stabilize prices and protect growers from excessive interest rates and charges for processing, prices did not keep pace with increasing costs. Coffee ceased to be a major export crop, falling from a level of 60 percent of the value of exports in 1895 to less than 1 percent by 1940. Production often failed to meet even the needs of the local market, and coffee was imported.[8]

Haciendas, which developed with the commercial production of coffee at the end of the nineteenth century, continued to produce most of the region's coffee in the 1950s. Ranging from 30 to more than 1,000 cuerdas, most haciendas were owner-operated. As a long-term investment, coffee favored large growers over small. Coffee bushes took four years to begin producing, and eight years to reach full productivity; they then produced for thirty years or more. Coffee is a seasonal crop; the peak demand for labor was from September to February or March. Harvesting was done by hand and ripe berries had to be picked quickly. Some processing was performed on the haciendas, the extent of mechanization depending on the hacienda's size and capital. For the rest of the year, coffee required only one-third to one-half of the workers needed during the harvest. Workers replaced dead or unhealthy bushes and built terraces and ditches around the coffee bushes, while tending pastures, livestock, and any food crops, and maintaining trails and roads. For most, there was very little paid employment for half of each year. While coffee haciendas were dominant, some farmers introduced or increased their production of sugar cane, tobacco, or minor crops as coffee became less profitable. Small farms, averaging three cuerdas, grew a variety of crops for home consumption, but were not entirely subsistence farms: the family either sold some crops or relied on income earned by working off the farm during the coffee harvest or in the home needlework industry.[9]

Agregados, landless laborers who lived on the haciendas, provided most of the coffee industry's labor. Housing was provided by the hacienda owner or built by agregados with the owner's permission. Homes, usually two rooms with a partial shelter on one side for a wood stove and an outside latrine or no toilet, had either no light or a kerosene lamp. Water was carried from nearby springs. Most haciendas paid the required minimum wage for coffee labor and for major tasks. Generally the whole family was expected to work for the hacienda, with women and children harvesting coffee, some women doing domestic work, and children running errands. Through a system of perquisites, agregados still met some of their subsistence needs, even as wages increasingly supplanted these less formal labor relations. Plantains, bananas, and shade trees were grown among the coffee bushes, which required partial shade. Many agregados harvested the plantains and bananas and made charcoal from the branches pruned from shade trees, giving half to the hacienda owner and keeping half to use or to sell. If they cared for a cow, most were entitled to a portion of the milk. Some agregados were permitted to grow food on small plots, usually a half cuerda or less, and to raise chickens and a pig or two.[10]

After 1898, tobacco production shaped the economies of the municipios in the east central highlands, including San Lorenzo. Import duties were removed, and the United States became the principal market for Puerto Rico's tobacco. Tobacco grew well on the mountainous slopes and was rotated with minor crops, including bananas, plantains, corn, and sweet potatoes. Sugar cane, the more profitable cash crop, was grown on the fertile lowlands of the Caguas Valley. Where neither sugar nor tobacco did well, farmers grew minor crops. Like coffee, tobacco's value as an export paled compared to sugar and home needlework, accounting for just 4 percent of the total agricultural income and 6 percent of export value during the 1940s. Nevertheless, Puerto Rico's Agricultural Experiment Station asserted, "Tobacco production is of great significance to the economy of Puerto Rico. In fact, it is the third most important agricultural enterprise of the Island, and is the main source of income of about one-fourth of its farmers." In the east central highlands tobacco was the livelihood of virtually all farmers.[11]

Tobacco production was characterized not by the haciendas of the coffee region, but by smaller farms. In his 1949 study of a tobacco municipio, anthropologist Robert Manners found that two-thirds of all farm area was taken up by farms of less than 100 cuerdas and that farms of less than 3 cuerdas could grow tobacco profitably. Rural houses were dispersed, sometimes a half a mile or more from the roads. Most were made of wood, often scrap lumber, and had wooden floors, but no electricity or privies. Water was carried from nearby springs, and sometimes barrels were used to collect rainwater from the roof. Labor relations varied with the size of the farm. Large farm owners relied on sharecroppers, who shared the costs of production and proceeds from the sale of the tobacco, or on wage laborers, mostly agregados. Men earned $.90 to $1.00 a day, which sometimes included coffee and lunch, while women earned $.40 to $.70 and children earned $.40 to $.50. Farmers with less land supplemented family labor with wage labor for planting and harvesting. On medium-sized farms of 8 to 35 cuerdas family labor was sufficient, and households were able to meet their subsistence needs and expenses. Although small farms of less than 8 cuerdas grew tobacco and minor crops, households also relied on wage work on nearby farms, sharecropping, or income from subsidiary economic activities.[12]

During the most active period in tobacco, from August to March, men, women, and children worked. Tobacco seeds were planted in seed beds, seedlings were transplanted to fields, the crop was weeded twice, and harvesting began seventy to ninety days after the seedlings were transplanted. Tobacco leaves were threaded and suspended from racks in barns for drying. Men prepared the fields for planting and harvested the tobacco crop, while women weeded seed beds, transplanted seedlings, applied fertilizer, removed plant pests from leaves, and sewed tobacco leaves for drying. Children weeded seed beds, transplanted seedlings, and brought water, coffee, and lunches to the fields for workers. While small shops in the region made handmade cigars, most tobacco was shipped to the States for advanced processing and resale. After the tobacco crop, food crops were planted in the same soil; land where tobacco was not grown was also planted in food crops.[13]

Because it was not very profitable, tobacco was considered "a poor man's cash crop." It required little capital investment in seed, fertilizer, or equipment, which consisted of hoes, an ox-drawn plow, and a tobacco barn or small storage shed. With a short grow-ing season of only four months, it also involved less risk than other cash crops, as hur-ricanes or a bad crop had fewer long-term consequences. Farms averaged 36 cuerdas, with 10 cuerdas cultivated, and most (88 percent) were managed by their owners, according to a 1952 survey of 150 tobacco farms. With an average profit of only $560 per year, there was little incentive to anyone but the owner to grow tobacco. Still, larger farms had higher tobacco production per cuerda, better labor efficiency, and higher profits than smaller farms. For smaller farms, the survey found "the area cultivated per farm was so small that it was not enough to provide a reasonable return to the farmer," and concluded, "In a region where tobacco represents almost the only effective income, the burden of so many people for so few cuerdas of tobacco cultivation seems more than the farms can support."[14]

Yet, because tobacco was rotated with other crops, farming was less seasonal than in coffee or sugar, and households were able to meet more of their subsistence needs. While tobacco provided 75 percent of farms' total income, it claimed only 27 percent of the cultivated land. The rest was dedicated to corn, sweet potatoes, and other food crops, which grew year round. During tobacco's dead season, households with larger farms relied on minor crops for food and for cash, selling to local retailers and to truckers who picked up crops and sold them in the San Juan metropolitan area and along the south-ern coast. Households also raised goats, chickens, and sometimes pigs. Sharecroppers worked in minor crops, earning wages even lower than those in tobacco or keeping a portion of the produce. Though some agregados were provided with small plots to grow food crops or with credit, others migrated to the south coast to work as cane cutters. Men also supplemented household incomes with unskilled carpentry or road building, while women turned to washing, ironing, and sewing.[15]

With the U.S. occupation, sugar came to dominate Puerto Rico's economy and was grown on the coastal plains in the north, south, east, and west. U.S. capital fueled the sugar industry, as U.S. corporations purchased large tracts of uncultivated land and hacienda owners sold or leased their lands. Irrigation was introduced, land concentra-tion increased, and processing was centralized. Anthropologist Sidney Mintz describes the impact, especially on the south coast: "The invasion of capital continued unabated for fully twenty-five years, within which time every feature of sugar production in Puerto Rico, and the very scale of the industry underwent revolutionary change." Prior to 1898, work on the haciendas was nearly year-round, with three growths of cane and grinding operations on the hacienda. Agregados were paid in scrip for the hacienda store and provided with subsistence plots to grow minor crops and raise animals. Wood was gathered in nearby woodlands. After 1898, U.S. corporations built *centrales* to process sugar cane and acquired the large tracts of land to operate them profitably. What Mintz calls the "corporate land-and-factory combine" was based on cash relations and wage labor. Work became more seasonal, and as more land was planted in sugar cane, "the local subsistence pattern of home-grown vegetables, livestock, free sugar, molasses and rum, and occasional gifts of fresh meat by the *hacendado* was largely upset."[16]

The sugar industry remained marked by centralization in agriculture and processing, as well as by continued dependence on the States. In five south coast municipios, more than 60 percent of land ownership was in excess of 500 acres, a degree of concentration unequaled in other parts of Puerto Rico. The agricultural and processing phases were linked, with sugar cane reduced to raw sugar close to the cane fields to prevent the loss of sucrose. Five small mills closed between 1938 and 1947, at which time four U.S. sugar corporations operated ten of the thirty-seven remaining mills, processing 30 to 40 percent of the total sugar output. With the United States as the only market for Puerto Rico's sugar and U.S. policies setting quotas for sugar production, Perloff noted, "the drawback lies in the dependence of the major sector of the economy on the uncertainties of political decisions made in Washington." Quotas, established in the Jones-Costigan Act of 1934 and the Sugar Act of 1937, limited the production and marketing of sugar for all areas supplying sugar to the United States, including Puerto Rico. The Agricultural Experiment Station criticized U.S. sugar programs in a 1944 study: "Soon after World War II started, the forces of demand and supply, aided by a rise in the general price level and by increased consumer purchasing power, would have brought the price of sugar and sugar cane to new peaks, had it not been prevented by governmental ceiling prices." Despite U.S. government subsidies to sugar cane growers, the study concluded that their income was "just high enough to maintain the industry in Puerto Rico but not sufficient to provide much incentive for production during the years of sugar shortages 1942 to 1945." The Sugar Act of 1948 further reduced Puerto Rico's quota.[17]

Sugar nevertheless continued to dominate the economy in the postwar era in terms of export value, land use, and employment. Sugar and its byproducts accounted for 57 and 60 percent of Puerto Rico's total export value in 1946 and 1948 respectively. Sugar also provided molasses for the rum industry and bagasse for the paper, carton, and wallboard industries. Thirty-five percent of cultivated land was dedicated to sugar, including the best soils. The sugar industry was Puerto Rico's largest employer: 130,000 to 140,000 worked in agriculture and another 13,000 to 15,000 in processing during the peak season. During the dead season, however, employment in sugar plummeted to just 50,000. Although sugar workers' wages were the highest in agriculture and among the highest in manufacturing, this seasonal nature meant that annual income for sugar workers was only about $400 to $500.[18]

The sugar industry defined household economies along the southern coast, including Salinas. In his 1949 study of a south coast municipio, Mintz concluded that "the people of the south coast are dependent almost entirely on the cane industry for their livelihood." Most workers were agregados, living on the owners' land, while others lived in villages or poblados along the main highways, either owning the land or building on the public domain. Most houses had two rooms with outside privies, and some had a lean-to for cooking. The population was still rural and agrarian, with less than 25 percent of the south coast's population living in towns. Most members of this "rural proletariat" did not own land or other property, depended on wages, bought their commodities in stores, and were employed by corporate entities. During the five- to six-month harvest, day laborers were hired for cane cutting, weeding, ditching, irrigating, wagon loading, and other tasks related to harvesting, transporting, and replanting cane. Workers were paid a minimum daily wage established for the different tasks, and some earned piecework rates. Cane cutting was considered the most physically demanding and unpleasant task; fibers irritated the skin and the cutting line was the hottest place on the field. Yet piecework rates sometimes enabled cutters to make two to three times the minimum wage. Mills operated twenty-four hours a day, six days a week. The overwhelming majority of field workers were men, although women occasionally spread fertilizer or cleaned cane debris from the fields. After the harvest ended, employment dwindled, as irrigation work and weeding required few workers.[19]

With land devoted almost exclusively to sugar and labor based entirely on wages, most found only six months of paid employment during the year. When the harvest ended in June or July, workers faced the "dead season" until another harvest began in late December or early January. As a result, "life is as dependent in many ways on successful subsidiary economic activities as it is on the main wage-earning activity." Without land or with plots of less than a cuerda, households grew very little food, but many had a pig or two, chickens, or some goats, which provided food, cash, and a vehicle for saving. Households relied on fishing for home consumption and for sale to local residents or wholesalers; they trapped land crabs, and gathered fruit, edible roots, and firewood. Some households supplemented their incomes by selling the illegal lottery or homemade rum. In addition to household tasks, women contributed to their household economies by tending livestock, preparing and selling food to workers on payday, and sometimes working in small stores. People also bought on credit, and most of the workers' money made its way to corporation stores. Still, Perloff concluded, "in the periods when sugar cane is not being harvested and ground, many families in the island go hungry."[20]

While sugar also defined the economies of the municipios of the north coast region, there were some regional distinctions. Prior to 1898 family haciendas produced sugar, as the north coast was rainy and irrigation was not needed. After 1898, haciendas continued dedicating most of their land to sugar, growing some mixed crops, using uncultivated land for pasture, processing their own cane, and having their own stores. Workers built their homes on the hacienda's unproductive land. Smaller farmers focused on subsistence production and met their needs for cash by growing food crops for the local market and by working for wages, usually on haciendas. Sugar production and land concentration increased. In one municipio former hacendados pooled their resources to build a *central* as a corporate enterprise. Their land holdings and control over subsidiary land companies increased, and they acquired a railroad. The government-owned, proportional profit farms of Puerto Rico's Land Authority were the other form of centralization. This region was the most affected by the Land Authority, accounting for 62 percent of the land owned and leased by the Authority.[21]

The Land Authority implemented agrarian reforms by enforcing the 500-acre limit on corporations' land ownership and redistributing the land. The 500-acre limit, established by the U.S. Congress in the Foraker Act of 1900 and the Jones Act of 1917, had not been enforced until a U.S. Supreme Court decision paved the way for the PPD's 1941 Land Law, which created the Land Authority. Land was distributed in three ways. First, proportional profit farms of 100 to 500 acres were government-owned lands that were leased to farm administrators for the continued production of sugar. Administrators and farm laborers received set wages and then split profits at the end of the season. Second, farms of 5 to 25 acres were sold, with financing, to individual families. The PPD hoped this would diversify agriculture, by increasing the production of food crops. Finally, the *parcelas* program distributed small plots of one-quarter acre to three acres to landless peasants and rural wage laborers, providing a permanent place to live and the ability to grow some food.[22]

Land reforms did not, however, lessen the region's or the island's dependence on sugar. By June 1948, the Land Authority owned or leased more than 110,000 acres or one-third of sugar cane land island-wide, employed 20 percent of sugar cane workers, produced 11 percent of sugar, operated two sugar mills, and had established 143 rural villages for 17,631 families. Nonetheless, in her 1949 study of a north coast municipio, anthropologist Elena Padilla Seda found "everyone is profoundly affected by the devotion of virtually all land to sugar production and by the control of most of this production by a centralized authority." Nor did government ownership eliminate the impact of the United States: sugar was sold to the States, stock market prices and tariff regulations had their effects, and food and manufactured goods were imported from the States. Similarly, family-sized farms continued to produce sugar. A study of 130 farms established on 4,171 cuerdas purchased from the San José sugar estate showed that the farms averaged 19 cuerdas planted in crops, with 13 cuerdas in sugar cane in 1943–1944 and 15 cuerdas the following year. As a result, "sugar cane accounted for 72 and 80 percent of the income from sale of crops the first and second year respectively." This nearly exclusive focus on sugar production appears to have been island-wide: a study of 134 farms in 1950–1951 found "that these farms were highly specialized," with 82 percent of their cultivated land in sugar cane, which accounted for 74 percent of the farms' income.[23]

As a result, seasonal work and low incomes plagued sugar workers on the north coast as well. During the dead season, households turned to informal economic and subsistence activities. Although some sugar workers owned their homes because of the *parcelas* program, they had very little land. Most houses, made of reeds and materials gathered from mangrove swamps, were one or two rooms with a lean-to kitchen and dirt floors with platforms for the bed or hammock. Houses on resettlement plots had aluminum latrines on cement platforms, while other houses had none. Candles or kerosene lamps provided light, and water was carried from public faucets. Despite plots of less than an acre, households grew some food crops, and a few had chickens and goats. Fish were caught and sold to a middleman for sale in town, while land crabs supplemented the household's diet. As both land and credit were scarce, earning additional income was a high priority. Men sought temporary jobs in carpentry, construction, plumbing, barbering, or handiwork, while women sometimes found work as laundresses, seamstresses, peddlers, herb gatherers, cooks, and maids. Some households supplemented their incomes with the illegal lottery or homemade rum. Other families hauled beach sand to the side of the road for sale to middlemen who resold the sand for construction purposes, or did stone quarrying, crushing limestone with pieces of scrap metal for sale to contractors for road and building repairs. Padilla Seda concluded that "most of the earnings of a cane worker are spent a few hours after he has been paid, for they seldom cover more than food and other immediate necessities. . . . In the dead season, the problem of making ends meet increases, and many families often go without food."[24]

Along with agriculture and agricultural processing, the other mainstay of Puerto Rico's rural economies was the home needlework industry. Puerto Rico's garment industry was, as Perloff noted in 1950, "developed chiefly by mainland capital" and "based essentially on cheap labor." The home needlework industry grew during World War I, when European imports to the States were cut off. The hand-sewing of gloves, previously imported from Czechoslovakia, and the hemming and embroidery of handkerchiefs increased. Materials were shipped from the mainland, a system of contractors and subcontractors handled the distribution and collection of materials, and rural women added the hand details at home, earning piecework wages. The finished products were shipped back to the States for marketing. Dependent on low wages, the value of needlework exports declined from $15.6 million to $5.8 million in just one year, when the U.S. Fair Labor Standards Act's (FLSA) minimum wages were enforced in Puerto Rico in 1940. The U.S. Congress responded by allowing minimum wages for Puerto Rico to be determined on an industry-by-industry basis. While the U.S. minimum wage stood at $.30 per hour, wages for Puerto Rico's home needlework industry were set at $.13 to $.23. The industry recovered.[25]

Concentrated in rural areas, especially near Mayagüez and in the surrounding coffee region, the home needlework industry remained an important part of household economies. During World War II, the home needlework industry grew, and by 1946–1947, the value of exports had increased to $39.2 million, second only to sugar exports. By 1948, 116,000 people worked in manufacturing island-wide, with almost 52,000 (mostly women) in needlework and another 18,000 in other textile manufacturing. As coffee continued to decline, people turned to other crops and relied more heavily on home needlework. In 1949, anthropologist Eric Wolf observed that "in one barrio, said to be the most 'traditional' and isolated in the coffee area, the writer found a hamlet surrounded on all sides by cane, and the people largely dependent on needlework farmed out from a nearby urban center." Within the region, home and workshop needlework was the only significant nonagricultural economic activity. Rural households in other regions also relied on women's work in the home needlework industry.[26]

In the immediate postwar era Puerto Rico's economy was still based on agriculture, agricultural processing, and home needlework. In 1950, 39 percent of the labor force was in agriculture, and most of the 17 percent in manufacturing were dependent on agricultural processing or the garment industry for their jobs. Of those employed in manufacturing, 50 percent worked in home needlework and other apparel, 16 percent in sugar processing, and 11 percent in other food processing. Rural households were dependent on commercial agriculture and the home needlework industry for income, as well as on a wide variety of subsistence and informal economic activities. Though commercial agriculture provided wage labor mostly for men, there were regional variations. In the sugar industry, women found few opportunities for paid employment in the agricultural or processing phases, and in the coffee industry women worked primarily during the harvest. Tobacco provided more paid jobs for women in both agriculture and processing, and women in the region also worked in minor crops. The home needlework industry, on the other hand, employed mostly women. Given the seasonal nature and low wages of this income-producing work, men and women contributed to their households through subsistence and informal economic activities—both men and women tended food crops and animals in the regions where they had access to land, men fished in the coastal areas, women made and sold food, men and women sold and played the illegal lottery in the coastal regions, and women took in laundry for wealthier families. For women in all regions, the reproductive work of raising children and maintaining the household was labor-intensive. Their houses did not have water or electricity, and their stoves required wood—or charcoal when they could afford it. Resources were limited and seasonal. The economic changes of the postwar era upset what was a delicate balance to begin with and sent Puerto Rico's rural peoples in search of paid employment.[27]

Regional and Gender Dimensions of Economic Development

Although elected with the slogan "Pan, Tierra y Libertad" (Bread, Land and Liberty), the Partido Popular Democrático (PPD) presided over the demise of Puerto Rico's agricultural economies. After a brief period of agrarian reform, the PPD replaced "Bread, Land and Liberty" with "The Battle for Production." By 1955, manufacturing income surpassed agriculture, and Puerto Rico's Planning Board conceded that "from that point industry took a definite precedence over agriculture." The PPD's economic development program was based on promoting industrialization by attracting U.S. capital. As employment declined, policy makers saw the problem as "overpopulation," and reducing the population as a crucial corollary to the success of industrialization. Emigration and the sterilization of women increased. More recently, scholars have questioned the inevitability of agriculture's demise. Describing the "flaw in the development program," economic historian James Dietz argues, "From the assertion that industrialization was required because agriculture *alone* could not provide an adequate economic base, a program was forged that functioned as if agriculture could be ignored altogether and industrialization, at nearly any cost, was the exclusive goal." Insisting that the problem was not "overpopulation" but the relationship between demographics and jobs, Frank Bonilla and Ricardo Campos conclude that "the steady expulsion of 'surplus' workers and efforts to attract greater amounts of capital together have governed all the plans and projects formulated by and for Puerto Ricans to solve the persisting problem of 'overpopulation' and to promote an economic development that remains elusive."[28]

Policy makers abandoned agrarian reforms and promoted industrialization, and the ensuing economic crisis was severe. Agrarian reforms had succeeded in weakening the sugar corporations' dominance, and had won support from those who received parcelas or family farms, as well as from *colonos*, individual sugar growers, who benefited from limitations on corporations. The PPD had also improved education, public health, roads, sanitation, and electricity in rural areas. Yet the PPD then abandoned agrarian reforms altogether, transferring the parcelas program to another government agency and leaving the Land Authority to operate existing proportional profit farms. Agrarian reforms had not revived or diversified agriculture. During the 1950s, an average of 9,100 agricultural jobs disappeared each year. At the same time, employment in home needlework plummeted from almost 51,000 workers to just 10,000. Meanwhile, manufacturing did not create enough jobs to offset the agricultural losses, and what jobs there were were concentrated in the metropolitan area and employed mostly women. There were fewer jobs island-wide: employment dropped from 560,271 to 551,656 during the decade. Between 1950 and 1970, employment in agriculture fell from 39 percent to 8 percent of the work force, while manufacturing remained steady (see Figure 2.1). The resultant economic crisis, while island-wide, was particularly acute in rural areas, where it threatened household economies based on the work, paid and unpaid, of men, women, and children. This crisis set the population in motion.[29]

In promoting industrialization, the PPD shifted from import substitution and government ownership to a strategy of industrialization by invitation. David Ross, a former employee of the Development Company, explains: "Prior to 1947, the development program was mainly one of government enterprise in manufacturing, while after 1947 it was mainly one of government promotion of private enterprise in manufacturing." In 1942, Puerto Rico's legislature created the Puerto Rico Development Company, a public corporation, and named Teodoro Moscoso the general manager. The corporation's mandate was to develop industrialization based on local materials and local markets. The company adopted one subsidiary from the Puerto Rico Reconstruction Administration and established four, producing cement, glass containers, paperboard, and shoes. With funding from the legislature, the company's role expanded to constructing factory buildings for sale or lease to privately owned industries. Divided in 1950, the renamed Puerto Rico Industrial Development Company (PRIDCO) continued as a semi-autonomous public corporation making loans and renting buildings. The Economic Development Administration, or Fomento, became an executive agency, making Moscoso a cabinet member. Fomento was responsible for promoting industrialization, conducting economic research, and providing labor training and recruitment services. By 1951 Fomento had sold the last of its government-owned industries and operated exclusively in the business of promoting private, mostly U.S., investment.[30]

Tax exemptions became a key component of the PPD's strategy. The U.S. Congress had exempted Puerto Rico from federal taxes in the Jones Act of 1917. In 1947, Puerto Rico's Industrial Incentives Act exempted new industries from income taxes, insular and municipal property taxes, certain excise taxes, and licensing and other fees. These exemptions made the island a "tax haven." Tax exemptions were available for firms manufacturing items not produced commercially in Puerto Rico and for designated items including gloves, men's and women's outerwear, and other items made primarily from textiles. Established as complete exemptions for 1947 to 1959, these tax benefits were then reduced over the next several years. For U.S. companies the benefits were

FIGURE 2.1.   Employment in Agriculture and Manufacturing,
Puerto Rico, 1940–1970

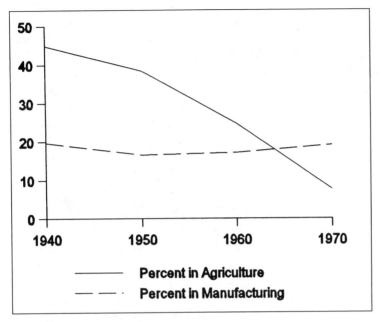

Sources: U.S. Bureau of the Census, *U.S. Census of Population: 1950*, vol. 2,
Characteristics of the Population, pt. 53, Puerto Rico (Washington, D.C., 1953), 40; and
U.S. Bureau of the Census, *Census of Population: 1970*, vol. 1, *Characteristics of the
Population*, pt. 53, Puerto Rico (Washington, D.C., 1973), 190.
Note: Percent is of total employed.

compounded—they could manufacture goods in Puerto Rico tax free and "export" those goods to the States without having to pay "import" duties. As Ross suggests, it was "freedom from taxes without leaving the United States."[31]

The other main attraction was cheap labor, especially that of women. Determined on an industry-by-industry basis, minimum wages in Puerto Rico remained lower than those in the States. The PPD recognized the impact of wage differentials in attracting U.S. industries and opposed the application of the federal minimum wage in Puerto Rico. In U.S. congressional hearings in 1949, Moscoso insisted that low wages and tax incentives did not give Puerto Rico an unfair advantage over the States in recruiting U.S. companies. He also asserted Puerto Ricans' willingness to work in the least desirable jobs:

> There are certain industries in the United States, Mr. Congressman, which are not looked upon as very desirable. . . . If you go to the United States, to New York, to almost any hotel, you will find that the bus boy or the fellow who scrubs the floor . . . is now being held by a Puerto Rican. Well, in Puerto Rico proper, we believe that a lot of jobs, from which people shy away in the States might eventually come down here.

Wages were low, he conceded, about 60 percent of those in the States, and yet workers were willing to take those jobs.[32]

Policy makers recruited labor-intensive, export-oriented industries, like the garment and textile industries. Moscoso explained: "Well, our interest in textiles started pretty much at the beginning of our program." Linking the relocation of industry with low wages, he noted that "a lot of people in New England just don't like to work in a textile mill, because now they can earn much better wages in more skilled operations," and suggested that if firms did not come to Puerto Rico, many would go to southern states where wages were low and labor was unorganized. Similarly, a 1949 pamphlet asserted the advantages of relocating to Puerto Rico for apparel and other industries, including an abundance of workers, extensive unemployment and underemployment, "orderly and tranquil" labor relations, and "very few strikes." Emphasizing the availability of women workers, it noted, "workers in the needlework industry, both men and women, but mostly the latter, are many and are noted for their dexterity and their industry." Labor laws had "recently been liberalized to permit night work for women in textile industries." Perhaps most important, wages in the needlework industry were only 26 percent of those in the States. The pamphlet concluded: "In virtually all lines and stages of textile and apparel manufacturing the current wage structure of Puerto Rico offers the possibility of substantial advantages to the entrepreneur."[33]

With their strategy dependent on U.S. investors' willingness to move to Puerto Rico, Fomento mounted an advertising campaign, hiring an advertising agency and a public relations firm. By the early 1950s "good press" finally counterbalanced "adverse publicity," an "effect [that] was deliberately manufactured." When the 1954 recession struck, "a spirit of super-salesmanship was promoted" to "intensify its promotional efforts on the mainland." Fomento doubled their advertising budget. In 1947, Fomento invested $7 million in a luxury hotel in San Juan, and two years later the Caribe Hilton opened its doors. Moscoso's goal, according to Ross, was to promote U.S. investment in manufacturing. Emphasizing "the 'good old USA' aspects of the Puerto Rico situation—the modern and efficient rather than the quaint and picturesque," the hotel would serve as "the needle's eye through which the rich man was to enter the tax haven." U.S. companies came. Between 1948 and 1950, "foreign" investment increased by $14 million. Of the 229 Fomento firms established by 1953, only 25 were locally owned. By 1960, 55 percent of capital came from outside of Puerto Rico, with the overwhelming majority from the States.[34]

Most new manufacturing jobs were in the apparel and food processing industries. Initially, home work increased, as the garment industry relied on the low-wage labor of women in their homes and in factories. By the 1949 congressional hearings, new U.S. plants employed 3,793 workers in shops and 3,440 home workers. Moscoso commented that "the Executive Council of Puerto Rico has adopted a policy that they don't want to stimulate home work," but concluded, "frankly, my personal point of view is that sometimes I get desperate and I wish that even if it were home workers, we wish we had them. Sometimes we just won't be able to avoid all of the evils of industrialization." In 1953, the U.S. Division of Wage Determinations described the needlework and fabricated textile products industry as "the most important manufacturing industry on the Island" and as "second only to sugar in its importance to the economy of Puerto Rico." The industry employed almost half of all workers covered by the minimum wage provisions of the FLSA, and in the early 1950s the value of shipments to the States had reached a new high of over $50 million annually. During the peak season, 15,000 factory and 40,000 home workers were employed. In 1957 wages for home needlework remained well below the U.S. minimum, at $.26 per hour in Puerto Rico—a striking contrast to $1.00 in the United States.[35]

By the mid-1950s, however, the home needlework industry was in rapid decline, displacing women workers and contributing to the rural economic crisis. From a peak of 54,000 in 1950, employment plummeted to 15,000 by 1957. Industry earnings decreased from $10 to $4 million between 1953 and 1956. Though significantly lower than in the States, wage levels were not low enough to compete effectively with imports from lower-wage areas, such as Japan and the Philippines. As home needlework declined, Fomento conceded that "even though homework is in fact very low-paid and has often been branded as a social evil, it has evident value in holding families together and supplementing rural incomes during the difficult transition period in agriculture." Similarly, Ross concluded, "no one could greatly lament the passing of an industry which made a sweatshop of every poor man's home in some sections of the island; except that this industry provided desperately needed income for several times the number of families that had been benefited by the Development Company." The new factory jobs failed to replace the lost jobs and were concentrated in the metropolitan areas, a dilemma characteristic of the development program during the 1950s.[36]

While the decline of agriculture and home needlework devastated rural areas, the San Juan metropolitan area was the magnet for industrialization (see Map 2.2). Between 1950 and 1953, the San Juan metropolitan area claimed 46 percent of the new industrial jobs for 23 percent of the population. By 1957, small towns received just one-sixth of the new jobs for more than a third of the population. Agricultural employment declined for men in rural areas, while the industrialization program employed women in metropolitan areas. By 1957, even Fomento was troubled by the regional and gender dimensions of their industrialization program. Touting industrialization's overall success, they nevertheless acknowledged that "even though our overall rate of economic progress and development is perhaps as rapid and as firmly grounded as in any part of our hemisphere, there remain groups of workers, individual towns, and even broader areas of Puerto Rico that have not shared fully in the measure of advance so far achieved." The beneficiaries had been "the major cities, their surrounding metropolitan areas, and city women." Fomento concluded: "It is in the country where additional jobs for men are most needed. . . . The bulk of the unemployment burden caused by the transition in agriculture has, therefore, fallen on older [male] workers." Rather than revitalizing agriculture, they called for more dispersed industrialization that would provide employment opportunities for men, especially heavy industries such as paper and pulp, forest products, meat packing, marble quarrying, and petroleum refining and petrochemicals. Fomento increased their publicity to and support for local investors and

MAP 2.2.   Location of Fomento Industries, 1956 and 1970

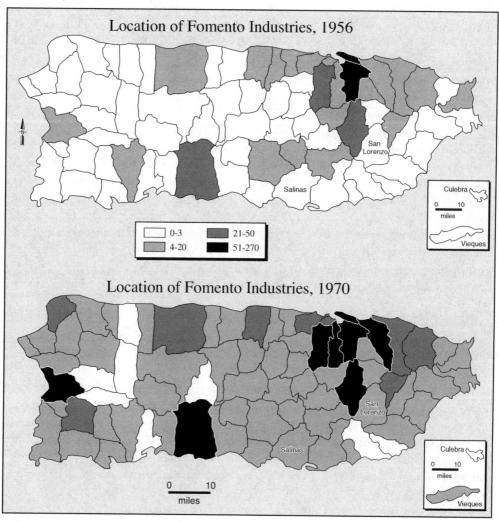

Location of Fomento Industries, 1956

San Lorenzo

Salinas

| | 0-3 | | 21-50 |
| | 4-20 | | 51-270 |

Culebra

Vieques

Location of Fomento Industries, 1970

San Lorenzo

Salinas

Culebra

Vieques

Sources: Puerto Rico Economic Development Administration, *Fomento de Puerto Rico* 3 (July 1956): 18; Rafael Picó, *The Geography of Puerto Rico* (Chicago: Aldine Publishing Company, 1974), 304.

offered mainland investors greater tax exemptions and rent subsidies for opening shop in the island's interior.[37]

With the second stage of their industrialization program, policy makers sought to address these issues. They promoted capital-intensive industries that would employ men, pay higher wages, bring jobs to areas beyond the San Juan metropolitan area, and be less likely to relocate when tax exemptions expired. As sociologist Palmira Ríos argues, Fomento worked within the accepted gender divisions of industrial labor in designing this stage. Petroleum refining and petrochemical industries became "Puerto Rico's top industrial priority" by 1965. Between 1967 and 1971, investment in the petrochemical industry increased from $500 million to $1 billion, the number of establishments from 24 to 36, and the number of workers from 2,851 to 5,616. New industries were established along the south coast between Peñuelas and Guayanilla. This apparent success was short-lived, however; 1973 witnessed the OPEC oil embargo and the U.S. government's imposition of fees on oil imports. The anticipated subsidiary industries never materialized, and environmental activists opposed the development strategy as environmentally unsound.[38]

Despite these efforts, labor-intensive industries continued to dominate manufacturing, remained concentrated in urban areas, and employed mostly women. By 1963, Fomento plants employed 70,000 workers, with 60 percent of new jobs going to women. Women's work, as Ríos contends, was "the key to the survival of these highly competitive industries in the new global economy." Growing from 18,736 to 36,819 workers between 1955 and 1970, the apparel industry remained the largest industrial employer, with 87 percent of its workers being women. In contrast, petroleum and related products employed 6,964 workers, 26 percent of whom were women. As a result, between 1950 and 1970 men's labor force participation decreased from 71 to 55 percent, while women's increased from 21 to 23 percent. Though Puerto Rico's Industrial Incentive Act of 1963 provided greater incentives for industries to locate outside the San Juan metropolitan area, Fomento conceded that the "greatest concentration of apparel plants is in and around the San Juan Metropolitan area." While seventy municipios had at least one apparel plant, the San Juan metropolitan area claimed 40 percent of the island's 2,367 manufacturing enterprises in 1967.[39]

Fomento continued to promote Puerto Rico as a profitable site for the U.S. apparel industry. Attributing their success to the "skill of the workforce" and "tax and other incentives," Fomento noted in 1973 that "three out of four apparel plants in Puerto Rico have [been] established with the guidance and assistance of Puerto Rico's Economic Development Administration (EDA) that maintains offices throughout the United States." Indeed, more than 50 percent of the plants were subsidiaries of U.S. firms. The wage differential between Puerto Rico and the States increased from $.71 to $.91 between 1965 and 1972, at which time garment industry wages in Puerto Rico averaged $1.76, compared to $2.67 in the States. In short, Puerto Rico offered "a very favorable profit record"; firms in Puerto Rico were almost two and a half times more profitable than those in the States before taxes, and more than four and a half times more profitable after taxes.[40]

Despite the substantial profits available to U.S. companies, employment in Puerto Rico declined during the 1950s, and policy makers found other ways to celebrate their industrialization program. Noting that employment decreased by 64,000 between 1950 and 1954, Ross advocated paying "tribute" to the development program's "effect on income rather than in the disappointing terms of its effect on employment," and insisted that the problem was not the industrialization program: "It was, rather, the rest of the economy that was out of step." Similarly, in a 1958 speech on "manpower," Secretary of Labor Fernando Sierra Berdecía revealed that the number of people "not in the labor force" increased by 108,000 between 1950 and 1956. Though manufacturing employment decreased by 10,000, Sierra Berdecía pointed to manufacturing's "growing importance in our economic set-up," asserting, "this is a bright spot in our economic development, wage and salary employment in the other manufacturing industries has increased considerably, to a point where it nearly compensates for the declines . . . there has been a definite improvement in both the quality and stability of employment in manufacturing." He did not contrast the loss of 51,000 jobs in agriculture to the gain of only 8,000 nonagricultural jobs.[41]

Policy makers also defined women's work as "voluntary" and "supplemental," and then discounted unemployed home needleworkers. While Sierra Berdecía identified 53,000 of the 108,000 people no longer in the work force as "housewives," employment in the home needlework industry had declined by 29,000, suggesting that some of his "housewives" were displaced women. Ross attributed the decreasing labor force first to migration, then to "the voluntary withdrawal from the labor force of unemployed home needleworkers for whom no alternative employment opportunities existed." Perhaps unaware of the contradiction, he did not explain how women's withdrawal from the labor force could be considered "voluntary" when no other "employment opportunities existed." Writing in 1965, Lloyd G. Reynolds argued that home needleworkers should be excluded from employment totals: "Since this is a sideline activity carried on in the household, many of these workers work and produce very little. . . . A second reason for considering home needleworkers as a special group is that, as opportunities in the area declined, most of these people simply vanished from the labor force." In the final analysis, he discounted "the disappearance of 41,000 'jobs' in needlework" during the 1950s.[42]

Instead of decreasing employment and the threats to household economies that included the labor of women, policy makers defined the problem as "overpopulation" and the solution as reducing the population through sterilization and emigration. Notions of "overpopulation" reinforced the view that agriculture was irrelevant and industrialization was imperative. For Ross, "the relationship of natural resources to population in Puerto Rico is such that if it is to become in any meaningful sense a developed economy, it must become industrialized." Considering it the dual battle of "population and production," Perloff advised that "while every effort is made to expand production, an effort of comparable proportions [should] be made to control the rate of population increase." Policy makers, according to historians Annette Ramírez de Arellano and Conrad Seipp, accepted "the view that fertility rates could be acted upon without changing the political, social, and economic context within which demographic decisions are made." Yet neither birth control nor emigration were politically popular approaches to reducing the population, so policy makers hesitated to admit that they were promoting either.[43]

A 1944 study by the Puerto Rico Planning Board focusing on women's reproduction suggested a consensus on "overpopulation" and revealed the emphasis on "mothers." According to the study, "that the basic problem of Puerto Rico is the maladjustment between resources and population is clearly the conclusion of most serious students." Predicting that "the pressure of population on resources, which is already great, will become intolerably greater," the authors called for "a conscious policy of emigration and birth control." Sensitive to legal restrictions, they noted that "the teaching of contraceptive methods in Puerto Rico has been restricted to mothers who require freedom from pregnancy or spaced pregnancies for their physical health" and that "post-partum sterilization is practiced to a certain extent on a voluntary basis to protect the mother whose health would be endangered by further pregnancies." Nevertheless, suggesting the potentials of expanding both, they called for "a continued expansion of the present work" in contraceptive education and considered it "a very small sum to pay annually for the stabilization of Puerto Rico's population." In regard to sterilization, they hinted only that "more could have been performed if facilities had permitted."[44]

The concern with "overpopulation" was coupled with political constraints on promoting population control. As a private citizen, Luis Muñoz Marín advocated birth control in 1923: "I favor Malthusianism, the voluntary limitation of childbearing, supported by the government . . . an active campaign should be carried out so that the largest possible number of poor families will want to learn" contraceptive methods. Once a politician, he tempered his enthusiasm, and as Ramírez de Arellano and Seipp contend, "Muñoz established the policy of private support for and public disavowal of birth control." Hence, in 1957, when the new secretary of health, Dr. Guillermo Arbona, wanted to pursue a family planning program, Muñoz Marín gave him a conditional "free hand." The Family Planning Association of Puerto Rico, a private organization established in 1954, would continue its promotion and education campaign. The Health Department, Muñoz Marín instructed Arbona, would provide the services the public requested as a result of the Association's efforts. Publicly, Muñoz Marín advocated increasing production to solve the population to resources problem.[45]

The increased sterilization of women coincided with the industrialization program. Although private hospitals led the way, between 1944 and 1946 the number of sterilizations performed in Puerto Rico's five public district hospitals doubled to about 1,000 per year. Researchers assumed that the procedure was prevalent in municipal hospitals as well. Fomento and the Family Planning Association "enlisted the industrialists' cooperation in checking population growth by stressing the conflict between reproduction and production." On a similar note, Ross hoped that manufacturing jobs for women would do "more to promote the cause of birth control than all the free clinics that have been operated since the 1930s." Ramírez de Arellano and Seipp conclude that "Muñoz's reluctance to espouse an explicit policy of population control, coupled with eugenic and medical pressures favoring sterilization, resulted in public laissez-faire, private prodding, and an acceleration of the existing trend" of increased sterilization. Medical reasons fell by the wayside, "informed consent" was perhaps questionable, and by 1965 one-third of Puerto Rican women between the ages of twenty and forty-nine had been sterilized, "a rate significantly higher than that of any other country."[46]

Policy makers also turned to emigration to reduce the population. Early in their administration, the PPD focused on "colonization," building on the Chardón Plan, which, in addition to agrarian reform and industrialization, considered "a policy of emigration" to be "desirable, probably imperative" and recommended "mass colonization projects in under-populated regions of tropical countries similar to Puerto Rico," like Cuba, the Dominican Republic, Costa Rica, Venezuela, and Brazil. In 1947, both the Emigration Advisory Committee and Clarence Senior's study explored the resettlement of Puerto Ricans in Latin American countries. Moscoso involved Fomento in the effort, sending a representative to Brazil to explore possibilities for a Puerto Rican colony and subsidizing Costa Rica's national airline as an incentive for Puerto Ricans to move to Central America. Few countries, however, seemed anxious to accept large numbers of Puerto Ricans, and some had "white only" stipulations. In addition, resettlement was an expensive proposition and a logistical nightmare. Nor was it clear that Puerto Ricans wanted to relocate to remote agricultural colonies.[47]

Insisting that the official policy was to neither encourage nor discourage migration, policy makers shifted their efforts from colonization to promoting migration to the States. In 1947, as the Director of the Social Sciences Research Center at the University of Puerto Rico, Clarence Senior expressed a common view: "The situation is so desperate, however, that emigration must be included in [any] well-rounded program for attacking overpopulation. It must be pushed intensively, with enthusiasm, initiative and imagination but also with balanced judgement." That year Puerto Rico's legislature established the Bureau of Employment and Migration within the Department of Labor. Senior became the Director of the National Office located in New York City. Tempering his statements, he now stated the official policy:

> The Commonwealth of Puerto Rico, as a matter of public policy, usually neither encourages nor discourages migration. It realizes that until the island's economic development has reached a point where it can offer job opportunities and economic security to its workers, ambitious citizens, who can, will search elsewhere. Therefore, the Government strives to help those who decide to leave to adjust more quickly in their new home community.

Repeated often, this language mirrored the legislation that created the Bureau. Yet the Bureau defined "help" broadly, opening offices in New York City and Chicago to keep migrants and potential migrants abreast of employment opportunities, and operating the contract labor program, which sent thousands of men to work on farms in the States each year.[48]

The Farm Placement Division of Puerto Rico's Department of Labor mounted an intensive recruitment campaign, with the same vigor Fomento used to recruit U.S. investors. Whereas the industrialization program concentrated in urban areas, the farm labor program concentrated on rural areas. "Recruitment was extended to remote wards in the interior of the Island," with municipal governments providing facilities for "the recruitment, selection and referral of workers in the various towns in the interior of the Island." In subsequent years, permanent satellite offices and temporary locations were established throughout rural areas. From 4,598 men in 1949, the number of Puerto Ricans who received government labor contracts for work in the States jumped to 14,930 in just four years. Policy makers attributed rural unemployment to increased mechanization, which they estimated would "displace" 40 percent of the agricultural labor force. They "expected that migration and industrialization, as both progress, will take care of displaced workers." Furthermore, with seasonal workers sending or carrying an estimated $18,532,000 back to Puerto Rico between 1951 and 1954, the Division asserted, "the contribution of this program to the economy of the island is evident." The following year the estimate was one and a half million dollars, and the Division concluded that "the migration program has greatly helped in solving local problems of unemployment and in improving the economic conditions of many families."[49]

The farm labor program highlighted the limited solutions policy makers offered for Puerto Rico's agricultural economies. Blaming the program, sugar and coffee growers complained of labor shortages. The general manager of the Coffee Growers Cooperative "confirmed . . . that workers from the coffee areas had moved out to settle in the towns or cities of the island or had gone to the mainland seeking better wages." Waging their battle in *El Mundo*, in 1952 the Association of Sugar Producers of Puerto Rico charged that mills were not operating at full capacity and insisted that "all efforts to take Puerto Rican workers to the continental United States should follow procedures that guarantee, before anything else, the number of workers that the agricultural industries of this country need and employ." Government recruitment fanned "the desire to travel and to see the world," making laborers ignore opportunities near their homes. The paradox was that "in an overpopulated country like ours, the farmer is forced to leave part of the crop in the fields because he cannot find the labor to harvest it," while Puerto Rican workers were in the States harvesting other crops.[50]

Instead of shortages, the Division insisted that Puerto Rico was "an island with a surplus of agricultural workers" and seasonal labor needs. The Division sought to coordinate this "surplus" by improving "local pre-season planning to avoid the referral of workers for migration while they are working in local industries." The "established policy" was that "no recruitment is made in areas of labor shortage." So, "in March and April, when the sugar cane season reached its peak, recruitments were restricted to the mountain areas," and "publicity and propaganda" were limited to "mail and telegraph notifications and direct contact with workers." When the harvest ended, "open publicity was put into effect, which included extensive use of radio programs and spots, sound vehicles, posters and handbills." Building on earlier patterns of internal seasonal migrations, they also organized day-hauling to areas of labor shortages and encouraged remote coffee growers to build camps and improve conditions for migrant laborers.[51]

The Division nevertheless grew increasingly defensive of its handling of contract labor and local agriculture. In 1952, the Division admitted that "this year our planning efforts were directed primarily to the migration of agricultural workers to areas of labor shortage on the mainland since this is the major activity of the Farm Placement Division." The next year, they reasoned, "we believe that a large segment of this labor force . . . is willing to migrate and could be used to fill the needs of manpower in the mainland farms without disturbing to any marked degree the agricultural economy of the island." By 1956, they insisted that "these two phases of the program do not conflict, as a matter of fact they supplement each other." Still, as the agricultural labor force shrank, they acknowledged that "the decline is due mainly to the migration of workers to the U.S." Finally, denying any conflict between contract labor and local agriculture, the Division reported that "despite the continued reduction in the local agricultural labor force and the local demand for workers during sugar cane harvesting, all clearance orders for agricultural workers received [from the States] were adequately served."[52]

Ultimately, policy makers claimed responsibility for only one of two migration streams. Senior explained: "Two streams of migration flow from the island; they differ significantly in origin, destination, and length of stay. One flows out in the spring and back in the fall; the other flows out and remains permanently. One is fairly highly organized; the other, spontaneous. The first consists of farmworkers; the second of city people." Assuming responsibility only for the "organized" migration, policy makers emphasized the "seasonal" nature of the farm labor program to quiet political opposition in Puerto Rico and to calm the fears of continental Americans that Puerto Ricans would stay in the States. The stated goal was for laborers to work Puerto Rico's peak season from January to July and then go to the States for its peak season from July to November. Despite their "intensive campaign," the Farm Placement Division insisted that they were not encouraging migration, reiterating the official policy: "The nature of the publicity employed in conveying information about employment opportunities in the continent to prospective migrants, neither encourages nor discourages the migration of Puerto Rican workmen to the United States." After all, "those who accepted referral did it on their own free will, as they have a right to do as citizens of the United States." This approach portrayed migration as an individual choice, ignoring the economic crisis, the industrialization program's failure to provide adequate employment, and the role of formal, government-sponsored programs in increasing migration.[53]

Rather than confronting rural economic decline, policy makers and scholars continued to emphasize "overpopulation." Geographer John Augelli used alarmist language in his 1952 essay:

> People to land ratios in San Lorenzo are oriental in intensity. . . . More than two people per acre cling to the mountainous farm land, and rural densities are constantly increasing. Even on the remotest peaks one can see a profusion of farmsteads and hear the *jíbaro's* voice echoing through the hills. . . . With the soils of the area already exhausted, the potential dangers of the situation become even more apparent.

Augelli's images of "oriental" people-to-land ratios, of people "clinging" to the mountainsides, and of "echoing" voices graphically portrayed his sense of "overpopulation," as well as a less than positive image of the people living in the region. The "dangers" he referred to were not the economic hardships confronted by San Lorenzo's residents but their negative impact on areas of settlement: "The supersaturated mountain lands have begun a retarded export of people which together with the export of the rest of the highland zones threatens to involve San Juan and New York in one of the largest slum developments in modern urban history." For Augelli, it seems, deteriorating economic conditions in rural areas were inevitable, while population ratios could change.[54]

Alternative voices, calling for improved agriculture or more balanced approaches to economic development, were not the ones that carried. Unlike Augelli, geographer Vernon Brockman concluded that "only through an effective type of land use planning and an increased efficiency in farm management can agriculture achieve the stability and security which is essential for the welfare of the Caguas–San Lorenzo area and for the island as a whole." Similarly, Perloff insisted, "It is not a question of industrialization versus agriculture." Instead, the interrelatedness of agriculture and industry meant that "Puerto Rico could not hope to achieve anything resembling an adequate level of living for its people unless it became an area of intensive and balanced agriculture, where farming was a scientific business as well as a way of life, and unless it processed and expertly marketed a wide variety of commodities for export and domestic use." As the PPD focused exclusively on industrialization, agriculture declined and Puerto Rico became a major importer of U.S. food products, a trend augmented with the introduction of federally subsidized food stamps in 1975.[55]

Puerto Rico's population did grow in the postwar era, as improvements in health care and sanitation in rural areas reduced the death rate. Geographer Déborah Berman Santana notes: "As is true of demographic transitions throughout the world, a rapid decrease in death rates and lag in the fall of birth rates resulted in a temporary increase in the natural growth rate—which was eliminated by massive emigration to the United States." Views of Puerto Rico as overpopulated and of Puerto Ricans as incapable of controlling their fertility, she argues, shaped Operation Bootstrap, as policy makers and scholars articulated the "doctrine of nonviability"—"that Puerto Rico was too small, too overpopulated, and too lacking in natural resources for less dependent economic and political strategies." Instead, it was the rural economic crisis and the resultant hardships for households that sent rural people in search of work.[56]

From the Country to the Cities

In addition to the regional impact of the development program, rural economies were negatively affected by shifts in world markets and in the States. Colonial ties defined Puerto Rico's place in the global economy, as the States remained the principal market for Puerto Rico's sugar and tobacco and imposed quotas on sugar. Coffee, on the other hand, did not have tariff protection and did not sell well in the States. Nor did Puerto Rico's coffee and home needlework fare well on the world market. Meanwhile, U.S. investment drove Puerto Rico's industrialization, and Puerto Rico became a major market for U.S. goods. As Weisskoff notes, "modern economic development, especially in the interior of Puerto Rico, has meant the replacement of all the simpler exchange relations by cash relations and the immediate integration into the world cash network." Faced with the rural economic crisis, migrants left rural areas in search of work, sparking Puerto Rico's rapid urbanization and massive migration to the States, including Philadelphia.[57]

Reflecting regional and gender dimensions of economic change and government policies, the postwar era in Puerto Rico witnessed an exodus from rural areas and rapid urbanization. During the 1950s, emigration peaked, as forty out of seventy-six municipios lost population (see Map 2.3). The population in the San Juan metropolitan area grew by 27 percent, compared to just 6 percent island-wide. During the 1960s, both trends continued. As the population in thirteen municipios decreased, the San Juan metropolitan area grew rapidly, with the populations in Bayamón and Carolina increasing by 876 and 2,965 percent respectively. Concerned policy makers turned their attention to rural areas in an effort to stem the tide. One goal of industrial dispersion, according to Ross, was to save "the City of San Juan from a still greater aggravation of its monumental growing pains."

MAP 2.3. Population Change, 1950–1970

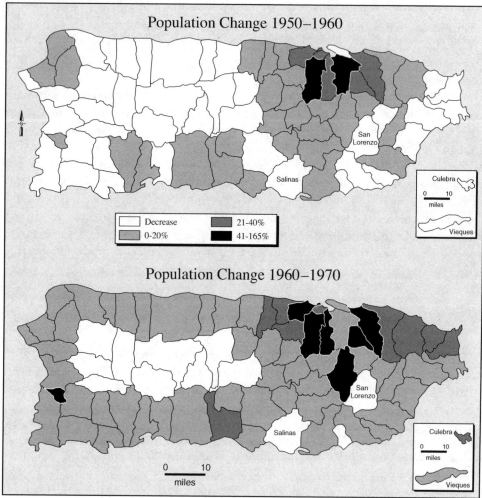

Sources: U.S. Department of Commerce, Bureau of the Census, *U.S. Census of Population: 1960*, vol. 1, *Characteristics of the Population*, pt. 53, Puerto Rico (Washington, D.C., 1963), 13–17; and *U.S. Census of Population: 1970*, vol. 1, *Characteristics of the Population*, pt. 53, Puerto Rico (Washington, D.C., 1973), 18–28.

Similarly, the Planning Board explained, "The change towards urban areas has been so rapid that the provision of services has not been able, in many instances, to keep pace with the rural-urban change." Attributing this massive migration to "the change in economic structure leading to adverse conditions in the rural areas of the country," the Planning Board undertook a study of rural municipios.[58]

Though agricultural decline affected all major crops and rural regions, there were variations in emigration and destinations. The coffee region experienced the heaviest emigration, as the population of all municipios except one decreased during the 1950s and 1960s. The region was devastated by the continuing decline of coffee and the sudden decline of the home needlework industry. Between the early 1950s and the early

1970s, the price of coffee beans in the world market fell from $80 to $50 per hundred-weight. It was a "vicious circle." Limited markets and low prices meant that growers lacked the money and incentives to invest in improvements. Crop yields decreased and coffee became less profitable. Citing labor shortages, high expenses, and inadequate government support, coffee growers ceased production and land abandonment was common, further reducing jobs in the region. Perloff concluded: "Cultivation is inefficient, yields are extremely low, and costs of production are too high for profitable operations. The levels of living of the people of the region are distressingly low."[59]

As the coffee industry declined, the practices of exchanging land use and goods for labor were undermined, leaving the rural poor with fewer means to meet their subsistence needs. Instead of granting subsistence plots, hacienda owners grew minor crops to sell, and milk was sold at market rather than given to agregados in exchange for tending cattle. Low seasonal wages replaced the previous arrangements. The rural poor had purchased rice, beans, codfish, lard, clothes, and metal tools when they had cash, and relied on subsistence crops when they lacked cash. As a cash economy penetrated the region and it became a market for U.S. goods, the household production of goods decreased. By 1949, Wolf found, "even in the center of the island the decline of the coffee industry has brought with it such phenomena as rapid out-migration, decline of private marketing, changes in the relations between owners and workers from a personal basis toward a cash economy, and departure of Spanish families." With the demise of the home needlework industry, the region lost its only other significant source of cash income for workers. The region was home to the highest unemployment rates and the poorest municipios. Acknowledging that "very little industry" had been established, even the Planning Board conceded that "migration is clearly here a matter of a push from the countryside rather than a pull from the cities."[60]

Migration from the tobacco region, including San Lorenzo, was also significant. During the 1950s, four municipios lost population, and in the next decade San Lorenzo and Orocovis continued to experience emigration that surpassed their birth rates. Tobacco's decline followed a brief period of growth; as Perloff noted, "the extremely favorable conditions existing at the end of the war and immediately after the war gave a temporary stimulus to the tobacco industry." The value of tobacco exports then plummeted from more than $22 million in 1945 to just under $9 million in 1948. Still the principal market for Puerto Rico's tobacco, the United States accounted for more than 99 percent of the total export value between 1950 and 1957. U.S. consumers' preferences were shifting, however, in ways that severely diminished the market for Puerto Rico's tobacco. Overall consumption of cigars declined, while that of cigarettes increased. Despite duties, Puerto Rico's tobacco was more expensive than filler tobacco imported from Cuba, the Philippines, and Indonesia. New methods enabled the use of less expensive tobacco in cigars. As a result, U.S. consumption of Puerto Rico's tobacco decreased, and consumption of foreign tobacco increased. Puerto Rican tobacco's market share in the States dropped from 37 to 32 percent between the early 1950s and the early 1970s.[61]

As agricultural jobs declined, tobacco processing suffered as well. Between 1950 and 1956, employment in tobacco decreased by 9,000. Sierra Berdecía reported that "since the beginning of 1957 there has been a very significant drop in employment in tobacco stemming and redrying," with employment dropping by 3,000, or 43 percent of 1956 levels. In 1949 there were 626 tobacco processing plants, but by 1954 only 259 remained. The Planning Board contended that crop diversity gave "these municipios a more solid economic basis than the coffee areas" and that the "availability of employment opportunities makes it unnecessary for the families of the area to move away." Yet as Brockmann noted in 1955, the region's economy was "predominantly agricultural" and "industrial activity is largely confined to processing and distributing agricultural products." He concluded that "the major island-wide problems of agriculture are present and they are more critical in the Caguas–San Lorenzo Region than, for example, in many sugar producing districts of the coastal areas."[62]

Indeed, during the 1940s "the population was still heavily concentrated in the main agricultural areas, especially those in sugar cane production," according to the Planning Board. As sugar's demise came later than other commercial crops, the southern and northern coasts attracted migrants. In 1949, Mintz wrote: "To the present day, small landowners and farmers working by share arrangements still descend in substantial numbers from the highlands during the harvest to augment their cash income by working in the cane." Pointing to higher wages in sugar and harsh living conditions in the highlands, he added, "now workers came from the highlands to the coast, and many stayed on after the cutting was over." Similarly, Padilla Seda observed inmigration to government-owned proportional profit farms, and argued that it was the "underemployment throughout Puerto Rico which caused an influx of workers from other regions seeking jobs." As agricultural employment decreased from 45 to 39 percent of the labor force during the 1940s, the proportion employed in sugar increased from 54 to 60 percent. In 1950, 48 percent of cultivated land was devoted to sugar, which accounted for 56 percent of agricultural income. The number of farms growing sugar cane had increased from 7,693 to 19,274 between 1935 and 1955. When production peaked in 1952, Puerto Rico had produced more sugar than its U.S. quota for five years in a row.[63]

Still, the agricultural crisis stuck sugar. Production dropped from 1,359,841 tons to 478,000 tons between 1952 and 1969, and by 1957 Puerto Rico no longer filled its annual quota. The Agricultural Experiment Station explained: "During the past few years a series of distressing conditions have harassed the sugar producers placing them in an unfavorable competitive position compared with those in other productive zones in the domestic sugar-producing area." Puerto Rico was not competing effectively with other areas producing for the U.S. market, including Louisiana, Florida, the U.S. sugar beet growing region, and Hawaii. Although workers' wages were lower in Puerto Rico, the labor cost per ton of sugar produced was the highest. Mechanization was not as extensive in Puerto Rico, where cane was still cut primarily by hand with machetes, in contrast to Hawaii where machines cut and gathered sugar cane. Puerto Rico's labor requirements were higher as a result. In addition, yields of cane per acre had increased for all areas except Puerto Rico, where yields decreased between 1949 and 1956. Puerto Rico's growers had a net loss in 1953 and 1955, and as sugar became less profitable, the cattle industry took over former sugar lands. Despite dropping from 56 to 34 percent of the value of all exports between 1950 and 1956, sugar remained "the most important single export product" and the largest employer, with 130,000 workers during the 1956 peak season. Nevertheless, employment in sugar plummeted to 23,000 by 1969. As in the tobacco industry, processing suffered as a result, and employment fell from 12,900 to 4,516 between 1949 and 1967.[64]

Seeking "an understanding of present critical conditions of the industry," the Agricultural Experiment Station revisited the impact of U.S. sugar programs in 1958. This time they concluded that the programs had a positive impact by providing a market, keeping sugar prices higher and more stable, and providing direct payments to sugar producers that accounted for more than 16 percent of their income. In short, "considering the cost situation of recent years it is not difficult to see that a large number of growers probably are still in business because of the effects of the sugar programs on the income of producers." Despite the "critical conditions" in the industry and producers' reliance on income subsidies, the study concluded that "there are very few alternative crops with a good market" and that "any adjustments made would probably have to be directed at reducing the costs of sugarcane production."[65]

As the sugar industry declined with nothing to replace it, the northern and southern regions experienced the population losses of the 1950s. In the southeastern region 12 of 16 municipios, including Salinas, lost population, as did 9 of 13 municipios in the southwestern region and half of the municipios in the northern region. During the 1960s, Salinas, Arroyo, and Vieques continued to lose population in the southeastern region. Meanwhile, no municipios in the southwestern region and only Rincón in the northern region lost population. The Planning Board attributed this leveling off to some gains in manufacturing along the southern coast. As for the northern coast, the Planning Board concluded, "the economic transformation of Puerto Rico is most evident" and "agricultural activity has been mostly replaced by manufacturing, commerce and service activities." Although agrarian reforms in the northern region had not prevented the sugar industry's decline nor diversified agricultural production, they may have slowed emigration by increasing land ownership through the parcelas and family farm programs.[66]

On leaving rural areas, some migrants went to metropolitan areas in search of manufacturing jobs. Although downplaying the rural economic crisis, economist Peter Gregory illustrated key elements of the rural to urban migration from 1953 to 1956. Interviewing 1,045 industrial workers in the San Juan metropolitan and northern coastal areas and in Ponce, Gregory found that 70 percent had lived in rural areas before getting their jobs, and 52 percent of their fathers had worked in agriculture, as had more than half of the men, most as wage laborers. Gregory argued, however, that migration was not an "escape from a life of mere subsistence," but rather that "a combination of desires to maximize income and to seek change for its own sake" were "more important." Nevertheless, the demise of agriculture was evident; those leaving agriculture felt that "the break was a permanent one," with 60 percent saying they would not return to agriculture under any conditions and 27 percent saying they would return only if they could own their own farms. Forty-six percent of men who had worked in agriculture wanted higher earnings, 13 percent disliked agricultural work, and 13 percent thought there was no future in agriculture. Gregory acknowledged that "land ownership, in itself, is viewed as only a limited source of social prestige and certainly as no effective substitute for income." With almost half the respondents women, Gregory's study revealed that this was a labor migration for women as well as men. For Gregory, "the appearance of factory employment opportunities was directly responsible for drawing a majority of the women in our sample into the active labor force." Manufacturing was the first job for 55 percent of the women; 26 percent had worked in home sewing and 12 percent as domestics. Like the men, women considered the change a permanent one: "In terms of their attitudes toward industrial employment, women seemed to be no less committed than men." Ninety percent of the unmarried women and 85 percent of all other women planned to continue working indefinitely.[67]

Given new industries' concentration in urban areas and their reliance on women's labor, another study suggested that women were more successful than men as internal labor migrants between 1955 and 1960. Positing a traditional labor migration based on men, John Macisco was surprised by "the lack of selectivity of male migrants in the labor force and the slightly higher proportion of unemployed migrants." In metropolitan areas, only 59 percent of male migrants were in the labor force, in contrast to 68 percent of nonmigrants. Migrating women, on the other hand, were more likely to enter the labor force than their nonmigrant counterparts—31 percent of migrants compared to 25 percent of nonmigrants. Pointing to "the poor job situation on the Island for males," Macisco concluded, "female migration may be more oriented toward real opportunity structures." In short, women migrated in search of work and were more able to find jobs in the metropolitan areas than men.[68]

Others left rural areas and migrated to the States, with the rural economic crisis and the farm labor program shaping migration. A 1952 airport survey of 1,141 migrants found that most, 69 percent, were from rural areas, where 66 percent of the men had been agricultural laborers and another 1 percent farmers. Women's occupations were not listed separately, but only 38 percent of 177 women were identified as "housewives." Both men and women were clearly labor migrants, stating that they were leaving because there was little work or little money in Puerto Rico. At the time of migration, 34 percent of the men and 62 percent of the women were unemployed. The overwhelming majority either had jobs lined up or planned to find work—99 and 64 percent of men and women respectively. Almost half of the men had farm labor contracts, accounting for 78 percent of those with jobs. These men had been farmworkers, laborers, and artisans. While only 29 percent of the migrants going to New York City had last worked in agriculture, fully 92 percent of those going to New Jersey and 80 percent of those going to Pennsylvania had last worked in agriculture.[69]

As a result, Philadelphia's migrants came largely from rural areas. Marriage records over a twenty-year period give a good approximation of migrants' origins, which correlates with other data. Catholic churches noted the place of baptism, while city marriage licenses sometimes listed the place of birth by municipio. Combined, these sources indicated the place of birth or baptism for 2,853 Puerto Rican migrants married in Philadelphia between 1945 and 1965. Growing from 1,910 to 7,300 between 1950 and 1954, Philadelphia's Puerto Rican population was overwhelmingly recent arrivals, with 83 percent born in Puerto Rico and only 13 percent born in Philadelphia. This was also a young population, with a median age of twenty-one. The timing of migration and the demographics of the Puerto Rican population suggest that migrants were likely candidates for marriage in the twenty-year period. Philadelphia's migrants had been born or baptized in seventy-five of Puerto Rico's seventy-six municipios. Yet eight municipios accounted for 39 percent of the migrants, and there were regional variations (see Table 2.1).[70]

Most migrants came from the tobacco and southeastern regions—31 and 22 percent respectively. Both regions witnessed the decline of agriculture and agricultural processing, without the significant growth of other industry. Four of the tobacco region's thirteen municipios had more than 100 migrants marrying, and San Lorenzo accounted for the largest single group with 244 migrants. As inheritance custom and law dictated the equal division of land among all children, land tenure in the region was marked by fractionalization, and the number of small holdings increased. In 1949, Manners noted that "many young people" of the rural middle class with farms of 8 to 35 cuerdas "became permanent migrants to the United States." Young people sought other economic options, including migration to rural areas, especially within the eastern highlands, to Puerto Rico's urban centers, or to the States. In the southeastern region, Salinas accounted for more than 100 migrant marriages. Mintz noted the increased migration from this region to the States in 1949, pointing to the U.S. Army and U.S. labor needs in urban and agricultural areas. In both regions, however, agricultural decline increased emigration, while the government's contract labor program facilitated migration to the States, including Philadelphia.

TABLE 2.1.   Origins of Puerto Ricans Marrying in Philadelphia, 1945–1965

Place of Birth or Baptism	Number of Migrants	Percent of Total
Puerto Rico	2,853	100.1
Tobacco Region	875	30.7
San Lorenzo	244	
Coamo	115	
Barranquitas	114	
Caguas	108	
Sugar: Southeastern	628	22.0
Salinas	122	
Sugar: Southwestern	318	11.2
Sugar: Northern	478	16.8
Arecibo	160	
Coffee Region	399	14.0
Utuado	135	
San Sebastian	112	
San Juan Metro	155	5.4

Sources: See Appendix II.

Note: The number of migrants reflects those married in Philadelphia between 1945 and 1965 for whom place of birth or baptism is identified in church records and/or on city licenses. Municipios are those with more than one hundred migrant marriages. Not all columns total exactly 100 percent due to rounding.

Another 11 percent of migrants came from the southwestern sugar region. Although negatively affected by economic changes, these were not the regions that experienced the severest decline of agriculture. Nor did they experience the most industrialization.[71]

Despite heavy emigration, relatively few migrants from the coffee region married in Philadelphia (14 percent), with Utuado and San Sebastián each accounting for more than 100. Apparently, migrants composed a larger segment of internal migration streams or traveled to other destinations in the States. Residents talked of sharecropping in tobacco and working in town or the sugar cane fields, according to Wolf, and "many people have indeed migrated to town, to the coast, and to San Juan." Wolf described the people as "too isolated by topography, social ties, and transportation facilities to move easily from one cultural situation into another" and as "too poor to migrate." Nevertheless, he concluded, "barring government intervention, more and more people will make the transition from the coffee way of life to other ways of living, and more and more workers will go 'to New York, New Jersey, Pennsylvania to harvest potatoes, asparagus, etc.'"[72]

Those areas most affected by industrialization, the San Juan metropolitan area and to a lesser extent the northern coast, had fewer migrants marrying in Philadelphia. The San Juan metropolitan area accounted for just 5 percent of migrant marriages, and no municipio had more than 100. The northern region accounted for 17 percent of the migrant marriages, with Arecibo having more than 100. Along the northern coast, Padilla Seda noted, "migration to the cities—in this case, largely to New York City—has drained off an enormous number of surplus workers, but many persons have found even the moderate cost of transportation to the United States prohibitive." She added, though, that "since the end of World War II, many young men have migrated to the United States a number of times as contract labor to work in the agricultural harvests. . . . Most migratory agricultural laborers, however, return to the community during winter when the sugar harvest begins." As the sugar industry declined, more contract laborers may have stayed in the States, and while industrialization provided some jobs, others sought economic alternatives elsewhere.[73]

In her 1965 anthropology dissertation, Joan D. Koss also concluded that the Puerto Rican population of Philadelphia was "predominantly rural," confirming the "general knowledge among Puerto Ricans resident in Philadelphia that the vast majority of 'the community' is made up of 'country' people." While 30 percent of the sixty-eight migrants she interviewed came from municipios with large urban areas, 59 percent were born and raised in the country, and 24 percent were born in the country but moved to a town as children or teenagers. Interviews with forty-five additional migrants found that 62 percent were rural, 24 percent were from towns or cities, and 13 percent were not identified. Her data on ninety-nine migrants reveals similar regions of origin, as well.[74]

Not surprisingly, many of Philadelphia's migrants came from farming families. On city marriage licenses, 36 percent of migrants identified their fathers living in Puerto Rico as farmworkers, the largest single category; 21 percent were retired or had no jobs, and another 20 percent were laborers, many of whom worked in construction. The overwhelming majority of mothers were identified as "housewives," 91 percent, probably contributors to their rural household economies. Most of those employed were domestics. Even several migrants born or baptized in the San Juan metropolitan area listed their fathers as farmers on city marriage licenses. In an oral history, one migrant from Bayamón, part of the San Juan metropolitan area, told of being a farmer's daughter. Like their fathers, more male migrants had last worked in farming in Puerto Rico than in any other occupation—27 percent, according to a 1954 study.[75]

Marriage records also suggest gender dimensions of the migration to Philadelphia. Agricultural areas had more male migrants married in the city, while industrializing areas had more female migrants. From the tobacco, coffee, and southern regions slightly more men than women appeared in the marriage records. The farm labor program may have contributed to the higher ratio of men from these agricultural areas. In contrast, both the San Juan metropolitan area and the northern region had more women than men represented. Women from these areas may have had higher expectations for gainful employment and migration to Philadelphia may have improved their options. Needlework employers in the San Juan area thought migration to the States was one of the primary reasons their workers quit, according to a 1953 survey. Meanwhile, 48 percent of women in Philadelphia had last worked as machine operators in Puerto Rico, and only 28 percent identified themselves as housewives in a 1954 study.[76]

Though most came from rural areas, some migrants, like Doña Margarita and Don Marcelino, came from the San Juan metropolitan area. As Don Marcelino's experience suggests, even those in the cities found little or no work and low wages, and used farm labor contracts to travel to the States. As manufacturing jobs for men were scarce, metropolitan employment offices offered seasonal agricultural work in the States instead. Don Marcelino was one of 10,637 men who got labor contracts in 1954. With eight regional offices throughout the island, the San Juan office referred 12 percent of these farmworkers, as men living in the metropolitan area and rural migrants who could not find jobs became candidates for farm labor contracts. Don Marcelino, however, left farm work within the first year and moved to Philadelphia, where he worked in agriculture for a few summers and in a metal factory for many years.[77]

While raising their eight children, Doña Margarita also found paid employment and contributed to her household through informal economic activities. Migration to Philadelphia eased her household tasks: "You know, when I got here, everything was different. . . . There I had to wash everything with a washboard, carry all that water. . . . There I had to cook with wood." In the city, she had indoor plumbing and a modern stove, and "the milkman came and left the milk outside; yeah, and in the morning you got up and got your milk, the newspaper, and the bread." The first two summers Doña Margarita had "the worst of my jobs," picking blueberries and strawberries on New Jersey farms with her husband and children. Later, she helped her *comadre* and neighbor, who provided day care and a guest house in her home. With her oldest children in school, Doña Margarita took her younger children with her. "After I finished my things in the house, I went to my comadre's house to help her with the children, to feed and bathe them. . . . So then on Fridays when [the parents] paid her, she always gave me something." Once the children were picked up, they cooked for the men who rented rooms. "So when they paid her, she always gave me a few dollars, and all the food that was left over." Doña Margarita took the food home for her family's dinner. After her husband died in 1972, she found paid employment cleaning people's houses, and working in a box factory and the garment industry. For rural migrants, the transition from their rural communities to life in Philadelphia was even greater than for those from the city, as they too struggled to recreate their household economies.[78]

Conclusion

Agriculture, agricultural processing, and the home needlework industry declined in the postwar era, threatening rural household economies and sending Puerto Rican men and women in search of paid employment. The government's industrialization program attracted labor-intensive industries that provided some jobs for women who migrated to metropolitan areas. It did not, however, compensate for the loss of jobs, and for Puerto Rican men the gap between lost jobs and new jobs was even greater. Displaced from agriculture and agricultural processing and finding few other manufacturing jobs, Puerto Rican men turned to government-sponsored labor contracts for seasonal farm work in the States. While the industrialization program bypassed rural areas, the contract labor program brought the full impact of the PPD's policies and the colonial relationship to rural communities. As a response to rural male unemployment, the farm labor program illustrated policy makers' focus on industrialization and reducing the population, as well as the limited solutions they offered rural economies.

The state promoted the farm labor program with a vengeance, enabling even poor rural men to migrate directly to the States without saving money for the trip or using the metropolitan area as a stepping stone. Providing information, transportation, and opportunity to travel to the States for seasonal work or permanent settlement, contract labor was one component of the massive rural-to-urban migrations that influenced migrants' origins and destinations. As Edwin Maldonado suggested, contract laborers framed the "socioeconomic nature" of Puerto Rican communities, as "one's relatives and acquaintances would be from the same area in Puerto Rico." The rural economic crisis, the farm labor program, and the rural origins of Philadelphia's Puerto Rican migrants challenge Senior's contention that there were two separate migrant streams and that "permanent" migrants were "city people." Instead the farm labor program contributed to the growth of Philadelphia's Puerto Rican community and its rural origins. While the economic crisis propelled emigration, the migration to Philadelphia was also shaped by the competing agendas of policy makers in the States, policy makers in Puerto Rico, and migrants.[79]

Chapter Three

Contract Labor:
The State-Sponsored Migration

The flier announced, "Opportunity for Agricultural Workers in the United States" and promised an eight-hour day, and the same wages paid to U.S. workers—about sixty cents an hour. It was an "intensive campaign . . . inviting interested farmworkers to register." The Farm Placement Division of Puerto Rico's Department of Labor also used radio spots, cars with sound systems, newspapers, and posters to recruit agricultural laborers for work in the States. Thousands of men responded and registered at the local employment office, providing a health certificate, a good conduct certificate from the local police, a birth certificate, their Selective Service card, a letter of recommendation from a farmer, and two photographs for their identification card. They signed labor contracts with employers and the contracts were approved by Puerto Rico's Commissioner of Labor. When they were needed, the workers were transported to *el ranchón*, the Embarkation Center at the airport in San Juan, where they boarded the twin-engine planes. In the States, workers were placed in farm labor camps or on individual farms, many of them in the Middle Atlantic states. Farmers requested Puerto Rican workers through the local offices of the U.S. Employment Service. The requests were forwarded to the regional office of the Bureau of Employment Security, which certified the need for laborers and contacted Puerto Rico's Employment Service for recruitment. This state-sponsored contract labor program was operated through the U.S. Employment Service's offices in Puerto Rico and the States.[1]

This chapter examines the competing agendas of the United States government, the Puerto Rico government, and the migrants, which shaped the outcomes of contract labor programs and their impact on the growth of Philadelphia's Puerto Rican community. In the postwar era, contract labor became a policy of the governments of the United States and Puerto Rico. These gender-based programs reflected the colonial ties between the United States and Puerto Rico and each state's underlying objectives. U.S. policy makers revealed a central paradox of labor migration—migrants were wanted for their labor, but not as permanent community members. Policy makers' fears that

Puerto Ricans would stay in the States limited recruitment during World War II despite labor needs. In the postwar era, however, the continuing search for cheap, seasonal agricultural labor and the cold war transformed Puerto Ricans' citizenship from a liability into an asset. At the same time, Puerto Rico's policy makers hoped contract labor would reduce the population, alleviate rural male unemployment, slow migration to Puerto Rico's metropolitan areas, disperse migrants beyond New York City, and minimize negative reactions to Puerto Ricans in the States. Although both governments promoted contract labor, Puerto Rico encouraged permanent settlement in the States for Puerto Rican migrants, while the U.S. government remained ambivalent.

Puerto Rican migrants, on the other hand, saw contract labor as an economic strategy in changing economic circumstances. Some migrants used labor contracts for seasonal income and others used them as a vehicle for permanent settlement. Julio Rosario, for example, left Cayey, Puerto Rico in 1948 with a labor contract for seasonal farm work. He was sent to the farm labor camp in Glassboro, New Jersey, and from there was sent to a farm in Lebanon, Pennsylvania. He returned to Cayey, but got another farm labor contract the following year. This time he was sent to Michigan, where he found the conditions harsh and left his farm placement within a month. After traveling in search of work and finding jobs in Wisconsin, Texas, West Virginia, and Hershey, Pennsylvania, Don Julio settled in Philadelphia in 1953. In the postwar era, thousands of Puerto Rican men like Don Julio signed labor contracts for farm work in the States. Most farmworkers were sent to New Jersey, Pennsylvania, and New York. Migrant farmworkers then came to Philadelphia from Pennsylvania and New Jersey farms. By 1953, an estimated 39 percent of Puerto Rican men in Philadelphia had come to the area as migrant farm laborers. Countless others made their way to the city via informal networks that started with the settlement of contract laborers. The state-sponsored migration interacted with migrants' own agendas, informal networks, and economic opportunities to increase Philadelphia's Puerto Rican population.[2]

World War II Precedents

During World War II, the War Manpower Commission (WMC) recruited only a limited number of Puerto Ricans for food processing and railroad work. Despite precedents in recruiting Puerto Rican workers, labor shortages in the States, and unemployment in Puerto Rico, U.S. policy makers were concerned that Puerto Ricans would stay in the States after their contracts ended. Policy makers therefore relied more heavily on foreign workers who could be deported when their labor was no longer needed. For their part, Puerto Rico's policy makers asserted that Puerto Ricans should not be excluded from contract labor programs, as a matter of citizenship rights. They worried, however, about the potential political and public relations problems of large-scale, government-sponsored emigration plans, and preferred to let people migrate on their own. Nonetheless, Puerto Ricans were recruited during the war, and most were sent to southern New Jersey for seasonal food processing jobs. The wartime experience revealed policy makers' and migrants' objectives. Some of those recruited stayed and settled in Philadelphia, contributing to the growth of the Puerto Rican community.[3]

Despite requests from U.S. employers, Puerto Ricans were not recruited for agricultural work. Policy makers hesitated, given the large-scale labor recruitment needed for agriculture. In 1943, a member of the Gloucester County Board of Agriculture in New Jersey, Willard B. Kille, wrote to Puerto Rico's Governor Rexford G. Tugwell. Kille wanted New Jersey's labor camps "filled with Puerto Ricans instead of Jamaicans." He described the Jamaicans as "slow and exceedingly contentious" and claimed that on wages they had "bested practically every grower." He wanted to know why these "English subjects" were "here working and demanding highest wages while our own Puerto Ricans were starving." He hoped Puerto Ricans would travel as families, eliminating "the necessity of living in crowded camps" and bringing along "youngsters old enough to work," and he assumed that "our own Puerto Ricans" would be more docile and would accept lower wages. The Division of Territories responded only that the WMC had brought Puerto Ricans to the States for industrial work, but the War Food Administration had not brought any for agricultural work.[4]

Congressional debates in 1944 revealed the perceived "difficulty" with Puerto Ricans and the benefit of foreign workers. Although much of the funding for agricultural labor recruitment and many of the workers were "domestic," the debates focused on the importation of foreign workers. Senator Langer suggested the use of Puerto Ricans. Noting that money was sent to Puerto Rico "to support the population because it is claimed that the island is over-populated," he asked, "I want to know what attempt has been made to bring Puerto Ricans to this country to perform farm labor here?" On receiving the answer that no attempt had been made, the Senator continued, "In other words, we send them money to support them and then pay laborers from other countries to come here and work for us." The response was a simple "yes." Earlier in this exchange, Senator Hayden had explained: "A proposal was made to import Puerto Ricans to do industrial labor, such as the maintenance of railroad tracks, and other work of that kind. Difficulty has been encountered in that respect. I will say frankly that one reason why the proposal is made to import aliens for laboring purposes is that we are certain they will return to their respective homes." This justified the program's expense—"aliens" were fingerprinted and "thoroughly identified," they were "kept under Federal control all the time . . . they were in the United States," and a portion of their wages were retained. He emphasized that government officials were "strictly enforcing" immigration policy and that they wanted "to be sure that [each worker] is deported after he is through with his work."[5]

This preference for foreign workers and deportation was widespread; during the war policy makers and employers relied on foreign workers instead of Puerto Ricans. The president of a Florida growers association revealed a common perspective: "The vast difference between the Bahama Island labor and the domestic, including Puerto Rican, is that labor transported from the Bahama Islands can be diverted and sent home if it does not work, which cannot be done in the instance of labor from the domestic United States or Puerto Rico." The *Washington Post* echoed this perspective: "Heretofore,

Puerto Ricans have been by-passed in the farm labor importation program because of the fear they might want to remain in this country when the war is over." The benefit of employing Jamaicans, Mexicans, and workers from Newfoundland, the article explained, was that they "could be returned because they are not American citizens." Between 1942 and 1945, 400,000 foreign workers were employed in agriculture, on railroads, and in industries essential to the war effort, such as food processing, metal-working, chemical manufacturing, and lumber. Repatriation was stipulated in bilateral agreements between governments and in contracts between employers and individual workers. U.S. authorities enforced these terms by deporting workers when their labor was no longer needed or when they failed to meet employers' demands.[6]

During World War II, Puerto Rico's policy makers criticized the exclusion of Puerto Ricans from contract labor programs. Governor Tugwell explained: "The Federal Government, by importing Jamaicans, Bahamians and Mexicans in large numbers, caused a serious resentment in Puerto Rico and seemed, so far as Puerto Ricans were concerned, to be ignoring the existence of a serious agricultural unemployment situation here." Hence, if a good plan evolved "Puerto Ricans should be entitled to share in it." Clarence Senior pointed to the role of citizenship: "Congressmen are reported to have objected to bringing Puerto Ricans on ground that they could not be sent back home after the need for them had ended." Similarly, in a memo to Governor Tugwell, Mason Barr of the Division of Territories and Possessions acknowledged that the "biggest obstacle" to recruiting Puerto Ricans was "the fact that they can't be deported or forced to leave at the end of their contract." Barr dismissed this rationale—"So what! they are American citizens."[7]

Policy makers nevertheless viewed state-sponsored migration as potentially problematic. Governor Tugwell was "skeptical of the success of large scale labor importation programs," but had "no objection to the importation of Puerto Rican farm laborers" and felt confident that "the Puerto Rican economy would not suffer." Barr, however, feared "a problem if large groups of Puerto Ricans were used in field work because of racial discrimination and social distinctions generally connected with that type of work where so many negroes are used." Concerned with public relations, Barr did not want Puerto Ricans to be associated in the public's mind with African Americans. For the Commissioner of Labor, Manuel Pérez, the wartime experience demonstrated that "while these groups, arranged under special circumstances, were generally successful in their industrial war activities, still they are a constant source of disappointments and complaints." He thought recruitment unnecessary: "We believe in a program for individual emigration. . . . Thousands of our people will leave without any pressure from the Government or enterprises willing to provide employment outside of Puerto Rico." The migration to New York illustrated his point. The benefit, he asserted, was that "when migration is effected individually, the Government is not bound to take measures or intervene in the contracts entered into by the individual himself."[8]

Nonetheless, in 1944 the WMC recruited approximately two thousand Puerto Ricans for war industry jobs. U.S. government agencies and employers cooperated in recruiting laborers for the least desirable and the most seasonal of jobs. Most were placed with two canneries in southern New Jersey, the Campbell Soup Company and the Edgar F. Hurff Company, or with the Baltimore and Ohio Railroad. Two hundred workers were sent to the Utah Copper Company of Bingham, Utah. The WMC made food processing plants in southern New Jersey a priority, insisting that "the importance of full cooperation between the canning industry and the Field Representatives of the War Manpower Commission cannot be over-estimated, and everything should be done that is possible to permit the United States Employment Service of the WMC to offer services to the canning industry." This cooperation and labor recruitment were necessary not only because food production was central to the war effort, but also because food processing paid less than other war industry jobs and was seasonal work. The WMC conceded that "it is difficult for canneries to compete with other industries in [the region] in the recruitment of labor on account of the differences in wage scales."9

The Campbell Soup Company, a large food processing company in Camden, New Jersey, exemplified the cooperation between employers and government agencies, but was distinguished somewhat by the relentlessness of their recruitment and their willingness to use all sources of labor. In 1943 the company was accused of "labor conspiracy" for bringing 438 African Americans from Florida without following the proper clearance procedures of the WMC. Later in the month, New Jersey Governor Charles Edison declared an emergency in the processing of tomato crops at Campbell. At the urging of manpower officials, thousands of civilians volunteered and soldiers were given furloughs from nearby Fort Dix. The company turned to recruiting Puerto Rican laborers and contracted 488 Puerto Ricans in 1943. In 1944 the WMC intensified its efforts to recruit southern migrants and returned to other sources of labor that had been effective in 1943—released war industry workers and civilians on vacation, soldiers on furloughs, and "housewives who do not normally work in any industry." Still anticipating a shortage, the WMC and food processors turned to prisoners of war and to areas identified as having surplus labor—specifically, "the surplus labor reported to be in the Island of Jamaica" and "the supply reported from Puerto Rico."10

With the support of the WMC, the Campbell Soup Company actively pursued "the supply reported from Puerto Rico." Personnel managers attended meetings with other canners and the WMC, and traveled to Washington, D.C. and Puerto Rico. Discouraged by the slow progress in recruiting Puerto Ricans, the company reminded the WMC of the magnitude of their need for labor and of their contribution to the war effort. "As for Campbell Soup Company, we feel we need 1500 migratory laborers to do the job that the United States Government has asked us to do." The WMC agreed: "Porto Ricans [sic] are considered to be excellent workers. The importance of this labor pool, maintained by the government and allocated by the War Manpower Commission cannot be underestimated." In April 1944, representatives of Campbell's and Hurff's recruited workers in Arecibo, Mayagüez, and Ponce, Puerto Rico. El Mundo advertised the interviews, providing the times, exact locations, and job requirements. The first group of workers arrived by ship in May, with 100 of the 858 laborers destined for Hurff and the rest for the B & O Railroad's eastern lines. The second group arrived in June, with 200 of the 680 men bound for the Campbell Soup Company and the rest for the B & O and the Anaconda Copper Company in Utah. The last group arrived in July, with another 300 workers for Campbell's and another 315 for Hurff.[11]

For Puerto Rico's policy makers, the wartime experience demonstrated the potential of contract labor programs. Gilbert Ramírez, from the Office of Puerto Rico in Washington, D.C., hoped that the contract laborers in food processing would "pave the way for a demand for more Puerto Ricans." He thought it "imperative that this migration be a success from the point of view of the employer as well as the workers." Greeting the first group of men who arrived by ship "in the name of the government of Puerto Rico and Governor Tugwell," he reminded them that "this was an opportunity for them to help the war effort and help Puerto Rico . . . by gaining a reputation as a worker and as a citizen." Government representatives visiting the Campbell and Hurff labor camps emphasized the positive and dismissed workers' complaints. The press release reported that "the company officials showed great satisfaction with the work being done by the Puerto Ricans" and that "the workers look healthy, wide awake and eager to work and make good." The factory was "a wonder of perfection in machinery" and "a fantastic undertaking," and the Puerto Rican workers were "amazed." Pointing to workers' adjustment to new conditions, the representatives explained, "some of the men are not used to American food and yearn for rice and beans but we wish to assure everybody that we ourselves went to one of several cafeterias in the plant for its workers, and the food is wholesome, plenty and served at cost. They even have posted a menu in Spanish." Similarly, "homesickness" was "natural." Described as happy and as wanting to stay, one worker was quoted: "You can say that I have come here to stay; I like it so much that they'll have to fight with me to take me away." The representatives concluded optimistically, "we are pleased to say that the Puerto Ricans have established a beachhead in Camden, New Jersey."[12]

While Puerto Rico's policy makers were "pleased" that a "beachhead" had been established, the WMC encouraged migrants to return "home" when their labor was no longer needed. The WMC acknowledged that "while the War Manpower Commission has no legal responsibility with respect to the contract, the WMC does have an implied responsibility to see that both the worker and the employer fulfill their contractual obligations." When workers wanted to leave their employment, the WMC instructed the local offices to try "to dissuade" the worker by reminding him of "the legal nature of his obligations under the contract." Workers were informed that they would lose free return transportation to Puerto Rico and Selective Service deferment, and would be subject to "existing controls over workers" under employment stabilization plans and to an increase in tax withholding. The local offices were to report individuals who left. Nonetheless, the WMC acknowledged their limited control and reminded the local offices, that "Puerto Ricans, as you know, are citizens of this country and have the same rights and privileges in regard to employment that obtain for other citizens." Ultimately, the WMC had little enforcement power over these U.S. citizens, and Puerto Ricans breaking their labor contracts remained one of the "typical problems."[13]

Policy makers and employers expressed concern that migrants might use labor contracts to settle in the States. While still on board the ship, some of the first arrivals requested "time off, varying from three days to two weeks, to stay over before starting to work." This request made B & O officials "apprehensive." Apparently, "some had relatives in New York, at least one had his wife there, and others just wanted to see the city." As a result, a dilemma emerged over transportation costs. While the government paid the transportation for agricultural field workers, the canners deducted transportation and maintenance costs from the workers' wages. The WMC explained the problem: "Workers demand the same free transportation permitted agricultural workers, and secondly, many workers disappear before full deduction can by made." It seems the workers wanted the government to pay transportation costs, while the employers complained that workers were quitting before the end of their contracts. Indeed, some war industry workers did choose to stay. The WMC reported that 60 percent of the workers left before their contracts expired, 25 percent completed their contracts, and only 15 percent returned to Puerto Rico.[14]

While some contract laborers returned to Puerto Rico, others settled in areas of Philadelphia where Puerto Rican communities grew in the postwar era. A clergy person who ministered to the Hurff workers revealed the range of options: "They have complied fully with their contracts and now some wish to return home and others to their homes in New York or Philadelphia." When they encountered problems returning to Puerto Rico, Hurff and Campbell workers contacted government officials, and the Resident Commissioner's Office had received many complaints. The director of the Division of Territories attributed the problem to "a misunderstanding on someone's part," as his "understanding" was that contracts stipulated return fare to Puerto Rico.[15]

Campbell workers were among those who settled in the city and sent for their families. In her 1965 dissertation, anthropologist Joan Koss found that of the one thousand workers brought to the Campbell Soup Company in the 1940s, 65 were still employed there in 1961. Men sometimes married Tampeñas, women of Cuban descent who migrated north from Tampa, Florida, in search of industry jobs. When the Reverend Oscar Rodríguez, who ministered to the Campbell's workers, moved to 16th Street between Vine and Fairmount, workers settled nearby. One woman recalled of her husband: "In 1944 he came alone to the United States to work in the Campbell Soup Company in Camden. In 1947 he sent for us and found an apartment in Philadelphia, on 6th and Green." In another instance, "Don Santiago came to work in the factory located in Camden. Three years later he sent for his wife and they moved to Mount Vernon Street." His child remembered, "I lived with cousins in an apartment house, with my cousins and my aunt. They came from Puerto Rico because my father sent for them after we got here and got established." Contract labor programs and informal networks had contributed to the growth of the Puerto Rican community in Philadelphia.[16]

Contract Labor as Government Policy

After World War II, Puerto Rico's policy makers became active promoters of emigration and of contract labor programs. Attributing Puerto Rico's economic woes to "overpopulation," they thought the success of their industrialization program hinged on slowing population growth. As a potential solution, their first contract labor program was designed to send Puerto Rican women to work in the States as domestics. In addition to reducing the population, policy makers hoped to foster more dispersed settlement in the States and to temper the hostility Puerto Ricans were encountering, especially in New York City. Policy makers then turned to a contract labor program for male agricultural workers, which became a large-scale and long-term program. They added the alleviation of rural male unemployment to their previous goals, and emphasized the seasonal nature of the program to avoid the political liabilities associated with encouraging emigration. With the farm labor program, the goals of Puerto Rico's policy makers intersected with U.S. policy makers' and employers' search for cheap seasonal agricultural labor. Differences remained, however, over whether or not Puerto Ricans' permanent settlement in the States was a desirable or undesirable consequence of the contract labor program.

Private recruiters demonstrated the potentials of contract labor programs for women as domestics and for men as seasonal agricultural laborers. Policy makers monitored these private recruiters, using the problems generated by the private ventures to justify increased government involvement. Private agencies brought Puerto Rican women to Chicago and Philadelphia to work as domestics. In September 1946, 362 women had been recruited to Chicago. Students at the University of Chicago, including the daughter of a Puerto Rico senator, became aware of the plight of the Puerto Rican domestics. Senator Vicente Géigel Polanco investigated. In his 1947 study, Clarence Senior suggested that about half of the women were satisfied, but acknowledged that others had returned to Puerto Rico, and "some landed in jail after becoming prostitutes and others went to hospitals with various diseases, among them tuberculosis." Senior was dismayed as "the Chicago group of houseworkers furnished headlines for some weeks early in 1947." Instead of condemning the exploitation of laborers, Senior noted optimistically that the experience "suggests the possibility of a well-organized program of training, recruitment, placement and follow-up which could give opportunities for work, travel and for education to many thousands of Puerto Rican young women in the next few years." The responsibility to "protect girls" working as domestics justified increased government involvement and shaped the contours of the program. Protecting "girls," however, was not seen as incompatible with fostering emigration.[17]

The private Philadelphia program, in contrast, served as a positive model. Senior noted that "the agencies working in the Philadelphia and New Jersey area seem to have had more experience. The groups they recruited have given rise to few complaints." In December 1946, Rebecca Smaltz, regional director of the Women's Bureau and chairperson of the YWCA's Metropolitan Industrial Committee, reported on the emerging plan by a private agency to bring Puerto Rican domestics to Philadelphia. The contract set standards below those recommended by the YWCA and below those prevailing in the city. Nonetheless, the Metropolitan Industrial Committee decided that "the Y.W.C.A. had some obligation to the girls who come to our city as strangers, for social and recreation activities, and to protect them from exploitation." The Committee agreed to contact the employment agent and send an invitation to the "girls." One group arrived in May 1947, and three months later the *Evening Bulletin* reported that the twenty-two women were finding "life in a strange country" to be "fun—and frightening." The International Institute, a nonprofit organization serving Philadelphia's foreign-born population, arranged day trips and afternoon teas for the women at the YWCA and invited Puerto Rican students from local colleges.[18]

The Committee also attempted to address the problems they encountered. In October 1947, the Committee concluded that "many of the problems that have arisen with this group are a result of the terms of the contract and the misunderstanding of the contract on the part of the Employer and Employee." The contract provided for fifteen-hour days and a salary of $15 per month for the first three months, with an increase to $16.25 for subsequent months. In contrast, the YWCA's "Standards for Household Employment" called for ten-hour days with a maximum of fifty hours per week, and a minimum weekly salary of $25. When Puerto Rico's Commissioner of Labor, Fernando Sierra Berdecía, proposed an orientation course for the domestics, the Committee stressed, "we hope that there would also be some changes in the contract as to hours and wages." The Committee also sent invitations for tea to all of the employers of the Puerto Rican domestics "for a discussion of their many problems." Only one employer attended, and the Committee was unable to get this employer to grant her domestic time off to study English.[19]

In addition to private agencies, the United States Women's Bureau and Puerto Rico's Department of Labor were involved in monitoring the venture. As the *Bulletin* observed, "the project has the permission of the United States Labor Department and the Puerto Rican Department of Labor, both of whom are keeping an eye on the handling of it." Along with Smaltz's participation through the Metropolitan Industrial Committee, staff members of the Women's Bureau visited both Philadelphia and Chicago "getting first hand information about problems arising for the Puerto Rican women brought to the Continental United States as domestic workers, for the employers, and for the community agencies." The Women's Bureau served in an advisory capacity as the government of Puerto Rico instituted their contract labor program for domestics, particularly on training and the involvement of community agencies. Daisy Reck hoped that organizations such as the YWCA would "provide guidance, language classes and recreational programs"—in short, protection and acculturation. Smaltz assured the Metropolitan Industrial Committee that "the Puerto Rican Department of Labor favors this movement," while the Office of Puerto Rico anticipated that "additional workers of this type will be brought to the mainland under arrangements made by a Philadelphia employment agent and the Puerto Rico Department of Labor."[20]

Yet the responsibilities of both governments were limited. When a disgruntled employer wrote to the U.S. Department of the Interior to complain about his Puerto Rican domestic breaking her contract, Barr responded:

Neither the Department of the Interior nor the Insular Government of Puerto Rico has any responsibility for the supervision of Puerto Ricans who come to the continent, or for enforcing the terms of contracts that are made by employment agencies. The Insular Government has given approval only to the form of contracts that are drawn up for Puerto Ricans, but has never assumed responsibility for enforcing the terms of such contracts.

Nonetheless, a month later, Smaltz noted, "In the future, [the] Puerto Rican Government will have a man to check up on what happens to the girls in this country." The Philadelphia program, however, was ending. By March 1948, Smaltz observed that "the Puerto Rican group coming to the Y has dwindled in numbers but that a new group has been brought to New York City." The Women's Bureau closed their field offices, and Smaltz remained "interested in the Puerto Rican household employees, though not in any official capacity."[21]

The government of Puerto Rico initiated its own contract labor program for domestics. A 1947 Emigration Advisory Committee meeting concluded that "rather than devote time to consideration of any broad-scale possibilities for emigration at this moment, it was decided that immediate energies should be concentrated on plans for a program for training domestic workers . . . and for helping them get established in the States." Daisy Reck, the Coordinator of Federal Activities for the Office of the Governor, announced, "the Department of Labor will not be a party to any more contracts for domestic labor until this program is operating." The government of Puerto Rico assumed responsibility for recruiting, screening, and training workers, and for administering the labor contract. Reck planned to meet with the United States Employment Service, but she was skeptical: "We have little hope that we can get cooperation from them on placement of domestic and agricultural labor, but we want to try." Despite her skepticism, the New York State Employment Service (NYSES) agreed to arrange placements for domestics.[22]

The program responded to perceived demands for domestics in the States. Puerto Rican women would replace European immigrants and "mainland girls." In 1947, Senior suggested, "household employment is one field which offers almost unlimited possibilities on the continent." He noted that half a million women had left the field during the war and that restrictive immigration legislation meant that positions previously filled by European immigrants were now "opportunities held out to Puerto Rican women." While European immigrants were no longer available, Donald J. O'Connor, chief economist of the Office of Puerto Rico, observed, "mainland girls prefer the routines of offices and factories to the requirements of domestic service which has had a long history of low pay, long hours, poor quarters, lack of privacy, no fixed days off, no severance pay, uncertain tenure and inconsiderate supervision." Nonetheless, Puerto Rican girls could "easily get a job," as "not a great deal is . . . expected. Ability and willingness to follow instructions, a reasonable familiarity with household appliances and practices, a strong back, docility, freedom from communicable diseases and the appearance of propriety."[23]

Although contracting women as laborers, the program for domestics was based on traditional notions of gender roles and sexual divisions of labor. Policy makers' focus on young women highlighted their goal of reducing the population. They were optimistic about the demographic effects, but hesitant to proclaim them publicly. O'Connor cautioned: "What need not be made clear, except in executive sessions of the legislative committees, is the demographic effect of female emigration." He estimated that three hundred jobs on the mainland per week for the next decade or so would halve the projected population figures. For a mere one hundred dollars, he calculated, "one young woman and five unborn children can be transported to the States." The cost to the Insular government compared favorably to the costs of education, relief, and health care should this "brood" remain on the island. The program for "young unmarried women" would compensate for the fact that they have "fewer opportunities to save enough for a trip to the mainland, and to work their own way than do boys." O'Connor concluded optimistically: "If Ireland could depopulate itself by emigration, Puerto Rico can."[24]

Planners foresaw additional benefits to the emigration of women, based on traditional gender roles. Women would spark informal networks, send money home, foster dispersion, and reduce the social tensions associated with settlement. O'Connor explained: "It is also obvious that girls, with their typically strong family loyalties will send for their kin" or at least "provide advance-guards which would make easy the entrance of late-comers." The "girl" would "send the amount of her loan, and more, back to her kin for family emergencies and for family travel." In addition, domestics were to be invisible migrants. The first group of thirty trained "girls" were sent to Scarsdale, New York, which was chosen as "a small community with civic agencies that have promised to cooperate in helping the Puerto Rican girls adjust to life in a new country." In the future, "groups may be sent to other small communities, but probably not to large cities where the adjustment problem is more difficult." Yet O'Connor assumed that even "our relatively wealthy Northeastern cities . . . could each take a hundred trained girls every month and be quite unconscious of their presence as a group in the city for a long time."[25]

Planners also emphasized the compatibility of the program with women's roles. Domestic training prepared the "girls" for domestic work in the States or in Puerto Rico and, O'Connor noted, "should serve them well as mothers and as locally employed servants." The training also kept women's limited options open, so that "they need not look forward to a lifetime of domestic service. The capable ones who display initiative will find opportunities in the field of hotel and other institutional housekeeping. . . . And there is always the possibility of marriage on the continent." Training was to cover how to "appreciate and use community opportunities for getting acquainted, getting along, getting ahead and getting married." The possibility that domestics would marry in the States increased the potential for depopulation, for dispersion, and for an invisible and problem-free migration.[26]

O'Connor's program was instituted with ambitious goals and a good deal of publicity. O'Connor hoped that "a program pitched toward an *eventual* teaching load of ten thousand girls (and women) per year would not be over-ambitious, inasmuch as the population is expanding so rapidly." While the initial proposal called for eight training centers throughout the Island, each of which would train sixty "girls" per three-month term, the Emigration Advisory Committee decided to run a trial project in one center. On October 25, 1947, *El Mundo* described the opening of the first training center in Caguas as a great civic, cultural, and recreational event. The Commissioner of Education, Francisco Collazo, emphasized the students' opportunity to benefit themselves, their families, and their towns, and the Mayor of Caguas added that the trainees should fulfill their duties in a manner that upheld the reputation of Puerto Rico. The director of the Women's Bureau in Puerto Rico saw the program as an opportunity to professionalize domestic work. Training covered household techniques, English, and personal hygiene. The flier recruiting trainees announced opportunities for employment in the States and a salary of $100 per month. Transportation to the required training course was free for those selected.[27]

Labor contracts stipulated working conditions and appropriate behavior for the domestics. Contracts were signed by the employer and the employee, and also by a legal guardian if the girl was under age, and were approved by the Commissioner of Labor of Puerto Rico. Although an improvement over the terms and conditions offered by private recruitment agents, the standards still fell below those prevailing in urban areas in the States. The one-year labor contracts provided a minimum wage of $25.00 per week with an increase of $2.50 every three months, and a minimum salary of $35.00 per week if employment continued at the end of the contract year. Hours were specified as a maximum of ten hours per day and forty-eight hours per week, with additional hours on call not to exceed three nights per week nor four hours per night. Yet the contract allowed work in excess of these hours provided they were compensated at double the hourly wage. The employers also agreed to provide one complete day off per week, seven holidays per year, "reasonable leave" to attend religious services, and "adequate health care and any necessary hospitalization." Employees were to have a private room and access to bathing facilities. The employees, in turn, agreed to perform their tasks "with diligence and due regard for the methods of operation desired by the employer" and "to respect the family way of living and to make every reasonable effort to adjust to it." In addition, employees were "to maintain a neat and appropriate personal appearance" and "to maintain the decorum of the household, especially with respect to her own guests and her deportment in public." Both parties agreed to take serious complaints to the Employment and Migration Bureau.[28]

In February 1948, the first group of twenty-one trained "girls," eighteen to thirty-five years old, were placed in households in Scarsdale, New York. Prospective employers had met with representatives of NYSES at the Scarsdale Women's Club, agreed to advance money for airfare and winter clothing that would be deducted from the domestics' salary, and signed labor contracts. A week after their placement, the *New York Times* reported that for the domestics, "the transition in their lives was wonderful," but that the "housewives, freed of some chores, were not quite as enthusiastic." Finding her domestic "eager to do the work," one employer was quick to assign blame: "But the Puerto Rican Government has been very unfair to these girls in choosing them to come north." She complained of her domestic's limited English and inability to cook or answer the telephone appropriately. Another newspaper account emphasized the employers' frustrations, as well as their financial motives. Most employers felt "that the original proposition was presented to them under false pretenses" and that the "girls" had been "oriented" but not "trained." They remained "hopeful" that the "girls" would become good "maids." While some of the "housewives" found "the girls . . . worth $25 a week now because they are available all the time," some felt "that $10 a week during the trial period would be more just." The article concluded: "Some housewives are holding on because they have not the heart to cast out a homeless kid in a strange land and because in no other way can they find a maid, even an inefficient one, to stay in for $25 a week."[29]

By June 1948, however, Puerto Rico's Department of Labor was expanding the program, even as the NYSES was expressing reluctance. At NYSES's suggestion, the training programs had been extended from three to four months with more emphasis on teaching English with a "continental accent." Two more training centers had been opened in San Germán and Guayama, and another sixty trainees would graduate by July 1. The government had funded vocational schools to teach household training, and an additional eight schools would be able to graduate trainees by December. NYSES, on the other hand, was hesitant about placing the sixty graduates. Instead they thought they could place twenty to thirty but wanted at least six weeks to prepare and to select a new area for placement. The Director of Puerto Rico's Bureau of Employment and Migration, Petro América Pagán de Colón, feared that most of the graduates would drop out. Puerto Rico's representatives negotiated. The Employment and Migration Office would arrange transportation to reduce the cost per placement for NYSES, and they agreed to modify the labor contract. The first two days in an employer's home would be an unpaid "breaking-in" period and the contracts would not provide for sick leave, even though it was customary in the New York City area. They did not, however, consent to suspending the provisions for overtime pay during the first two weeks. Finally, they were willing to consider individual placements and even asked about possible placements in New York City. Puerto Rico's Department of Labor had received inquiries from individuals interested in employing domestics and had placed some workers. In sharp contrast, a NYSES representative "pointed out the risks of individual placements outside the project and without staff for follow up."[30]

Despite ambitious goals and considerable fanfare, the program was short-lived. In Scarsdale, a year and a half after the initial placements, twelve of the twenty-one women were still employed, with seven in the original households. Yet only five were receiving the salary of $35.00 per week stipulated in the labor contract; the others were receiving $32.50 or $30.00, according to the local newspaper, by "agreement between the girls and their employers." Three had returned to Puerto Rico; six had moved to New York City, where one was a housekeeper for a wealthy family, two worked in factories, two had gotten married, and one was living with relatives. All of the employers had recouped their expenses before the women left. In October 1949, Pagán de Colón declared the program a "success" and "suspended." The number of placements was not high enough for Puerto Rico's policy makers. Writing to the Employment and Migration office in New York, Pagán de Colón noted that "the New York Employment Office could not help us in the placement of large groups of girls" and that "this Program has been suspended and the funds are being used in the training of workers for the hotel industry." She continued that "in spite of all the circumstances, we believe that the Household Program was a success from the vocational training point."[31]

The Department of Labor still made individual placements. Pagán de Colón had "fourteen girls available for job[s] in the States." The Department of Labor responded to inquiries by individuals interested in Puerto Rican domestics by sending the contract and the address of the Employment and Migration Office in New York. Similarly, when they received inquiries from young women in search of domestic jobs, they responded with the address of the New York office and told the women they would have to pay their own way and bring enough money to cover their own expenses until they were placed. The Assistant Director of the Employment and Migration Bureau in New York, however, was concerned about public relations. When asked by Pagán de Colón about placing five trained domestics, Estella Draper responded, "it would be a better service to Puerto Rico to leave them there. . . . My feeling is that it is much better not to incur the ill will of five American employers if these girls are not exceptionally good."[32]

Women who traveled with contracts for domestic work sometimes had plans of their own. Puerto Rican women were not as docile as expected. The YWCA staff had assumed that "the girls will be timid" and made efforts to "reassure them." Instead, they found that the "Puerto Rican girls" were "very undisciplined and difficult," and "had picked up boyfriends or gotten to know the city well enough so they were not interested in a group" for social activities. For some, the contracts were a way to travel to Philadelphia. In September 1947 a disgruntled employer from the suburbs of Philadelphia wrote to the U.S. Department of the Interior. He had contracted a domestic worker in May for a year, but by September she had moved to Philadelphia to live with her husband. He was "convinced that the girl entered into this contract with the premeditated intent to defraud." The contract "showed the maid as a single girl" but when a man "besieged her with telephone calls . . . the girl confessed to the fact that it was her husband who had followed her to Philadelphia." Apparently, he too had come with a labor contract for work in New Jersey but chose to stay in Philadelphia instead. The employer complained: "We feel they are a definite menace to society if not properly apprehended. If they are permitted to remain in this country under breech [sic] of contract, I am confident it is only the beginning of similar complications for others. . . . Puerto Rican domestics should not be turned loose in this country without definite supervision." Implying that the woman had no right to be "in this country," this former employer demanded that the matter "be investigated by the proper authorities," or, he threatened, "the matter can be left in the hands of my attorneys for proper follow-up."[33]

Philadelphia's economy made contract labor for women unnecessary. This woman left her job as a live-in domestic, not only to live with her husband, but also to work "in a sugar factory in the center of the city." Indeed, a 1950 survey of fifty-four Puerto Rican women in Philadelphia found over a third working as domestics, but more than half working in the garment industry sewing by machine or by hand, and the rest in other factory work. Domestic workers in Philadelphia were, for the most part, not "girls." Only three were under twenty years old, and the overwhelming majority were married and living with their husbands. Puerto Rico's policy makers proclaimed the program a success, but considered it expensive. It was, perhaps, not the most cost-effective way to reduce the island's population. They also acknowledged that women sent as domestics preferred industrial work, which was readily available in the States. Here Philadelphia's economy and women's own agendas undermined the contract labor program.[34]

While Puerto Rico's policy makers were promoting the program for domestics, a private labor agent was demonstrating the potentials of a contract labor program for men as seasonal agricultural laborers. Samuel Friedman, a private employment agent licensed by the state of Pennsylvania, was building his program on wartime precedents. Friedman served the farmers who supplied the Campbell cannery and the Glassboro labor camp, which was owned and operated by the Gloucester County Board of Agriculture. This was the organization that had tried to secure Puerto Rican agricultural workers during the war. Efforts to recruit Puerto Ricans for seasonal agricultural work, which had failed during the war, were now underway again. The government supervised and the newspapers publicized Friedman's efforts. In May 1946 Friedman approached Puerto Rico's Commissioner of Labor, Manuel Pérez, about Puerto Rican laborers for the States. El Mundo's front page announced the emigration plan for 1,000 workers and Pérez's approval of a small trial group. A few days later, job requirements were detailed in what amounted to free advertising. Two weeks later, Pérez authorized an additional 200 workers. Between May and August, 900 farmworkers were placed in southern New Jersey and eastern Pennsylvania.[35]

Puerto Ricans were placed in one of two large labor camps, one in eastern Pennsylvania and the other in southern New Jersey, or directly on farms. The labor camps either placed laborers on smaller farms in the area or arranged for daily transportation from the camps to nearby farms. The Glassboro camp in southern New Jersey housed 250 Puerto Rican laborers, and another 150 were on smaller farms administered by Glassboro. In eastern Pennsylvania, 100 workers were in Chalfont, which was identified as the key to the project in Pennsylvania, and another 100 were on smaller farms in the Chalfont area. Friedman opened the Chalfont camp in July. In Perkasie, Pennsylvania, Conte and Sons Packing Company, a small tomato sauce factory, employed 22 Puerto Ricans, while George Seidel employed 5 Puerto Ricans on his Perkasie farm. Another farmer had 18 Puerto Ricans in his home and held a party and a dance for them every Saturday night.[36]

El Mundo reported the success of Friedman's program, increasing Puerto Ricans' familiarity with Pennsylvania and Philadelphia. Providing detailed information on transportation, crops cultivated, and salaries, El Mundo declared that the boricuas were working well in Filadelfia. According to Friedman, one Pennsylvania farmer was satisfied with the two Puerto Ricans he had hired and added that other Pennsylvania farmers might contract 15,000 laborers in the coming years. With the trial group of 30 workers placed on ten farms in the Philadelphia area, "both groups—the workers and the farmers—are evidently pleased with the arrangements made." Friedman offered his own version of the success story: "The initial group of agricultural workers that I took to New Jersey and Pennsylvania have won the respect and friendship of the farmers they work with, and have left such a good impression that many farmers have called me and written me saying they want to sign a contract with me to provide more Puerto Rican workers."[37]

Echoing the reports on the food processing laborers, government reports and newspaper articles stressed the good relations between workers and employers in both the labor camps and the smaller farms, using patriotic and paternalistic terms. One newspaper reported the story of Miguel Marcano, who was the first to arrive at Chalfont. Marcano took personal responsibility for the appearance of the living quarters, insisting on an American flag for the farm and painting the dining room in red, white, and blue. The camp also had a Puerto Rican cook, and the Reverend Enrique Rodríguez held services every Sunday in Chalfont and Glassboro. Friedman was described as available twenty-four hours a day, with his phone ringing constantly. The farmers' support for the program was described as more than commercial interest. One farm family provided fruits and vegetables and helped "take care of our boys." On Seidel's farm, Puerto Rican workers were treated as "part of the family." Santiago Ortiz, from the Office of Puerto Rico, thought this "typical" where farmers and laborers lived on the same farm, often eating and working together. As for the workers in the Glassboro camp, "the men in general enjoy the life in the camps and the directors do everything possible to maintain a high level of morale among them." The camp provided a variety of services and facilities, a Puerto Rican cook, and a Puerto Rican assistant to the camp director who is "an important bond between the necessarily impersonal operation of the Government and that Puerto Rican that for some reason finds himself displeased in a foreign land, so far from his home." Workers' relations with the camp directors and Friedman were so good, they were said to mitigate the workers' misgivings about the wire fence that surrounded the Glassboro labor camp.[38]

Complaints about wages, working conditions, housing, and food were mentioned only in passing. In Glassboro, workers complained about the lack of cleanliness in the barracks, bad coffee, and the frequency with which spaghetti was served. Ortiz found the sanitary conditions "unsatisfactory" at Conte and Sons Packing Company and noted that the men were working seven days a week, averaging 80 to 90 hours. Despite these conditions, he emphasized that the men were pleased with the food and their relations with the family. For Ortiz, the farmers worked intensively several months out of the year and expected their laborers to do the same. Complaints about pay were attributed not to low wages, but to the deductions required by the government of Puerto Rico. Twenty percent of workers' salary was withheld and sent to their dependents in Puerto Rico. An additional $3.50 per week was saved in Philadelphia toward their return fare to Puerto Rico. In one example, an average weekly salary of $30 was reduced to $10.70—$6 was sent to dependents, $3.50 went towards return airfare, and $9.80 bought the food the workers so often disliked. One article concluded, "the primary problem that employers face and the principal 'bother' for workers are the deductions that are taken from their salaries." Emphasizing the deductions diverted attention from low wages and absolved employers of any responsibility. From the workers' perspective, the "hope to earn good money" was not achieved.[39]

Like domestics, these farmworkers sometimes had agendas of their own. By August 26, 650 of the 900 laborers were still working; the others "abandoned the project and went to New York or returned to their homes in Puerto Rico." One farm owner, Mr. Conte, sometimes invited the men to go out with him. He had, however, limited the men's trips to New York for fear that they would not return to work. Those workers not wanting to return to Puerto Rico received the cash equivalent of the money deducted for their return fare. In contesting the 20 percent deduction for dependents, some workers argued that they had no dependents and others that they wished to send money personally rather than through the government of Puerto Rico. Elimination of the 20 percent deduction for dependents did not increase their salaries, but it did enable migrants to decide whether money was best sent to Puerto Rico, or perhaps used to bring "dependents" to the States. Friedman conceded that 25 percent of his workers failed to complete their contracts and that "the 'city boy' often uses this job as a way to arrive on the continent to join his friends in New York."[40]

Nevertheless, Friedman's program was deemed a success, and in 1947 the government of Puerto Rico assumed responsibility for the contract labor program. The Glassboro camp was described as "an example of how a project of large scale importation of workers could function." Friedman's role was now limited to placing farmworkers. Although the focus shifted from female domestics to male farmworkers, the goals of Puerto Rico's policy makers did not change. The Migration Division still hoped to encourage migration and settlement in areas beyond New York City. Policy makers reinforced gender divisions of labor in their contract programs. Although women worked in agriculture in Puerto Rico, they were not contracted for agricultural work in the States. Instead policy makers sought to alleviate rural male unemployment, and the farm labor program provided them with a way to increase migration and dispersion while reassuring potential opponents that migration was seasonal. They expanded the program, mounted an intensive recruitment campaign in Puerto Rico's rural areas, and encouraged U.S. policy makers and employers to use Puerto Rican labor. Policy makers' promotion of the program in the States, their intensive recruitment, and their interest in dispersing the Puerto Rican population revealed their underlying goals of increasing emigration and permanent settlement.[41]

In Puerto Rico, political leaders defended the program as seasonal employment, protection for workers, and within Puerto Ricans' rights as citizens. The stated goal was a seasonal migration. In 1947 Governor Jesús T. Piñero justified the farm labor program on the front page of *El Mundo*. He wanted the organized migration to the farms to replace the "disorganized flow" to the "congested slums" of New York, which he said created "potential dangers." Migrants could be channeled to jobs and favorable living conditions, and well-prepared citizens could be sent to the farms where they had proven to be good workers, doing work of "unprecedented importance." Then, the migrant would "be considered a desirable citizen in any community, not a social problem." In a rare admission, he noted that the government of Puerto Rico had recognized migration as "one of the most important factors in our plans to combat the economic problems of the Island." Politicians also championed the labor contract as advancing the status and working conditions of agricultural workers. Manuel Cabranes, director of the Office of Employment and Migration in New York, boasted that the contract was "setting standards for workers on the mainland," and that "there is nothing like it anywhere in the United States or in the world." Yet, as with the domestics, policy makers balanced protecting workers with promoting the program.[42]

Policy makers encouraged the U.S. government to use Puerto Rican laborers instead of British West Indians. Meetings between Puerto Rico's policy makers and the United

States Employment Service (USES) were underway by June 1948, when work on a standard contract was started. Expressing disappointment with the 4,500 placements made in 1949, however, Sierra Berdecía blamed "unfair competition on the part of the British West Indians." USES director Robert Godwin stated that "the USES was ready to tighten up as much as possible on the use of British West Indians" and expected "that a larger number of Puerto Ricans will be used."[43]

Citizenship remained a central concern for U.S. policy makers. The assistant director of USES, A. W. Motley, revealed that "because most of these B.W.I.'s have been here for over five years immigration authorities are concerned over the fact that they will soon become eligible for citizenship and that Immigration does not favor this." Yet he was no less concerned about Puerto Ricans' citizenship and "asked what percentage of our agricultural workers had been returning to Puerto Rico at the end of the season." He was reassured that about 95 percent returned and that workers reported stranded in Lorain, Ohio and in Florida had involved men who had traveled on their own. Policy makers continued their criticism of the use of foreign workers and took the issue to the press. Sierra Berdecía was quoted in the *New York Times*: "Since Puerto Ricans are American citizens and there are a substantial number of them ready, willing and able to do the work, the admittance of foreign workers under the circumstances is not only an invasion of the rights of citizens but also the perpetuation of a serious American unemployment problem."[44]

For U.S. policy makers after World War II, Puerto Ricans were becoming a preferred source of labor. The search for cheap agricultural labor continued, criticism of foreign contract labor programs increased, and the cold war added a patriotic tone to the reliance on domestic labor, which came to include Puerto Ricans. Demands on production remained high, and the conditions for agricultural laborers were deteriorating. The gap between farm wages and manufacturing wages was increasing. Farm work was becoming more seasonal, as a result of the uneven pace of mechanization and of an increase in the acreage of crops that required harvesting by hand. There was no unemployment insurance, no minimum wage, no old age and survivors' insurance, no disability insurance, and no workmen's accident insurance in most states. In short, the President's Commission on Migratory Labor found that "conditions have become worse because employment is more brief and uncertain" and that migrant workers were "expected to work under conditions no longer typical or characteristic of the American standard of life." The cooperation between the government and employers that had emerged as a wartime emergency continued as the USES took over where the WMC had left off. While Puerto Ricans' U.S. citizenship was transformed from a liability to an asset, the tension between wanting Puerto Rican laborers and not wanting Puerto Rican community members remained.[45]

In 1947 congressional debates Puerto Ricans were referred to as both "citizens" and "foreign laborers." The controversy centered on the importation of foreign workers, and Representative Andresen suggested, "there may be one way out of it, and I think it could well be explored by the Congress. We have an overpopulation in Puerto Rico. What is the matter with bringing in about 25,000 Puerto Ricans to do some of this work? They claim status as American citizens." Yet most still viewed Puerto Ricans as "foreign labor," and even Andresen conditioned Puerto Ricans' citizenship with the phrase that they "claim status." Senator Lucas warned: "As a result of the last 5 or 6 years of importation of foreign labor from the Bahamas, Puerto Rico, and Mexico, it will be found more and more troublesome . . . to get the average American agricultural worker to go into the fields and do the stoop labor." He included Puerto Ricans with "foreign labor" and not with "the average American agricultural worker." Nevertheless, a 1948 bill authorized the U.S. government "to recruit foreign workers within the Western Hemisphere and workers in Puerto Rico for temporary agricultural employment in the continental United States." The next year, the Bureau of Employment Security "specifically acknowledged the Puerto Ricans to be part of the domestic labor force," implying "that they should be given preference of employment over alien labor." Hence, Puerto Ricans, who had been U.S. citizens since 1917, had become "part of the domestic labor force."[46]

Puerto Ricans were now portrayed as U.S. citizens in competition with foreign contract laborers. The *New York Times* reported: "United States citizens, including Puerto Ricans, were available for the jobs for which British subjects were imported, according to those seeking an end to the practice." The regional representative of the Bureau of Employment Security, Paul M. Kenefick, explained: "The Bureau of Employment Security has a policy of not issuing certifications for foreign workers until the employer has demonstrated . . . that the use of Puerto Rican workers will cause undue hardship." Meanwhile, USES instructed their offices, "the local office will explain to the employer that Puerto Rican labor is to be considered for employment prior to any foreign labor, and all efforts must be made to encourage the employer to use this source of labor supply." The President's Commission on Migratory Labor reemphasized the hiring of domestic workers, including Puerto Ricans, recommending that, "to meet any supplemental needs for agricultural labor that may develop, preference be given to citizens of the offshore possessions of the United States, such as Hawaii and Puerto Rico."[47]

In the midst of the cold war, the hiring of citizens took on patriotic dimensions. In a speech on Puerto Rican migration, Arthur Gernes of the Bureau of Employment Security quoted Secretary of Labor James Mitchell: "It is necessary for the sake of all our people and for the survival of our country that we utilize the best talents of all Americans. . . . I cannot foresee with certainty the demands to be made upon our nation by the communist threat. But of this much I am sure—we do not have so much manpower that we can afford to waste any of it." Similarly, the U.S. Department of Labor's *Employment Security Review* made the connection between the "defense" of the United States and the use of domestic labor, proclaiming, "Farm Work is Defense Work: Maximum Utilization of the Domestic Labor Force." The issue included articles on the recruitment of Puerto Ricans, Native Americans, women, and youth. The Chief of the Farm Placement Service, Don Larin, warned, "job discrimination against any minority group can be especially costly at a time when all hands are needed." Puerto Rico's policy makers emphasized Puerto Ricans' role as patriotic citizens, as they promoted the labor recruitment of Puerto Ricans. Describing the 11,735 farmworkers sent in 1951 as "probably the world's largest nonmilitary airlift operation," Pagán de Colón reiterated the issue's themes: "During 1951, the people of Puerto Rico made a real contribution to democracy. While one group of the male population was fighting in Korea, another group was serving on the home front, for 'Farm Work is Defense Work.'"[48]

The active participation of Puerto Rico's Migration Division and the U.S. Employment Service drastically increased the scope of the farm labor program. In February 1949, the *New York Times* announced, "U.S., Puerto Rico Map a Labor Pact," and reported that a "standard labor contract" was "being worked out by representative of the Puerto Rican Government, the United States Employment Service and the major farm and food processing groups in this country." In 1951, the Pieser-Wagner Act was extended to Puerto Rico, making the Bureau of Employment and Migration a branch of the U.S. Bureau of Employment Security and eligible for federal funding. The Bureau of Employment and Migration office in Puerto Rico became the Bureau of Employment Security, while the offices in New York City and Chicago became the Migration Division. Federal monies were behind the farm labor program. The labor contracts were signed by the employer and the worker and approved by Puerto Rico's Commissioner of Labor. The contract guaranteed the worker 160 hours of work every four weeks, the prevailing wage, and no discrimination in employment or housing. The employer provided free housing, and workmen's compensation for industrial accidents, and could provide either free cooking and eating facilities or meals at specified prices. Deductions from the workers' pay covered the transportation arranged by the employer, and "reasonably necessary medical and dental services, care, attention and surgery."[49]

Despite this cooperation, differences remained in the underlying goals of Puerto Rico's and the United States' policy makers. Although wanting to reduce Puerto Rico's population, Puerto Rico's policy makers feared the implications of Puerto Ricans' concentrated settlement in New York City. Employment opportunities seemed limited and racial tensions seemed to be mounting. As historian Michael Lapp notes, "the Puerto Rican government was concerned, however, about the possibility that massive and uncontrolled migration would sour the spirit of cooperation and good feeling that was developing between Puerto Rico and the United States." As "American investment and tourism in Puerto Rico were so important to the island's development strategy," Lapp continues, "increasing hostility toward Puerto Ricans on the mainland could only hinder such efforts." The Migration Division "issued publicity in Puerto Rico announcing the greater supply of jobs in the Midwest" and tried to find jobs there for unemployed Puerto Ricans living in New York City.[50]

While insisting publicly that most migrants returned to Puerto Rico, Puerto Rico's policy makers continued their efforts to disperse the population. In 1949, Cabranes assured Philadelphia's social service workers "that more than 90 percent of the migrant workers . . . returned to Puerto Rico." Yet in 1952 Division representatives visited Chicago "to look into work opportunities in that area for Puerto Ricans residing in New York and the Island," and by 1957 they were pleased that 70 percent of those registering in the Migration Division's Chicago office had come directly from Puerto Rico. Another approach was the "efforts . . . made by the Migration Division to shift farmworkers into industry." In 1951 the Division suggested that "a pool of agricultural workers in south Jersey be utilized in an attempt to secure industrial placements of the men as they completed their agricultural contract." The goal was to send two hundred men from the Glassboro farm labor camp to Illinois. While considering new offices in the farming areas of Keyport, Camden, and Hamburg, "much greater emphasis was placed on community relations and work with urban employers to secure jobs in areas outside New York City." Public relations remained an area of concern, with the Division noting in 1955 that the public's opinion of Puerto Ricans living in the States affected programs on the Island. In opening nine small offices in farming areas in the northeast the following year, the Division kept public opinion very much in mind.[51]

Policy makers also sought to increase migration by manipulating informal networks. Writing in 1954, Clarence Senior revealed the government's awareness of the connection between contract labor, informal networks, and areas of settlement. He observed: "When we find Puerto Ricans in substantial clusters far from New York City we almost invariably find that either private or governmental organization has been responsible." The legal restrictions on private agencies since 1947 meant that "recent group placements" had all been of the governmental variety. The "seasonal farm labor program" was partly responsible, as "a small proportion of these men" remained on the continent and "contrary to popular notion, few move to New York City." Instead, settlements in New York, Illinois, Michigan, Ohio, and eastern Pennsylvania were "traceable to these migrants." Contract labor sparked informal networks, as "once the individual is established he looks for opportunities to bring his family and his relatives and friends." Communities then grew as a result of "the relationship between the newly arrived Puerto Rican and his entire environment . . . plus the close blood and ritual family ties of the Puerto Ricans." Senior admitted that "the tendency toward dispersion is encouraged and facilitated by the Commonwealth." Contract labor, sparking informal networks to areas with opportunities for permanent settlement, was a means to this end.[52]

In the States, however, the tension between wanting Puerto Rican laborers and not wanting Puerto Rican community members persisted despite the new emphasis on citizenship and the patriotic tone. The President's Commission on Migratory Labor put it this way: "The public acknowledges the existence of migrants, yet declines to accept them as full members of the community. As crops ripen, farmers anxiously await their coming; as the harvest closes, the community, with equal anxiety, awaits their going." The contradictions emerged even as Friedman recruited small numbers of Puerto Ricans to Pennsylvania and New Jersey. The Glassboro labor camp director, Robert Moore, preferred "to work with Puerto Ricans before any other class of immigrant workers." He found that the Puerto Ricans were "more trustworthy, hardworking, and get along better with each other" and the farmers praised their work. There was concern, however, that the "community" would not agree with the farmers' praise. A Philadelphia social service worker explained that Friedman and his wife were "not desirous to give the project publicity, because there are too many people who do not want people who sound foreign brought here, but these are American citizens and they have a right to come." Friedman defended the workers—they not only provided needed labor for "the nation and Truman's emergency project" but also served as "good will ambassadors" from Puerto Rico to rural areas of the States. As government involvement and the numbers of Puerto Rican migrants increased, concerns mounted. Just beneath the *New York Times* caption, "Jersey Welcomes Migrant Workers," the supervisor of the New Jersey migrant labor bureau was asked, "do all your Puerto Ricans go back to Puerto Rico?" He responded, "The first year we used them, some went to New York." He continued on a more reassuring note for his readers: "New Jersey has not had a single case of relief for Puerto Ricans, however. Most of them go back to their home island with a good roll of bills in their pockets."53

In Pennsylvania, some farmers requested Puerto Rican laborers while one elected representative insisted that Puerto Ricans were not wanted in his region. Representative Gross of Pennsylvania asserted: "It is not true that farmers want this help because they are cheap. . . . I have seen Puerto Ricans and Jamaicans getting $16 a day picking cherries." He continued: "They are sick and tired of these foreigners who come in here, 70 percent of whom it can be proven by the records have venereal disease." A year later, Representative Gross doubted that Lancaster County farmers had requested 250 Puerto Ricans to work in the tomato fields. He retorted, "I do not think a single soul in Lancaster County is looking for anybody to pick tomatoes." He accused the Department of Agriculture of "looking for something to do," whereupon he was reminded that these hearings and the program were the responsibility of the USES and not the Department of Agriculture. Many farmers preferred local laborers because they saw them "as good workers who presented no housing problems, no language barriers, and who created no social or other tension in the community." The availability of industry jobs, however, had reduced local labor to school youth, "idle industrial workers, house wives, and other persons not generally considered to be in the labor market." So, farmers turned to Puerto Rican laborers. By the late 1950s, Pennsylvania farmers relied on approximately 45,000 seasonal workers annually, and a labor force that was 80 percent local labor, just over 10 percent southern African American, and just under 10 percent Puerto Rican.54

Contract Labor as Economic Strategy

For Puerto Rican migrants, labor contracts were an economic strategy. Securing labor contracts because of deteriorating economic conditions at home, Puerto Rican men used the farm labor program in a variety of ways. For some labor contracts provided seasonal income, while for others they provided the means to settle permanently in the States. Because some workers stayed, the state-sponsored contract labor program shaped the origins and destinations of Puerto Rican migrants to the States. During the late 1940s and the 1950s, the farm labor program had its greatest impact on the Mid-Atlantic states. It fostered the growth of the Puerto Rican community in Philadelphia and contributed to its rural origins.

Don Julio used labor contracts for two years before settling in Philadelphia in 1953. Born in Aibonito, Puerto Rico in 1925, Don Julio moved to a barrio in Cayey when he was five years old. It was, he recalled, "the countryside, the mountains, from our house you couldn't see another house." The family, his mother and father and the eleven children, combined wage labor in tobacco with subsistence agriculture. His father worked as a farmer on someone else's farm, but was given a plot to live on and grow food. They relied heavily on the food they grew and the animals they tended:

> Corn, *batata, yautía*. Well, he grew hot peppers, he grew tomatoes, he grew sweet peppers, lettuce. There was so much food at home. . . . We had goats, we had cows, we even had a, no we didn't have horses, but a mare, was what we had. I remember I used to ride that mare a lot. . . . There wasn't any money, no, no, no. . . . And then in order for me to have one cent, I had to sell one egg. When I went to school, you see, I never had, not even one *penny* to take to school. That you didn't have. Shoes you didn't have. . . . During that time, in the country, we lived poor.

Don Julio left school in fourth grade and went to work on the farm with his father. When there was no work on the farm they lived on, "a man with tobacco farms hired us and we worked picking tobacco. My sisters sewed the tobacco, my mother destemmed them. All of them worked in tobacco."[55]

Don Julio, however, was working in sugar cane when he decided to sign up for agricultural work in the States. Cayey's economy was shifting from tobacco and minor crops to sugar cane. "When I was little, there wasn't any sugar cane," he remarked, "but later, later, since sugar cane brought a lot of money, there was a lot of sugar cane." Don Julio, however, felt that the money was not evenly distributed. When he started working in tobacco, he earned a quarter a day. Although the wages in sugar were higher than tobacco, he still did not earn very much, $1.88 a day. Because the work was seasonal, he worked in tobacco in the summer and sugar cane in the winter. He concluded: "There were a lot of people, the rich ones, that took advantage of the poor, they lived off of us, see. We didn't have anything, we had to work cheap." As a twenty-two-year-old, he was spending many of his evenings socializing in town. It was there that he heard of the program to bring farmworkers to the States and signed up. He explained his decision to get a labor contract in 1948: "Well, you see, I've always worked. Well, then I went to work to earn money, and the work that there was, was sugar cane. Work in sugar cane is really tough. Sugar cane, it irritates [your skin] badly, ooh. I worked for about a year. Then I heard the news that they were going to bring people to work in the United States. Then, I went and filled out a paper. I came." The program enabled him to make the trip by paying his airfare and then deducting it from his salary. "They took it out of what you earned, well, because if not, you couldn't go. And where would I have gotten it [the money] from?"

Don Julio was sent to the farm labor camp in Glassboro, New Jersey. About three days after he arrived, a farmer came from Lebanon, Pennsylvania and took Don Julio and three others to his farm. The four men were given a room on the side of the house. Don Julio recalled, "when his work was finished, he would get us work with other *farmers*. I picked tomatoes, I even went to work in tobacco, a *farmer* that had tobacco, and since I knew tobacco, they took us there. And that's how we worked." But the work was only for three months—August, September, and October—and then the tomatoes were gone and there was no more work. They were taken back to Glassboro. It was November, and Don Julio was sent to a farm in New Jersey, where for two weeks he followed the tractor, picking up potatoes and putting them in sacks. Then it was back to Glassboro, where Don Julio and five other men decided to take a taxi to Florida in search of work. They each paid thirty-five dollars for the taxi, but when he got to Florida, he decided to return to Puerto Rico instead of getting work in a restaurant. "I didn't have anything, enough for the trip nothing more. . . . You earned very little there, you earned almost nothing. . . . And then to spend it on the airfares, to go there, and then the airplane. So, I arrived in Puerto Rico with ten dollars. What did I do? I spent it the same night!" Don Julio had completed the terms of his contract, traveled to Florida on his own, and then returned to Puerto Rico.

He returned to work in sugar cane, until they called for workers to travel to the States again in May 1949. This time Don Julio stayed in the States, eventually settling in Philadelphia. He signed up with his older brother, who was married and had two children. "Everyone was coming, believing that there was a lot of money here." There were ads in the newspaper and offices, and as Don Julio saw it, "there were people dedicated to that, because it was a business like any other. Because these, these Puerto Ricans, it's like selling you, you see—because they bring you here, they bring you sold. That's why they pay them, you see. It's a business like any other." Don Julio and his brother were sent to Michigan and placed on a sugar beet farm with about eighty other Puerto Ricans and eighty Mexican families. He described the conditions:

> And when they took us to Michigan and shut us in that camp, and without paying us! . . . Well, they took us out during the day to work in those *farms,* in those *fields* that were there, you know. And that hot sun! *Man!* And there were no trees, the trees were way over there, over there. And you in that hot sun getting burned. . . . We went the first week and they didn't pay us. And I said, "What is this?!" They gave each of us five dollars. Look, five dollars. . . . Listen, what those people did to us was an abuse. And not just with the two of us, with the 80 of us that were there. And they had us there, about, about a month. Every week they gave each of us five dollars. Nothing more, you hear! And well, we didn't know how to defend ourselves, we couldn't speak, we didn't know English, you see.

With their ten dollars, Don Julio and his brother bought food, and in the evenings his brother cooked for them both.

When the opportunity presented itself, Don Julio and his brother left the farm to search for better work and better conditions. After about a month, a Mexican *troquero* came by, announcing that he was going to Texas and looking for work along the way. Don Julio, his brother, and three Mexican workers went with him. First they found work in a plant processing corn, where the pay was good but the work lasted only a week. Then they went to another farm and picked tomatoes until a storm came and destroyed the crop. Next they picked cotton. Finally, they arrived in San Antonio, Texas, where the truck driver left them, taking most of their money with him. Don Julio's brother, a Baptist, found help at a Baptist church just two blocks away, and they went to court and managed to recover their back wages. Through a member of the church, they found construction jobs and stayed in San Antonio for a year, earning $40 a week. His brother sent money home every week to his wife and children, saved $700, and decided to return to Puerto Rico. Don Julio, on the other hand, had spent his money at the bars, and had $35. When they laid him off because of his drinking, he found out they were recruiting people to work in West Virginia on the railroads. "Well, I filled out the papers and came to West Virginia. Eighty, they brought eighty Mexicans, one Cuban, and me, Puerto Rican." He lasted only two weeks, working on the railroad. Accused in a stabbing incident in town, he spent one night in jail, paid a twenty-five-dollar fine, and was told to leave town.

Don Julio turned from labor recruitment to social networks of family and friends for his next two moves. He packed his bags, got on a Greyhound bus, and headed for Hershey, Pennsylvania, where a friend of his from Cayey was working. Don Julio recounted: "As soon as I arrived at Hershey, the next day they gave me a job in the kitchen. I had, thank God, a lot of luck with jobs." He cleaned the kitchen and washed pots and pans at night, earning $70 a week. But his "vices" cost him his job again. In 1953, he left Hershey, Pennsylvania and settled in Philadelphia where his cousin and nephew were living and working. They gave him a place to live and helped him find work. He found jobs in construction, in cafeterias and restaurants, and finally at the Progress Lighting Company packing lamps, where he worked for eighteen years. He remarked, "I always, thank God, got another job right away." Don Julio gave up his "vices," became a religious man, and settled down. He got married in 1960, to a woman who already had three children, and they had two more, and in 1963, they bought a house. His wife worked in the garment industry, got involved in local politics, and then worked in the city's welfare office. He described their routine: "And then she got a job and kept working. We worked, me at night, and her during the day. We lived well. She went to work and I stayed with the kids, taking care of them. She came home and I went to work. We never lived off the government, we both always worked."

While Don Julio's route to Philadelphia may have involved more stops and turns, other migrants also used labor contracts in a variety of ways. In a 1954 study, the U.S. Department of Labor expressed the possibilities: "The majority are using this organized migration as a stepping stone toward eventual settlement on the continent, as an experiment to see whether they would be able to adjust to life on the mainland, or as a means of supplementing their incomes for one or two seasons." Of the 487 migrants interviewed, more than half planned to return as farmworkers the following year. Only 8 percent planned to return to Puerto Rico permanently; 31 percent planned to settle in the States permanently. For year-round agricultural work they could return to Puerto Rico or migrate to Florida. Most, however, wanted manufacturing jobs. Employers complained of Puerto Ricans quitting before completing their contracts and pointed to migrants' "desire to earn more money" or "opportunities to get jobs in factories or food processing plants." Another study found that most of Pennsylvania's Puerto Rican farmworkers wanted manufacturing jobs: 89 percent stated they would work in industry if they could, citing better wages and steady employment as the reasons. Most—72 percent—did seasonal farm work because of insufficient employment at home, and another 9 percent explained that other opportunities were closed to them.[56]

Because some farmworkers stayed, Puerto Ricans' settlement patterns reflected the destinations of contracted farmworkers. From the 1950s through the mid-1960s, most contract laborers were sent to New Jersey; New York and Pennsylvania were the next most common destinations (see Table 3.1). In 1953, for example, the three states combined received approximately 86 percent of all farmworkers. In the thirteen-year period, 93,155 contracted farmworkers went to New Jersey, 27,013 went to New York, and 20,420 went to Pennsylvania. During the 1950s Puerto Rican communities grew rapidly in the Mid-Atlantic states, especially Philadelphia. Fewer contract laborers were sent to Delaware and Maryland each year. During the 1960s Connecticut and Massachusetts became more important as destinations for farmworkers, and Puerto Rican communities grew rapidly in those states. This contract labor program continued.[57]

Other regions received relatively few contract laborers. Contract laborers were not sent to the segregated South. Labor contracts stipulated that "the Employee shall not be subject to discrimination in employment, housing facilities or any other regard because of race, color, creed, membership in or activity in behalf of any labor organization." Sierra Berdecía stated the policy: "We agreed that should the communities make definite arrangements for non-discrimination of any kind then we should agree to let Puerto Ricans work in the respective communities." He continued, "inasmuch as this might necessitate changing of laws in certain communities, many of them would not be able to comply with this requirement." Similarly, Senior asserted that "there is the question of recruiting Puerto Ricans to work on a 'share-cropping' basis which certainly does not appeal to me!" He considered it "extremely unwise to send Puerto Ricans under contract and through the official machinery of the Puerto Rican government into the eastern or southern sections of Maryland." In addition to not making placements, they investigated when Puerto Ricans were recruited through other channels and reprimanded the Glassboro Service Association for placing workers recruited for New Jersey in areas that had not been approved.[58]

Nor did Puerto Ricans replace Mexican or Mexican American farmworkers. Policy makers did, however, experiment with contracting workers for Michigan's sugar beet fields. In 1949, Sierra Berdecía, referring to "Mexican workers who are being used in the west and southwest," noted, "we do not want to compete with them in contracts providing for a minimum wage of 40 [cents] per hour." Nonetheless, policy makers explored the transfer of five hundred Puerto Rican workers from New York state to Michigan. Michigan Field Crops, Inc. represented thirty-eight companies that employed between 7,000 and 8,000 men from May to November, primarily in the planting and harvesting of sugar beets. The organization's representative, Max Henderson, thought that "if this experiment with a small number of Puerto Ricans works out satisfactorily the Michigan Field Crops, Inc., may make a major change in their labor policy and next year use Puerto Ricans instead of Mexicans." Several issues emerged in the negotiation of contracts. Workers in the area were expected to work ten-hour days instead of the eight-hour days provided for in the contract, and workers were paid on a piecework

TABLE 3.1. Contract Farm Laborers, Destinations by State, 1952–1965

	Total #	% NJ	PA	NY	DL	MD	CN	MA	NH	RI	MN	MI	OH	WI	IN	IL	CA	WA
1952	12,277	50.0	16.1	20.7	2.6	0.8	5.1	3.2	0.2	—	—	—	1.5	—	—	—	—	—	—
1953	14,930	36.2	27.0	23.1	1.1	1.0	5.8	5.5	0.2	—	—	—	—	—	—	—	—	—	—
1954	10,637	43.5	20.7	22.2	0.2	2.6	5.3	5.2	0.3	—	—	—	—	—	—	—	—	—	—
1955	10,876	48.6	17.7	18.6	0.4	1.9	7.0	5.1	0.4	—	—	—	0.5	—	—	—	—	—	—
1956	14,979	50.8	15.2	19.3	1.9	0.6	6.1	5.1	0.3	0.5	0.1	—	—	—	—	—	—	—	—
1957	13,214	51.2	13.6	18.8	2.0	1.2	5.4	6.3	0.6	0.3	0.2	0.4	—	—	—	—	—	—	—
1958	13,067	60.5	11.0	10.4	4.5	1.5	7.3	3.2	0.8	0.2	0.2	0.4	—	—	—	—	—	—	—
1959	10,012	54.7	7.5	10.0	8.0	1.5	9.4	6.3	0.8	—	0.3	0.3	0.3	0.4	0.2	0.9	—	—	—
1960	12,986	52.8	7.0	7.4	9.0	1.4	11.1	9.5	0.6	—	0.3	0.3	0.1	0.1	0.1	0.5	—	—	—
1961	13,765	49.1	6.6	12.3	9.5	1.7	10.4	8.9	0.6	0.1	0.3	—	—	—	0.1	0.2	0.1	—	—
1962	13,526	58.2	5.1	11.4	5.7	1.2	9.3	8.1	0.5	—	0.2	0.2	0.1	—	0.1	0.2	—	—	—
1963	13,116	53.3	3.2	11.2	9.2	2.2	10.1	7.0	0.4	0.2	0.2	0.2	2.9	—	0.1	—	—	—	—
1964	14,628	50.5	3.3	11.5	11.4	2.0	10.7	6.4	0.3	0.1	0.2	2.3	—	—	—	—	0.7	0.6
1965	17,385	46.6	3.4	9.0	9.1	1.7	12.9	8.2	0.2	0.1	0.1	3.5	—	0.1	—	—	5.0	—

Sources: Puerto Rico Department of Labor, Employment Service, Farm Placement Division, *Annual Agricultural and Food Processing Reports*, 1952–1965.

Note: 4,906 contract laborers were sent to the States in 1948; 4,598 in 1949; 7,605 in 1950; and 11,747 in 1951. Puerto Rico, Department of Labor, *Informe Anual del Departamento del Trabajo, 1950–1951*, 45.

basis instead of being guaranteed an hourly wage matching the prevailing wage. Henderson declined to pay workers a bonus and increased the wage deduction for transportation to cover the round trip. A representative of the Seattle Aviation Corporation offered a round-trip rate of $100 from San Juan to Michigan. In 1950, 5,300 Puerto Ricans were contracted to Michigan despite a plane crash in June that killed 29 of the 65 passengers en route to Michigan. Governor Luis Muñoz Marín banned the use of nonscheduled airlines to transport the workers, enlisting Pan American and Eastern Airlines to continue the flights. The migration to Michigan was small-scale, as policy makers continued to focus on the Mid-Atlantic states and increased their efforts in the New England states, especially Massachusetts and Connecticut.[59]

Those with labor contracts for Pennsylvania and New Jersey often chose Philadelphia for permanent settlement. Given the nature of seasonal farm work, many Puerto Rican migrants who had already traveled to the States were willing to continue their search for adequate employment. Some migrants tried to find manufacturing jobs close to farming areas, while others made their way to Philadelphia. The desire for manufacturing jobs also created the potential for fraud. In December 1950 several people were convicted for a recruitment scheme. They had charged several Puerto Rican migrants at the Glassboro labor camp a twenty-dollar "fee," promising jobs at the Illinois Steel and Pipe Tubing Company at South Bend, Illinois. Nine Puerto Rican men, who were left waiting at the corner of 6th and Brown Streets in Philadelphia, had filed the complaints.[60]

A few small Puerto Rican communities emerged in Pennsylvania's farming areas. By 1970, more than four hundred Puerto Ricans lived in each of ten Pennsylvania counties other than Philadelphia, and all were in areas that relied on Puerto Rican agricultural workers. As early as 1949, fifteen to twenty-five farm laborers settled in Lancaster to take jobs in industry, and ten years later, more than a thousand Puerto Ricans lived in the area, with most working in factories and restaurants. By 1954, Chambersburg claimed more than six hundred Boricuas, who were described as agricultural workers that were making material and spiritual progress. That year, fifty Puerto Ricans attended a meeting in Allentown to address relations between Puerto Ricans and the larger community. Victor Carmona, who had migrated to the area "to serve as an interpreter for fruit-pickers," called the meeting. By 1958, four hundred Puerto Ricans lived in Allentown.[61]

More migrants settled in Bethlehem—anywhere between five hundred and five thousand by 1958. Farm laborers were among the early settlers, as "more than one migrant worker . . . has jumped his contract with the Puerto Rican government or his farm job to come to Bethlehem and work in industry." In Bethlehem, the steel industry was "the lure," since "it offers the best money." Puerto Ricans also worked for the city, for contractors, in woodworking, and in other factories, and did "farm labor in the summer," joining the "migrant help who are in the Bethlehem area only during the hot months." Informal networks played a role in the migration, as one newspaper reported: "The Puerto Rican who comes to Bethlehem today will probably have friends and relatives already here. He will often find a job waiting (though the recession has made it much more difficult) and a place to stay right away." Yet in smaller communities, job opportunities may have been limited and Puerto Ricans' roots in the community may have been tenuous. As Bethlehem's steel industry slowed, most thought migration had slowed, too, and that some Puerto Ricans had "gone back to the island or to New York or Philadelphia because of the layoffs."[62]

Racism and discrimination in rural areas and a sense that cities were less hostile may have fostered settlement in Philadelphia. Both the Allentown and Bethlehem series of articles began with comments on racism against Puerto Ricans. The Bethlehem series began with an attention-getting "Spik." It continued, "you very seldom hear the vile word in Bethlehem. Instead you hear 'pork chop.' It means the same thing: Puerto Rican. It is far from flattering, too." The Allentown article began: "People are funny," and reported that a "second generation Italian-American family . . . just beginning to be a part of the community" threatened to move if Puerto Ricans moved in next door. The articles documented discrimination in employment, housing, bars, and attitudes. Police relations created problems as well. One resident explained, "Allentown police have just been a little rougher on customs which in Puerto Rico 'tourists might find picturesque.'" Puerto Ricans were arrested for "loitering" and "disturbing the peace." While this suggested a clash of customs, the Migration Division thought local police in the area of Freedom, Pennsylvania "seem to be discriminating against Puerto Ricans in the nearby towns as a method of discouraging them from coming there."[63]

In a 1955 study, the New Jersey Department of Education's Division against Discrimination found a regional pattern to discrimination in New Jersey, with more discrimination in central than in northern New Jersey, and even more discrimination in southern New Jersey where the majority of Puerto Rican farmworkers were employed. In the smaller communities in southern New Jersey, Puerto Ricans were unable to get a haircut; so, "for convenience, and elimination of embarrassing situations, the Puerto Ricans at the Glassboro Service Association Camp have their hair cut in camp by one of their own group." As "community pressures prevent the majority of white girls from keeping company with Puerto Ricans," Puerto Rican men socialized "almost exclusively with Negro girls." In contrast, "in the large cities where individuals know less about what their neighbors are doing and prejudices seem less intense towards Puerto Ricans, the Puerto Ricans find companionship with Puerto Rican girls, many more Negro girls, and some white girls." Migrants in search of more hospitable environments could move north in New Jersey or to nearby Philadelphia, and the study found that they did both.[64]

While representatives of Puerto Rico's government claimed that the majority of farmworkers returned to Puerto Rico, Philadelphia residents and social service workers thought differently. As early as 1949, Philadelphia residents and social service workers noticed farmworkers moving to the city. When Manuel Cabranes claimed that 90 percent of the farmworkers returned to Puerto Rico, Ella Harris, director of the Philadelphia District of the Health and Welfare Council, disagreed. She had heard that 75 of the 175 Puerto Ricans on the King Farm in Pennsylvania "had left their jobs before the end of the season and had not bought return tickets." She concluded that "a much larger percentage of this group had not returned." Cabranes conceded "that a few of them do stay, obtaining jobs in industry, as had some 15 or 25 Puerto Ricans he had seen recently in Lancaster." Santos Montalvo, director of a radio station's Spanish hour, suggested that most contract laborers stayed and that their impact was intensified by informal networks. He "thought that his people needed direction as to how to adjust to the community as they were coming to Philadelphia so fast." Montalvo summarized an interview with the Governor, who told him that 1,500 Puerto Ricans had come to New Jersey in May 1949 with labor contracts. Montalvo thought that "most of them came on to Philadelphia to reside" and that "at the end of July there were 11,000 Puerto Ricans in Philadelphia alone that had come as a result of the first 1,500 because, as soon as they get their hands on any money, they send for their families and have no intention of coming back."[65]

Farmworkers knew of Philadelphia. Beginning with Samuel Friedman's recruitment and *El Mundo*'s publicity, Puerto Ricans were made aware of Philadelphia, as the farm labor program became synonymous with Friedman, New Jersey, and Pennsylvania (or "Philadelphia"). Transportation to farms was often arranged through the city. Puerto Ricans worked in farming areas that bordered Philadelphia, in the southeastern and south central areas of Pennsylvania and southern New Jersey, a proximity that increased migrants' familiarity with the city and facilitated relocation there. Once on the farms, religious and social service agencies linked migrant workers to the city. The city seemed to offer jobs, housing, and a more hospitable environment.

Philadelphia churches and social service agencies provided an early and persistent link between the city and the agricultural migrants in the area. At the Glassboro labor camp, "the Catholic priest who stays in camp from Friday to Sunday is also in charge of the recreation as well as the English classes." The Reverend Enrique Rodríguez provided services at the Chalfont and Glassboro camps every Sunday. In 1948, the Pennsylvania Council of Churches hired "three full time summer teacher-evangelists" to "fill this missionary role" to the several thousand migrants, including "Negroes from the South; Mexicans and Puerto Ricans . . . not reached by regular churches." At King Farms in Morrisville, "one of the States' largest migrant centers," a chapel had been provided. Services were also provided at Quakertown and in Lancaster County "where several hundred Puerto Ricans are being served."[66]

The Friends Neighborhood Guild, a settlement house in Philadelphia, also became involved with the migrant laborers. In October 1949, the Guild hosted the first, and perhaps only, meeting of the Puerto Rican–American Agricultural Labor Union. The meeting was held in Philadelphia and the first president of the union lived in Philadelphia, but many of the fifty-seven Puerto Rican workers who attended arrived by truck from south Jersey. The Guild also hosted a meeting of Philadelphia Health and Welfare Council's Subcommittee on Puerto Rican Labor, which focused on Puerto Rican agricultural laborers. Marcia Bacchus, a Guild staff member and the chairperson of the Subcommittee, had "questions concerning the importation of Puerto Rican labor and the responsibility of the Puerto Rican government for its citizens after they reached the United States." Bacchus "pointed out that the Puerto Ricans in New Jersey as well as Pennsylvania come to Philadelphia for their social life and contacts." Guild staff members were aware of informal networks; one thought "that conservatively 150 families represents the potential about which large numbers will gather in the course of the next few years."[67]

Hence, while some farmworkers settled in smaller communities in farming areas, most migrants settled in Philadelphia. By 1970, more than half of the 44,535 Puerto Ricans in Pennsylvania lived in Philadelphia and 96 percent lived within the metropolitan area. As migrant farmworkers moved to Philadelphia, the Puerto Rican community grew rapidly. The Puerto Rican population of Philadelphia grew from 1,600 in 1950 to 7,300 in January 1954, with 2,600 Puerto Ricans arriving in the city in 1953 alone. That year 11,400 Puerto Ricans worked on farms in Pennsylvania and New Jersey, more than in previous years. When farmworkers settled in Philadelphia, whole families often followed. A 1954 study found that one-fourth of all respondents said they knew of people coming to live in Philadelphia in the year following the study.[68]

Interviews conducted during the mid-1970s confirmed the key role of farm work in the migration to Philadelphia. One son explained that his father came to a New Jersey farm in 1951 to work in the tomato crops: "My father came over first and he found a job here in the farm picking tomatoes or whatever till he saved up some money. And it was me and my mother, so he sent for us. And from him many others from my family came." In another family, the older brother migrated first, going to New Jersey in 1946. His younger brother recalled that his brother was married and wanted to establish his family independently. His independence was short-lived, however, as his father came to Philadelphia for a vacation, liked it, and made plans to move the family. Then, "little by little all of us filtered here to Philadelphia." With his father coming to New Jersey farms in 1950, one son thought that "*he probably did go to* an agency because they made a stream of passages to there, and contracts with the farmers." A couple of years later, the father was joined by his wife and two children. They had five more children, and the family worked picking blueberries and strawberries. When the father died six years after a tractor accident had left him unable to work, the mother cooked for all the workers so that her family could stay in housing provided by the farmer. Eventually, the family moved to Hamilton, New Jersey, then Camden, and finally to Philadelphia. Another told his father's story: "He came and went to farming, then he worked in some hotels. Then he told me he had got a job at a mill, a steel mill." The family followed the father to Philadelphia in 1953. The pattern was repeated: "My father came first looking for a job, better money. . . . When he first come over here he was working in the farms in Jersey. He worked there a while and then did factory jobs." His father migrated in 1954, with his wife and children coming to Philadelphia later.[69]

As migrants settled in the city, the farm labor program contributed to the rural origins of Philadelphia's Puerto Rican community. The program's promoters emphasized the rural origins of Puerto Rico's migrant laborers, and employers requested rural workers. Friedman asserted that the "*jíbaro* of the interior of Puerto Rico" made "the best agricultural laborer" and encouraged the government to finance their transportation. Similarly, referring to sugar cane workers, the Migration Division contended that "work in the cane fields is so hot and heavy that the Puerto Rican does not find so-called 'stoop labor' difficult" and that "having worked steadily during the winter, he does not have to get back into the swing of regular work habits." It worked. Robert Moore, director of the Glassboro farm labor camp in New Jersey, wanted men "from country districts who are working in the sugar cane industry." Moore had recruited Puerto Ricans from New York but found most Puerto Ricans "living now in New York have not come from farming backgrounds and therefore are unable to do a satisfactory job in farm work." Don Larin, Chief of the U.S. Farm Placement Service, hoped "new arrangements would permit more use of workers from the interior of Puerto Rico."[70]

Farm labor contracts for 1949 and 1950 reveal that the majority of farmworkers were from rural areas and that there were regional variations. The regions of origin for farmworkers paralleled the regions of origins for Puerto Ricans in Philadelphia. In 1949, 26 percent of the men identified their residence or that of their contact person in the tobacco region (see Table 3.2). Twenty-four percent were from the southwestern sugar region and 19 percent were from the southeastern region. Despite the economic crisis there, few came from the coffee region. Even fewer came from the San Juan metropolitan area. In addition to sending the largest cohorts of contract laborers, the tobacco region and southern sugar regions had significant proportions of their contract laborers sent to southern New Jersey and Pennsylvania, and elsewhere in the northeast. Similarly, the municipios of origin that were well represented among Philadelphia's Puerto Rican migrants were also well represented among the contracted workers. In 1950, the tobacco region again sent the largest cohort of laborers, and the southern sugar regions followed. The destinations of contracted workers were unusual in 1950, however, as large numbers were sent to Michigan and St. Croix. By 1952, the Mid-Atlantic states had reemerged as the primary destination.

Although Puerto Rico's policy makers wanted to promote settlement, Philadelphia was not their first choice of destination. Migration Division officials may have feared that Philadelphia was too similar to New York. Instead they encouraged migrants to move to the Midwest, and opened an office in Chicago in 1949. A 1953 newsreel was to "play up Puerto Ricans living in the smaller towns and cities of the middle west, the fact that they are building their own homes, they own cars and businesses, etc." The Migration Division focused on farmworkers in the areas surrounding Philadelphia, responding to farmworkers' complaints and supporting community groups in Lancaster, Chambersburg, and Bethlehem, Pennsylvania. The Division opened service centers in Keyport and Camden, New Jersey, and in Hamburg, Pennsylvania, to better serve farmworkers and to explore possibilities for permanent settlement in these areas. When the Division decided to open the Delaware Valley Regional Office, it chose Camden as the location. Thus in 1949 Cabranes had recently visited the fifteen to twenty-five Puerto Ricans living in Lancaster, yet asked social service workers "for information concerning the number of Puerto Ricans in Philadelphia" and "felt that he was not in a position to offer an estimate of the number in Philadelphia." He reported nonetheless that "there are now two small but growing permanent Puerto Rican settlements" in Philadelphia, and Camden and was "encouraged at the evidence he found that permanent and growing communities may result from migratory labor."[71]

TABLE 3.2. Contract Farm Laborers, Origins and Destinations, 1949 and 1950

	1949					1950				
	# of Contracts	% of Total	South NJ and PA	Northeast	Other	# of Contracts	% of Total	South NJ and PA	Northeast	Other
Puerto Rico	4,291	99.9	37.3	53.1	9.6	7,350	100.0	21.6	11.9	66.5
Regions										
Tobacco	1,098	25.6	29.6	54.2	16.2	1,855	25.2	24.5	21.2	54.2
Coffee	570	13.3	39.8	50.7	9.5	750	10.2	22.1	12.1	65.7
Southeastern	812	18.9	47.7	41.6	10.7	1,683	22.9	15.4	11.9	72.7
Southwestern	1,019	23.7	35.8	64.2	—	1,499	20.4	24.9	0.6	74.4
Northern	594	13.8	38.7	46.0	15.3	777	10.6	11.5	11.5	77.1
SJ Metro	198	4.6	34.3	64.6	1.0	786	10.7	31.2	11.6	57.3
Municipios										
Tobacco										
San Lorenzo	160	3.7	40.0	43.8	16.3	261	3.6	9.2	22.2	68.6
Barranquitas	207	4.8	21.7	45.4	32.9	213	2.9	48.4	11.7	39.9
Caguas	154	3.6	37.7	62.3	—	318	4.3	11.6	22.6	65.7
Coamo	155	3.6	26.5	54.2	19.4	287	3.9	25.8	34.8	39.4
Coffee										
Utuado	185	4.3	33.5	64.9	1.6	193	2.6	15.0	25.4	59.6
San Sebastian	87	2.0	63.2	36.8	—	44	0.6	4.5	18.2	77.3
Southeastern										
Salinas	73	1.7	53.4	46.6	—	123	1.7	7.3	14.6	78.0
Northern										
Arecibo	211	4.9	25.1	52.1	22.7	191	2.6	1.0	17.8	81.2

Sources: Farm Labor Contracts, 1949 and 1950, Puerto Rico Department of Labor, Record Group 61-55, Archivo General de Puerto Rico, San Juan, Puerto Rico.

Note: Origins are based on the residence of the contract laborer or of their contact person. For destinations, Southern NJ and PA includes growers served by Gloucester Farm Service Association in Glassboro, New Jersey, which became the Glassboro Farm Service Association in 1950, and King Farms in Morrisville, Pennsylvania. Northeast includes growers served by the Garden State Service Association and its subsidiaries. Other includes growers' associations serving the Midwest, the Northwest, and the Virgin Islands. Not all columns total exactly 100 percent due to rounding.

Conclusion

Sending thousands of Puerto Rican men to the States each year, the state-sponsored farm labor program was partially successful in meeting the objectives of the United States' and Puerto Rico's policy makers. The program met the States' immediate need for cheap seasonal agricultural laborers, as Puerto Ricans became part of the seasonal agricultural labor force. Yet Puerto Ricans also stayed. As they settled in Philadelphia, some policy makers and social service workers defined the migrants as a community problem. For Puerto Rico's policy makers, contract labor tempered seasonal unemployment and increased emigration and settlement. Farmworkers' permanent settlement in Philadelphia signaled success for the government of Puerto Rico in reducing the island's population, although Philadelphia may not have been policy makers' chosen destination. The program failed, however, to disperse the population as widely as hoped, dispersing the Puerto Rican population primarily within the northeast. Furthermore, while planners preferred small communities, migrants settled in metropolitan areas—a trend evident in internal migration and in migration to the mainland.[72]

For farmworkers, the search for work, especially manufacturing jobs, fostered emigration from rural to metropolitan areas in Puerto Rico, and from the farms of Pennsylvania and New Jersey to Philadelphia. Changing economic conditions propelled emigration from rural municipios and made labor contracts an economic strategy for preserving household economies. Thousands of Puerto Ricans came to the Philadelphia area with labor contracts, first for war industry jobs and later for positions as domestics and farmworkers. Economic conditions in Puerto Rico and Philadelphia influenced the outcomes of contract labor programs. Philadelphia's economy rendered the contract labor program for domestics unnecessary, as women had other employment options. For Puerto Rican men, however, manufacturing jobs were not readily available. With other options limited, the contract labor program for seasonal agricultural workers continued, and Pennsylvania's farm economy provided jobs for Puerto Rican men above and beyond the scope of the contract labor program. Informal networks could complement government efforts, as Senior hoped, or undermine them. In this case, the state-sponsored contract labor programs interacted with migrants' economic strategies, economic conditions, and informal networks to foster emigration from Puerto Rico's rural municipios and to increase the Puerto Rican population of Philadelphia.

Tobacco production defined the economy in the East Central Highlands, including San Lorenzo. Scattered tobacco farms dot this landscape between Coamo and Aibonito. The larger structures are tobacco barns and the smaller ones are houses, July 1946. (Photo by Jack Delano, Puerto Rico Office of Information. Source: Fondo Fotográfico del Departamento de Instrucción Pública, Archivo General de Puerto Rico, San Juan.)

Tobacco was planted on the steep slopes. Though men did most of the planting, a young girl helps in this photograph taken near Comerío, November 1945. (Photo by Edwin Rosskam, Puerto Rico Office of Information. Source: Fondo Fotográfico del Departamento de Instrucción Pública, Archivo General de Puerto Rico, San Juan.)

Tobacco processing employed women. Here, women strip tobacco in a growers' cooperative in Comerío, October 1945. (Photo by Edwin Rosskam, Puerto Rico Office of Information. Source: Fondo Fotográfico del Departamento de Instrucción Pública, Archivo General de Puerto Rico, San Juan.)

Salinas and other municipios along the southern coast encompassed highland areas, level plains, and coastal areas, as seen from the road between Salinas and Cayey, March 1958. (Photo by Ramírez. Source: Fondo Fotográfico del Departamento de Instrucción Pública, Archivo General de Puerto Rico, San Juan.)

Sugar cane defined the economy along the southern coast, including Salinas. As seen in this July 1946 photograph of sugar cane harvesting outside the San Francisco sugar mill, Guayanilla, workers were men, and limited mechanization meant that cane was cut by machete and transported by ox carts. (Photo by Jack Delano, Puerto Rico Office of Information. Source: Fondo Fotográfico del Departamento de Instrucción Pública, Archivo General de Puerto Rico, San Juan.)

Households in this region supplemented seasonal incomes in sugar cane with fishing. Men did most of the fishing, while children sometimes sold the fish locally. Here, fishermen bring in their catch with a young girl looking on, in the village of La Parguera in Lajas, July 1946. (Photo by Jack Delano, Puerto Rico Office of Information. Source: Fondo Fotográfico del Departamento de Instrucción Pública, Archivo General de Puerto Rico, San Juan.)

Throughout Puerto Rico's rural areas, women contributed to their household income through garment industry work at home. This woman is sewing in her home, near Comerío, October 1945. Note the tobacco farms in the background. (Photo by Edwin Rosskam, Puerto Rico Office of Information. Source: Fondo Fotográfico del Departamento de Instrucción Pública, Archivo General de Puerto Rico, San Juan.)

Here a woman does home needlework in the doorway of a sugar mill's company house near Lajas, July 1946. (Photo by Jack Delano, Puerto Rico Office of Information. Source: Fondo Fotográfico del Departamento de Instrucción Pública, Archivo General de Puerto Rico, San Juan.)

For women and the daughters who helped them, maintaining their rural households was labor-intensive. These women are washing clothes in a stream near Caguas, May 1946. Water was also carried from streams for other household tasks. (Photo by Jack Delano, Puerto Rico Office of Information. Source: Fondo Fotográfico del Departamento de Instrucción Pública, Archivo General de Puerto Rico, San Juan.)

Domestic workers arrive in Philadelphia, April 10, 1947, under a contract labor program later sponsored by the governments of Puerto Rico and the United States. The newspaper caption read, "Heartening News for City Housewives." (Photographer not identified, *Philadelphia Bulletin*. Source: Urban Archives, Temple University, Philadelphia, Pennsylvania.)

These men are on an airplane ready to leave from Salinas to the States in July 1948; labor contracts also brought men to the States for seasonal farmwork. (Photo by Louise Rosskam, Puerto Rico Office of Information. Source: Fondo Fotográfico del Departamento de Instrucción Pública, Archivo General de Puerto Rico, San Juan.)

Julio Rosario signed up for a labor contract for farm work as a young man in 1948 and eventually made his way to Philadelphia. With his friends in Cayey, Julio is in the front row, on the right, with the hat, ca. 1946. (Courtesy of Julio Rosario.)

These farmworkers are in the barracks at the farm labor camp in Glassboro, New Jersey, August 26, 1946. In a newspaper article the next day, U.S. Representative Vito Marcantonio charged that the camp was "virtually a barbed-wire concentration camp," while New Jersey state inspectors responded that it "was a model migrant's camp" and that "the barbed wire has been kept up and a watchman hired on 24-hour duty at the gate to protect the men's belongings." (Photo by Martin, *Philadelphia Inquirer.* Source: Urban Archives, Temple University, Philadelphia, Pennsylvania.)

While the contract labor program for domestic workers was short-lived, Philadelphia's garment industry offered Puerto Rican women jobs. This is Ninth and Filbert Streets, October 18, 1959. (Photo by Wagner, *Philadelphia Inquirer*. Source: Urban Archives, Temple University, Philadelphia, Pennsylvania.)

In 1954 Genara Aponte migrated from San Lorenzo to Philadelphia to work in the garment industry. When she married in 1958 at St. Peters, she and her husband worked in the same garment shop, where she sewed and he ironed; they each earned about $40 a week. (Courtesy of Genara Aponte.)

Chapter Four

Leaving Local Communities:
San Lorenzo and Salinas

Philadelphia's migrants emphasized the economic reasons behind their decision to leave their local communities, describing Puerto Rico as *flojo* or slow, the work as scarce, and the work that was available as low paid and seasonal. Doña Carmen recalled her and her husband's decision to leave San Lorenzo for Philadelphia in 1947: "This period of '47 was pretty slow, there wasn't work. There were schools, there was a life, you see, in town, but there wasn't enough for everyone to have a better life. So, what we did was plan for the family, like us, we planned to go to the United States." That there was a life in San Lorenzo was important to Doña Carmen, as she remembered San Lorenzo nostalgically and emphasized its beauty. Living in town, she made a business of cooking from her home, catering to the town's wealthier residents and providing lunches for the women who worked at the nearby tobacco factory. Her husband, Don Quintín, drove the town's ambulance. Yet rationing during the war had hurt her business. She reiterated the economic motivations: "We didn't want to, nobody wanted to leave. It took a toll. There wasn't any alternative." Although he had never worked in agriculture, in 1946 Don Quintín came to the Philadelphia area with a labor contract for seasonal farm work. Within a year, Doña Carmen sold all of their possessions and migrated to Philadelphia with their four children. Leaving seasonal farm work behind him, Don Quintín joined them in the city.[1]

Similarly, Don Florencio reminisced: "Salinas was a poor town, there were a lot of thatched houses. Some, not many, were wood. There weren't many made of concrete." It was getting harder to find work in sugar cane or in fishing, "especially for the youth, the young men." He explained: "The farmworker that was used to cutting cane, already, the sugar cane was disappearing. Already, you almost couldn't get sugar cane to make sugar." Meanwhile, government licensing requirements made fishing more expensive and hence "more difficult for the poor." Don Florencio's route to Philadelphia was less direct than Doña Carmen's. In 1952 he joined three siblings who were already in New York City. He was drafted and served in Korea, then returned to Salinas in 1957. Not finding work, he went back to New York, but stayed less than a year. In 1960 Don Florencio migrated to Philadelphia; thirty-seven years later, he still lived there.[2]

Both San Lorenzo, a municipio in the tobacco region, and Salinas, a municipio in the southern sugar region, sent significant numbers of migrants to Philadelphia. Located in the regions with the largest migrant streams to Philadelphia, these municipios were two of only eight that had more than a hundred migrants marrying in the city between 1945 and 1965. Indeed, more migrants from San Lorenzo were married in the city than from any other municipio.[3] Although they produced different cash crops, both municipios were dependent on agriculture and agricultural processing. Households relied on commercial agriculture and subsistence activities. As agriculture and agricultural processing declined during the 1950s and 1960s, neither municipio was an early recipient of Fomento industries. The industries that eventually came were labor-intensive ones, like the garment industry, that employed mostly women. While the government's industrialization program brought few jobs to these rural areas, its farm labor program offered men seasonal agricultural work in the States. As employment decreased, emigration offset the birth rate and both municipios had population losses in the 1950s and 1960s.

This chapter explores the impact of economic change and government policies on San Lorenzo and Salinas and the ways people perceived and responded to changing conditions from within their local context. Migrants from San Lorenzo and Salinas became part of Puerto Rico's internal migration and of more dispersed settlement in the States, which included Philadelphia. Their destinations reflected the regional nature of economic change in Puerto Rico, the contract labor program, and informal networks. Confronting the rural economic crisis in their communities, the men of San Lorenzo and Salinas were among the thousands who secured government-sponsored labor contracts for agricultural work in the States. Many of the early contract laborers were sent to farms in the Philadelphia area. Others came *por su cuenta* or on their own. Informal networks of family and friends played a role for migrants who came with and without labor contracts. In this way San Lorenzo and Salinas illustrate the causes of migration, the decisions migrants made, and the migration processes that brought Puerto Rico's rural peoples to Philadelphia.

San Lorenzo's Changing Economy

As one of the municipios of the tobacco region, San Lorenzo's economy was defined by its reliance on tobacco as a cash crop. Yet sugar was also grown, and was in fact the more profitable of the cash crops. Born in 1936 and the oldest of seven children, Doña Gloria described growing up in the San Lorenzo barrio of Jagual. Doña Gloria's father was a foreman for a farm owner who had several farms, growing tobacco and sugar cane. She recalled: "The sugar cane and the tobacco were the only things. So you left, for example, from sugar cane and started in tobacco. You left the tobacco and started in the sugar cane. That was the only work that you could get at that time." In addition to her father's wages, her household relied on financial contributions from her mother and the children, as well as a variety of subsistence activities. For Doña Gloria, however, the demise of San Lorenzo's agricultural economy was apparent by the mid-1950s. "There wasn't sugar cane or tobacco anymore. Here, at least, because in other places, there in Salinas and all those other places, there was still sugar cane. . . . So, people here turned more to growing *yautía*, yams, bananas, plantains, for sale." Nor were there other employment options. Describing San Lorenzo as "very small," she noted, referring to her brothers, "there weren't factories, there wasn't anything. So, the poor had to work in agriculture." As San Lorenzo's agricultural economy continued to decline and employment decreased, Doña Gloria, her siblings, her cousins, and other Sanlorenceños left the municipio in search of work.[4]

Nestled in the East Central Highlands of Puerto Rico, San Lorenzo is thirty miles south of the capital, San Juan, about midway between Puerto Rico's northern and southern coasts (see Map 2.1). The East Central Highlands include rounded hills and more rugged mountain peaks, with an average elevation of 900 feet, but with heights of 1,800 to 2,100 feet not uncommon. The mountainsides are very steep in places. The town of San Lorenzo was built on a bend in the Loíza River, where the river changes from a narrow valley stream and flows into the lowlands of the Caguas Valley. "From its earliest history," according to geographer John Augelli, "San Lorenzo's leading function has been that of service center for the surrounding agricultural area." With the U.S. occupation and the rise of tobacco, a large component of serving the agricultural area meant tobacco processing and a cigar industry. By 1935, San Lorenzo ranked third among Puerto Rico's municipios as a producer of tobacco. It had the most tobacco farms (1,424) and the most cuerdas planted in tobacco (24,206). Farms averaged 19 cuerdas, and most—78 percent—were owner-operated.[5]

San Lorenzo's agriculture and manufacturing were intertwined; most manufacturing was tobacco processing. In 1940 the overwhelming majority of San Lorenzo's men (81 percent) and a significant proportion of the women (24 percent) worked in agriculture (Table 4.1). In addition to tobacco, men worked in minor crops and sugar, while women worked in minor crops but not sugar. The majority of those employed in manufacturing, 76 percent, worked in tobacco processing. Although this was not the region in which it was concentrated, the garment industry was San Lorenzo's only other significant industry. Whereas the tobacco industry employed both men and women, the garment industry's workers were overwhelmingly women. Because of these labor-intensive industries, 38 percent of working women had manufacturing jobs, in contrast to only 5 percent of men.

In the 1950s, tobacco and tobacco processing continued to define San Lorenzo's economy. Most people, 68 percent of the work force, were employed in agriculture, with most in tobacco. The five tobacco *fábricas* were the largest employers in town, with each employing as many as five hundred workers at the height of the season. These large buildings served as factories for fermenting, stemming, and sorting tobacco and as warehouses for storing the tobacco until it was shipped. They were "owned by large tobacco interests both local and American" and produced leaf tobacco for export to the States. The overwhelming majority of workers were women who were paid twenty-five cents

TABLE 4.1.   Industry of Those Employed, San Lorenzo, 1940

	Total	Male	Female
Number Employed	6,897	5,740	1,157
Percent in:			
Agriculture	71.2	80.7	23.7
Sugar	20.9	22.0	2.6
Tobacco	42.8	42.0	56.9
Coffee	—	—	—
Other	36.2	36.0	40.5
Manufacturing	10.9	5.4	38.4
Sugar	2.0	4.9	—
Tobacco	75.8	80.6	72.5
Other food	3.8	8.7	0.2
Home needlework	14.3	0.3	24.1
Other apparel	2.0	0.3	3.2
All other	2.1	5.2	—
Construction	1.6	1.9	—
Transportation	0.9	1.1	0.1
Trade	6.3	6.7	4.4
Professional services	1.4	0.7	4.8
Other services	6.7	2.5	27.7
Domestic	87.7	57.8	97.5
Government	0.6	0.6	0.7
Not reported	0.4	0.5	0.2

Source: U.S. Bureau of the Census, Sixteenth Census of the United States: 1940, Special Reports, Puerto Rico: Population, Bulletin no. 2, Characteristics of the Population (Washington, D.C., 1943), 61–64.
Note: Other services include personal, business, and repair, entertainment, and recreation services.

an hour. Devoted to the rolling of cigars, cigar *chinchales,* in contrast, were small, single rooms, and most employed fewer than five workers, all men. *Chinchales* relied on locally grown tobacco and wrappers imported from Florida, Maryland, Connecticut, and other states. All of the cigars were handmade and they were sold only in Puerto Rico, costing from two to twenty cents apiece.[6]

This was the economic context that shaped Doña Gloria's parents' household economy as she was growing up. Her father worked five-day weeks, overseeing workers and managing the farms owned by another. His days were long: "Sometimes at midnight, there were times when he still hadn't gotten home, and by 4:00 in the morning, he had to get up to go." In addition to his weekly wage, he grew tobacco on their own three-cuerda plot. Her mother sold coffee to the farmworkers, and her father collected the money every Friday afternoon. Selling fifty bottles of coffee at ten or twenty cents each, her mother contributed to the household's income. Although she considered her family poor, Doña Gloria thought that both of her parents had been even poorer, recalling that when her mother was young, "she did all kinds of work," because she "was so poor, even poorer than us." She worked in tobacco, planting it, harvesting it, removing insects, and earning wages. Doña Gloria's household managed:

We did without necessities, not without food, because thanks to God and the Virgin, food we had, always, always. . . . At that time, there wasn't electricity. There wasn't anything. . . . My father was working basically for the food, for whatever medicine, whatever things. My mother, everything she earned was for us, for clothes. She sewed it for us herself, because she knew how to sew.

While her mother sewed most of their clothes, there was money to buy special items and pants, which she did not know how to make. Her mother also raised pigs and chickens, and grew plantains and bananas.[7]

Her household managed in part because Doña Gloria and her siblings started working for wages at a young age, in addition to helping with household tasks. As the oldest, Doña Gloria and her brother carried water from the stream and gathered wood for the stove. Sometimes Doña Gloria went with her mother to do the laundry in the stream, but other times she stayed home, making lunch and learning to cook. The children also helped their mother sell coffee, collecting the glass bottles that she filled with coffee, cleaning them in the stream, and delivering the coffee to the workers. When she was twelve years old, her father sent her and her brother to school, but just for two years. Her brother then went to work with her father. Meanwhile, Doña Gloria recalled, "I stayed at home, sewing tobacco and helping my mother with household things, and with my father, when my father grew his own tobacco. Because when it was for other people, I didn't go." Although she worked in the agricultural phase of tobacco only with her father, she sewed tobacco leaves during the season, for one or two months, earning piecework wages. Working in groups of ten to fifteen girls aged eight to fifteen, they moved from one farm to the next depending on the work available. With her earnings she bought clothes and other items, and helped her mother and father. Her younger siblings had a few more years of education, but all of her sisters sewed tobacco, and by the time they were fifteen years old, her brothers worked in tobacco, sugar cane, and in minor crops after the sugar cane harvest had ended.

This agricultural way of life, however, dissipated rapidly in the postwar era. Between 1940 and 1970, agricultural employment in San Lorenzo plummeted from 71 to 14 percent of those employed (see Figure 4.1). Agricultural decline began during the 1940s, when employment in minor crops decreased sharply, and sugar absorbed a larger proportion of workers. As a result, women's agricultural employment declined more than men's. Tobacco's dramatic demise during the 1950s, from 41 to just 7 percent of agricultural workers, affected both men and women. By 1970, just 20 percent of men and 1 percent of women worked in agriculture. Both farm owners and farm laborers felt the impact. Hard times in tobacco followed a "brief prosperity of the tobacco industry in the early forties." The proportion of men who were farmers increased from 24 to 26 percent during the 1940s, before dropping to 16 percent by 1960 and to just 7 percent by 1970. Farms were disappearing. In 1949 there were 1,646 farms, but by 1964 only 398 remained, with smaller farms under ten cuerdas accounting for 20 percent of the loss. At the same time, the proportion of men working as farm laborers declined from 56 to 12 percent between 1940 and 1970. For women too the declines were continuous, with farmers decreasing from 7 to less than 1 percent and farm laborers from 16 to 1 percent between 1940 and 1970.[8]

FIGURE 4.1.   Employment in Agriculture and Manufacturing, San Lorenzo, 1940–1970

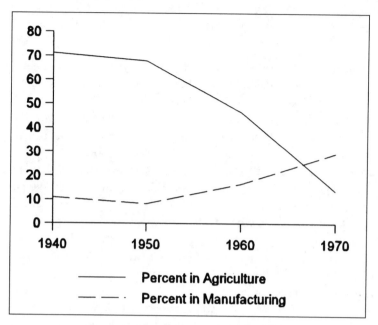

Sources: U.S. Bureau of the Census, *Sixteenth Census of the United States: 1940,* Special Reports, *Puerto Rico: Population,* Bulletin no. 2, Characteristics of the Population (Washington, D.C., 1943), 61–64; U.S. Bureau of the Census, *U.S. Census of Population: 1950,* vol. 2, *Characteristics of the Population,* pt. 53, Puerto Rico (Washington, D.C., 1953), 91–92; U.S. Bureau of the Census, *U.S. Census of Population: 1960,* vol. 1, *Characteristics of the Population,* pt. 53, Puerto Rico (Washington, D.C., 1963), 204; and U.S. Bureau of the Census, *Census of Population: 1970,* vol. 1, *Characteristics of the Population,* pt. 53, Puerto Rico (Washington, D.C., 1973), 490.
Note: Percent is of total employed.

As tobacco declined, some men turned to sugar. Between 1939 and 1949, the number of farms devoted to sugar increased from thirty-three to sixty-two, with the cuerdas cultivated increasing from 1,478 to 3,294. By 1969, however, only four sugar farms and 468 cultivated cuerdas remained. Sugar workers also traveled beyond the municipio's boundaries. In his anthropological study of a municipio in the tobacco region, Robert Manners found that the "rural lower class" or agricultural laborers had "a real problem during the dead periods in tobacco." As a result, "they are the ones most often forced to migrate or commute to the cane fields to survive during these periods." Responding to sugar growers' complaints of labor shortages, the Department of Labor's Farm Placement Division formalized this seasonal commute by organizing it. During April, May, and June 1958 about 85 men per week were transported from a pick-up point in San Lorenzo to the sugar areas to work, with as many as 150 workers commuting during the peak weeks.[9]

While agricultural employment plummeted, manufacturing failed to replace the lost jobs. The decline of tobacco took tobacco processing with it, accounting for 76 percent of manufacturing workers in 1940 but only 41 percent in 1960. Manufacturing employment decreased from 11 to 8 percent during the 1940s, and then increased to 29 percent in 1970 (see Figure 4.1). By 1956, Fomento had established only one small industry in San Lorenzo—a plant for polishing diamonds. The diamond factory was owned by a large New York City firm "attracted to Puerto Rico by low cost labor." The diamonds were sent from New York City, polished in San Lorenzo, and then sent back to New York City. The plant employed about 45 workers. This one small Fomento industry could not compensate for the decline of agriculture and the tobacco processing industry in San Lorenzo.[10]

Between 1954 and 1963, both the number of industrial establishments and the number of employees in these establishments decreased. In 1954, San Lorenzo had 22 industrial establishments—19 of them in tobacco processing. Most were small, with 14 employing fewer than ten people. The smaller workshops were cigar-making enterprises that employed men; the larger ones, for tobacco stemming and redrying, employed women. The other two industries, apparel and furniture, each had fewer than ten employees. Altogether, 1,235 people worked in industrial establishments. By 1963, San Lorenzo had 21 industrial establishments. Only 9 of these were tobacco-related, and most were small, with 6 employing fewer than ten people. The other industries were diverse in terms of products, but not in terms of size: 10 employed fewer than fifty people. Products included bread, curtains, leather, concrete block, and metal work. Combined, these industries employed 484 industrial workers—751 fewer than in 1954.[11]

Recognizing the limited impact of the industrialization program on rural areas, Puerto Rico's legislature provided additional incentives for industries outside the San Juan metropolitan region. In the late 1960s, tax exemptions ranged from ten to seventeen years, and San Lorenzo was given one of the longer periods, fifteen years. By 1970, San Lorenzo had 20 Fomento factories, many of which were in labor-intensive industries. Eight were in the apparel industry and 5 of these were U.S. subsidiaries by the early 1970s. In 1964, Robin Undies, Inc., based in New York City, opened Saint Lawrence Garments, Inc., making women's and children's underwear. The other subsidiaries made ties and shirts, ladies' sportswear, acetate draperies, and mosquito nets. The three Puerto Rico–based companies made ladies' dresses and ladies' underwear.[12]

In San Lorenzo, the decline of agriculture and limited industrial growth had a devastating effect on the municipio's labor force. From 6,897 in 1940, employment decreased to 5,380 in 1960 and to just 4,881 in 1970. The gender dimensions were pronounced, as the labor-intensive industries coming to the municipio employed mostly women. In 1970, manufacturing employed 48 percent of working women but only 19 percent of the men. After increasing slightly during the 1940s, men's employment fell, from 5,794 to just 3,201, between 1950 and 1970. Male labor force participation dropped to less than half (see Figure 4.2). Women's employment, on the other hand, decreased from 1,157 to 835 during the 1940s, and then recovered to 1,680 in 1970, with their labor force participation following suit. In addition to manufacturing jobs, women found work in the professional services. In 1950, more women worked in personal services (25 percent), the

FIGURE 4.2.   Labor Force Participation, San Lorenzo, 1940–1970

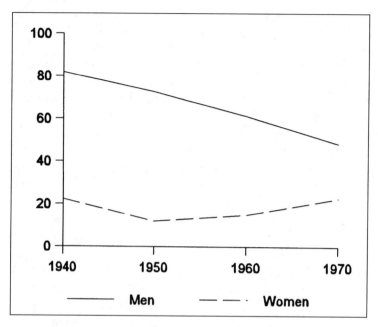

Sources: U.S. Bureau of the Census, *Sixteenth Census of the United States: 1940,* Special Reports, *Puerto Rico: Population,* Bulletin no. 2, Characteristics of the Population (Washington, D.C., 1943), 61–62; U.S. Bureau of the Census, *U.S. Census of Population: 1950,* vol. 2, *Characteristics of the Population,* pt. 53, Puerto Rico (Washington, D.C., 1953), 92–93; U.S. Bureau of the Census, *U.S. Census of Population: 1960,* vol. 1, *Characteristics of the Population,* pt. 53, Puerto Rico (Washington, D.C., 1963), 186; and U.S. Bureau of the Census, *Census of Population: 1970,* vol. 1, *Characteristics of the Population,* pt. 53, Puerto Rico (Washington, D.C., 1973), 454.
Note: Labor force participation is for those fourteen and older in 1940, 1950, and 1960, and for those sixteen and older in 1970.

overwhelming majority (99 percent) as domestics. By 1960, however, only 9 percent still worked in personal services, while those in professional services had increased from 20 to 27 percent, most in education. These trends continued during the 1960s, and women's employment in manufacturing and professional services eventually offset the loss of jobs in agriculture and tobacco processing.[13]

As agriculture declined and industries did not materialize, San Lorenzo's politics reflected its strong attachment to tobacco and the negative impact of economic change. During the Partido Popular Democrático's political reign from 1940 to 1968, many of San Lorenzo's voters opposed the PPD. In their landslide electoral victories in 1944, the PPD lost in only four municipios. Two of these, San Lorenzo and Aguas Buenas, were in the tobacco region; the other two were the offshore islands of Vieques and Culebras. In the first gubernatorial election in 1948, the PPD received 61 percent of the votes island-wide and only 38 percent in San Lorenzo. The PPD also won all of the local races,

except for San Lorenzo's. *El Mundo* described San Lorenzo as "a small island of opposition." The PPD finally won in San Lorenzo, in the 1952 and 1956 elections, though
with a smaller margin of victory than island-wide. San Lorenzo returned to form in
1960, when the PPD lost by a mere sixteen votes to the Partido Estadista Republicano
(PER), the pro-statehood party. As in 1948, San Lorenzo became the only municipal
government controlled by the opposition.[14]

The continuing significance of tobacco for Sanlorenceños was evident in both local
and island-wide politics. Local government was dominated by farmers and cigar-
makers. In 1948, the municipal assembly represented the three opposition parties and
included three republicans, three socialists, and three liberals. There was less variety in
occupations—five were farmers, two were cigar-makers, one was a shoemaker, and one
was a "housewife." The mayor, Pedro Borges López, was a former socialist and a cigar-
maker. The mayor-elect in 1960, Dolores "Lolo" González Díaz of the PER, shared a
similar background. González Díaz had left school in the sixth grade to begin work in
the tobacco industry. He had been a socialist and the president of a local union of agricultural workers. Sanlorenceños also identified with the leaders of the pro-statehood
parties, especially Santiago Iglesias Silva. Iglesias Silva was the president of the Partido
Reformista in 1948, a former socialist, a cigar-maker, a native son of San Lorenzo, and
was described by *El Mundo* as an "institution." This was, however, not just loyalty to
native sons; the PPD's candidate for resident commissioner, Antonio Fernós Isérn, won
in every municipio except his native San Lorenzo in the 1960 elections. Sanlorenceños
also identified with the more devout Catholicism of opposition leaders. In the 1960 elections, the Partido Acción Cristiana (Christian Action Party) received 23 percent of the
votes in San Lorenzo in contrast to only 7 percent island-wide.[15]

Nor was San Lorenzo a clear beneficiary of the PPD's economic policies. Land reforms
based on enforcement of the 500-acre limit had a limited impact given the smaller size of
tobacco farms. Yet in Barrio Cerro Gordo, the PPD divided an 800-cuerda farm into 10-
and 24-cuerda parcels and built a road. Nevertheless, the opposition won the barrio by 233
votes in 1948. Similarly, while the PPD emphasized industrialization, San Lorenzo had
received only two Fomento industries by 1956. Arguing that San Lorenzo's opposition to
the Partido Popular Democrático was the result of the local economic crisis, historian Luis
Martínez Fernández contrasts the Great Depression of the 1930s to the 1950s in San
Lorenzo. In 1935 San Lorenzo's unemployment rate was lower than island-wide, agricultural salaries were higher, and the work was less seasonal. By the 1950s, agricultural and
manufacturing salaries in tobacco were lower than for other crops, and by the 1960s there
were fewer workers in industry than in 1935. Noting that Puerto Rico's economic trans-
formations had a more severe impact in tobacco municipios precisely because the decline
in tobacco affected secondary tobacco activities, Martínez Fernández questions whether the
Depression arrived in San Lorenzo in the 1930s or in the 1950s with Operation Bootstrap.
For Martínez Fernández, San Lorenzo's contribution to the 1968 defeat of the PPD was a
continuation of the search for alternatives to the party's economic development program.[16]

By the mid-1950s, Doña Gloria's family had been affected by the changes in San
Lorenzo's economy. Her father's employer was selling portions of his farms and was only

growing sugar cane on plots closer to town, not on those surrounding her home. Nevertheless, her father still worked five days a week. For her brothers and cousins, however,

> it was very difficult for them, because already, the work here was in agriculture, for example, plantains, *yautía*, those things. But it wasn't for everyone, it wasn't a group. One or two people, and if four or five people were working on one side they couldn't hire anyone else. It wasn't like in sugar cane, where even a large group of one hundred people could work.

Whereas workers used to come from other areas to work in the sugar cane, now there was not enough work, even for her brothers, who sometimes found work for only one or two days of the week. Their wages in minor crops were also significantly lower than those for sugar cane, and they could not find other jobs.[17]

The Navarros too were working hard to make ends meet. Married in 1946, Don Justino and Doña Ana Luisa had four children by 1954. They were living in a small house on her father's farm in barrio Quemados. They grew tobacco, and Don Justino also worked in sugar cane. Before he was eleven years old, Don Justino had started working on a farm that grew sugar cane and had a dairy. His father had died, and his mother had six children to raise by herself. In the mornings, he worked in the dairy and delivered the milk to town on a horse. When he returned, he worked in the sugar cane earning seventeen cents for six hours of work. For delivering the milk seven days a week, he earned even less—two dollars a month. For Don Justino, not much changed: "When we were married, well, I continued the same struggle, the same route, working in sugar cane, in all kinds of agriculture." Don Justino and Doña Ana Luisa's days started at 5:00 A.M., when they went to the stream to get water for the day and then worked in the tobacco they planted on her father's farm. At 6:30 Don Justino went to work in sugar cane and "she stayed at home dealing with the children." He was making $1.50 for an eight-hour day, and when the weather was bad, he lost the day's work and his wages. When he came home at 5:00 P.M., they went back to working in tobacco. They also grew plantains, corn, beans, and *yautía*, as Don Justino explained: "During the summer there wasn't any work in the sugar cane or in tobacco, and that's how I spent my life, not just me, but everybody, until the sugar cane harvest and the tobacco planting came." He saw few alternatives: "All the workers here in Puerto Rico worked like that, because that's the industry that there was, the major industry was tobacco and sugar." As for factories, he added, "the only ones were tobacco, there were no factories here in San Lorenzo." Doña Ana Luisa reflected, "it was incredible, sometimes I ask myself, I say to myself, 'How did we survive this?' I don't understand it, how we survived it."[18]

San Lorenzo's Internal Migrations

As employment declined, the people of San Lorenzo left their municipio in search of work. The impact of economic change was widespread. Agricultural decline affected farm owners and farm laborers alike, threatening rural household economies to which men, women, and children contributed. As tobacco declined, so did the tobacco processing industries in town, displacing the women who stemmed and sorted tobacco and the men who made cigars, threatening households in town that were dependent on wages. Women, who contributed to their households not only through subsistence activities but also by processing a cash crop and working for wages, were displaced from San Lorenzo's economy and migrated in search of paid employment. Shaped by the regional and gendered nature of economic change, Sanlorenceños' emigration and their destinations within Puerto Rico mirrored the island-wide trends in this period.

San Lorenzo, like most other rural municipios, experienced its largest population exodus during the 1950s. As employment declined sharply, an estimated 10,000 Sanlorenceños left their municipio. Emigration counterbalanced the birth rate, and the population declined by 4 percent. During the 1960s, emigration continued. Another 7,000 Sanlorenceños left, and the population decreased by 1 percent. In 1950 just under 30,000 people lived in the fifty-four square miles of the municipio—23 percent in town and the rest in the ten rural barrios (see Map 4.1). The settlement in town was dense, centered around the town plaza, while rural settlement was dispersed and characterized by isolated farmsteads.[19]

During the 1940s San Lorenzo's population had increased by 10 percent, and the town had grown by 30 percent (see Table 4.2). Much of the growth in town could be attributed to Barriada Roosevelt, a "pueblito" or a "low class urban growth resulting from the country-to-town movement," founded in 1935 when a flood destroyed rural homes north and east of town. The town purchased eight cuerdas a quarter mile north of town and gave free building lots to those in need. From 36 houses in 1936, the pueblito grew to almost 400 houses and more than 3,000 people by 1950, as the town purchased more land and people continued to move in from the rural areas. Women found jobs in the tobacco *fábricas* and as domestics for wealthier Sanlorenceños, while the men sharecropped in tobacco and minor crops, kept small garden plots and animals, worked in the sugar cane fields and in other agricultural work when it was available, did heavy work in the town's stores and the tobacco industry, and got jobs on public works projects when they could.[20]

During the 1950s, however, the population in town decreased by 18 percent, and eight of San Lorenzo's ten barrios lost population. Reflecting the decline of agriculture, the greatest emigration was in the rural barrios east of the Río Grande de Loiza, including Quebrada and Quebrada Arenas. The barrios bordering the municipio of Caguas lost less population, and Hato was the only barrio with a significant increase in population. Located between the town of San Lorenzo and the municipio of Caguas, Hato was situated on the road to Caguas and San Juan. In the aftermath of World War II with the increased use of automobiles, "kilometer hamlets," comprising at least two stores, residences, and sometimes a church or a school, emerged along the main highways. Suburbs also appeared, with houses of the "upper class" developing "string-like" along the highway. In 1955, Augelli found a dozen such houses, with more under construction. During the 1960s the barrios east of the Loíza River had the largest population losses again, while the two barrios with growth, Quemados and Jagual, were close to the town of San Lorenzo and bordered Caguas. Yet the population in town grew by 39 percent,

MAP 4.1.   San Lorenzo, Puerto Rico, ca. 1950

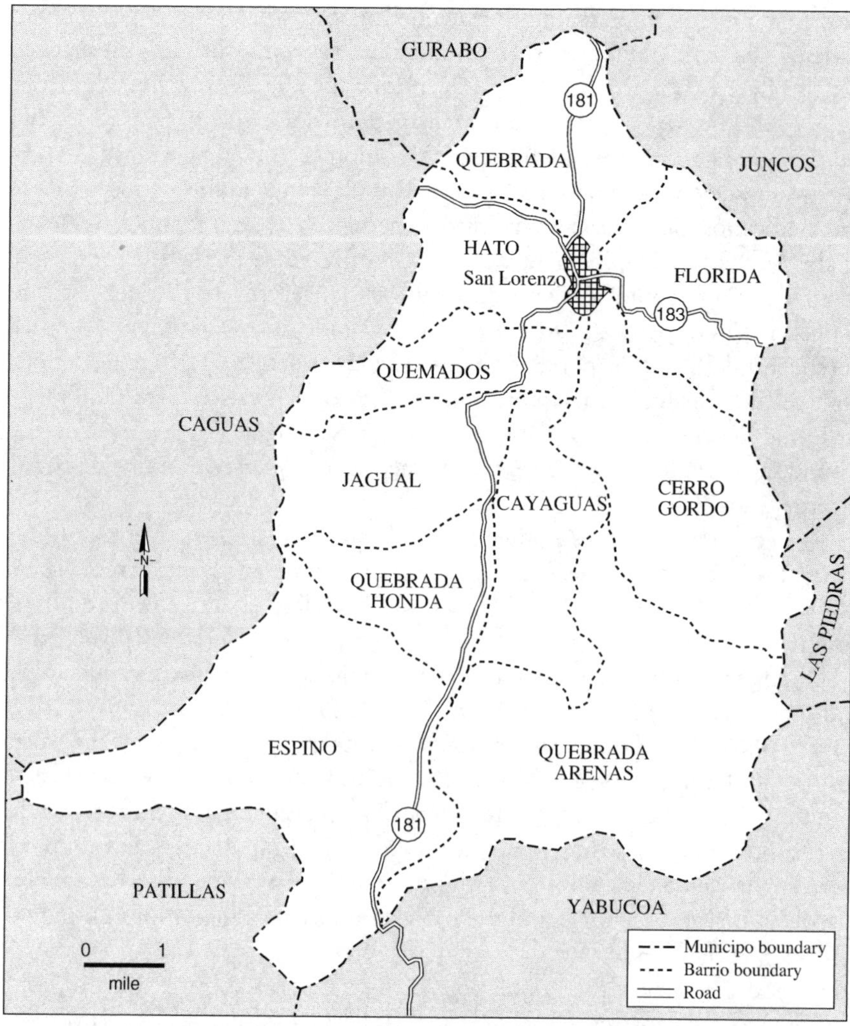

Sources: Puerto Rico, Planning Board, *Municipio de San Lorenzo: Memoria Suplementaria al Mapa de Límites del Municipio y sus Barrios* 22 (1955): 1.

indicating the continued decline of agriculture and some employment in those sectors concentrated in town—manufacturing, professional services, and construction.[21]

The decline of tobacco and the growth of industry in Caguas shaped migration patterns for the tobacco region. In contrast to San Lorenzo's one Fomento industry, Caguas was home to twenty-seven new Fomento industries by 1956 (see Map 2.2). During the 1950s Caguas's emigration rates were lower than those for the tobacco region as a whole, and during the 1960s Caguas had immigration, while all of the other tobacco municipios had continued emigration. Initially, cigar manufacturing increased, with Fomento providing subsidized facilities and tax exemptions. "If that trend holds," the Agricultural Experiment Station concluded, "the cigar industry in Puerto Rico is des-

TABLE 4.2.   Population Change by Barrio, San Lorenzo, 1940–1970

	1940 Population	1950 Population % Change	1960 Population % Change	1970 Population % Change
San Lorenzo (municipio)	26,627	29,950 + 9.8	29,248 − 4.4	27,755 − 0.7
Town of San Lorenzo	5,181	6,745 + 30.2	5,551 − 17.7	7,702 + 38.7
Cayaguas	1,277	1,497 + 17.2	1,280 − 14.5	838 − 34.5
Cerro Gordo	2,689	3,073 + 14.3	2,752 − 10.4	2,327 − 15.5
Espino	3,237	3,472 + 6.1	3,104 − 10.6	2,888 − 7.0
Florida	1,763	1,899 + 7.7	1,561 − 17.8	1,473 − 5.6
Hato	1,790	1,669 − 6.8	3,773 + 126.1	2,264 − 40.0
Jagual	2,223	2,408 + 8.3	2,347 − 2.5	2,626 + 11.9
Quebrada	1,697	1,207 − 25.2	1,012 − 20.3	989 − 2.3
Quebrada Arenas	3,108	3,459 + 11.3	2,757 − 20.3	2,144 − 22.2
Quebrada Honda	1,856	2,145 + 15.6	2,089 − 2.6	1,988 − 4.8
Quemados	1,770	1,611 − 9.0	1,724 + 7.0	2,516 + 45.9

Sources: U.S. Bureau of the Census, U.S. Census of Population: 1960, vol. 1, Characteristics of the Population, pt. 53, Puerto Rico (Washington, D.C., 1963), 16; and U.S. Bureau of the Census, Census of Population: 1970, vol. 1, Characteristics of the Population, pt. 53, Puerto Rico (Washington, D.C., 1973), 24–25.
Note: Parts of the barrios of Hato, Quebrada, and Quemados were added to the town of San Lorenzo between 1960 and 1970.

tined to become one of the most important sources of income in the Puerto Rican economy." Yet of 381 tax-exempt industries established island-wide by 1954, only 3 were in tobacco, and they employed 777 people. The demise of tobacco assured that Caguas's industrialization would have to take another route.[22]

Sanlorenceños were increasingly migrating and getting married beyond the municipio's boundaries. The baptism records of Parroquia Nuestra Señora de las Mercedes in San Lorenzo suggest the timing and the destinations of San Lorenzo's migrants. To get married in Catholic churches, migrants requested confirmation of their baptisms and the place of marriage was entered in the baptism register. Estimating a period of about twenty years between baptism and marriage, the increase in marriages outside San Lorenzo coincided with the increased emigration of the 1950s. These requests for proof of baptism increased, first from other parts of Puerto Rico, and then from the States. For example, of the 105 people baptized in San Lorenzo in 1912 and later requesting information for marriage, 87 percent were married in San Lorenzo, 8 percent were married in other parts of Puerto Rico, and 4 percent were married in the States. In contrast, of the 279 people baptized in

1932, only 53 percent were married in San Lorenzo; 15 percent were married in other parts of Puerto Rico, and 31 percent were married in the States. Very few of San Lorenzo's migrants married in other countries and those who did were often in countries where the United States had a strong military presence, such as Panama.[23]

In the late 1940s, those who left San Lorenzo formed part of the massive internal migration that characterized Puerto Rico, with 77 percent of men and 84 percent of women marrying in other parts of Puerto Rico (see Table 4.3). Between 1945 and 1949, migrants settled in nearby sugar-producing municipios, especially Yabucoa, Juncos, Las Piedras, Patillas, and Humacao. For San Lorenzo's men, this migration continued earlier traditions of seasonal migration to the sugar cane fields. Men's frequent marriage in Yabucoa may have reflected the municipio's proximity to San Lorenzo, the sugar industry's slower decline, or the increase in cultivation of minor crops. While this migration may have been an attempt to preserve an agricultural lifestyle that was becoming more difficult to maintain in San Lorenzo, by the early 1950s fewer men and women married in the southeast region. Throughout the period, very few migrants went to agricultural regions other than the southeast.[24]

With the widespread decline of Puerto Rico's agriculture, San Lorenzo's migrants settled increasingly in metropolitan areas, contributing to rapid urbanization. For the period as a whole, about a third married in the San Juan metropolitan area, another third in the southeast region, and just about a quarter in the tobacco region. Those staying in the tobacco region settled overwhelmingly in Caguas (83 percent). Increasingly Sanlorenceños migrated to the San Juan metropolitan area. The U.S. census confirms this internal migration pattern without providing a sense of the timing of migration or of the migrants' gender (see Table A.1).

The migrants to the San Juan metropolitan area were diverse. The migration of "upper-class groups," according to Augelli, began with World War I and "increased sharply with World War II," when they "were joined by people from the lower ones." The "migration initiated by the war was made up of *jíbaros,* poor town dwellers and returning veterans." Noting that not one in five of those born in San Lorenzo and listed in the 1949 edition of *Who's Who in Puerto Rico* were living in the municipio by 1952, Augelli concluded that "few of the successful professionals tend to remain in the area." Founded in 1954, the club Hijos Ausentes de San Lorenzo (the absent sons) confirmed that wealthier Sanlorenceños were among the migrants. Focusing on the San Juan metropolitan area and holding meetings in Santurce and Hato Rey, the club organized the parade of *ausentes* during the annual celebration of the town's patron saint, worked "to establish personal relations with university students from San Lorenzo," and raised funds for a public library and a recreation center to be built in San Lorenzo. Reflecting a concern for prestige, mayors and former mayors were frequent guests of honor. Resident Commissioner Dr. Antonio Fernós Isérn presided over the 1954 annual parade as the honorary president of the organization, and engineer Francisco Fortuño was selected as the "Most Distinguished Ausente for 1964."[25]

Underestimating the impact of the farm labor program, Augelli posited a serial migration for the "people driven off the land by the decline of tobacco" who "represent the

TABLE 4.3. Place of Marriage by Region of San Lorenzo's Migrants, 1945–1965

	1945–1965		1945–1949		1950–1954		1955–1959		1960–1965	
	Male	Female	Male	Female	Male	Female	Male	Female	Male	Female
Total Number	1,367	1,211	98	95	246	284	538	469	485	363
Percent in:										
Puerto Rico	41.0	48.0	76.5	84.2	55.3	57.4	35.7	37.1	32.6	45.4
United States	58.7	51.9	23.5	15.8	43.9	42.6	63.9	62.9	67.4	54.3
Other Country	0.3	—	—	—	0.8	—	0.4	—	—	0.3
Number in Puerto Rico	561	586	75	80	136	164	192	173	158	169
Percent in:										
Tobacco	26.0	31.6	24.0	23.8	19.9	29.3	27.6	31.2	30.4	37.9
Coffee	2.0	0.5	2.7	—	2.2	—	2.1	1.2	1.3	0.6
Southeast	35.3	29.5	56.0	45.0	40.4	32.9	31.8	24.3	25.3	24.3
Southwest	2.1	0.7	—	1.3	2.9	—	1.5	1.7	3.2	—
North	3.2	1.2	2.7	2.5	1.5	0.6	4.7	2.3	3.2	—
S. J. Metro	31.2	36.0	14.7	27.5	33.1	36.0	32.3	39.3	36.1	36.7
Military	0.2	0.5	—	—	—	1.2	—	—	0.6	0.6

Source: Baptism Records of Parroquia Nuestra Señora de las Mercedes, San Lorenzo, Puerto Rico.

Note: Data is for baptisms between 1910 and 1940, with the place of marriage recorded as outside of San Lorenzo, between 1945 and 1965. Not all columns total exactly 100 percent due to rounding.

poorest emigrant element." For "lower-class groups" who had moved to town, he concluded, "all these types of work are not sufficient to give employment to all the surplus rural population, so that some of them move to Metropolitan San Juan, other urban centers of the island, and even to New York City." Revealing a less than positive attitude toward these migrants, he noted their movement from the country to the "slum districts" of San Lorenzo, to "San Juan's infamous Fanguito," and then on to foster "slum development" in New York City. He estimated that thirty people left San Lorenzo for New York City every month—twenty from Barriada Roosevelt, the "slum district," and the remainder from town. Suggesting some early migration from the barrios to the States, baptism records for 1913 to 1921 identified 268 residents by their barrios. Migrants left from town (30 percent) and from the barrios (70 percent); almost two-thirds of these migrants married in other parts of Puerto Rico, and the other third married in the States. It was the farm labor program, however, that made this type of serial migration unnecessary for many of San Lorenzo's migrants and facilitated migration from the rural barrios directly to the States.[26]

Since migration was shaped by economic opportunities, men and women from San Lorenzo chose different destinations. Throughout the period from 1945 to 1965, a larger proportion of women settled in Puerto Rico, while more men went to the States (see Table 4.3). Of those staying in Puerto Rico, the women were more likely than the men to move to the rapidly urbanizing areas of Caguas and San Juan. Women responded to employment opportunities in metropolitan areas, as the industrialization program attracted U.S. industries that were concentrated in the metropolitan areas and that relied on women workers. Men, on the other hand, migrated to the southeast sugar area more often than the women. With the decline of tobacco, some of San Lorenzo's men sought work in sugar cane either by commuting or by relocating, while women rarely worked in sugar cane. Men found fewer employment opportunities in the metropolitan areas. Faced with few manufacturing jobs in the cities and only declining sugar cane production in agricultural areas, San Lorenzo's men were more likely than the women to migrate to the States. The farm labor program encouraged this pattern of migration by contracting only men for agricultural work. Increasingly, Sanlorenceños responded to economic changes in their municipio by migrating to the States, and between 1955 and 1965 those getting married in the States outnumbered those married in other parts of Puerto Rico.

Salinas's Changing Economy

Salinas's economy was defined by the production of sugar. Households supplemented men's seasonal wages in sugar cane with fishing. Don Florencio was born in La Playa, Salinas, in 1929 as one of eleven children. He described his father's work: "This work in sugar cane, what we call *la zafra* in Puerto Rico, he got four or five or six months, no more. Because at that time, when there wasn't work, he went fishing. . . . That's the work that there was, agriculture and fishing." While fish provided food for the family,

Don Florencio's father also sold fish to a wholesaler. The family managed, he explained, as "my older brothers were always helping too," by working in sugar cane. Yet by the 1950s sugar "was already going down." Government requirements for licenses and life jackets had also made it more expensive to enter the fishing industry. As for manufacturing jobs, "in Salinas, there was one factory before 1957. There was the Paper Mate factory. . . . There was a *central,* too, that's mostly what there was." Don Florencio did not work in sugar cane, but he did not have a manufacturing job either. Instead, his only job in Salinas was working in an "American store": "That was my first job and I earned $8 a week to help my family. . . . I worked from six in the morning until six in the evening, from Monday through Saturday. My only day off was Sunday. They gave you lots of work for a little money." In Salinas, new manufacturing jobs did not compensate for declining employment in the sugar industry. As employment decreased, Don Florencio and other Salinenses migrated in search of work.[27]

Bordering the Caribbean Sea on Puerto Rico's southern coast, Salinas is 50 miles southwest of San Juan and 23 miles east of Ponce, Puerto Rico's second-largest city (see Map 2.1). Its coast encompasses Jobos Bay, one of the most protected harbors on the southern coast. The alluvial plains near the coast are relatively level lands with excellent soils. While these plains account for about half of the municipio's territory, Salinas's terrain also includes highland areas. Although sugar had been grown along with coffee and food crops, with the 1898 occupation the United States brought irrigation, capital, an increase in sugar production, and land concentration. Irrigation divided savanna forest lands into irrigated sugar cane land along the coast and the semiarid crop and grazing land beyond the reach of irrigation. This dry area was dedicated to grazing and food crops, with small patches of coffee, food crops, and some tobacco grown along the streams. Farther north, there was a small area of humid uplands with remnants of earlier coffee production, interspersed with oranges, bananas, and shade trees. The result was "two distinct classes in the agricultural population; a group of large land owners who grow export crops on the best lands, and a group of small land owners who grow subsistence crops on the poorer lands." Coffee and tobacco production declined, and "the growing of subsistence crops has been relegated to the less productive lands; those with rougher terrain, poorer soil, less available water, and poorer transportation." The settlement pattern changed from one of haciendas and isolated peasant settlements to one of densely settled workers' villages.[28]

The south coast was, as anthropologist Sidney Mintz noted, "one of the regions most altered by the economic effects of the American occupation." Between 1898 and 1930, Central Aguirre came to dominate Salinas's economy, becoming a sugar mill complex, with docking facilities, a railroad, and a company town. At the end of the War of 1898, four U.S. businessmen purchased Hacienda El Nuevo Aguirre, the sugar mill and equipment, and two thousand cuerdas of sugar cane land. They also purchased twelve miles of railroad and two smaller mills in the neighboring municipio of Guayama. The Aguirre Corporation continued acquiring land and equipment and constructing the irrigation system. With more than 20,000 acres of cane fields, the mill was grinding 9,000 tons of sugar a day. In addition to the factory and warehouses, the company town had a hospital, schools, stores, bungalows to house workers, more elaborate residences for the U.S. executives, a golf course, a theater, a swimming pool, and two racially segregated social clubs. The company owned and operated most of the commercial businesses in the southern region, with the main store in Central Aguirre and branches on other sugar plantations. Aguirre employed 8,000 workers during the busy season and created thousands of ancillary jobs, employing workers from Salinas and neighboring municipios.[29]

Sugar continued to define Salinas's economy, assuring that agriculture and manufacturing were thoroughly intertwined. By 1940, 58 percent of the work force was in agriculture, with 87 percent in sugar (see Table 4.4). Of those in manufacturing, 82 percent worked in sugar processing. Employing primarily men, the sugar industry shaped women's options. Very few women worked in agriculture, and because of the predominance of sugar processing, few worked in manufacturing. Those who did worked in home needlework and other apparel. Instead, with only 13 percent of women in the labor force, half worked in the nonprofessional services, where the overwhelming majority (96 percent) were domestics.

Doña Nilda was born in 1933 in Santa Isabel. Her family moved to San Felipe in barrio Aguirre, Salinas when she was young. She described growing up as the oldest of eleven children, with her mother, her stepfather, and their ten children. Her stepfather worked at Central Aguirre, but had work for only six months of the year. She recalled: "Then, during the time when there wasn't that work, well, he fished a lot and we sold the fish. Even I sold fish. And with that, we ate fish and bought other things too. . . . You bought rice, you bought beans, you bought everything. I went one way, my brother went another, my sister another." While fish provided food for the family, it also provided needed income during the dead season, in what was largely a cash economy. In addition to taking care of eleven children, Doña Nilda's mother contributed income to the household, taking in laundry, washing and ironing clothes for the Americans who worked at Central Aguirre, as her mother had done before her. Doña Nilda noted, "there were a lot, a lot of women from San Felipe that worked in those jobs." Her mother had also worked in the garment industry: "There was a factory and there were women that embroidered the edges of handkerchiefs and earned some money." When Doña Nilda was about eleven years old, her mother worked in a government-funded breakfast program for children, from 7:00 to 10:00 A.M. She then came home to her household tasks, and continued taking in laundry. Doña Nilda attended school until the sixth grade, and then sold fish, delivered laundry, took her mother's government payroll papers to town, and helped her mother with cooking, taking care of her younger siblings, and doing the household's laundry at the stream. She also gathered food for the family: "There were times when she didn't have anything to cook and I would say, 'well, look, I brought shrimp' and she would get and put on a pot, put them to cook, and that's what we ate." Despite their poverty, she concluded, "Life before, even though we were poor and we didn't have a lot of good or expensive things, was better, much better than life today. Because now, you work, you earn good money and everything, but there's more ruin."[30]

Because of sugar's dominance, land ownership was concentrated, and the jobs available were in the agricultural and processing phases of the sugar industry. In 1959, Sali-

TABLE 4.4.   Industry of Those Employed, Salinas, 1940

	Total	Male	Female
Number Employed	5,355	4,663	692
Percent in:			
Agriculture	57.6	65.2	6.1
Sugar	87.4	87.6	76.2
Tobacco	1.8	1.8	2.4
Coffee	0.8	0.8	2.4
Other	10.0	9.7	19.0
Manufacturing	17.3	17.3	17.1
Sugar	81.8	97.2	6.8
Tobacco	0.9	0.7	1.7
Other food	2.5	2.7	0.8
Home needlework	9.1	—	71.2
Other apparel	2.4	—	18.6
All other	3.5	3.8	0.8
Construction	2.0	2.3	—
Transportation	2.6	2.8	0.9
Trade	8.2	7.6	11.7
Professional services	2.5	1.0	13.0
Other services	8.8	2.7	50.3
Domestic	80.1	36.3	95.7
Government	0.9	0.9	0.9
Not reported	0.1	0.1	0.1

Source: See Table 4.1.
Note: Other services include personal, business and repair, entertainment, and recreation services.

nas had 103 farms, in striking contrast to 1,519 in San Lorenzo. Salinas's farms were large: 22 had more than 260 cuerdas, and the number of small farms of from 3 to 9 cuerdas had decreased from 43 to 22 between 1950 and 1959. As a result, 52 percent of men were farm laborers in 1950, but only 2 percent were farm owners or managers. Similarly, there were few industrial establishments in Salinas—only six, in contrast to twenty-two in San Lorenzo in 1954. Half were in food processing, including sugar, and together these six industries employed 1,003 workers. A 1955 article revealed Central Aguirre's importance in the economy and the seasonal nature of the work. At the end of March, Central Aguirre employed 5,736 workers in the fields, and paid out $97,783 in wages. By August there were 3,317 agricultural workers with combined earnings of $48,017. From 854 people earning a total of $23,736, employment in manufacturing declined to 488 people and earnings of $12,164. While Central Aguirre's manager asserted that the Central provided more employment than others during the dead season, for Salinas's mayor the unemployment could already be felt.[31]

Despite the hardships for workers created by a seasonal one-crop economy, a 1950 study revealed that sugar production was still profitable, especially in the southern region. Though labor costs had "increased substantially in the past few years," so had the price of sugar. The larger farms were the most profitable, as farms of 500 cuerdas or more had the most efficient labor use for harvesting. The southern region had the most level terrain, the most efficient use of labor, and the highest sugar yield per cuerda. Salinas fit this profile, as twenty-four holdings of 260 cuerdas or more claimed 90 percent of the land in farms in 1950. That year, the Central Aguirre Sugar Company processed 133,290 tons of sugar, surpassing their previous record of 130,240 tons in 1934. The company ordered a new, high-speed mill to replace one installed in 1905 and anticipated that it would be operating for the 1952 crop. For the fiscal year ending July 31, 1950, the company declared a net profit of $2,184,701.[32]

Nevertheless, agricultural decline came to Salinas. Agricultural employment decreased during the 1950s and even more sharply during the 1960s (see Figure 4.3). Even as agricultural employment decreased, the concentration of workers in sugar increased from 87 to 90 percent during the 1950s, as what little work there was in other crops vanished. Not surprisingly, farm laborers were hit hard, accounting for 60 percent of working men in 1940 but only 18 percent in 1970. At the same time, even the small proportion of farm owners or managers decreased from 2 to 1 percent. The number of farms decreased from 103 to 53 between 1959 and 1969. Continuing the earlier trend, small farms of less than 10 cuerdas were disappearing; only seven remained in 1969. For large farms of more than 260 cuerdas, the decline struck between 1964 and 1969, when the number dropped from twenty-three to fifteen.[33]

As in San Lorenzo, the decline of Salinas's commercial crop had a negative effect on agricultural processing. Sugar processing declined, from 82 to less than 36 percent of those in manufacturing between 1940 and 1970.[34] Aguirre Sugar Corporation remained profitable until 1967, when it changed ownership. Between 1967 and 1970 the company lost $14 million, losing $6 million in 1969 alone. In 1970 the owners closed the factory, leaving 3,000 workers unemployed. The municipio would have lost one-half of the income it derived from tax revenues. The government expropriated all of the property and assets, and reopened the Central as part of the Puerto Rico Sugar Corporation, operating the mill until 1990, when they closed it citing losses. During the first phase of the shutdown 114 workers lost their jobs, and another 653 workers lost theirs with the final shutdown.[35]

Emphasizing sugar's seasonal nature and the impact of mechanization, Salinas's municipal and civic leaders called on the government to establish other industries as early as 1949. Speaking to the Unión de Damas de Oficios Domésticos (Ladies Domestic Workers Union), Inés Mendoza de Muñoz Marín, the governor's wife, pledged her support to help the women of Salinas and to bring industries to the community. Two years later, a recently formed civic organization, El Comité Pro-Bienestar Público, urged the government to mount an advertising campaign to bring other industries to Salinas, especially needlework industries and those that used the byproducts of sugar cane. The committee was organized by José Caraballo, the president of the sugar workers union, who also served as the committee's president. It included representatives of the Catholic, Methodist, and Pentecostal churches; of the sugar workers', railroad workers', and domestics' unions; of Central Aguirre's administration; and of social clubs, the veterans'

FIGURE 4.3.   Employment in Agriculture and Manufacturing,
Salinas, 1940–1970

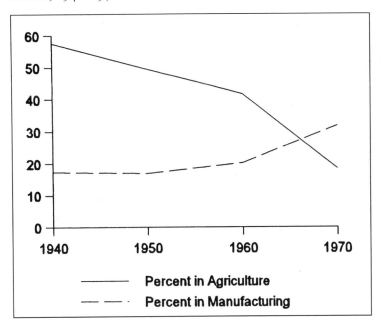

Sources: See Figure 4.1
Note: Percent is of total employed.

post, and the parent and teachers' association. In making their case, the committee
emphasized four points. First, they noted that the growing population and unemployment required immediate attention. Second, they pointed out that the only existing
industry, sugar, was mechanizing rapidly and eliminating large numbers of workers.
Third, observing that both the government and the town had recognized mechanization
as the only way to reduce the cost of production and compete effectively with other producers of sugar, they asserted that the government had the responsibility to protect the
industry for the benefit of workers and of the government. Finally, they argued that
since mechanization benefited the government and hurt the workers, "the Government
is obligated to create some industry in this area to alleviate the precarious economic situation of the residents."[36]

Yet Salinas received few Fomento industries, and the first one established, the Paper
Mate Company, exemplified both the promise and the limitations of the industrialization program. Starting with a single factory in 1952, the company had three factories
in Salinas by 1955. Making 100,000 ball point pens daily, these factories accounted
for 60 percent of the company's total production. The company's other factory was
in Culver City, California. In Salinas, the company employed 450 workers, mostly

women. The work was year-round, and workers made 57 cents an hour during three months probation and then a minimum wage of 75 cents an hour, with benefits including hospitalization, life insurance, unemployment compensation, and a cafeteria. Ignoring the gender dimensions of male unemployment in the sugar industry and women's employment in the new industry, *El Mundo* reported that the company solved part of Salinas's unemployment problem. Similarly, Salinas's mayor, Victor Figueroa, called for additional industries to be established close to Central Aguirre, where unemployment had its greatest impact. Yet a 1956 *Christian Science Monitor* article noted that the company employed 355 women and 120 men. Instead of pointing to employers' hiring practices, the reporter thought that few men wanted to work at Paper Mate, figuring that the factory would not last long in Salinas, and that women had the agile fingers needed for the work. For the reporter, women's work in the factory represented a major change in gender roles, as women worked outside the home for the first time, made more than their husbands or boyfriends, and were able to make purchases at the new jewelry store in town. While women were still seen taking hot lunches to the men at the *central,* men were sometimes seen taking lunches to the women working at Paper Mate.37

By 1957, however, Paper Mate was contemplating relocation to the San Juan metropolitan area. Noting that sugar cane, the principal industry, provided employment for only four months of the year, the factory was identified as practically the only source of income for the residents. At least four hundred workers earned a minimum wage of $1.00 an hour, generating an income of $15,000 to $40,000 a week in the municipio. Closing the factory, according to one source, "would leave the town dead." The original owners, the Frawley Manufacturing Company, had sold the operation to the Gillette Company two years earlier. Municipal and civic leaders responded in an effort to prevent the relocation. Meetings were held with Governor Muñoz Marín, Fomento's Teodoro Moscoso, and the Mayor of Salinas. Some of the problems noted by the company's owners had been addressed, such as improved telephone service and a commitment to construct another road to the factory. Others, such as the lack of air transportation in the region, were not easily resolved. Fomento responded with a study to address the owners' concerns. An editorial in *El Mundo* stressed the importance of keeping the factory in Salinas, not only for the immediate community, but also for the industrialization program's efforts to bring jobs to the smaller towns of the island, to prevent further congestion in the metropolitan area, and to address the difficulties that would likely confront other industries. Nonetheless, the factory closed in 1960, displacing three hundred workers and maintaining a temporary workforce of only seventy to pack and ship the remaining materials. Other businesses felt the impact, including a beauty parlor and a clothing store, for whom the factory workers constituted 80 percent of their business. Company officials cited the cost of transportation and the challenges of communication between Salinas and California. While thirty workers transferred to the company's California factory, municipal and civic leaders again called for new industries.38

Although Fomento promised special incentives for industries to set up shop in Salinas, few Fomento industries came. Special incentives included rental of the former Paper

Mate building and another Fomento building at rates lower than those available in the San Juan metropolitan area; up to $20,000 to be used for rent, salaries for instructors or supervisors, and/or shipping expenses; and the availability of trained garment workers. Fomento's employees were instructed to promote industries in Salinas with priority over other more developed areas of the island, and Salinas received one of the longer periods of tax exemption, fifteen years. In the aftermath of Paper Mate's closure, Fomento revealed that one other factory was operating in Salinas and that another was coming. Tempo Glove, which made leather gloves, occupied a Fomento building and employed 140 workers. Embroideries, Inc. was in the process of moving into another Fomento building and anticipated employing 250 workers.[39]

Despite the second stage of Puerto Rico's industrialization program, which emphasized capital-intensive, heavy industries, many of Salinas's industries remained labor-intensive ones, like Paper Mate, that employed mostly women and were prone to relocation. Between 1956 and 1970, the number of Fomento industries increased from two to twelve. In 1965, Phillips Oil Refinery came to Salinas; policy makers anticipated the creation of 30,000 direct and indirect jobs. Instead, 2,000 people were employed, with many coming from outside the municipio, and the only subsidiary established was Fibers International in 1966. Meanwhile, apparel firms, especially affiliates of the Kayser-Roth Corporation based in New York City, set up shop in Salinas. Making women's undergarments, Kayser-Roth opened Bratex Corporation in 1961, and then expanded their operations with Bratex Corporation #2 in 1966 and Salinas Manufacturing Corporation in 1967. In 1968 they added Salinas Pressing. Salinas Manufacturing became the second largest manufacturing employer, after Central Aguirre. Two Puerto Rico-based apparel firms opened in the early 1970s. Yet the same factors that brought garment factories to Salinas—low-wage labor and special incentives—also encouraged them to relocate elsewhere.[40]

Here, as in San Lorenzo, agriculture and agricultural processing declined, while other industries failed to replace the lost jobs. After increasing slightly during the 1940s, employment then fell from 5,611 to 4,644 by 1960 and to 4,470 by 1970. While agricultural employment declined dramatically between 1940 and 1970, manufacturing increased modestly during the 1950s and more significantly by 1970 (see Figure 4.3). Economic change affected men and women differently. Since it employed primarily men in the agricultural and processing phases, as the sugar industry declined men's labor force participation decreased from 82 to 56 percent between 1940 and 1970 (see Figure 4.4). In contrast, the decline had little impact on women's employment in agriculture, which fell from 6 to 4 percent from 1940 to 1970. Instead, as manufacturing shifted from sugar processing to apparel and other industries, women found more opportunities for paid employment. Between 1940 and 1970 women's labor force participation increased. By 1970, 42 percent of employed women found jobs in manufacturing, compared to 28 percent of men. Women also found work in the professional services, where 33 percent worked in 1970, while fewer worked as domestics.

Throughout the rural economic crisis, politics in Salinas, unlike in San Lorenzo, were characterized by close association with the Partido Popular Democrático. According to

FIGURE 4.4.   Labor Force Participation, Salinas, 1940–1970

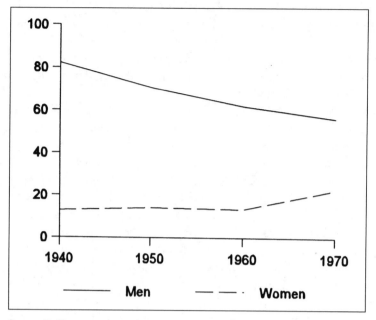

Sources: See Figure 4.2.
Note: Labor force participation is for those age fourteen and older in 1940, 1950, and
1960, and for those age sixteen and older in 1970.

Mintz, "it was precisely to the now disillusioned, now politically awakened workers of
the south coast—and sugar workers everywhere—that the new party made its appeal."
Political reforms decreased the dependence of agregados on the sugar corporations and
increased the significance of the town center, which had paled in comparison to the centrality of the sugar corporation. Agregados could not be summarily evicted from their
residences on company land, and resettlement programs were initiated that provided
former agregados with parcels of land on which to build their homes. Laws required
that company stores become separate entities from the sugar corporations and abolished
the practice of paying workers with scrip. Workers also benefited from wage and hour
legislation and from improvements in health and educational services. The new party
asserted workers' rights to participate in political and union activities without the threat
of being fired. Yet while an enforcement of the 500-acre limit and a government purchase of corporate land was made in 1948, most land on the southern coast remained
in the possession of private corporations.[41]

The union representing sugar workers was closely affiliated with the PPD, especially in
Salinas. As the PPD came to power, a new labor organization emerged, the Confederación
General de Trabajadores (CGT). In 1942, the Sugar Syndicate of Puerto Rico was orga-
nized to represent sugar workers within the CGT. Two of the Syndicate's leaders,

Armando Sánchez and José "Chepo" Caraballo, were based in Salinas; both were PPD leaders and former sugar workers. When the CGT split into an anti-PPD, pro-Independence faction and a pro-PPD faction in 1945, the links between the pro-PPD faction and the party were solidified. José "Chepo" Caraballo, siding with the pro-PPD faction, received government posts and organized workers with the American Federation of Labor. In 1961, with the support of the PPD, he organized the United Southern Workers' Syndicate (SOUS), which worked to keep Central Aguirre open, represented workers, and ran a pharmacy. The union's headquarters were in Salinas. Despite this support for the PPD, Salinas's agricultural economy declined and sufficient new industries did not materialize.[42]

By the late 1940s, Don Julio was affected by the changing sugar industry. He and Doña Nilda had married in 1949 and were expecting their first child. Don Julio was working at Central Aguirre, where he had started working when he was eighteen years old. He rarely worked in the sugar cane fields, working mostly on the docks. He emphasized that the work was not "steady," but seasonal: "There was some unemployment, but some people turned to work in fishing, to work in agriculture, doing other things, not in sugar cane." Wages for sugar cane workers had improved: "At the beginning, they didn't pay much. They paid us almost nothing. At the end, they raised it. The workers were making good money in sugar cane, at the end." Yet there was less work: "It lasted six months, I worked at the *central* six months, until at the end, there were times that we worked two months. That's why the sugar cane ended in Puerto Rico." Don Julio contrasted the past to the present: "A lot of people worked, a lot, a lot . . . several *centrales* and a lot of jobs, a lot, a lot. This southern section [had] a lot of work. Now, there's nothing. There's nothing."[43]

Salinas's Internal Migration

Like Sanlorenceños, Salinas's residents responded to declining employment by migrating in search of work. As sugar and sugar processing declined, Salinenses had few economic alternatives and few subsistence activities to rely on. The rural economic crisis affected Salinas's highland and lowland areas. During the 1950s an estimated 7,000 people left, reducing the municipio's population by 1 percent. In the next decade an additional 7,000 people left, and the population decreased more sharply, by 6 percent. The 1940s, in contrast, had witnessed a 21 percent increase in population, with the population in town growing by 38 percent. As Puerto Rico's fourth largest municipio, with sixty-nine square miles of territory, Salinas was home to 23,435 people in 1950, with 19 percent in town and the rest in five barrios (see Map 4.2). Leaving from highland and lowland areas, Salinas's migrants became part of the internal migration streams that fostered Puerto Rico's rapid urbanization.[44]

During the 1950s the population in town decreased by 16 percent, and two of the five barrios lost population as well (see Table 4.5). The United States continued to have a major impact on Salinas. Established as a U.S. Army training camp during World War II, the U.S. Army's Military District, Camp Santiago, was expanded during the 1950s.

MAP 4.2.   Salinas, Puerto Rico, ca. 1950

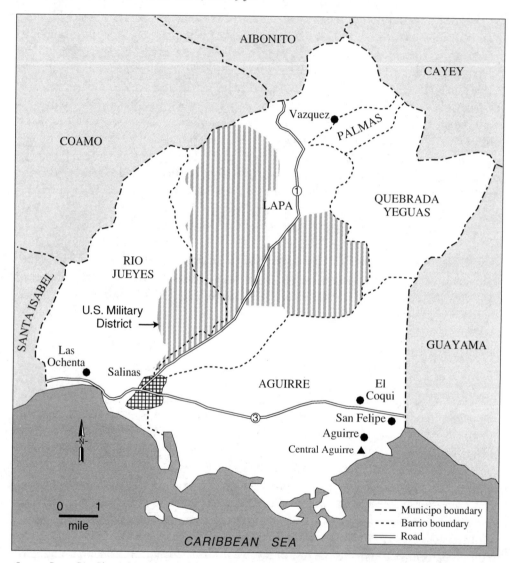

Sources: Puerto Rico Planning Board, *Municipio de Salinas: Memoria Suplementaria al Mapa de Límites del Municipio y sus Barrios* 38 (1955): 1; and George Beishlag, "Trends in Land Use in Southeastern Puerto Rico," in *Symposium on the Geography of Puerto Rico*, ed. Clarence F. Jones and Rafael Picó (Río Piedras: University of Puerto Rico Press, 1955), 282–283.

TABLE 4.5.   Population Change by Barrio, Salinas, 1940–1970

	1940 Population	1950 Population % Change	1960 Population % Change	1970 Population % Change
Salinas (municipio)	19,400	23,435 + 20.8	23,133 − 1.3	21,837 − 5.6
Town of Salinas	3,176	4,367 + 37.5	3,666 − 16.1	4,461 + 21.7
Aguirre	7,811	9,152 + 17.2	8,645 − 5.5	6,435 − 25.6
Lapa	3,822	4,621 + 20.9	6,078 + 31.5	5,848 − 3.8
Palmas	240	446 + 85.8	519 + 16.4	429 − 17.4
Quebrada Yeguas	540	528 − 2.2	833 + 57.8	1,172 + 40.7
Río Jueyes	3,811	4,321 + 13.4	3,392 − 21.5	3,492 + 2.9

Sources: See Table 4.2.

Note: Parts of the barrios of Aguirre and Río Jueyes were added to the town of Salinas between 1960 and 1970.

Occupying one-third of Salinas's territory, mostly in barrio Río Jueyes and partly in barrio Lapa, the Camp displaced small-scale farmers and disrupted the highland populations. The expropriation of 6,143 cuerdas displaced some four hundred people, and the total settlement was expected to reach $636,258, with payments ranging from $115,192 for the more than 1,000 cuerdas expropriated from a widow to $15 for a shed made from straw and wood. In seventy-two cases settled in July 1952, payments totaled more than $20,000, with the largest payment $4,277 for a 9-cuerda farm. Some of those displaced settled in El Coco, a parcela community in barrio Lapa, and perhaps in other upland communities. As a result, Río Jueyes lost 22 percent of its population, while the populations of Lapa, Palmas, and especially Quebrada Yeguas increased. The establishment of parcela communities increased the population in the highlands, with El Coco and Vásquez in barrio Lapa and La Plena in Quebrada Yeguas. Las Ochenta was established closer to town, in barrio Río Jueyes. Coffee was still grown in the highlands, as no other crop had replaced it, but was so unprofitable that growers relied on the sale of bananas and of firewood from the shade trees to remain solvent. By the early 1950s, wealthy sugar cane growers had introduced the dairy industry into the area. Meanwhile, the resettlement of agregados, who had previously lived in barracks in the sugar cane areas, resulted in a depopulated area and the uninterrupted growth of sugar in the lowlands. Aguirre's population decreased by 6 percent.[45]

Emigration during the 1960s affected both highland and coastal areas. Quebrada Yeguas's population continued to increase, by 41 percent. Without the influx of those displaced by Camp Santiago, however, other highland areas, Palma and Lapa, had population losses. Reflecting the demise of the sugar industry, Aguirre lost 26 percent of its population. Home to Central Aguirre, the barrio encompassed much of the munici-pio's sugar lands and had several communities where sugar cane workers lived, including Coquí and San Felipe. The population in town, which had decreased by 16 percent dur-ing the 1950s, now increased by 22 percent. As agriculture declined in the rural areas, some settled in town in search of what few manufacturing jobs had been established.

Migrants from Salinas went to other parts of Puerto Rico, and many then migrated to the States, according to the baptism records of Nuestra Señora de Monserrate de Sali-nas. More than half, 57 percent of the thirty people baptized in 1913, had married in Salinas, while 27 percent married in other parts of Puerto Rico and 17 percent married in the States. Emigration increased and more migrants went to the States. Of those bap-tized in 1932, only 32 percent were identified as marrying in Salinas, while 32 percent married in other parts of Puerto Rico and 27 percent married in the States. These records suggest that Salinenses migrated to the States between the world wars and then contin-ued this migration in the postwar era.[46]

Like their counterparts from San Lorenzo, Salinas's migrants' destinations reflected the decreasing opportunities in agricultural regions and the increasing urbanization that accompanied industrialization. During the late 1940s, most of Salinas's men and women married in other parts of Puerto Rico (see Table 4.6). Initially, migrants settled primarily in the southern sugar regions, with about one-third marrying in the southeast and another third in the southwest. Very few went to the coffee or northern regions. Increasingly, Salinas's migrants headed for metropolitan areas. During the 1950s the proportions marrying in the southeast and southwest decreased somewhat, while the tobacco region and the San Juan metropolitan area accounted for more of the migrant marriages. For the twenty-year period, about a quarter married in the southeast and the San Juan metropolitan regions, and just under a quarter married in the southwest and tobacco regions. The trend toward urbanization was apparent even among migrants to regions other than the San Juan metropolitan area. Of those marrying in the southwest region, the overwhelming majority, 80 percent, married in Ponce, Puerto Rico's second-largest city. For those staying within the southeast region, most (57 percent) married in neighboring Guayama, and for those in the tobacco region, 49 percent married in neigh-boring Cayey. In addition to bordering Salinas, both of these municipios had more Fomento industries than Salinas by 1970. The gender differences in destinations were less pronounced than for San Lorenzo's migrants, perhaps because Salinas's men headed more often for urban areas, the same destinations as for women. The U.S. census con-firms these internal migration patterns (see Table A.2 in Appendix I).

Leaving Local Communities

Salinenses' and Sanlorenceños' internal migrations reflected Puerto Rico's rural eco-nomic crisis and the regional impact of industrialization. Although Salinas's economy was defined by sugar and San Lorenzo's by tobacco, both municipios experienced a decline in agriculture and agricultural processing. The different cash crops created dif-

TABLE 4.6. Place of Marriage by Region of Salinas's Migrants, 1945–1965

	1945–1965		1945–1949		1950–1954		1955–1959		1960–1965	
	Male	Female	Male	Female	Male	Female	Male	Female	Male	Female
Total Number	562	481	23	25	98	85	220	189	221	182
Percent in:										
Puerto Rico	40.6	43.9	78.3	68.0	54.1	47.1	30.9	36.0	40.3	47.3
United States	59.3	56.1	21.7	32.0	45.9	52.9	68.6	64.0	59.7	52.7
Other Country	0.2	—	—	—	—	—	0.5	—	—	—
Number in:										
Puerto Rico	228	211	18	17	53	40	68	68	89	86
Percent in:										
Tobacco	21.9	23.2	5.6	5.9	22.6	17.5	23.5	26.5	23.6	26.7
Coffee	1.8	0.9	5.6	—	5.7	—	—	—	—	2.3
Southeast	24.6	26.1	38.9	29.4	20.8	32.5	19.1	22.1	28.1	25.6
Southwest	22.8	22.7	33.3	29.4	20.8	20.0	29.4	19.1	16.9	25.6
North	3.5	0.9	5.6	—	3.8	2.5	1.5	—	4.5	1.2
S. J. Metro	25.4	26.1	11.1	35.3	26.4	27.5	26.5	32.4	27.0	18.6
Military	—	—	—	—	—	—	—	—	—	—

Source: Baptism Records of Parroquia Nuestra Señora de Monserrate de Salinas, Salinas, Puerto Rico.
Note: Data is for baptisms between 1911 and 1940, with the place of marriage recorded as outside of Salinas, between 1945 and 1965. Not all columns total exactly 100 percent due to rounding.

ferences in land-holding patterns, in the nature and extent of subsistence economic activities, and in gender divisions of labor. The different commercial crops also altered the pace of the economic crisis. During the 1940s the number of people employed in Salinas increased, while the number of those employed in San Lorenzo had already decreased. The divergent gender divisions of labor and women's employment were largely responsible, as the labor force participation of San Lorenzo's women declined from 22 to 12 percent, while Salinas women's participation increased slightly from 13 to 14 percent. Tobacco's demise began earlier than sugar's and affected San Lorenzo's women, who were much more likely to work in agriculture and in agricultural processing than their counterparts in Salinas and elsewhere on the island. Sugar's decline, in contrast, affected primarily Salinas's men. Yet even as they combined wages and subsistence activities or different kinds of income-producing activities, and even as they relied on the economic contributions of men, women, and children, households in Salinas and San Lorenzo could not withstand the economic changes without seeking alternatives beyond their municipios' boundaries.

Although Salinas supported the ruling political party and San Lorenzo opposed it, neither municipio benefited from the PPD's industrialization program. Few Fomento industries came to either municipio, highlighting the regional aspects of the program and the concentration of industry in the San Juan metropolitan area. When industries did arrive, both municipios found that these were mostly labor-intensive, export-oriented industries, seeking the low-wage labor of women and prone to relocation. Salinas's sugar workers benefited from the political and social reforms of the PPD, and both municipios saw the extension of water, electricity, health care services, and education. These improvements, however, could not compensate for the lack of jobs. Employment in both municipios decreased in the 1950s and the 1960s. San Lorenzo's men were displaced in staggering numbers; their labor force participation decreased from 73 to 48 percent between 1950 and 1970. Agricultural employment was limited; only 20 percent found agricultural work, and of the 19 percent of men working in manufacturing, only 5 percent were in food processing, including tobacco. For Salinas's men, labor force participation decreased as well, from 71 to 56 percent. Sugar still provided a few jobs; 24 percent worked in agriculture and 28 percent worked in manufacturing, with 53 percent in food processing, including sugar. Manufacturing accounted for a larger proportion of the workforce in both municipios. Reflecting the labor-intensive nature of the new industries, however, women's labor force participation increased, from 15 to 23 percent in San Lorenzo and from 14 to 23 percent in Salinas. Yet for San Lorenzo's women this was comparable to the 22 percent who had been in the labor force in 1940, suggesting the limited gains of the industrialization program. As employment declined, both municipios saw their populations decrease in both decades.

Responding to the rural economic crisis and looking for work, migrants chose their destinations within Puerto Rico based on regional economic changes. Neither Salinas's nor San Lorenzo's migrants went to the coffee region or the north coast. What variations there were in their destinations stemmed from migrants staying closer to home, in nearby agricultural and urbanizing areas. Early destinations, especially for San

Lorenzo's men, may have indicated an effort to preserve agricultural ways of life, as well as familiarity with the area and the feasibility of the move. They also reflected pockets of increased industrialization and urbanization outside the San Juan metropolitan area. Hence, Salinenses were more likely to stay in the southern sugar regions, especially Ponce, while Sanlorenceños were more likely to stay in the tobacco region, especially Caguas. Perhaps because Ponce provided an urban alternative, a smaller proportion of Salinas's migrants married in the San Juan metropolitan area—a quarter of the men and women, in contrast to a third of San Lorenzo's men and women.[47]

Internal migration, however, could not solve Salinenses' or Sanlorenceños' economic problems. It was, after all, an island-wide economic crisis. Employment and labor force participation decreased island-wide during the 1950s, and the decline would have been even more severe had migrants not pursued another option—traveling to the States—in greater and greater numbers. By the late 1950s, more than half of Salinas's men and women married in the States, as did more than half of San Lorenzo's men and women (see Tables 4.3 and 4.6). For the period between 1945 and 1965, more than half of Salinas's and San Lorenzo's migrants were married in the States. Island-wide, demographer José Vázquez Calzada found similar migration patterns. Women were more likely to be internal migrants, especially to the metropolitan area. While there were 93 men for every 100 women among internal migrants, there were only 88 men per 100 women among those migrating to the metropolitan areas. In contrast, there were 118 men for every 100 women among migrants to the States. Noting the increased migration to the States, Vázquez Calzada estimated that during the 1940s 266,000 people left their municipios, with 72 percent going to the States, and that during the 1950s 97 percent of those leaving their municipios went to the States. Thus Salinas and San Lorenzo illustrate the rural economic crisis that sent migrants in search of work in Puerto Rico and the States.[48]

Coming to the States

Displaced from Puerto Rico's rural economies, Salinenses and Sanlorenceños made their way to the States, with many settling in Philadelphia. Migrants from both municipios came with farm labor contracts and *por su cuenta*, on their own. The government's use of the contract labor program to combat "overpopulation" coincided with migrants' use of labor contracts as an economic strategy, increasing the Puerto Rican population in Philadelphia. As some migrants used contracts as a vehicle for permanent settlement in the States, the farm labor program made their migration financially feasible and shaped their destinations. Although some migrants came with contracts and others came without, the distinctions between "formal" and "informal" means of migration were not clear-cut. Informal networks of family and friends played a role in the migrations and destinations of those who came with labor contracts as well as for those who came on their own. Similarly, many of those who "came on their own" were recruited for farm work in the States. Both the formal labor contract program and informal networks brought Salinenses and Sanlorenceños to Philadelphia, fostering the growth of the Puerto Rican community and contributing to its rural origins.

Contract labor became one option for San Lorenzo and Salinas residents, who found themselves displaced and in search of work, and many were sent to farms in the Philadelphia area. In 1946, Samuel Friedman, the private labor recruiter, opened an employment office in San Lorenzo and began bringing men from San Lorenzo and other parts of Puerto Rico to New Jersey and Pennsylvania. In 1948 the government of Puerto Rico assumed responsibility for the farm labor program, and at least 22 men from San Lorenzo and 33 men from Salinas came to the States with labor contracts. Their applications for labor contracts reveal their backgrounds, goals, and destinations. All of the men from Salinas were sent to farms in New Jersey, Pennsylvania, and New York. San Lorenzo's men, on the other hand, had a variety of destinations, with 10 going to New Jersey and Pennsylvania, 3 to New York, and others to Delaware; Lorain, Ohio; and Gary, Indiana to work with the Illinois Steel Corporation. All told, 10 men from San Lorenzo and 21 men from Salinas came to farms in the Philadelphia area. Their contracts stipulated a minimum hourly wage of $.55 and set piecework wages according to tasks. They were to work not more than six days a week, but not less than 80 hours in a two-week period. Workers were to pay $85 for their transportation to the States. Employers could advance the cost of transportation and then deduct it from the workers' wages, along with a deduction of $1.50 per day for three meals.[49]

Most of the men applying for contracts were agricultural laborers, and most were unemployed. In their twenties, these were young men looking for work and a way to improve their economic situations. Juan Bautista de Jesús Rodríguez, from San Lorenzo, signed a labor contract with Samuel Friedman to work on a farm in Pennsylvania. Unemployed and twenty-one years old, he stated that he was getting a labor contract to improve his economic situation. Growing up in barrio Quebrada Arenas, he had completed two years of schooling. For four years he had worked as an unskilled agricultural laborer, making $3.15 a day. Then, in 1947, he went to Michigan and the Philadelphia area for four months with a farm labor contract from Friedman. As a single man, he listed only his mother as a dependent. Like Juan, most of the other seven contract laborers for whom detailed information is available had worked in sugar and/or minor crops, earning between $2 and $3 a day. At the time they applied, five were unemployed, one was packing coffee for $8 a week, another was described as "in business," and the last was cultivating his own land. Most were in their twenties and single. While five of the eight did not have children, some had other dependents. Half of them had four years of schooling or less, and the other half had between five and eight years of schooling. Most were getting labor contracts in search of opportunities and a better life, *buscar ambiente*. Others expressed their reasons in explicitly economic terms, including wanting work or an occupation. They financed their trips, paying from $35 to $60, in a variety of ways. Some had saved the money, others sold their furniture or a cow, and one borrowed the money from his mother-in-law who was living in New York.[50]

Similarly, most of Salinas's contract laborers were agricultural laborers and unemployed. Raimundo Dávila de Jesús signed a labor contract with the Gloucester County

Board of Agriculture, stating that he was unemployed and needed to earn money. Unable to read, he had worked only as an unskilled agricultural laborer, including eight years in sugar cane at Central Aguirre, earning $2.56 a day. At the age of twenty-six, he was in a consensual marriage, had a two-year-old daughter, and was living in barrio Coquí, Aguirre. He paid $35 of the travel expenses with money he borrowed from his mother to pay back little by little, left $12 for his family, and was taking no money with him. Most of the other twenty workers had also worked in sugar cane, earning between $2 and $3 a day, or in sugar processing, earning between $3 and $4 a day. A few had been unskilled laborers and one had been a driver. When they applied, more than half were unemployed. Salinas's contract laborers were somewhat older, in their twenties and thirties, and more often married with children than were those from San Lorenzo. More than half (thirteen) were married either civilly or consensually and all but seven had children. Like those signing up in San Lorenzo, most had four years of school or less, and the others had between five and eight years. One had attended some high school. Explicit about the economic hardships in Puerto Rico, several described the situation as bad, pointing to the lack of work, unemployment, the end of the harvest or a bad harvest, and their need to earn money and improve their economic situation. Paying between $35 and $60, they financed their trips with money they had saved and by selling their possessions, including a bicycle, a cow, a Singer sewing machine, and a house. Another mortgaged his house. Several borrowed money, and one had money sent to him from a brother living in New York City. To provide for their families during their absence, they left money, set up credit accounts at stores, or designated someone to look after their families until they could send money.[51]

Several of these early contract laborers seemed to be contemplating settlement in the States. The applications asked if they were considering taking their families to the States, if they had been to the States before, and if they knew anyone in the area to which they were being sent. From San Lorenzo, Juan was the only one who had been to the States before and the only one who said he knew someone in the area. Although his sister lived in New York City, he stated that he was not considering taking his family to the States. Five other contract laborers responded that they were not planning to take their families, and three responded that they did not know. More than half of Salinas's migrants left open the possibility of settlement in the States. Two stated that they were thinking about taking their families to the States, and nine said they did not know; the other ten were not planning to take their families to the States. None had ever been outside of Puerto Rico, however, and only two knew people in the States. Most were leaving Salinas with no more than $10 or with no money at all.[52]

Men from San Lorenzo and Salinas continued to sign up for farm labor contracts, with significant proportions being sent to farms in the Philadelphia area. In 1949, 160 men from San Lorenzo got farm labor contracts, compared with 73 from Salinas (see Table 3.2). Although fewer came from Salinas, a higher proportion of these farmworkers went to southern New Jersey and Pennsylvania. As in 1948, the rest of Salinas's farmworkers went to other parts of the northeast. In contrast, the destinations of San Lorenzo's contract laborers varied more widely, as they had the previous year. Forty percent of San Lorenzo's contract laborers were sent to farms in southern New Jersey and Pennsylvania, 44 percent were sent to other parts of the northeast, and the remaining 16 percent were sent farther west. In 1950, the number of farmworkers from San Lorenzo and Salinas continued to increase, with 261 contract laborers from San Lorenzo and 123 from Salinas. Yet the destinations for farmworkers in 1950 were unusual. Whereas New Jersey, Pennsylvania, and New York received the majority of farmworkers between the late 1940s and 1965, in 1950 most farmworkers were sent to Michigan and some were sent to St. Croix (see Table 3.1). As a result, few of San Lorenzo's and Salinas's contract laborers were sent to southern New Jersey and Pennsylvania, with most going to the Midwest, the northwest, and the Virgin Islands instead.

Migrants from San Lorenzo and Salinas farming families were among those who settled in Philadelphia. Of the Sanlorenceños getting married in the city between 1945 and 1965, 43 percent listed their father's occupation as "farmer," more than any other category (see Table 4.7). Another 22 percent were laborers, while 19 percent were not working. Salinas migrants' fathers were also more likely to be "farmers" than any other category, 30 percent. Twenty-seven percent were not working, while another 20 percent were laborers. Although no distinction was indicated between farm owners and farm laborers, most from Salinas would have been farm laborers while some of those from San Lorenzo may have owned the land they farmed. Mothers in San Lorenzo and Salinas were overwhelmingly identified as "housewives," perhaps unpaid contributors to rural household economies. When employed, San Lorenzo's mothers were service workers and operatives; Salinas's mothers were operatives, laborers, and service workers.

Anthropological studies from the late 1940s suggested that migrants to the States came from diverse backgrounds; however, they sometimes underestimated the impact of the farm labor program, which was just getting underway. In his study of a tobacco municipio, Manners found that migrants to the States were "the middle-class rural group," made up of those farming between eight and thirty-five cuerdas, and "lower-class rural and urban men." Among the "rural upper class," migration to other municipios was more common than migration to the States. The rural middle class faced economic instability and little hope of a substantial inheritance, especially if their families were large, which made migration an alternative to agricultural day labor. These potential migrants could afford the airfare. Meanwhile, "in the last few years migration of lower-class rural and urban men has been increased by labor contract arrangements." For these men, the farm labor program provided an alternative to migration to the cane fields and meant they did not have to come up with the money for airfare, because the cost of transportation was deducted from their earnings.[53]

Similarly, in his study of a southern sugar municipio, Mintz found that members of the middle class were among the migrants to New York City but had also gone to Ponce, San Juan, and Miami. Returning veterans did not stay long; the twenty-nine members of a veterans' social club started in 1947 had dwindled to two by 1949. The others had migrated to New York and started another social club there. For sugar cane workers, Mintz noted, "the United States Army, and the need for labor in such urban United States centers as New York City and in commercial and agricultural areas, as well, have

TABLE 4.7.   Migrants' Parents, Residence and Occupation, 1945–1965

	Puerto Rico		San Lorenzo		Salinas	
	Male	Female	Male	Female	Male	Female
Total Number	1,147	1,147	203	203	79	78
Percent:						
In Puerto Rico	47.3	50.6	39.9	43.8	38.0	44.9
In Philadelphia	18.9	26.9	25.6	34.0	26.6	34.6
Unknown	6.6	2.6	8.4	1.5	7.6	3.8
Deceased	27.1	19.9	26.1	20.7	27.8	16.7
Number in Puerto Rico	543	580	81	89	30	35
Percent:						
Professionals	1.1	—	—	—	—	—
Managers	6.4	—	7.4	—	—	—
Clerical/Sales	1.7	—	2.5	—	—	—
Crafts	8.3	—	6.2	—	16.7	—
Operatives	4.2	1.0	6.2	2.2	6.7	2.9
Laborers	19.7	0.5	22.2	—	20.0	2.9
Service	2.0	2.9	1.2	4.5	—	2.9
Farmers	35.9	0.3	35.8	—	30.0	—
Housewives	—	91.0	—	87.6	—	82.9
Retired/None	20.6	4.1	18.5	5.6	26.7	8.6

Source: Philadelphia Marriage Licenses, 1945–1965, Court of Orphan Pleas, City Hall, Philadelphia, Pa.

provided rural sugar cane workers with opportunities to escape the economic and social limitations." They financed migration through the pooling of family resources and winnings from the lottery. Yet he concluded, underestimating the significance of the farm labor program and hence the emigration of sugar cane workers, that "for many sugar cane workers, emigration is economically impossible."[54]

Migrants from San Lorenzo and Salinas had choices other than Philadelphia, and migrants from both municipios settled in other parts of the States. While Sanlorenceños and Salinenses were well represented in Philadelphia's growing Puerto Rican community, their other destinations in the States varied, influenced by the timing of emigration and by the contract labor program. Between 1945 and 1965, Sanlorenceños' destinations reflected the relative size of the Puerto Rican communities in the States. Most of San Lorenzo's migrants went to New York City, Chicago was second, and Philadelphia was third (Table 4.8). The proportion marrying in New York, however, decreased over the years to less than half of the migrants. At the same time, more Sanlorenceños were settling in Chicago and Philadelphia, a pattern indicative of the increasing dispersion of the Puerto Rican population in the States. This trend continued, and between 1960 and 1965 San Lorenzo's migrants married not just in New York City, Chicago, and Philadelphia, but also in New Jersey, Ohio, Massachusetts, and Connecticut.

Salinas's migrants, on the other hand, remained more concentrated in New York. Throughout the twenty-year period, more than two-thirds of the migrants married in New York (Table 4.9). Philadelphia was the second most common destination, with

TABLE 4.8. Place of Marriage in the United States of San Lorenzo's Migrants, 1945–1965

| | 1945–1965 | | 1945–1949 | | 1950–1954 | | 1955–1959 | | 1960–1965 | |
	Male	Female	Male	Female	Male	Female	Male	Female	Male	Female
Number in the States	806	625	23	15	110	120	346	296	327	194
Percent in:										
New York	38.9	46.5	78.3	93.3	57.4	55.4	37.8	42.0	31.2	44.2
Philadelphia	8.7	11.0	4.3	—	8.3	8.3	11.9	15.9	5.8	6.1
Mid-Atlantic	5.4	4.9	—	—	3.7	3.3	2.9	5.1	8.9	6.1
Chicago	29.2	23.1	4.3	6.7	20.4	14.9	30.2	26.1	32.7	24.9
Other Midwest	10.7	9.6	4.3	—	6.5	12.2	11.9	7.5	11.3	11.7
Other U.S.	7.1	4.9	8.6	—	3.7	5.8	5.2	3.4	10.1	7.1

Source: Baptism Records of Parroquia Nuestra Señora de las Mercedes, San Lorenzo, Puerto Rico.
Note: Data are for baptisms between 1910 and 1940, with the place of marriage recorded as outside of San Lorenzo, between 1945 and 1965. Not all columns total exactly 100 percent due to rounding.

TABLE 4.9. Place of Marriage in the United States of Salinas's Migrants, 1945–1965

	1945–1965		1945–1949		1950–1954		1955–1959		1960–1965	
	Male	Female	Male	Female	Male	Female	Male	Female	Male	Female
Number in the States	333	270	5	8	45	45	151	121	132	96
Percent in:										
New York	68.8	69.6	100.0	87.5	86.7	82.2	68.2	62.8	62.1	70.8
Philadelphia	10.5	10.4	—	—	2.2	2.2	14.6	18.2	9.1	5.2
Mid-Atlantic	10.2	9.6	—	—	6.7	6.7	7.9	11.6	14.4	9.4
Chicago	2.4	3.0	—	12.5	—	2.2	2.0	1.7	3.8	4.2
Other Midwest	1.8	1.5	—	—	2.2	—	3.3	2.5	—	1.0
Other U.S.	6.3	5.9	—	—	2.2	6.7	4.0	3.3	10.6	9.4

Source: Baptism Records of Parroquia Nuestra Señora de Monserrate de Salinas, Salinas, Puerto Rico.

Note: Data are for baptisms between 1911 and 1940, with the place of marriage recorded as outside of Salinas, between 1945 and 1965. Not all columns total exactly 100 percent due to rounding.

others marrying elsewhere in the Mid-Atlantic states. In contrast to San Lorenzo's migrants and to the size of the Puerto Rican community there, very few married in Chicago or in the Midwest. Salinas's migrants also married in other states, especially Connecticut and Massachusetts. The timing of emigration and the contract labor program may have influenced these destinations. Baptism records suggested an earlier migration to the States, between the world wars, and informal networks may have built on a preexisting community in New York. Whereas San Lorenzo's contract laborers were sent to a variety of destinations, most of Salinas's early contract laborers were sent to Pennsylvania, New Jersey, and New York. Labor contracts might have fostered their settlement in the Mid-Atlantic region, while limiting their settlement in the Midwest. San Lorenzo's men also seem to have relied more extensively on labor contracts than those from Salinas. Finally, heavy emigration during the 1960s may have contributed to the presence of migrants from Salinas in Massachusetts and Connecticut, as the Puerto Rican populations in these states grew more rapidly during that decade.

As with internal migration, there were discernible gender patterns in the migration to the States. San Lorenzo's women were more likely than the men to migrate to New York and Philadelphia. Both New York and Philadelphia employed large numbers of women in the garment industry. As in Puerto Rico, there were fewer manufacturing opportunities for men. Men who found themselves participating in the farm labor program and working in agriculture in the States were more likely to migrate to all other areas in the States. The gender gap among migrants to Philadelphia was smaller than for New York, perhaps because the farm labor program had a greater impact on the migration to Philadelphia than it did on the migration to New York. While Philadelphia's garment industry encouraged the migration of Puerto Rican women to the city, the farm labor program encouraged the migration of Puerto Rican men to the agricultural areas surrounding the city. For migrants from Salinas there was less of a gender gap in destinations in the States, just as there was in Puerto Rico. San Lorenzo's women may have migrated more intentionally to places where they could find paid employment, since they were more likely than their counterparts in Salinas to be in the labor force, and even those who worked at home often processed a cash crop. On the other hand, the destinations chosen by Salinas's women may have been more similar to the men's because men's primary destinations were New York and Philadelphia, places where Puerto Rican women could find paid employment.

The farm labor program facilitated the settlement in Philadelphia of San Lorenzo and Salinas migrants. Oral histories revealed the widespread impact of the farm labor program; even those who came on their own were aware of the program. Puerto Ricans in Philadelphia made a distinction between those who came "in the migration" with labor contracts, and those who came "on their own" without contracts. Yet these migrants' stories also highlight the interplay of formal and informal means of migration. Contract laborers sometimes signed up with family or friends, and those who broke their contracts or stayed after completing them relied on family and friends already living in the city. Other contract laborers came first, sending for family and friends after they settled in the city. Still others bypassed farm work, coming to Philadelphia directly, or sometimes through New York. Like farmworkers, however, they relied on and/or sparked informal networks of migration.

Illustrating another aspect of formal and informal means of migration, farmworkers came both with and without contracts. Although the government of Puerto Rico encouraged all farmworkers to use contracts, private employers and agencies recruited workers, and farmworkers chose to make their own arrangements. Despite legislation passed in Puerto Rico in 1947 restricting labor recruitment by private agencies, both formal, government-sponsored contract labor and noncontract labor for farm work continued. While Puerto Rico's Farm Placement Division tried "to keep the workers in the sugar farms as long as they are needed," they admitted that "there is a factor beyond our control which has created a problem to local employers." Their efforts were undermined by "walk-ins, who on their own communicate with employers in the continent or buy their own tickets and report to farms in the states without referral from our offices." Walk-ins were encouraged by labor recruiters and farmers on the mainland who "through known workers stimulate others to go." Estimates of the number of workers traveling without contracts varied greatly and seemed to increase. In 1954, for example, almost 7,000 farmworkers were thought to have left without contracts, while 11,323 were sent with contracts.[55]

For the Apontes, farm work and family in Philadelphia provided a way to settle in the city. As economic changes affected those living in town, Doña Carmen described San Lorenzo as "slow" and concluded that "there wasn't enough for everyone to better their conditions." Although she enjoyed working for herself, cooking for wealthier residents and selling lunches to the workers at the tobacco factory nearby, rationing during the war had hurt her business: "The war came . . . there was no food, I couldn't buy rice, I couldn't buy anything, everything was rationed. *I couldn't cook, there was nothing to buy. So we decided to come here. My husband came first . . . he was the driver of the town ambulance. . . . I sold every little thing I had for fifty dollars.*" The crisis in her business fostered their decision to leave. In 1946 Friedman was recruiting in San Lorenzo, and "everybody knew" about the program. Although he had never worked in agriculture, Don Quintín got a labor contract. Returning farmworkers told stories of money on the ground in the United States—so much money you could kick it with your feet. Doña Carmen acknowledged, "that was the ambition and that's why we left."[56]

Yet family networks were important, as well. "Most went to New York. We came to Philadelphia because my husband's cousin was living here." Her husband's cousin ran a guest house in Philadelphia. "That was where everyone from San Lorenzo arrived. . . . The ones that came to work on the farms, they gave them room and board." Don Quintín sent Doña Carmen the first $50 he earned, she sold all their possessions and flew to Philadelphia with their four children, hiding the youngest in a blanket because she did not have enough money for his airfare. Recalling that her husband found agricultural work "difficult," Doña Carmen explained, "my husband worked until he doubled over, picking those long ones, what are they called, asparagus. When he came home he had to lean against the wall to straighten up, little by little. You know he was picking those things all day." Within the year, Don Quintín came to the city, leaving agricultural work behind him. While economic need was paramount, Doña Carmen also expressed a sense of adventure: "We came to adventure, like everyone came from Puerto Rico. We saw the whole world coming and we wanted to see what would happen too." She recounted her trip with a sense of drama—a frightening flight in a twin-engine plane, hiding her youngest child, and arriving late at night in New York instead of her intended destination, Philadelphia. Hers was a sense of economic necessity, ambition, and adventure.

Don Justino came to work on Pennsylvania farms on his own, without a labor contract, relying instead on informal networks and borrowed money. His brother, however, had gone to work on a farm in Gettysburg, Pennsylvania with a labor contract in 1952. He explained his decision to go with his brother the following year:

> In '53 I went with him because in Puerto Rico at that time, you didn't earn much money. And so, I went for the first time that year, to work there on the farms, in agriculture, and looking for a better life. In Puerto Rico, when the work in sugar cane and tobacco ended, well, there wasn't anything else. . . . In tobacco you earned a dollar a day, it wasn't enough for anyone to live on and that was the reason that I went to Philadelphia, to the farms, for the first time.

Unlike Don Quintín, Don Justino had worked in agriculture all his life. That year, too much rain had damaged the tobacco crop. They lost about a cuerda of tobacco and what they had did not fetch as good a price as usual. Recalling that "we worked night and day," Don Justino said it was the last straw. "I didn't want to plant more tobacco, so then I went there and worked for six months in the farms." Don Justino, his brother, and several friends went back to the same farm: "My brother had gone, so he told me I could work there. We went for several months, with a lot of others from here, from San Lorenzo. . . . All friends. That year we went, about eight or ten went to work in the same place."57

Although he knew about the government program, he did not sign up:

> I didn't go through that program. I knew about it but I didn't want to go through that program because at the end they put you all together, a huge group to take to a camp there. Then the bosses went there to get people from that camp and took them sometimes. Sometimes it was better because they had to find, because they had to give you work quickly and change the work quickly. I didn't like that, so I looked for money to borrow. . . . There was a woman in San Lorenzo that lent you money, to the people, and we paid her back. And from there you went to work. I know people who liked it, but the people here that I know, we all went like that—we had already paid. If we didn't want to work, we got our money and we left.

Desiring more autonomy, he avoided the labor camps: "I didn't like it because—and a lot of people didn't like it—because in that place, every kind of person came to the camps. You know, good people and bad people, and I never wanted to be in places like that. . . . They didn't treat them very well either." Making the trip on his own, however, was a costly proposition: "I borrowed the money from someone, for the trip, to buy, for the trip and to buy clothes, suitcases and all of those things for me to go. I remember it was like one hundred, one hundred and twenty dollars, I think, that I borrowed."

After his first trip, Don Justino returned to Puerto Rico. He had worked as long as he could in the States, picking apples in October. He summed up his expenses and his earnings:

At that time, it was 60 and 65 cents, and so I went, I worked six months, I saved. I paid the trip both ways, to go and to return, I paid the money that I still owed that was almost $200. I paid the store, because I had told her [his wife] to get what she needed for the kids. . . . Well, I remember how I saved, and when I got home, I arrived with $10 in my pocket.

Nonetheless, he went back to the farm the following year. This time, however, he went to Philadelphia instead of returning to Puerto Rico. He explained:

I worked during the sugar cane harvest, and when the sugar cane harvest was over, I went to the United States again. So, I went to the farms, to the same place in Gettysburg, and it turned out to be a terrible year, that year. That was when the people, you saw the people in the streets because there wasn't work because of a drought in the United States. And I couldn't return to Puerto Rico, I had to stay. After Gettysburg, I picked Philadelphia, my brother and me. I had a *compadre* and so I stayed in his house and when the summer came, I started working in construction then.

While farm labor brought him to the area, his *compadre* helped him settle in the city. Don Justino returned to Puerto Rico once more, during the winter layoff in construction work, but then he returned to Philadelphia, got work in construction, and sent for his family. Doña Ana Luisa came to Philadelphia in 1956, with their four children and another on the way.

Don Julio made a distinction between those who came through the farm labor program, the "migration" or "immigration," and those who came on their own. He explained, "I paid my own airfare. I paid. A migration, they say a migration, but I paid for my airfare. A lot went that way, they took them from here to work there. I went on my own. . . . I wanted to work where I wanted to work." The Quiñones migrated to Philadelphia by way of New York. Don Julio left Salinas in 1949, at the age of twenty-six. He was still working at Central Aguirre on the docks. Doña Nilda explained their decision:

Well, when we left in 1949, since there wasn't much work, the work that there was was sugar cane and things like that. So, he worked but seasonally, seasonally more than anything. Well, there was always enough to eat, thank God. But, well, he thought that since he was already married, that he was going to have a child, that in order to get ahead and then, well, he decided to go there.

While Don Julio went to New York City to find a job, Doña Nilda stayed with his parents. The separation was difficult, she recalled, not because she lacked what she needed, but because they were recently married, she was having their first child, and they missed each other. Emphasizing the difficulties and the economic necessities, she commented, "he wanted to return to Puerto Rico, but his mother told him no. His mother told him to stay there and send me money, because if he came back here it would be the same—that maybe he would work a week or a month, and then there wouldn't be any more work." He sent her money every week or every other week, her in-laws helped her a lot, and her own mother was nearby. The baby was born in 1949, and the following year Don Julio sent the airfare and they joined him in New York City. Although Don Julio thought that he "would be there for a very little time," they lived in New York City until he got a job transfer in 1965 and they went to Philadelphia.[58]

Like Don Julio, Don Florencio left Salinas on his own and went to New York. Three of his siblings were already living in New York when he joined them in 1952. His sister left Salinas first, migrating to New York with another family, to take care of their children. His older brother migrated next, going first to another part of the States with a farm labor contract, and then making his way to New York and getting a job as a cook, making pizzas. His younger brother was in New York, too, working in a factory in shipping. They had migrated, Don Florencio explained, "with the intention of helping my family, my mother and my father." Having completed high school, Don Florencio had another goal as well: "I had to look for, well honestly, money so I could study." Going to New York and staying with his younger brother, he recalled, "it was easy, because everyone—there was work for those that wanted to work. There was work. Well, I myself got a job in a factory right away." He did not work for long, though; he was drafted into the U.S. Army in 1953 and served in Korea. Returning first to New York and then to Salinas in 1957, he found "the town of Salinas very different." The houses were now made of concrete and "very, very pretty," and the government had brought modern conveniences, so that houses had water and electricity. Nonetheless, he concluded, "for me it was bad because I didn't find work." By 1960 he was back in New York, but for less than a year; he then made his way to Philadelphia. While he came looking for work and the money to study, he explained, "I decided to come here to Philadelphia, and I found myself playing music and here I am, involved in the music, because I like music." Don Florencio was also a musician.[59]

In 1956, at the age of twenty, Doña Gloria left San Lorenzo to come to Philadelphia to do child care. Doña Gloria had met Doña Armenia several years earlier at a party, and had stayed in touch with the family, going to town to help Doña Armenia's mother with cleaning and laundry. Doña Armenia migrated to Philadelphia, and married Don Mundo, who was from Salinas; the couple had three children. As she was working in a factory making candles and he was working in construction, they wanted someone to live in and take care of the children. They sent Doña Gloria the airfare and she came to Philadelphia, where she took care of the children and cleaned, working seven days a week and making $30 to $40 a month. When Doña Gloria first arrived at the Philadelphia airport, she was met by Hipolito Amaro, who was from Salinas and a friend of Don Mundo's. Don Hipolito had migrated to work on a farm in the Philadelphia area in the mid-1940s. Doña Gloria recalled the hardships of his youth in Salinas: his father had abandoned the family, and "he started to work when he wasn't even twelve years old, he started to work in sugar cane, because he was left alone with his mother and they were seven children, and he was the oldest." He also worked in a bakery, and she emphasized his low wages: "They gave him a quarter, for working an hour, a quarter, twenty-five cents, but he took home bread, they gave him bread, they gave him cakes, they gave him little things." He came to the States, and after three to four years of farm work, he settled in Philadelphia and got a job in a sugar refinery. Doña Gloria and Don Hipolito were married in 1958. Years later, he encouraged their children to finish their food, reminding them of the times he had gone hungry.[60]

Over the next several years, much of Doña Gloria's family joined her in Philadelphia, coming to the area both with and without labor contracts. Don Hipolito had already helped his brother migrate, before they were married, while other members of his family had gone to New York. Now it was her siblings and her cousins, who had grown up with her, that made their way to Philadelphia, with their help. Highlighting the connections between formal contract labor and informal networks, her two cousins got labor contracts, but as Doña Gloria recalled, "When they left from here, they took my telephone number and the address where I lived and everything." Both of her cousins left the farms, coming to stay with Doña Gloria and Don Hipolito until they found jobs and places of their own. Next, she brought one brother and then another directly to Philadelphia from San Lorenzo, and they were all living at the house. Her sisters came too, and two of them got married in Philadelphia, one to a man from Salinas. As for San Lorenzo, she explained:

> Things were getting slow, so that, well, my brothers and all of my cousins left. A lot of people that were here [in San Lorenzo], well they looked in other places or went to apply, because there were a lot that left for other places. I left. . . . Most are in the United States, in some part, a lot went to Philadelphia. . . . When my brothers left, the work here by then— there was practically no work, you couldn't get it, it wasn't easy to get a job.

As the rural economic crisis deepened and as labor contracts and informal networks provided an alternative, the migration to Philadelphia continued and the Puerto Rican population in the city grew.

Conclusion

As residents of San Lorenzo and Salinas were displaced from Puerto Rico's rural economies and left to search for work, they became part of the internal migration streams and of the increasingly dispersed settlement of Puerto Ricans in the States, including Philadelphia. The Puerto Rican population in Philadelphia grew as a result of the rural economic crisis and the intersections of formal and informal means of migration. It was the formal contract labor program that enabled rural men to migrate directly to the States, without having to save the money for the trip. Less formal forms of labor recruitment persisted, and the lines blurred as workers sometimes used contracts initially and then went on their own. Even migrants who bypassed the farms were aware of the farm labor program, and everyone seemed to know someone who had come to the farms first. They were not always sure, however, whether people had come with contracts or without, since as we shall see in the next chapter, the conditions were not always that different. Either way, family members and friends signed up together for farm work in the States. Those that came directly to the city also relied on the help of family and friends already settled in the city and helped others to come.

Puerto Rican migrants who settled in Philadelphia confronted their new urban environment as young adults from the countryside, with little formal education, who had worked mostly in agriculture, agricultural processing, and the garment industry. The Puerto Rican population in Philadelphia reflected the backgrounds of farmworkers. In 1953, Puerto Rican farmworkers were men, 91 percent were between twenty-one and thirty-nine years of age, and most had a fourth-grade education. Although 60 percent were married, almost none had their wives with them. In the city there were more men than women, but the gap narrowed from 57 to 53 percent between 1950 and 1954. Puerto Ricans were young, with a median age of twenty-six in 1950 and twenty-one in 1954, as compared to thirty-three for other Philadelphians in 1950. Nor did Puerto Ricans in the city have very much formal education, with about a quarter having five years or less and another quarter having six to eight years in 1950. Compared to the economic conditions in their municipios and in the rest of Puerto Rico, migrants perceived Philadelphia as having a lot of jobs. Philadelphia's economy sustained the migration, providing jobs as Puerto Ricans in the city worked to recreate their household economies. Once in the city, informal networks continued to operate, as migrants helped each other find housing and jobs.[61]

Chapter Five

A Plethora of Limited Opportunities: Philadelphia's Economy

As Puerto Rican migrants came to Philadelphia looking for work, the city's economy provided jobs and sustained the migration. Coming from San Lorenzo in 1954, Doña Genara emphasized the ease of getting work in the city's garment industry: "As soon as I arrived from Puerto Rico, I started in that factory." She left and reentered the work force as needed: "Before, it was good here. You left one factory and you could get work in another. And since I had five children, I had to stop working for a while. But when I could, I returned to a factory and started to work again." She worked, on and off, in the city's garment industry until she retired. Similarly, Don José, who came from San Lorenzo in 1947, thought that in those early years "there was more work," and "it was a lot of factories, like every corner there was a factory." It was not easy, however, for Puerto Rican men to get good manufacturing jobs. Instead Don José washed dishes at the Warwick Hotel, made soup at the Campbell Soup Company, and worked on farms outside the city. He was then able to get two manufacturing jobs—the first with low wages and poor working conditions, and finally a "good" one with decent wages, benefits, and conditions, where he was still working in 1998.[1]

Though they sensed that there was an abundance of work, Puerto Rican migrants were confined to the secondary labor market, in jobs that paid poorly, required few skills, and offered poor working conditions, little security, and few avenues for economic mobility. As labor migrants, Puerto Rican men and women filled particular niches in a labor market segmented along racial and gender lines. Puerto Rican women became overwhelmingly concentrated in the city's manufacturing jobs. Puerto Rican men, on the other hand, were overrepresented in the service sector, especially in hotels and restaurants, and also found manufacturing jobs. Despite limited options, jobs were available. As a result, more Puerto Rican women were in the labor force than women citywide in 1950—36 and 34 percent, respectively. At the same time, 74 percent of

Puerto Rican men were in the labor force, compared to 77 percent of men citywide. Similarly, a 1954 study found 69 percent of Puerto Ricans employed, a higher proportion than for others living in the same neighborhoods. Those who settled in the city helped family and friends come and find work. While they sustained the migration, these informal networks were more effective in helping migrants get some types of jobs than others. As Puerto Ricans struggled to recreate their household economies, many found themselves living in poverty even though men, women, and sometimes even children worked.[2]

Philadelphia's Postwar Economy

Philadelphia was an industrial city notable for the diversity of its manufacturing. In addition to garment and textile production, the city led the country in metal items, machine tools and hardware, locomotives, hats and caps, boots and shoes, jewelry, shipbuilding, and other industries. During World War II much of Philadelphia's industry had turned to war production. Policy makers, planners, and journalists anticipated few postwar reconversion problems and a "normalizing" of the labor force along with economic reconversion. Returning veterans, they thought, would replace "temporary" workers—prisoners of war, immigrants, southern African American migrants, women, and youth. Yet because the city's labor market was segmented along racial and gender lines, the equation was not quite so simple. The postwar reshuffling of the economy left certain jobs unfilled, many of which were eventually filled by Puerto Rican men and women. Initially, Puerto Rican migrants who came to the city in search of work encountered a plethora of jobs in a limited range of occupations.[3]

Philadelphia's diverse manufacturing economy was considered an asset for postwar reconversion, with one reporter proclaiming, "Everyone concerned paints an optimistic picture for post-war Philadelphia, 'workshop of the world.'" The War Manpower Commission's regional director, Paul Lewis, described the Philadelphia area as "fortunate in having diversified industries" and reported that "nearly 75 percent of the major war plants were facing no serious reconversion problems." As a result, the WMC's 1945 study of seventy-five large labor markets found "the Philadelphia industrial area, second largest in the United States, to be the least affected by reconversion." Labor-starved industries, including thirty-nine industries that had been declared less essential in the war effort, were expected to provide jobs for returning veterans and laid off war industry workers. So, while 30,000 workers had been laid off, the WMC's area office had been "deluged" by requests for workers from "labor-starved" industries, including stores, candy manufacturers, hat manufacturers, breweries, and trucking firms, which were "the very industries from which WMC was 'drafting' workers a few months ago to fill war plant needs," according to the office's director, Levy Anderson. The hat industry, for example, employed 2,900 workers in 1941 but only 1,100 in 1945. The cigar and cigarette industry was "in immediate need of 2500 workers, of whom 60 percent are to be women." More than 1,000 workers were needed for the "seriously undermanned" service industries, especially hotels and restaurants, which were "hard hit through employees going into the armed forces or war plants." The search was on for men and women "to operate elevators, work in kitchens, serve as maids and perform other similar duties." All told, an estimated 52,000 workers were needed to compensate for wartime labor shortages.[4]

Additional jobs were anticipated because of booms in certain sectors of the economy and public works projects. The most new jobs were expected in manufacturing, with one report estimating that employment would increase from 252,600 to 329,400, while nonmanufacturing employment would increase more modestly, from 447,900 to 495,000. Textiles and hosiery, "two major industries in the area," were already seeking workers—3,500 for the hosiery industry and at least 1,500 for textile plants. During the war, 80 percent of the plants producing cloth and 90 percent of those producing fine woolen yarns were engaged in war production. The hosiery industry had operated at only 60 percent production, as nylon was unavailable for civilian use and "many workers went into war plants." Consumer demand had mounted, as "it has been a long time since the Philadelphia housewife has been able to get a choice of towels, pillow cases, sheets, better grade cloth, and fine woolen yarns." Analysts also predicted new job growth in construction, trade, financial and insurance services, and business. Meanwhile, Mayor Bernard Samuel announced that the city was "at the forefront among major cities of the country in its plans for post-war public works." Planned was "a gigantic post-war reconstruction program which, experts say, will create a wave of prosperity that will last at least five years." Half a billion dollars had been earmarked for public works and new factories, hospitals, churches, stores, theaters, and housing projects that would "provide jobs for many thousands of workers here for years to come."[5]

Although labor relations were part of the initial postwar optimism, strikes affected the industries cited as areas of job growth, including food processing, textiles, and services. In August 1945, Philadelphia's Chamber of Commerce encouraged firms to establish branches in the city with a brochure "pointing out that labor relations in the city are exceedingly good." One business leader added that "living expenses are more favorable to the worker here than in many leading cities throughout the country." Yet Philadelphia's workers were among those nationwide who fought to secure wartime gains and to get wage increases that would offset wartime inflation. By the end of September 1945, 15,200 workers were on strike in the Philadelphia-Camden area. When 1,200 employees walked out of Stephen F. Whitman and Sons candy firm, the *Inquirer* reported, "several hundred pickets, mostly girls, paraded outside the factory carrying placards and singing 'We Want a Nickel.'" A sit-down strike at the Campbell Soup Company "completely halted production" until the company agreed to a three-cent increase in wages. Sugar refineries were struck by 1,050 workers. The largest manufacturing employers, textiles and hosiery, also experienced strikes, with an estimated 5,000 workers affected by contract disputes in the hosiery industry and many others by plant closings in the textile strike. Nor were the service industries immune: 120 striking bellhops, maids, waitresses, and maintenance workers at the Ritz-Carlton "compelled scores of guests to climb stairs and go to other establishments for their meals." Philadelphia newspapers kept a running tally of the number of people involved in work stoppages and printed editorials condemning the strikes.

One letter to the editor of the *Inquirer* considered the strikes "a shameful betrayal of veterans" who were "eager to return to work and to take up again normal, contented lives in a world of peace."[6]

For some, the vision of "normal, contented lives" encompassed a shift in the composition of the work force from temporary war workers to returning veterans. Between 1940 and 1943 the labor force grew from 876,000 to 890,000, even as 146,000 men entered the armed forces. Pointing to "the entry of thousands of women, school children and retired persons who normally would not have been employed" and to "immigrant workers, drawn here by high wages," one article noted, "with the end of the war, thousands of these emergency workers are expected to retire to the home, to the classroom or to their residences in other parts of the country."[7]

Prisoners of war and "foreign workers" were among the first to be "removed" from their jobs and "shipped home." Nationwide, 315,000 jobs held by "war prisoners and foreign workers" were "being filled gradually by American workers," according to reconversion director John W. Snyder. By the end of 1945, 68,000 Mexicans and 15,000 West Indians were to "have left for home," and prisoners of war were to "be shipped home by early 1946." While Snyder's wording implied a voluntary departure for Mexicans and West Indians, the *Inquirer* reported, "Jamaicans Riot on Way Home." The 2,200 "imported Negro farm laborers" had been "assembled" at the former Army camp in Stuart, Florida "to await transportation to their homes in the Bahamas and Jamaica." Rioting erupted as some "were impatient to get going" after being held in the camp and "others reportedly didn't like the idea of leaving the United States." Twenty-seven people were hospitalized, six were arrested, the rest were "confined" to their barracks, and everything was reported as "sweet and lovely." In the Philadelphia area, 7,647 German prisoners of war "would be removed from industrial and agricultural jobs in the area to provide work for returning veterans and unemployed war workers."[8]

While prisoners of war and foreign workers could be "shipped" home, migrants presented a different situation. In September 1945, the Philadelphia Housing Authority conducted a survey to determine "the number of vacancies that would become available to war veterans in need of housing accommodations." The survey found that "only about nine percent of the workers who came to this city to take war jobs plan to move away during the next 12 months." Mass evictions seemed eminent, as "only those migrant war workers now engaged in the completion of war contracts" and "distressed families of service men and of returning war veterans" were "eligible for occupancy in the project." Implying that migrant families had neither servicemen nor returning war veterans, the prospect that migrant families would be evicted was surely intended as an incentive for migrants "to move away." Although southern African American migrants could not be "shipped" home, they could be "removed" from their wartime jobs. Historian Allen Ballard suggests that the patterns of the World War I period were repeated in the aftermath of World War II. African American migrants, recruited by Philadelphia industrialists during the wars, lost these jobs when the wars were over.[9]

In an effort to get young war workers to relinquish their jobs, policy makers mounted "persuasion" campaigns. Local offices of the United States Employment Service started "a back-to-school campaign for youth of high school age," counseling them "to return to school instead of seeking jobs." Meanwhile, the WMC's local office sent letters to 500 employers and 500 local labor unions suggesting they urge "youth to complete or further their education." Although policy makers stressed the "voluntary basis" of the programs, which were "not designed to relieve from jobs youth who would not return to school anyway or who are seeking employment because of economic necessity," these programs were clearly designed to reallocate jobs in a labor market flooded by 80,000 workers laid off from war industries and 70,000 local men discharged from the armed services. Hence, policy makers emphasized the "employment pool of some 150,000 workers available for replacements of youth of high school age released from full-time jobs." One month later the *Inquirer* reported some success: "Three hundred and five boys and girls who left school 'permanently' to take war jobs have changed their minds and returned to classes this fall."[10]

For Philadelphia's white, middle-class women, the image of the happy housewife quickly replaced that of "Rosie the Riveter." With a letter to the editor of the *Inquirer* in August 1945, Leo Rosner unleashed a storm of controversy, asserting: "Now that peace has come, thank God, it is time to consider seriously the advisability of putting women back into the homes where they belong." With "service men coming home" and "millions of male war workers being laid off," Rosner considered it "only fair and just that the available jobs should go to them." Besides, he continued, "nature created women to be home-makers and mothers and they don't belong in business or politics, but in the home." K. L. Bell agreed: "Now that the war has ended and lay-offs . . . are under way, don't you think it would be the honorable thing for the women employees to leave their jobs voluntarily, to give the male help with a family or the returning veterans the chance they are entitled to?"[11]

Women responded by asserting their need to work and by reminding Rosner that the war, for many, was not over yet. One woman wrote: "Perhaps if Mr. Rosner will think again, he will tell us that he really meant that all married women whose husbands are physically capable of working should be compelled to give up their jobs." Asking, "just who will give these girls the means to fulfill the financial obligations which have been forced upon them because of the deaths of their loved ones?" she signed her letter, "A Girl Who Must Work." Identifying themselves as "service men's wives," other women stressed that until "the men return to assume the responsibility that we have shouldered," they were committed to keeping "things as they were before they went away." For two women, however, women's work was tied to gender roles, albeit in different ways. One, hoping for a return to "traditional" gender roles, wondered: "Now that the war is really over and women aren't working in factories to get their men home quicker, will men at home reconvert with the war industries and turn into gentlemen again, and give a woman a seat on a bus?" The other criticized "traditional" gender roles and a "Germanic attitude toward womankind," insisting, "this nation has been built on women's work, inside and outside the homes." Women, she asserted, "are individuals and have talents, which they have a right to express, just the same as men." Besides, she continued, "there are just as many men fitted for household duties as women."[12]

Despite the exhortations to "Keep Jòb Pledge to G.I. Joe" and make jobs available for returning veterans, veterans' skills and interests did not always match the jobs available in the city. Initial optimism for veterans' job opportunities gave way to an "employment problem." In September 1945, the *Inquirer* reported that "the returned war veterans in Philadelphia are not expected to cause any serious labor problem"; older veterans "were skilled in various trades and professions and will have no trouble getting back their old jobs," and younger veterans were "eager to continue their education . . . instead of trying to get jobs [as] the rate of pay is not attractive to them." By 1947, however, Pennsylvania's Employment Service conceded, "veterans continue to represent more than half of the unemployed group. . . . Despite the advantage of youth, the veteran represents an employment problem since many have had little or no experience in industrial establishments or have trades or skills not needed in the present labor market." A similar dilemma arose with policy makers' other priority—men laid off from war industry jobs. The WMC acknowledged that "numerically, at least, there is a sufficient demand to absorb all displaced war workers. . . . Not all of them will be absorbed, of course, because of the differences in job specifications, wage rates and other factors." So, with 34,600 workers laid off from war industry plants, most of the 20,900 jobs listed at the United States Employment Service's local office were in textiles, apparel, iron and steel, and the railroads at the end of August 1945. These jobs in labor-intensive industries, like textiles and apparel, and in the harshest industrial work, like railroads and steel, were unlikely to employ skilled veterans or war industry workers, who expected higher wages and better working conditions.[13]

Meanwhile, women remained unemployed in spite of labor shortages in industries that traditionally employed women. Women laid off from war work were not, it seems, willing to take any job. Nationwide, as historian Alice Kessler-Harris indicates, "in the food, clothing, and textile industries, where they had traditionally been employed, women quit jobs at an incredible pace. Women in well-paid jobs—chemical, rubber, and petroleum—quit more slowly than from other manufacturing jobs." Women accounted for 52 percent of the workers receiving unemployment in Philadelphia in September 1945. For the WMC, "the high proportion" of unemployed women "was due to the fact that women were less willing than men to accept jobs in private industry after high war-time wages." Wages in cigar-making, textiles, clerical work, and the "posts for 26,000 women" anticipated as a result of the upcoming Christmas shopping season did not compare favorably to those in war industries. By 1947, the Pennsylvania State Employment Service concluded, "female employment in the Philadelphia area during the past five months has not conformed to the national trend upward. . . . It does not appear that a return of women into the labor market has taken place in this area." The number of women workers had decreased by 2,900 between January and May.[14]

As Philadelphia's economy and labor force shifted, pockets of labor shortages remained. Puerto Rican migrants responded to these labor shortages and ended up in jobs where employers sought out cheap labor, and where postwar strikes had made little gain in securing workers' interests. As prisoners of war and foreign workers were "removed" from agricultural jobs, few veterans or laid-off war industry workers took their place. Instead, Puerto Rican men were recruited for farm work. At the same time, the "labor-starved" hotels and restaurants continued to need dishwashers and other workers, and Puerto Rican men became concentrated in the city's service sector. They also found manufacturing jobs, sometimes in the same labor-intensive industries that employed Puerto Rican women—the garment and food processing industries.

Puerto Rican women found jobs in labor-intensive industries, traditionally defined as "women's work." In reporting labor shortages in the food processing and apparel industries, the Pennsylvania Bureau of Employment Security revealed that these were not popular jobs. In food processing, the "demand is the result of high turn-over because of night work and is for replacement purposes primarily." Likewise, in the apparel industry "marked shortages are apparent among sewing machine operators of all types, tailors, hand sewers and certain types of pressers," as a result of "high turnover among entrants." These were precisely the jobs laid-off women war workers were unlikely to take if they had a choice. African American women, on the other hand, had fewer choices. As historian Jacqueline Jones notes, "like their white counterparts, they were loathe to leave relatively well-paying jobs. . . . but unlike white women, they had few options other than institutional or domestic service." While African American women continued to be excluded from industry, the Women's Bureau mounted a "postwar campaign to improve the image of household service" and encouraged African American women to return to work as domestics. This campaign, combined with employers' preferences and racial stereotypes, may have locked African American women into domestic and other service jobs and out of manufacturing, while Puerto Rican women were recruited to fill the low-wage jobs in the garment and food processing industries.[15]

Because the labor market was segmented by gender as well as by race, Puerto Rican men and women had access to different economic opportunities, which shaped migration patterns, the impact of contract labor programs, and informal networks. By 1954, most Puerto Ricans (52 percent) came to Philadelphia directly from Puerto Rico. Women, however, were more likely to come directly from Puerto Rico—60 percent compared to 47 percent of men—or from New York City. More men came via New Jersey, Pennsylvania, or elsewhere in the States—39 percent compared to 14 percent of women. While garment and other manufacturing jobs brought women directly to the city, farm work brought men to the region. At the same time, manufacturing jobs for women in the city rendered the contract labor program for domestics ineffective. With fewer employment options in the city, men continued to rely on the farm labor program and on noncontract seasonal agricultural work.[16]

As Puerto Ricans came to the city, they encountered an economy that was similar to earlier eras. Historian Walter Licht characterizes the period from 1800 to 1950 as "Philadelphia's age of industrial enterprise." Still a major manufacturing center in 1950, the city produced diverse products in a wide variety of work settings. Manufacturing was marked by significant numbers of small and medium-sized enterprises and by continued family ownership and partnerships. Yet specialized and flexible production meant seasonality, high turnover of firms and workers, and underemployment for many. Manufacturing jobs were still located within the city, as a 1976 study observed:

"In 1950 the region looked much like it had 20 or 30 years before. . . . Philadelphia remained a tightly organized patchwork of rowhouse residential neighborhoods alternating with high employment-density strips of industry and business." The city's economy, however, was on the verge of major economic restructuring. While there were early signs of deindustrialization during the 1950s, the major shifts, which will be discussed in Chapter 7, were yet to come.[17]

Women's Labor Migration

Puerto Rican women came to Philadelphia as labor migrants in search of paid employment. Most women, 64 percent, were migrating to the States because they had a job offer or were looking for work, according to a 1952 survey. The others were joining family members, and perhaps would look for work as well. In Philadelphia, the Commission on Human Relations identified just 17 percent of Puerto Rican women as "housewives" in their 1954 study. Not surprisingly, then, in their oral histories women recalled looking for work the day after they arrived in the city or finding a job "right away." Puerto Rico's policy makers facilitated women's labor migration not only through the contract labor program for domestics, but also by providing vocational training in Puerto Rico and alerting women to the availability of garment industry jobs in the States. Indeed, once in Philadelphia Puerto Rican women found garment and other manufacturing jobs. While some women got union jobs with benefits, others worked under poor conditions, with low wages and no benefits. Nevertheless, social networks played a role, as women helped each other find jobs and settle in the city.[18]

Garment workers' migration was in part facilitated by Puerto Rico's policy makers and in part the "unorganized" or "spontaneous" flow that had concerned them at the outset. Though there was not a contract labor program, policy makers were aware of job opportunities for garment workers. In promoting migration, Clarence Senior had envisioned domestic work for women and agricultural work for men. The third area of labor shortages, manufacturing, was more complicated. Senior noted that "women may prove to have many opportunities in this field" and quoted a U.S. Employment Service report: "In Scranton, Pennsylvania a huge male labor surplus exists, a large portion of which is veterans, while a shortage of semiskilled female workers exists in the textile, apparel, and tobacco industries." Similarly, Donald O'Connor of the Office of Puerto Rico had commented that "any man or woman who can earn a sub-standard living at needle work in Puerto Rico can earn a standard living at the hosiery plants around Philadelphia." Policy makers were interested in dispersing Puerto Rican settlement beyond New York City, as Senior noted: "The tendency toward dispersion is encouraged and facilitated by the Commonwealth." Yet Pennsylvania was not on his list of fourteen states where "attention should be concentrated" in terms of desired destinations. Policy makers may have feared that Philadelphia was too similar to New York and that migrants would encounter comparable obstacles, such as declining economic opportunities and hostility from others. Nonetheless, government-sponsored training programs provided skills and information about jobs in the States. Knowing through these training programs and from each other that they could find work, Puerto Rican women came to the city.[19]

Doña Genara's experiences illustrate the role of the garment industry in Puerto Rican women's migration. Born in a rural barrio in San Lorenzo in 1926, she described growing up on a family farm of 17 cuerdas with her eight brothers and sisters:

> Life wasn't so good. It was good in one way, but we had to work hard. My father had a farm. We had to do everything to be able to survive in Puerto Rico. . . . We had to go barefoot when we were kids and we had to work hard helping our parents on the farm and everything. . . . There was no water in the barrio, there was no electricity. We had to carry water, we had to pick *gandules,* we had to sew the tobacco, do everything. But it was nice to live like that, it was honorable. The parents were treated with respect. The children, we respected our parents. There weren't vices, everything was good.

Changing economic conditions, however, sent Doña Genara and her siblings in search of work. "The first that left was my sister. And she got married, she married a boy that was a prison guard in town and moved to town. And we started to leave the barrio little by little and to look for work." Doña Genara went to live with her sister in the town of San Lorenzo in the early 1950s.[20]

It was there Doña Genara heard about a vocational training program. "They were announcing it on the radio. So I said, 'I want to study something. Since I don't have much schooling, I want to take something in any kind of manufacturing.'" In order to attend the program in neighboring Caguas, she had to earn the money for her transportation. "I remember that I was very poor and in the morning, I cleaned for a woman so that she would give me the money because I had to travel to another town. I only took four hours of class, but since we needed to work, we made sure to learn everything in a little bit of time." Her need to work also limited the length of her training. "Actually, I had to leave because I had to work, but I took six months, nothing more." The course taught embroidering, knitting, and sewing by machine, and alerted students to the availability of jobs in Puerto Rico and in the States. Doña Genara explained, referring to her sewing teacher, "she always talked with me—she told me, told us, 'You can work here and in the United States there are also good jobs on the sewing machine.' She told me, she told us, 'Try to do well on the machine because this is the most important work that all of you are going to find.'"

Her first two garment industry jobs were in San Lorenzo, first working in a shop and then doing piecework at home. She recalled, "in the town, I worked about three years. I always worked in knitting, because there wasn't anything else, I mean in my town." The knitting shop employed twenty-two women, most of them single, and made ballet slippers and hats. Working eight-hour days, Monday through Friday, she earned $12.80 for the week: "Well, I was really fast at the work. Yeah, we could talk, we listened to *novelas* on the radio. We could talk, we had friends. Yeah, I lived happy at least because before $12 was a lot of money. . . . But we had to produce an average of four pairs of slippers a day. We had to work fast, if not, they fired you." After two years, the shop closed and Doña Genara began to do homework, knitting hats. Every week she went to Río Piedras to get materials, made the hats at home, and returned them the following week. She continued living with her sister: "During that time, I stayed mostly at my sister's house because in the country there still wasn't any electricity. So I stayed to do my work." Doña Genara now worked longer hours and earned less money: "Three dozen, it was thirty-six hats to earn $4. . . . It was several hours. I didn't have time for anything. I worked about 10 or 12 hours [a day]."

Doña Genara came to Philadelphia in 1954 with the help of another sister, who was living in the city. As garment workers had to pay their own way, she noted, "if you didn't have family, you couldn't emigrate quickly." She explained her decision to migrate: "I wanted to come for a better life, because everyone was looking for a better life. So I decided to come here to Philadelphia. I had a sister here, and I came to my sister's house, I worked as much as I could. . . . I wanted to earn more money. Here I started with $38 a week." She found her first job as a machine operator right away. "A man in a store told me, 'So are you looking for work?' I kept looking for work when I got here. And then he told me, 'Look, in this factory where I work, they're asking for machine operators.' I didn't know a word of English, but I knew how to work. I started and I kept working." Her first job was at the Charlie Singer Company, making jackets and boys' clothing. The factory was much larger than the shop in Puerto Rico, occupying two floors, and at that time "there were almost no Puerto Ricans. When I came to this country, in that factory there were two—one Peruvian woman, one Cuban woman, one Puerto Rican man, and me, a Puerto Rican woman. . . . The rest were Americans . . . whites. Blacks, too. . . . Later, more Puerto Ricans came." She considered it a good job: "I earned more money. I, for example, in Puerto Rico I earned $12 a week and here I earned $40, they took out two, I kept thirty-eight." She concluded: "The factory was good. The bosses were good. It was good work." The workforce continued to change, as Doña Genera observed:

> Most of the factories where I went to work in the earlier times had a lot of Poles. They worked hard. And the factories where I worked, I worked with Italians, Jews. But every day there were more *hispanos*. They came from different countries. They came from Cuba, they came from Peru, they came from Mexico, from different ones. They came, every day more people immigrated here, more and more and more.

Recalling the 1970s, she noted, "when I worked at Richard, there were already a lot of *hispanos*."

Finding work readily available, Doña Genara worked at a variety of garment industry jobs. "They announced it on the radio. There were factories close to the houses, around here there were a lot of garment factories open. So when I had to stay at home with the children, well I returned to another factory and could work right away. It was very easy to work before." After working at the Charlie Singer Company for a year, Doña Genara returned to Puerto Rico for six months, then returned to Philadelphia and worked with the same company for another three years. In 1958 she got married, and in 1960 she and her husband returned to San Lorenzo, where their first daughter was born. "Sometimes, when you come from Puerto Rico, you're nostalgic to return to your country, to see the place, to be there. I thought that I was going to stay, but it wasn't like that, because you couldn't get work, and I came back here." Four days after returning to Philadelphia, she started working in another garment factory. She described her employment pattern: "Then I went to Puerto Rico, I returned, and continued in the same factory. I worked in different factories. Then when I had the children—since there were a lot—I worked with three, but when the fifth one came I had to leave [work]. But when they went to school, I returned to work, and I retired as a machine operator." She concluded, "every time I wanted to work, I could work."

While Doña Genara considered most of her jobs to be "good" ones, she understood the range of working conditions. Other Puerto Rican women did homework. "I returned to the factory, I didn't sew at home. Well, since I came from Puerto Rico, I sewed in the factory, but I saw a lot of people sewing at home. . . . They got homework, they could work at home, because the factory gave them clothes to sew at home." Her worst factory job was after she got married in 1958, when she and her husband worked in the same factory, making mattress covers. She sewed and he ironed. The shop paid the minimum wage but was not a union factory. "That factory, I didn't like it much. They didn't turn in social security, they found themselves in trouble. . . . It seems they didn't pay taxes or something, I don't know. And we had to go to another factory." The shop closed. Yet most of the factories where she worked were represented by the Amalgamated Clothing Workers of America. She considered these good shops, where she earned good money, and had health coverage for herself but not the children. In 1974, when her youngest daughter was six years old, she went to work at the Richard Singer Company. "Well, it was still good work. You could still get machine work, you could get a lot of work. If you left a job, you could still work in another. But I liked the work at Richard a lot and I stayed there. It was good." She retired from the Richard Singer Company with social security and a pension.

Informal networks played a role in women's labor migration to Philadelphia and in their employment in the garment industry. Like Doña Genara, Doña Juanita's migration to Philadelphia was facilitated by her sister and by garment industry jobs. Leaving Naguabo, she came to the city for the first time in 1951 to take care of her sister's children after her sister had an operation. At their father's insistence, Doña Juanita also continued her high school education, even though she knew very little English. After a year she went back to Puerto Rico and finished high school. In 1953 she returned to Philadelphia and to her sister's home, this time looking for work:

> There wasn't any work [in Naguabo]. The girls worked in different stores, clothing stores, or something like that. Naguabo is a town, at that time there weren't many advances. . . . Yeah, to work, that was all. There wasn't any other reason. And then we saw that the neighbors were coming too, my friends. That's all, you know, to work and that your friends are there.

Her first job was working with her sister in a garment factory making men's suits. There was only one other Puerto Rican working in their shop. "It was Italian, German women, a lot of Italians with less English than us." Unlike Doña Genara, however, Doña Juanita did not know how to sew. "I sewed too even though I didn't know how to sew anything. . . . I learned to sew what they gave me there [at the factory], but I didn't like the idea of that, of *piece work,* to earn your money." She and another sister were sharing an apartment. "We recognized it very quickly, that we were going to work and going to get an apartment, and going to pay [our way]." She described her earnings and expenses: "I started off earning $.75 an hour. After a little while came $1.00 and it was $1.00 for a long time, you know, it was $1.00 for a long time. You got $30 or $35 dollars a week, because it was $40 but they deducted those things, you know. I don't know how we did it, but we did it." The trolley cost $.10, they paid $35 per month for their apartment, and split their other expenses.[21]

Puerto Rican women like Doña Juanita's sister helped each other get jobs in the garment industry. Doña Juanita recalled of her sister, "after she came to Philadelphia, she was a garment worker. And she, well if someone came, well she said, 'Look, in the garment industry you do well,' or something like that, you know. And it was true because there were a lot of garment factories in Philadelphia. You would get a factory job anywhere in Philadelphia." Their neighbors in Naguabo were a family of twelve that gradually made their way to Philadelphia with help from her sister. "The wife lost her husband. So, they were still young women that hadn't gotten married or anything, and they wanted to come to the United States. They wrote to my sister, and we helped each other out. But it was my sister who first received them and got them work." All of the daughters in the family worked in the garment industry. After she got married in 1954, Doña Juanita continued working. When her two children were still young, she worked a night shift downtown making women's clothing.

Her sister continued working in the garment industry until she retired, but Doña Juanita found other manufacturing jobs, which were readily available. "I always got my jobs—the other jobs after my sister—I got them from the newspaper. You looked in the newspaper, and you got a job. . . . I started to look for the things that I was most able to do. I always looked for *assembly*. . . . Things I could do with my hands." For several years in the early 1960s she worked the 4:00 to 10:00 P.M. shift at a donut factory. They made the donuts during the day, and she worked the cash register, selling the donuts. The factory was "very hygienic, everything was very clean, and all the machinery," and the owners were "good people," who were always working. Although she left work late, she recalled, "we weren't afraid that anyone was going to harm us. . . . We worked and I tell you, we weren't afraid because in that area there were enough Puerto Ricans, because there was a Puerto Rican theater." Her bosses and a friend of hers also gave her rides. Yet as the work force changed, the owners closed the factory:

> The place was very good but then, it was, they were all white, Germans, but then they had to hire other people, you know. I was the first Puerto Rican, and I was the first of any group, you know how it is. And then they had to hire other people and I don't know if it was the people that came, or that they didn't want to work anymore, you know, they closed the building and everything there. . . . The workers changed, they came from other places, or something like that because that was when, it was already that they had to give work to other people, it couldn't just be one group of workers anymore.

It was the mid-1960s; the work force and the city's economy were shifting and some factories had started to close down or relocate—a trend that continued.

Doña Juanita's next employer took a different approach. For almost ten years she worked in a jewelry factory putting stones in bracelets. In contrast to the donut factory, the jewelry factory relocated within the city and expanded. "There they opened the doors to the whole world. There were Colombians, a boy who was very good and that studied and put in the emeralds—very fine work. Then later there was another Colombian, then came Koreans and then came more Puerto Ricans and then came more African Americans. . . . It was the United Nations there." The owner was an Italian, whom she considered a good man; he gave Christmas parties and gifts of jewelry. She felt that she had learned something and liked the job. Even her children worked there. "It was huge and he was such a good man that he gave *part-time* work to students and that's how my children went there. . . . When they were in *high school* they went to work for two or three hours in the afternoon. He gave them both work for me in *shipping* and they liked it a lot." Despite her emphasis on his kindness, there was a drawback to the job:

> We all worked very well and he was very delightful, but look, there weren't any kind of benefits. There weren't benefits for anything. We joked a lot there that when we were old that we would all be working there and the only thing we would be able to collect was social security. But, it didn't happen like that, you know, because we all left, going to different places.

Like Doña Genara, she stressed that jobs were available, and concluded:

> I think that the majority of Puerto Ricans, during the '50s and '60s and '70s, they were working here, everyone was working. It didn't matter what kind of work they did, you know. . . . They could find it because, like I told you, there were so many factories of many things, of many things. There were candy factories, there were sugar factories, you know that Jack Frost was in Philadelphia, but they closed it only about fifteen years ago, and there were a lot of people that worked there. Whitman's was here in Philadelphia and there were a lot of Puerto Rican people working there, and well so many that I don't remember. . . . In the garment industry, the women, the Puerto Rican women worked, like that very good family I mentioned, all of them worked in the garment industry.

Doña Juanita, however, stayed at the jewelry factory until she and her husband bought a bodega.

The city's food processing industries were another major employer of Puerto Rican women. Doña Nilda described the first job she had on coming to Philadelphia from New York City in 1965 with her husband and five children:

> Well, there I started packing almonds. Then they put me, one day they called me to work downstairs in pineapples, and there I stayed, cutting—you know how in those cans of fruit salad there are those small, square pieces of pineapple? Well, I cut those on a machine.

For Doña Nilda, "it was good work, I liked it a lot," and she explained why:

> I liked the work in that it was a job that I did alone. Nobody was on top of me, like telling me "you have to do this, you have to do that." The *foreman* that I had—because the *boss* was always upstairs in the office—he had a *foreman* in each department and the *foreman* that I had he told me what they were going to do that day, in the morning right at the beginning or in

the afternoon of the day before. And when I arrived, I did that. I turned on the radio, I went
to the bathroom when I wanted, came back to keep working and nobody bothered me.

The job was also convenient, as she could walk to and from work, leaving at 4:30 in
the afternoon and getting home by 4:45. Referring to the union, she added, "it was
good, it was good. It always helped us." And it provided benefits: "It had a union and
the union paid you if you were out and there was more than three sick days. . . . It had
vacation, when I left I had almost three weeks of vacation." The workforce was diverse,
"Puerto Ricans, there were whites, there were blacks, and even I think there were Chinese, and even Colombians," and she appreciated the relations among coworkers: "It
was good, there was good comradeship, we got along well." When she left her job in
1981 to return to Puerto Rico, her coworkers threw her a party.[22]

Like the garment industry, there were a range of working conditions in the food processing industry, and for many Puerto Rican women the choice was between these
industries. In contrast to Doña Nilda's food processing job, one son recalled his
mother's jobs:

> I remember she used to work peeling potatoes in a factory. . . . It was wet on the ground and
> her feet used to get wet and she was sick all the time. But we had to survive one way or the
> other so she had to go to work. She used to be sick a lot. . . . I remember a couple of times
> her missing work because she could not take it any more and she eventually had to quit to
> find something better so she ended up sewing. . . . She sews in a factory today. . . . She works
> piece work.

Even piece work was considered a step up from her food processing job. Another son
explained that his mother "came over and found a job and an apartment . . . she got the
money to bring us both back. . . . We come over in 1950." His mother's job was "at a
factory. Making belts at 8th and Race St. Chinatown. She's been off and on at the same
job for seventeen years. . . . She doesn't like the job." Hence, while Puerto Rican women
could find work, some of the jobs labeled as "women's work" were not very pleasant.[23]

Doña Carmen's first job reflected the opportunities available to most Puerto Rican
women. Although she came to the city as a married woman with four children and her
husband had come to the area for farm work, she did not just follow her husband.
Instead she came with the intention of finding paid employment and went looking for
work the day after she arrived. Referring to two friends, she recalled:

> I went with them at sunrise to look for work. We came to a garment factory and they needed
> two people but not three and I told him give it to them and I left. But the *boss* said that you
> needed these little scissors and nobody had them, and I went searching for them. I got lost. . . .
> I didn't know where I lived. I arrived late at night, everyone was looking for me.

Although she never found the scissors, she did find a job, packing shoes at the J. Edward
Shoe Company, where she worked for seven years. She worked on the fourth of
ten floors, where "everyone was Latino" and most were women. Doña Carmen remembered fondly that they "sounded like a bunch of hens, '*yacate, yacate, mira Carmen, mira Rosa*,'" and she formed several lasting friendships. She did not earn much,

however—$.45 an hour, $18.00 a week—and it did not go very far. "There was no refrigerator, you bought some ice and put it in an icebox, we ate what we could, we paid $7.00 a week for rent, and that's how we started." But there were benefits, Blue Cross and a plan for mothers with children. In telling her story, Doña Carmen emphasized the hardships early migrants encountered. "At first everything was like that, we had to pass through many things."[24]

Unlike most Puerto Rican women, however, Doña Carmen had a long career in human services. Some women found jobs serving the growing Puerto Rican population. Doña Carmen had been attending the 5th Street Methodist Church for religious services in the evenings and on Sundays, and keeping the guest register as a volunteer. While she was on vacation from the shoe factory, the pastor hired her to work in the Church's community center, which was serving more and more Puerto Ricans. According to Doña Carmen, the pastor told her to forget about her other job, "that better things were coming," and "he hired me as a social worker and that's how I began." For thirteen years she organized after-school activities for children and the Christmas party, and helped people with food and clothes. Later she worked for the city and continued her studies at Temple University, something very few Puerto Rican women achieved. In the early 1970s she became the director of the Norris Square Senior Citizens' Center, where she worked for more than twenty years.

This was an era when jobs for Puerto Rican women were readily available, even though the types of jobs were limited. Puerto Rican women were overwhelmingly concentrated in the city's manufacturing sector, especially the garment industry. In 1950, 56 percent of Puerto Rican women worked as operatives, in contrast to 28 percent of women citywide (see Table 5.1). In the same year, a survey by the Friends Neighborhood Guild found more than half of the fifty-four Puerto Rican respondents working in the garment industry, sewing by machine or by hand; more than a third working as domestics; and the rest in other factory work. Four years later, fully 72 percent of Puerto Rican women worked as operatives, with the Commission on Human Relations concluding that they "were largely employed as operatives in various clothing factories." Despite the contract labor program, few Puerto Rican women were domestics or service workers. African American women, on the other hand, were overrepresented as service workers, more than half of them working in this area. As sales and clerical work became the largest employers of women citywide, Puerto Rican and African American women were left by the wayside. These patterns continued. In 1970 Puerto Rican women were still more likely than their counterparts to be operatives, and African American women were still more likely to be service workers. While the proportions of Puerto Rican and African American women in sales and clerical work increased, they were still less likely than women citywide to work in these jobs.[25]

Philadelphia marriage license records confirm the centrality of manufacturing and garment industry jobs for migrant women. Of women marrying between 1945 and 1965, 41 percent worked as operatives, with at least 30 percent in the garment industry (see Table A.2 in Appendix I). Women from both San Lorenzo and Salinas found

TABLE 5.1.   Female Occupations by Race, Philadelphia, 1950 and 1970

	1950			1970		
	Puerto Rican	Black	Total	Puerto Rican	Black	Total
Number Employed	34	53,973	274,532	1,907	106,929	313,718
Percent:						
Professional/						
Managerial	20.6	5.1	12.8	11.4	11.3	16.1
Sales/Clerical	11.7	6.8	36.3	22.1	31.0	44.7
Crafts	2.9	1.1	2.1	3.5	2.6	2.4
Service	8.8	53.2	19.3	11.0	32.3	18.9
Operatives/						
Laborers	55.9	32.3	27.9	51.9	22.3	17.7
Farm work	—	—	0.1	—	0.5	0.2
Not reported	0.2	1.6	1.6	—	—	—

Sources: U.S. Bureau of the Census as compiled in Philadelphia Commission on Human Relations, *Puerto Ricans in Philadelphia: A Study of Their Demographic Characteristics, Problems and Attitudes* (April 1954; reprint, New York: Arno Press, 1975), 126; U.S. Bureau of the Census, *Census of the Population: 1950,* vol. 3, *Census Tract Statistics,* pt. 42, Philadelphia (Washington, D.C., 1952), 205–211; U.S. Bureau of the Census, *Census of the Population: 1950,* vol. 2, *Characteristics of the Population,* pt. 38, Pennsylvania (Washington, D.C., 1952), 205–211, 135; and U.S. Bureau of the Census, *Census of the Population: 1970,* vol. 1, *Characteristics of the Population,* pt. 40, Pennsylvania (Washington, D.C., 1973), 500, 452, 396.

Note: For 1950, data are for the "nonwhite" population living in census tracts with 250 or more "nonwhite" persons. Most of the "nonwhite" population was African American, and these census tracts included 53,973 of 55,810 employed, "nonwhite" women. Not all columns total exactly 100 percent due to rounding.

work as operatives, and many were garment workers. Compared to women from San Lorenzo, however, Salinas's migrants were more likely to be "housewives," and those with paid employment were more likely to work as domestics. This may have reflected their work experiences in Puerto Rico. In Salinas, women had lower labor force participation rates, but a high proportion of working women were domestics. For migrants' mothers, those living in Philadelphia were more likely to find paid employment than those living in Puerto Rico (see Table A.3 in Appendix I). Like their daughters and other Puerto Rican women in the city, most working mothers were operatives.[26]

For women, paid employment was a very real and constant possibility, as well as an economic necessity. Women were important contributors to their household's income and viewed paid employment as part of their responsibilities in caring for their families. Although most found it challenging to balance household and paid work, they did not express this as a conflict in roles. Instead, the nature and rhythm of paid employment was shaped by their other responsibilities to their households. The availability of jobs meant that women could enter and leave the work force as needed. Hence, women balanced reproductive and productive tasks, at a time when paid employment was readily available and when much of the work available to Puerto Rican men was low-wage and seasonal.

Men's Labor Migration

Migrating to the region in search of paid employment, most Puerto Rican men hoped to find manufacturing jobs. Yet many of the manufacturing jobs available in Philadelphia, like those in Puerto Rico, were low-wage jobs defined as "women's work." Instead Puerto Rican men were recruited for seasonal farm work. Pennsylvania's agriculture provided jobs beyond the contract labor program, and many came without contracts to work on farms in the area. Dissatisfied with working and living conditions on the farms and in the camps, many migrants continued their search for better jobs and made their way to the city. Like the women, Puerto Rican men emphasized that they could always find a job. The problem was that the available jobs were often seasonal, low-paid, and unpleasant. They found work in restaurants and hotels, as well as manufacturing jobs that sometimes paralleled those available to women in the garment and food processing industries. Faced with poor wages and working conditions, some men changed jobs frequently and resorted to seasonal agricultural work, while those with decent manufacturing jobs kept them for decades. Although Puerto Rican men helped each other find work and settle in the city, informal networks had a greater impact in some areas of work than in others. Informal networks intersected with contract labor programs to get men seasonal agricultural jobs. Networks also helped men get jobs in the services and lower-level manufacturing jobs, but in many good manufacturing jobs men often found that they were the only Puerto Rican or one of very few.

Puerto Rican men were recruited to meet Pennsylvania's need for seasonal farm laborers. In 1954 the Pennsylvania Farm Placement Program declared that "seasonal farm labor is a major element in the economy," and about 45,000 seasonal workers were needed annually throughout the decade. The Farm Placement Program emphasized the recruitment of local workers and of workers from the more economically depressed regions of the state. Although expressing a preference for local laborers, Pennsylvania farmers turned increasingly to Puerto Rican and southern African American migrants, citing limited local labor and the loss of crops. By 1952, the seasonal labor force was one half local labor, one quarter southern African American, and one fifth Puerto Ricans from the island, with the remainder northern blacks, Puerto Ricans living in the States, and migrating whites. Between 1954 and 1960, an estimated 22,800 Puerto Ricans worked on Pennsylvania farms. As a regional phenomenon, seasonal agricultural work employed 15,000 Puerto Ricans on farms in the Middle Atlantic States in 1954: 7,000 in New Jersey, 3,700 in Pennsylvania, and 3,000 in New York. Fifty-four of the sixty-one employers asked said they expected to hire the same number or more Puerto Ricans the following year, two said they would hire fewer, and the rest were undecided.[27]

Puerto Rican men came to farms in the region with labor contracts and as walk-ins without contracts. In 1954, for example, 4,630 Puerto Ricans employed on New Jersey farms had contracts and 3,668 were walk-ins. An agricultural agent described the non-contract arrangements:

Originally most or all of the farmers received Puerto Ricans from the migrant camp. After the first year or two the farmer gets his help directly from Puerto Rico. If a farmer and a Puerto Rican like each other very much, and have good working relationships, the Puerto Rican will return to him every year . . . [and] good workers will bring along one or two relatives if his employer requests him to do so.

The Migration Division intercepted letters making these informal arrangements. A farmer from Barto, Pennsylvania wrote to a former employee named Roberto: "I can not at this time use the other boys but maybe I can later and I will let you know." The farmer had already made arrangements for other workers, including one who "was with me last year." Another farmer in Gettysburg, Pennsylvania wanted and wrote to twelve men who had worked for him in previous years. The Migration Division stopped the departures because the local employment office had not certified the need for laborers.[28]

The Pennsylvania State Employment Service oversaw the state's labor recruitment program. While the government of Puerto Rico recruited workers and monitored labor contracts, private employment agencies placed Puerto Rican farmworkers in Pennsylvania. Prior to 1953, the Glassboro Labor Association made placements on Pennsylvania farms. Puerto Rican workers came from the island to the association's labor camp, where they were either transferred to other farms or kept in camp and day-hauled to nearby farms. The association charged employers a fee, equivalent to about 8 percent of the wages paid by the employer to the worker. In 1953 the Farm Service Association in Hamburg, Pennsylvania began operating in much the same way. That year, 57 percent of Puerto Rican workers were placed through a private employment agency, 29 percent through personal search, and 10 percent through crew leaders operating in Florida. The state's employment service played a more active role in the recruitment of southern African American crews. Crew leaders organized migrant workers, many of them in Florida, and were paid by deductions from the workers' pay, or less frequently by the employer. Representatives from the Pennsylvania State Employment Service, joined by those from other states along the east coast, made annual trips to Florida to recruit and organize the Florida crews. The "Florida Itinerary" aimed to assure the most efficient use of crews and adequate numbers of laborers when farmers needed them. In 1953, 74 percent of 102 southern African Americans secured employment through crew leaders, and 22 percent through personal search.[29]

Puerto Rican and southern African American migrants were concentrated in particular sectors of Pennsylvania's agricultural economy. Most Puerto Ricans worked in the counties of southeastern Pennsylvania. Although they worked in a wide variety of crops, many found themselves working in tomato crops. In Adams County, Puerto Ricans provided 28 percent of the seasonal agricultural labor, locals 54 percent, southern African Americans 12 percent, and southern whites 5 percent. Puerto Rican migrants worked mostly in tomatoes and apples, while locals provided most of the labor for cherries and were the only workers in raspberries. In Lebanon County, Puerto Ricans provided 65 percent of the labor, with locals and local youth providing the rest. Here Puerto Ricans worked in tomatoes, peaches, and apples. Few Puerto Ricans worked in other counties, such as Union and Potter, where employers relied mostly on southern African American migrants. While employment of Puerto Rican and African American migrants varied by region and by crop, the greatest differences remained between migrant and local labor.[30]

Despite labor recruitment during the war, food processing jobs were rare for Puerto Rican and African American migrants in the postwar era. While there was a "substantial demand for seasonal labor in the processing of fruits and vegetables," it was largely met by local labor. In 1951, locals provided 79 percent of the labor with most of the workers women; Puerto Ricans provided 3 percent of the labor, and southern African Americans 1 percent, with most of that unreported assumed to be local. Economist Morrison Handsaker explained in 1953: "Although the work is not easy, local labor seems to prefer it, in many instances, to field labor. Better earnings, better personnel practices, protection of Workmen's Compensation and Social Security are among the factors which increase the attractiveness of cannery work as compared with field work." For those few in food processing, Puerto Ricans worked in Adams and Erie counties, while African Americans worked in Potter county.[31]

While the number of seasonal farmworkers declined, the proportion of labor provided by Puerto Ricans and southern migrants increased. Between 1955 and 1965, local labor decreased from 80 to 62 percent of the seasonal work force (see Table 5.2). Southern African Americans assumed a larger portion of the remaining jobs than did Puerto Ricans. During the decade, the portion of Puerto Ricans coming with labor contracts decreased from more than two thirds to less than one third. In addition, fewer southern migrants were organized by crew leaders. Yet southern African Americans were more likely to come to Pennsylvania via organized crews than Puerto Ricans were to come with labor contracts, and the gap widened. Although employers' control over crew leaders was limited, the operation of the crew leader system cost them nothing. Employers may also have benefited from the family labor of southern migrants, who sometimes traveled in family groups while Puerto Ricans came overwhelmingly as men alone.

Working and living conditions were harsh for seasonal agricultural workers in the state, and Puerto Rico's labor contracts provided only limited protection. Handsaker concluded:

> Puerto Ricans, thanks to the regulations of their government and to centralized recruiting, have more regular employment, and, as a result of the amount of work provided, they often have higher earnings although the rate per hour is the same or sometimes less. They also have medical care, and workmen's compensation coverage and are not subject to some of the abuses, petty or major, to which an undetermined proportion of Negro workers are subject under the crew leader system.

Yet even Handsaker tempered his praise for the contract system, noting poor housing and Puerto Rican workers who had been stranded and "victimized in other ways." As Handsaker implied, employers met the clause requiring that workers be paid the prevailing wage by paying Puerto Ricans less per hour but requiring more hours of work. Similarly, employers met the guaranteed hours of work by overworking laborers in the fourth week to make up any lost time. In addition, it was the employers who determined what constituted "reasonably necessary" medical care, "adequate meals,"

TABLE 5.2.   Seasonal Farm Labor, Pennsylvania, 1955, 1960, and 1965

	1955	1960	1965
# Seasonal Workers	40,000	30,100	20,100
% Local	80.0	76.7	62.2
% Puerto Rican	7.5	7.3	10.0
% Southern	12.5	15.9	27.9
# Puerto Rican	3,000	2,200	2,000
% with Contracts	66.7	47.5	29.7
# Southern	5,000	4,800	5,600
% with Crews	80.0	72.7	64.8

Sources: Pennsylvania, Bureau of Employment Security, *Farm Placement Program: Annual Report: 1955*, 5; Pennsylvania, Bureau of Employment Security, *Farm Placement Program: Annual Report: 1960*, 4, 6–7; and Pennsylvania, Bureau of Employment Security, *Farm Placement Program: Annual Report: 1965*.

Note: These figures are estimates and are provided to show general trends. "Southern" refers to African American migrants from the southern states, especially Florida, many of whom came under the crew leader system. Not all columns total exactly 100 percent due to rounding.

and "adequate hygienic housing," since provisions for inspection and channels for complaints were insufficient.[32]

Housing was a persistent problem. While stressing the range, Handsaker admitted, "persons are in many instances virtually compelled to live in places hardly fit for human habitation." He called for the enforcement of existing legislation, especially 1948 provisions for licensing and inspecting labor camps. In 1958, however, the Farm Placement Program acknowledged, "experience shows that the migratory farmworker and his family is perhaps the most easily exploited, the lowest paid, and lives and works under more substandard conditions than any other single group in the labor force." New regulations in 1958 required improvements in hundreds of labor camps, and between 1954 and 1970 regulations and services increased, including health and child care. In addition to the "social and humane standpoint," Handsaker noted, "it appears clear that improvement in housing and other conditions will be an important factor in insuring a steady and reliable labor force to harvest the seasonal crops." From the economic standpoint, the increased cost to employers of improving conditions would pay off in workers finishing their contracts and returning the next year.[33]

A wide variety of working and living conditions for farmworkers persisted, and Puerto Rican migrants experienced the full range. For Puerto Rico's rural migrants, farm work in the States was not new, but it did not provide the opportunities they had hoped. For others, farm labor provided the means to travel to the States, and hopefully some income to ease their settlement. Whether they had worked in agriculture in Puerto Rico or they were new to farm work, migrants left the farms, went to the city in search of work, and sent for their families. Doña Gloria recalled that Hipolito Amaro, her future husband, had worked on a farm for several years before settling in Philadelphia. In the mid-1940s Don Hipolito migrated from Salinas to the farms surrounding Philadelphia. According to Doña Gloria, "he was working there about three or four years, because he got along fine," and "he never complained." "The work was difficult at first. Then he learned to drive those machines, the machines that plow, that plow the farm. He learned to drive all of those and he did all of that work. He picked fruits at first, he worked with the machines, he did everything on that farm. . . . He was the one that was in charge of everything there was on the farm. He was the one that took the *trucks* to town, to Philadelphia." His responsibilities, and presumably his pay, had increased. After they were married, Don Hipolito and Doña Gloria went to visit the farm and were given baskets of cherries and apples.[34]

In contrast, Doña Gloria's cousins, Andrés and Manolo González from San Lorenzo, found much harsher conditions in the late 1950s. She and her husband went to visit Manolo on the farm where he had been working for a couple of months, with about fifteen other men, picking peaches, apples, strawberries, and other crops. "Well, we couldn't enter there to register, or to look, or to see anything, because it was prohibited. But, by what we saw, they cooked outside, in some pots outside. The camp, that's what they call it, well it wasn't fit to have people. . . . Because that was really bad there. It was a terrible, terrible thing." For Doña Gloria, "it made us really sad because we found them all piled up in a little house there, living together, and they weren't eating well. They had a lot, a lot of mosquito bites or something like that. . . . They were practically boys, very young. And I came home, but I came very, very upset." Although they wanted Manolo to come home with them, they considered his labor contract to be legally binding: "But of course, we couldn't do anything because they made like a contract, [and the workers] had to pay, because those people sent him his airfare—they had to pay that airfare. If not, they couldn't leave from there. If they saw them leave or something, they could send the police after them." Nonetheless, "Manolo was the one who ran away and he had to come on foot. So, he got to the house a wreck. This one got to my house and he couldn't even speak. Nothing. With an unlit cigarette in his hand, because he hadn't even been able to ask for a match to light it. This one came to me really bad, really bad, really bad." A few months earlier, Andrés, Manolo's brother, had arrived at Doña Gloria's having experienced "more or less the same" working and living conditions. They both stayed at the house and Don Hipolito helped them find work.

Don Justino came to work on a Pennsylvania farm on his own, without a labor contract, in 1953. For five or six months he worked and lived on a farm in Gettysburg, Pennsylvania. To get there, he took an eight-hour flight from Puerto Rico to New York and then a two-hour train ride to Gettysburg. On the farm, he picked tomatoes, apples, peaches, cherries, strawberries, and pears. When there was not enough work on the farm, the owner sent them to work on other farms in the area: "There were six of us there. But there were other farms. One farm that we visited there, where sometimes we worked with them, right, had 25 or 30 [workers]. There was another apple farm where I went to work too, that had more than a hundred workers. . . . All Puerto Rican and some blacks, but the majority Puerto Ricans." Don Justino and the other workers lived in a small house that the owner built, where they cooked and washed their clothes. He described it as "a very poor house, very poor," with no water. His wife, Doña Ana Luisa added, "it didn't have heat in the winter." Although he did not earn much, he recalled,

"I sent her money, not much, but I sent it until the work ended. The last work that I found was in apples, that was the last you picked, as it was already getting cold, October. . . . At the end of the apples, well there wasn't any more work, so we returned to Puerto Rico, all of us. Some people went to Florida, but I never liked the idea." Don Justino concluded, "at first, it wasn't that easy there either," and Doña Ana Luisa agreed, "it was very difficult there."[35]

Whether they came to Philadelphia from farm work or directly from Puerto Rico, the men faced the same options in the city. Although aware of the contract labor program, Don José, who came from San Lorenzo in 1947, saved the money for his airfare and came on his own. "I didn't come in the immigration. I come in my own, I pay my own money, I work in my own job. But this people, they come already with a job, and this is why a lot of people come that way. I never came that way." Nonetheless, Don José experienced the range of jobs available to Puerto Rican men in the postwar era. Unlike many migrants, however, Don José had completed high school, knew some English, and had money in his pocket. Although his sister was already living in the city, she was working as a live-in domestic. With nowhere to stay, he got a hotel room until his money ran out.[36]

Don José got his first job, washing dishes at the Warwick Hotel, with the help of someone from his church: "There was about fifteen, twenty families, and I think that one of them guys by name Alberto, he was working in that place. And he told me, so I went there. I got that job because nobody wanted that job. It was too hot. I was making 28 dollars a week." For about seven months he worked the night shift until 1:00 A.M. and then walked home from 17th Street to his apartment on 6th and Fairmount. Next, he tried farm work, but he lasted only about four days. "Oh, I couldn't take it. I never worked in farms before and I couldn't take it. I can't—picking tomatoes, oh man! Oh no!" He added, "I don't want to remember. . . . When I remember, I cry, I tell you, that was like an animal, that was." Nor did he find the conditions at the Campbell Soup Company much better. "I have a callus in my hands, and up and down all day long, you know, because its going fast. You gotta take the soup and put it here, all day long, like this, I mean this is for animals." The cans were hot and burns were not uncommon. In five months he was looking for another job. He spent the next several years in New York, working in a shoe factory, a lamp factory, and a bicycle factory.

When he returned to Philadelphia in 1953, Don José was able to get manufacturing jobs. He considered these better jobs:

> The manufacturing jobs were better. Dishwasher, that's what you do. When you work in an industry, you start getting some experience in some other jobs. . . . Because when you work in a farm, it's just like you are, you are [at] the last resort. That's when you can do nothing else. . . . In manufacturing, one hundred percent better. Of course, it's better pay. They had the unions, you know, you'd be protected more. It's, you know, more benefits.

The jobs, however, were not ideal. First he worked at Fogel's Refrigeration for close to ten years with a lot of other Puerto Ricans, mostly men. He described the working conditions: "Very poor, very bad. We were working with insulation, you know that fiberglass stuff and all that crap and asbestos and—very poor. And the money wasn't there, the money was peanuts. I think, I remember, I was making $45 or something like that. That was tough." Nor did he feel that this union protected the workers' interests. "And some of the unions, like when I worked in Fogel's, it's a union but the people that work with the union, the group of people supposed to be working with the employee, they together with the company owners. So you know, so you only pay the dues but you ain't got no protection really."

Don José searched continuously for better jobs. In 1966, he got what he considered his best job, with Boeing. Yet even here there were layoffs. "When I started my job, the first years, you always get laid off when the job is slow. I got laid off about five or six times. . . . But in those years, you could get a job everywhere. . . . Every time they give me layoff, I always found something. I never was in the house, sitting down waiting. No, I always found a new job." His temporary jobs included working at the federal reserve bank, another refrigeration factory, at a hospital, driving a SEPTA bus, and cleaning at the airport. For Don José, it was about meeting his financial responsibilities:

> See, when you have responsibilities—I put it this way—and you came to this country looking for a better living, but you have to get what you can get. They don't like to do no dishwashing jobs. . . . It's a big job today. But those years there was really nothing. So, that's why I said I worked in a couple of months in that place as a dishwasher, I mean, I was making my living, I don't care. But I had no intentions to stay there for the rest of my life.

Similarly, while he was working at Fogel's, he kept looking for a better job. "You don't make enough money in a job, you're gonna, you're gonna fail in your responsibility. So, so you have to keep on looking around. So, I was there working and then I put in an application in Boeing and they called me and so I went there." He considered leaving Fogel's a risk, and felt he had been lucky. "I was thinking, if I get out of here, to go to another place for another job, maybe they're gonna pay less, maybe I'm not going to find it. So you know, I stayed there for years and years. Some of the people that were working there, they're still there. Some of them already left, like me, I left. But I was lucky that I left and I got this job with Boeing." At Boeing, Don José was the only Puerto Rican working in his department.

Don Florencio, who came to Philadelphia from New York City in 1960, emphasized the availability of work and the role of social networks in getting jobs. He recalled: "That construction job, I got it through a friend of mine that saw I was here. So, he took me, he got me that job working in construction with him." It was a "good company," according to Don Florencio, "but they paid nothing! I was working, they paid $1.25 an hour at that time." From 1962 to 1968 he worked in a garment factory. "That job I got through a friend that I met that told me that he was the *foreman* in a factory and that I should go there, that he was going to take me." Not recalling what town his friend was from, Don Florencio explained, "Once you were Puerto Rican, we were almost like a family here. If you needed me, well, 'let's go there and I'll get you work.' It didn't matter what town you came from." When the friend that got him the job left, Don Florencio became the foreman and reciprocated. "I got a lot of people work there." With help from his friend and a *compadre*, he got his next job. "The same friend got me papers for the Merchant Marines, and a *compadre* of mine got me a contact, so I went and applied for the Merchant Marines. I went to sail, but I didn't have to sail for long." Discovering that he disliked being at sea, he lasted less than two months, while his friend and his *compadre* continued. Social networks were also important in getting his next job, in a metal factory. "I got the job because a *compadre* of mine that was working, well he told me that they were hiring in the factory and I took advantage." Then he helped others to get jobs: "I got a lot of people work, too, after I was working there, I brought many people to work. . . . The same *compadres* of mine. We were always helping each other out."[37]

Like Don José, Don Florencio had several different jobs before getting a "good" job in a metal factory. He described the garment factory where he worked with about one hundred workers, "Puerto Ricans, Americans and from everywhere." Women sewed the skirts by machine and finished the garments, while the men pleated the skirts: "We pressed it, secured it, put it in the place to get the *steam* . . . so it would get the form of the skirt. . . . It did a lot of damage to my eyesight, because when you opened the door a lot of smoke came out and it damaged your eyesight." He added, "There was a union but the union wasn't, at that time you didn't earn much either." He started at $1.25 an hour, and his pay did not increase while he was there; the only benefit they had was a health clinic, which he thought few used. In contrast, describing the metal factory where he made pipes and elbows of different sizes, Don Florencio remarked, "it was a good job. I was working with Americans, Italians. It was good, especially, the boss was really kind with the workers. I left that job because he decided to leave the factory, to close it, because he wasn't in any condition to work. He was already very old." Initially he earned "very little," $1.50 an hour, but over time his wages increased to $8.00, and it was steady work. He contrasted the union at this factory with the other: "In this place, the union pretty much backed up the worker. The other union, the other company that had a union, since the older representatives had already died and all, the representatives got involved with the company. The worker didn't have the backing of the union." When the metal factory closed, he found a similar job, where he stayed until he retired. He reminisced: "It was easy, it was easy because everyone—there was work for those that wanted to work, yeah, there was work. So, me, I got work in the factory right away." Throughout, he found satisfaction and supplemented his income by playing music: "I liked it and I even earned a few bucks, too. I say a few bucks because it really didn't pay enough."

After working in a plastics factory and then being unemployed, Don Julio got a "good job," which he followed from New York to Philadelphia in 1965. He recalled, "I had a good job there on the Brooklyn naval base, it was a pretty good job. I liked it a lot. I don't complain about the United States." He was a painter, working on the ships that were built and repaired, including carriers, submarines, and destroyers. The job provided for the family, as Doña Nilda noted: "Well, thank God, we always, always had enough for food, to dress modestly, not to dress as millionaires but always we could wear something new, once in a while." He valued autonomy from his bosses: "They were good, yeah, since they worked in the office, we were below, we almost never saw them. . . . They taught us the work, we did the work, and they didn't bother us." When they closed the Brooklyn naval base, they gave the workers alternatives, as Doña Nilda recalled: "They gave us Philadelphia, Boston, and California. I told my husband that I wasn't going to California or to Boston either, that was too far. . . . And my mother already lived there [in New York], exactly, so we came, they gave us Philadelphia and that's how we lived in Philadelphia for sixteen years." According to Don Julio, it was a diverse work force with good relations—"I never had problems with anyone." Yet there were few Puerto Ricans:

> There weren't Puerto Ricans, in New York, in Brooklyn there were a few there, twenty or so Puerto Ricans. And then, this was the same one that gave *transfers* to Philadelphia. A lot did it, a lot went. But in neither of the places, there weren't many Puerto Ricans. There were many blacks, black people, many whites, Italians and others, but there weren't many Puerto Ricans.

He worked at the naval base until he left with a disability, and with "a lot of memories, a lot, a lot of good friends, good people."[38]

Others never got manufacturing jobs, working instead in the services or in construction. In contrast to his wife Doña Carmen's career in human services, Don Quintín had a series of jobs. After leaving agricultural work behind him and coming to the city, "He got work at Girard College helping to paint, and after that he came to the shoe factory. Later, he worked in a hospital, cleaning, and after that he worked at Concilio for many years—he was the one who took care of the building. After that he worked in a hospital, Temple Hospital, he worked there as an orderly." Perhaps not surprisingly, he considered returning to Puerto Rico. In San Lorenzo he had driven the town ambulance—a job with perhaps more autonomy and prestige than those he could get in Philadelphia.[39]

When Don Justino came to Philadelphia from the farms near Gettysburg, Pennsylvania, he found a construction job with the help of his *compadre*. Arrivng in Philadelphia during the winter months, he recounted: "He told me—I am a bit worried—so he told me that I would find work when the summer came. Well, we went one day, during the month of February, we went to the office where he worked, which was seventeen miles from Philadelphia, and with the Italians. We went to the office, then the boss told me that he would give me work when it came, they resumed [work] when summer came." While the bosses were Italian, the majority of workers were Puerto Rican. He worked during the summer of 1955, but when winter came, "they sent us to collect unemployment, and I didn't collect anything because I was thinking of coming to Puerto Rico. So I came." After six months in Puerto Rico, he came back to Philadelphia, this time planning to send for Ana Luisa and their four children. Don Justino remarked, "I went to look in construction because they gave me something right away." Although he had no trouble finding a job, the work was seasonal and physically demanding:

> In the winter we worked as long as you could, until we couldn't work anymore because of the cold, then they sent us to collect. . . . Imagine that what they gave, I think, was $35 for unemployment, but since things weren't too expensive, well we managed. . . . When winter passed and they saw that you could work in construction, well, they called us to work again.

They called a man that had a telephone—we didn't have one—so he would tell all of us that worked together and we returned.

The only benefit they had was unemployment. After eight years in construction, Don Justino worked at the Cathedral, cleaning and doing maintenance. It was year-round employment, he formed lasting friendships with the two men he worked with, both of whom were from Utuado, and he felt appreciated by the priest. Reflecting on his work life, he concluded, "I would say that they were more or less the same—the jobs. . . . I have always worked in hard jobs."[40]

Doña Gloria revealed that the men in her family found different kinds of jobs because some were easier to get than others and because informal networks worked for some jobs and not others. When Don Hipolito left agricultural work, he got a job at a sugar refinery, and kept it for thirty years. He tended the machines that ground the sugar. The work was in three shifts, and every two weeks his shift rotated—from 8:00 A.M. to 4:00 P.M., from 4:00 P.M. to midnight, and from midnight to 8:00 A.M. For Doña Gloria, this meant "I practically raised my kids, I would say that I raised my kids, almost always, I was alone. Or that all the time, he was working." They had eight children. His was a union job with benefits, and he got a month and a half of vacation, and before he retired he had two months vacation. He took his vacations during the summer and took his family to New Jersey and New York in their car. He was involved with the union and became the shop steward. By 1969, he was earning $12 an hour, and his salary continued to increase. They bought a house in Philadelphia, and later had a house built in San Lorenzo.[41]

As others arrived, Don Hipolito helped them find work. Yet informal networks had a limited impact for Puerto Rican men in securing quality manufacturing jobs. When his younger brother came to Philadelphia in the early 1950s, Don Hipolito was able to get him a job at the sugar refinery. As Doña Gloria explained, however, "where my husband worked, they couldn't get in, it wasn't easy. . . . It was the sugar refinery and there you couldn't get in easily. There you had to have a little, well, my husband had to go study." When Doña Gloria's cousins came to their home from the farms and her brothers started arriving directly from San Lorenzo, Don Hipolito helped them find work, but in construction, "because at that time, to get into construction, well there were a lot, a lot of Latinos in construction, working, the majority were Latinos. Because for a Latino to arrive in Philadelphia and enter a factory, it was very difficult." She described how they got their construction jobs:

> My husband got a job for Andrés . . . because the man that got Andrés a job, was a good friend of my husband. My husband spoke to him, he got him work. . . . Then when Andrés told him about Manolo, his brother, and told him that he was living in [my] house too, well the man found work for Manolo. Then, my brother Catalino arrived, and they hired him too, they hired him there. Cheo arrived, my brother, and he went there too. In other words, they all worked together.

In this case informal networks worked. Once Cheo was settled in his own household, he brought over the youngest brother, Alfredo. Cheo helped Alfredo find a job: "He was practically a boy, too new to start working in construction, so my brother got him a job

there. . . . In a factory that made dog food, because my brother knew a man [there]."
When Andrés brought over one of his younger brothers, he got him a job at the dog
food factory as well. At just twenty years of age, an industrial accident left him collecting Social Security. "The machine, I don't know, it cut off his hand, I don't know what,
something happened there, with the machine that he was working with that was to grind
the meat, and it caught him and took his arm." He returned to San Lorenzo. For Doña
Gloria, the difficulty of getting jobs like her husband's meant that Puerto Ricans were
found only in certain jobs: "Almost the majority, you went to construction and you
found Latinos. To the country, to the farms, you found Latinos. But to get into a factory, it was very difficult."

Indeed, Puerto Rican men were overrepresented as service workers and, to a lesser
extent, as operatives. In 1950, 37 percent of Puerto Rican men were service workers, in
contrast to just 9 percent of men citywide (Table 5.3). An even larger proportion of
African American men were service workers. Just over a third of Puerto Rican men were
operatives, compared to just under a third of men citywide. Four years later, fewer
Puerto Rican men were service workers and more were operatives—29 and 42 percent
respectively. More were also farmworkers—6 percent. A 1958 study described the jobs
available: "Puerto Rican men have found jobs in the construction business as pick-and-
shovel men, form setters, and carpenters' helpers; in hotel and restaurant kitchens (as
dishwashers, vegetable men, salad men, etc.); as pressers in laundries and dry cleaning
establishments; as packers and simple machine operators in light industry." Revealing
the low level of occupations even within particular areas, the study concluded, "few
have become waiters or even busboys. . . . nor have many found their way into the heavy
industry of the city or into skilled trades, despite their marked manual dexterity and
industriousness." The shift from service to manufacturing continued through 1970,
with more than half of Puerto Rican men working as operatives. As the city's manufacturing sector declined, both Puerto Rican and African American men assumed a
larger proportion of the remaining jobs. At the same time, the growth in service jobs
was mostly in the professional and related services, which employed few Puerto Ricans.
The impact of the city's shifting economy is discussed in Chapter 7.[42]

Migrants from San Lorenzo and Salinas occupied similar niches in the city's economy.
Of those marrying in the city, most were operatives, laborers, and service workers, with a
few continuing to rely on farm work (see Table A.2 in Appendix I). Salinas's men were
somewhat less likely to work as operatives or service workers than San Lorenzo's, and
slightly more likely to work as laborers or farmworkers. For migrants' fathers, it seems
those with jobs stayed in Puerto Rico. In contrast to migrants' mothers, fathers were more
likely to be working in Puerto Rico than in Philadelphia. In Philadelphia, fathers from San
Lorenzo were much more likely to work as operatives than those from Salinas, while
fathers from Salinas were more likely to be service workers and farm laborers (see Table
A.3 in Appendix I). Overall, fewer fathers were operatives. The difficulty of landing a good
manufacturing job was perhaps more pronounced for older men, who turned instead to
seasonal work in agriculture and in construction. Unlike Puerto Rican women, Puerto
Rican men were not concentrated in just one sector of the city's economy. As service

TABLE 5.3.   Male Occupations by Race, Philadelphia, 1950 and 1970

	1950			1970		
	Puerto Rican	Black	Total	Puerto Rican	Black	Total
Number Employed	90	80,732	552,711	4,363	125,263	449,802
Percent:						
Professional/Managerial	10.0	5.7	18.4	5.8	10.2	18.3
Sales/Clerical	6.7	9.0	17.3	14.7	21.6	29.2
Crafts	7.8	11.5	22.0	12.2	9.8	12.5
Service	36.7	49.0	9.1	14.6	24.5	14.8
Operatives/Laborers	35.5	22.7	31.9	51.8	33.4	24.9
Farm work	1.1	—	0.2	0.8	0.6	0.2
Not reported	2.2	2.0	1.2	—	—	—

Sources: See Table 5.1.

Note: For 1950, data are for the "nonwhite" population living in census tracts with 250 or more "nonwhite" persons. Most of the "nonwhite" population was African American, and these census tracts included 80,732 of 81,195 employed, "nonwhite" men. Not all columns total exactly 100 percent due to rounding.

workers, operatives, and laborers, however, Puerto Rican men were concentrated at the lower end of the city's economy. For both men and women, this concentration was more pronounced for migrants arriving after January 1951 than for earlier arrivals. The post-1951 migrants were more likely to work as operatives, laborers, and farmworkers and less likely than their predecessors to be professional, clerical, or sales workers.[43]

As opportunities for Puerto Rican men were limited, some continued to work in agriculture. While farmworkers under contract decreased, those day-hauled from the city to farms in the area increased. As early as 1949, a State Department of Labor and Industry employee "described how New Jersey farmers come to Philadelphia and pick up laborers at Franklin Square and at 13th and South Streets." Implying that this practice would continue, he noted that there were "legal ways of controlling this interstate traffic but they are complicated." Instead, in 1953 the Employment Service office in Philadelphia hired a "Puerto Rican Community leader in anticipation of an influx of resident Puerto Ricans in the near future." Their "recruiting program" used "radio, sound equipment, posters and other media to recruit seasonal labor during the harvest season." While the Mid-City Local Office referred 350 Puerto Ricans to work on nearby farms in 1954, by 1958 they referred 5,000 workers, mostly Puerto Rican. Doña Margarita and her husband were among those who lived in the city and worked on farms in the area. She recalled: "The worst of my jobs was when my children were growing, here, when we first got here with my husband. So, during the summer we took them to the farms to pick fruits, blueberries. We took them during the summer, to not leave them alone." The practice continued. In 1971, journalist Charles Thomson observed, "in the Philadelphia ghetto, meanwhile, the only work that separates many Puerto Ricans from unemployment is 'day-haul.'" Puerto Ricans boarded "ramshackle buses before dawn," rode to farms where they were paid for how much they picked, received wages that rarely exceeded $1.50 per hour, and returned to the city each night. In short, with opportunities limited, "the Puerto Rican finds himself trapped in the blueberry or tomato fields of southern New Jersey or bent over a steaming sink." Thomson made no mention of Puerto Rican women workers or their plight, but concluded, "for most Puerto Ricans in Philadelphia, the promised pot of gold proves empty indeed."[44]

Recreating Household Economies

Philadelphia's economy enabled Puerto Rican migrants to find work and recreate their household economies. Men and women worked, and young people sometimes found jobs as well. Women emphasized the continuities in contributing to their households, even as migration changed the contexts of those contributions. For women, recreating the household meant caring for their children in a very different environment, finding paid employment, and participating in informal economic activities. Some women focused on the work of raising their children and tending to household responsibilities, at least until their children were in school. For others, it was the classic "double day"; they retained primary responsibility for domestic duties even as they secured paid employment. In some instances women and men worked different shifts and took care of the children in shifts. These women's eldest daughters often helped them with household tasks and child care, much as they had helped their mothers in Puerto Rico. Despite limited options and low wages, some families managed to purchase homes in Philadelphia or in Puerto Rico. Yet for many, the low-wage, seasonal jobs available to them left their families in poverty, even with more than one person working.

Migration created new challenges for families, and the change from rural Puerto Rico to Philadelphia was significant. When she joined Don Justino in Philadelphia in 1956, Doña Ana Luisa was pregnant with their fifth child. She described the long, bumpy, loud, and frightening flight from Puerto Rico to New York City: "I went on that flight, eight hours, the kids were dying on me. I thought that the kids were going to die, they threw up, they got pale, everything from throwing up so much." Conditions improved. By 1960, Don Justino could get a direct flight to Philadelphia, the flight took three and a half hours, and the price had increased from $52 to $72. For Doña Ana Luisa, however, her first day in the city was no less trying than the flight:

> I found it very different, that we went to live on the third floor, and I had never climbed to the third floor, because in Puerto Rico, the houses always—now they have two stories—but before, at that time, they were only one story, except the houses of the rich in town and over in the metropolitan area. We arrived on Sunday. So the next day, he went to work and he didn't tell me that it got dark at 9:00 at night. And when I saw the sun at 7:00—and he didn't tell me that he was going to work overtime either—and it was 8:30 and still day, and I said, "What is happening?" The children got scared and me too because it didn't get dark and he didn't come home from work either. We spent the day there a bit uncomfortable, without knowing anybody, without being able to go downstairs, because we had gone to mass on Sunday, to the church, but we didn't know anything.

Moving to a first-floor apartment made her life a little easier and a little more familiar:

> Well, then we kept getting adjusted. . . . It wasn't good to have [the children] on the third
> floor and we moved to the first floor. Then we were calmer on the first floor because they
> could go out on the patio, on the third floor we didn't have a patio. We could sit on the
> patio, and I could put the clothes outside on the patio, we could sit on the stairs. I couldn't
> let them go downstairs alone. I have always been very strict with my children . . . because I
> didn't let them out of my sight for even a minute. I had to know where my children were 24
> hours a day.

While everyday tasks were easier in Philadelphia than in San Lorenzo, this ease was tempered by the challenge of adjusting to life in Philadelphia and by their growing family. Don Justino thought, "in terms of hard work, I would say that for her the work increased because the kids kept coming, but that there [in Philadelphia] it was easier to do things, because here [in Puerto Rico] she had to carry [water] from the river, [and] walk to town." For Doña Ana Luisa, "in Philadelphia, well, there I had water in the house, I could wash, I didn't have to go to the stream to wash. In that way the change was easier. It was easy but then you had to know English, you had to struggle with people who weren't the same as you, from the same culture. It was very difficult, the adjustment was very difficult."[45]

Doña Ana Luisa emphasized her responsibilities in caring for their ten children: "I have always worked more at home." She reflected on parenting: "That was our responsibility and I considered it more my responsibility than his because he left the house, sometimes at 5:30 in the morning and didn't come back until 9:00 at night, at least in the summer when he always worked extra. And the responsibility was mine, the responsibility that I had before society and before God." Working in construction, Don Justino had seasonal layoffs, and their resources were limited. He remarked, "so with what I earned. . . . It wasn't really enough but I told her better that you stay home, because the other alternative was worse. . . . I earned $75 a week, the week, six days. And from there I had to pay transportation, the rent." They paid $14 a week to rent a two bedroom apartment in the Spring Garden neighborhood. Doña Ana Luisa added, "it wasn't enough in the sense that, well there were hardships and things, limits, but we adjusted. We always told the children that right now the situation wasn't very good but that over the years things would get better." When one of their children got very sick, they had no health coverage. Referring to one of the Sisters at the Cathedral, Doña Ana Luisa explained:

> She always said to my husband, "Justino, why don't you ask so that welfare would give you
> a supplement." And Justino was very proud, he never wanted to, he never wanted to. When
> he came to accept help from welfare it was because Rosa Nilsa got very sick, with pneumo-
> nia, and because we didn't have insurance, our baby almost died. And then I told him, "For-
> get your pride, and I am going to go with the Sister to that office". . . . Because he didn't
> want it, but I went. Well, they gave $28, $28, but they gave me a card and they gave me,
> with that card, the children and I had the right to a health plan and thank God.

Their daughter recovered, but despite Don Justino's hard work, they were just getting by.

Doña Ana Luisa also contributed to the household by sewing their clothing, and by getting paid employment when the children were older. A Cuban woman who worked with the Cathedral taught her to sew:

> So she would come to the house and I learned to sew from her. First, I learned to sew by hand because I didn't have the money for a machine. I sewed . . . for the family. No, Justino never let me [sew] for other people because he didn't want anyone to make problems for me. But I sewed for the kids, I made his shirts and things, I made the wedding dresses for all of my daughters.

When their youngest child went to school, Doña Ana Luisa went back to school and got a job. She explained: "Well, I got tired of being alone in the house, I got bored, and then we talked, my husband and I. And I had a really good relationship with the nuns where the children went to school. So I went to talk with them." They told her about a training program for teachers' aides; she enrolled, and then worked as a teacher's aide at the Cathedral. For Doña Ana Luisa:

> It was a very good experience. While I was working at the Cathedral, I had always wanted to finish high school, and so I also registered at the institute at 19th and Girard, they had a GED course, high school equivalency, and I also went to school at night. I worked during the day and went and cooked—we cooked because they helped me. And he took me to school at night and came to get me.

She added: "The good thing about this job was that I left the house with the children and came home with them, because I never wanted to have a job where the children would be in the house alone and I would be out. He never permitted that, to work before the children went to school because of that, to supervise the children." Don Justino was also working at the Cathedral, and it was close enough to their home that they could walk.

In Puerto Rico Doña Ana Luisa and Don Justino had contributed to a household economy based on growing tobacco and food crops, and on his wage labor in sugar cane. She had primary responsibility in caring for their children, while he helped her carry water. She spent the evenings sewing tobacco. In Philadelphia, she continued to have primary responsibility for the children, while he worked first in construction and then in maintenance. She learned to sew and then found paid employment when their youngest child started school. Don Justino contrasted what he could earn in Puerto Rico with what he earned in construction in Philadelphia. While he was in Puerto Rico, "a man asked our *compadre*, 'look, how much does his brother make,' my brother. 'Well, he worked with me six days and I paid him $12.' And I said . . . $12 in a week and I make $12 in a day." In Philadelphia, Doña Ana Luisa recalled, "we were able to buy the house. We rented for more time than we owned, yeah, we rented more. When we bought it that was when I had already started to work. . . . The kids were in school, so I started to work and every *penny* that we could save, we saved it."

They borrowed $1,000 from Don Justino's sister, bought a house at 18th and North Streets from a man who was returning to Puerto Rico and gave them a good price, and then they fixed it up so that it was "very nice." They also bought a house in San Lorenzo, returning in 1973. Don Justino concluded: "Life in Puerto Rico and life in the United States were very different. It was better there [in Philadelphia] economically and it was easier there. We don't complain." Doña Ana Luisa agreed: "There were many, many trials, many, many very difficult moments, but there were also beautiful moments, precious moments that you wouldn't change for anything." Nevertheless, recalled Doña Ana Luisa, "I felt, outside of Puerto Rico, I felt alien, like something was missing."

For Don Julio and Doña Nilda, recreating their household economy in New York and then Philadelphia meant periods of relying on just Don Julio's wages, on welfare, and on both their incomes. Doña Nilda recalled: "There was a time when we got *welfare,* because we have to say it, we got *welfare.* He was without work and I wasn't working and we already had five children, six children. And then, well, after that, when he started working on the naval base, well everything stopped, the *welfare* stopped, everything stopped. And then, I could work too." Initially, they managed, as Doña Nilda noted, "with the little that he earned and with the little bit I worked." She described her household tasks: "It's easy because you, the minute they go to sleep, you can take advantage to do laundry, you can take advantage to mop. Look, I raised those five, six children until my baby died at eight months, and I did laundry, I ironed, I cooked, I did everything and the girls didn't complain about anything because when they wanted something, I left what I was doing and got it for them." Although she worked for brief periods in New York, making shoes and sewing on buttons, it was when they came to Philadelphia in 1965 that she was able to work steadily: "There were times when we had shifts where he was already home and I went to work. Well, then, I didn't work any more until I came to Philadelphia. Because when I came to Philadelphia the littlest one was already pretty big, and well, I got her things ready the day before, she got herself dressed for school and so there, I had my opportunity to work." Like Doña Ana Luisa, she found paid employment primarily when her children were older. Her eldest daughters helped with the household tasks: "They made the rice for me, they had the beans for me, and they were getting the house ready. When I got home, I made the meat, I made the salad and at 5:00 or 5:30 we were already eating." Their household's economic well-being improved when Don Julio worked on the naval base and when she secured paid employment in Philadelphia. They bought their first house in the city, not having owned a house in Salinas or in New York, and in 1981 they returned to Salinas and to a home they had bought there.[46]

Doña Genara, on the other hand, worked outside the home when her children were young. She emphasized the challenges of balancing raising five children with paid employment: "I worked outside and I worked inside [the home]. Well, so I worked too much, but it was good because it didn't kill me!" For Doña Genara, the balance meant both trading off between paid employment and staying home, and balancing paid employment and household tasks during the periods when she worked outside the home:

I worked continuously. When I had the first, I looked for a *babysitter*. When I had the second, I worked 35 days after her birth. When I had the third, I returned to work. With the second I worked and with the third, too. I looked for a *babysitter* and I went to work. When I left work was when I had, when the fourth was born. Then I couldn't. It was too much for me. But when they went to school, I went back to work.

Initially, her niece, who was married and had a baby of her own, took care of her daughter in her home for $5 a week. Later, she found another Puerto Rican woman who cared for the children.[47]

Although she and her husband had paid employment, the household tasks remained hers: "We took care of, I took more care of the children, because, I don't know, he had to sleep. . . . I did everything. I cooked, did the laundry, ironed, and worked outside [the home]." After their third child was born in 1963, Doña Genara was working in a factory making boy's clothing, and her husband was working in a bread factory on the night shift. She described their daily routine:

So my husband worked at night, and he took the children when he came home from work in the morning, he took them to be looked after. And when I came, he went to get me, and then since he worked at night, we went to get the children, brought them home, and I cooked, did laundry, ironed, did everything. . . . A lot of work. But I'm already seventy-one years old and look at me here. Work doesn't kill. . . . I worked, hard. I think that it was good to work.

Nonetheless, when their fourth child was born in 1966 and another followed in 1968, Doña Genara considered it "too much" and stayed home until the youngest went to school. Even for Doña Genara there was a point where extensive household responsibilities made it impossible to work outside the home. For her it was after her fourth child was born. Similarly, she commented, "my sister never worked outside [the home]. She had eight children, she couldn't work outside." When she and her husband had marital problems and eventually separated, Doña Genara became the sole support for their five children, staying home until the youngest went to school and then getting another job in the garment industry. She explained how they survived:

[I did] everything and supported my five children, with what *welfare* gave me, supplemented, and the job. . . . The first thing I did was to teach my children to work, that they had to work. When I came home from work, when they were older, I gave them, I said to the oldest, "You are going to clean that part and prepare the meat [for dinner]" or whatever. I told the other, "You clean the second floor for me," and to the other, "You clean the bathroom." . . . They learned young and worked hard.

By the time she returned to the factory, her oldest children could and did help with household tasks.

Doña Juanita and her husband, David Rodríguez, balanced their employment and household responsibilities by working different shifts and by sharing the household responsibilities. "My husband and I had to fix it so that we could work, with the children and all of those things." He worked in a metal plating factory for many years.

"During that time, you made good money, and we bought our first house when [our first child] was only three months old." Meanwhile, she worked the evening shift at the donut factory:

> The children were already pretty big. Well, then I worked at night because my husband worked during the day. We also had a girl, who was very good, that came to the house. We were relatives and she took care of [the kids] until my husband arrived at about 5:00. She came at 3:00, I left at 3:00 and she stayed there, and [was] really good, really good. And well then, that way we worked our hours and we both worked and struggled and all of those things.

She felt that they "worked together a lot," and "when we talked about something, we agreed, it was decided. I was going to look for work and that was it, you know, and 'I am going to help you because the kids are already grown,' you know. It wasn't that we didn't miss each other, because we missed each other all the time, and I got frustrated a lot." Whereas paid employment for many women meant a burdensome double day, for Doña Juanita and her husband, "we had a system, my husband and I, after a time—when we got married was when he learned to cook—and if I got home first I started to cook, and if he got home first he started to cook. Well, it was a very good relationship."

As times were hard and unskilled jobs were available, young people also contributed to their household economies, with their own jobs or by working in family-owned bodegas. One son explained: "My first job was in a place called 'Premier Food Market,' it was an American grocery and they paid me $4 for the week. The owner of the store gave me groceries to take home on Fridays and Saturdays . . . rice, beans, potatoes, things he knew he wasn't going to sell." Another recalled, "when I was very young I worked selling *Inquirers* at the corner and little jobs, odds and ends. Every little penny I would give to my mother because we had very little." *Bodegas,* small grocery stores selling Puerto Rican and other products, were based primarily on household labor, including men, women, and children. Most were "owned and operated usually by a husband and wife," and sometimes children helped after school. As the Puerto Rican community grew, so did the number of bodegas. Domingo Martínez opened the first one in 1948; by 1953 there were twenty-two, and by 1960 there were about eighty. Don Domingo had become the wholesaler supplying the bodegas. Other small businesses catering to the Puerto Rican community emerged as well, including restaurants, newsstands, and barber shops. Don Domingo and his wife Esther opened a travel agency serving the Puerto Rican community. They started out helping farmworkers return to Puerto Rico, and had five branch offices by 1971.[48]

After years of working in manufacturing, Doña Juanita and her husband became bodega owners. Don David had been laid off after twenty-five years in the metal industry. He had always wanted to have a small business, and as Doña Juanita explained, "he wasn't the kind of man to stay at home." She added, "my husband was already fifty years old. So when there are people already thinking that they are going to retire, my husband was thinking about working more." She was still working at the jewelry factory and he was collecting unemployment. "I kept telling him not to worry, that soon something good would turn up. Then, one day, very close to my house, there was a small business that was like a house. It was like what we Puerto Ricans call a bodega." Yet there were obstacles, and when they went to inquire, "[the owner] didn't seem very interested in us or that there would be in the neighborhood a bodega with Puerto Ricans. Because in reality, they were all Americans, very few Puerto Ricans." When the owner failed to get back to them, a friend of hers suggested they contact the Spanish Merchants' Association. With the help of the Spanish Merchants' Association and of her cousin who worked for the city in licenses and inspections, they were able to get a loan and purchase the business.[49]

Doña Juanita left her job at the jewelry factory to work in their bodega. Initially, they were open seven days a week, from 7:00 A.M. to 7:00 P.M., but after about two years they started closing at 2:00 on Sunday. They were the only store in the neighborhood with extended hours, and Doña Juanita recalled that before they opened there was nowhere in the neighborhood to buy milk after 5:00. Although they carried products of special interest to Latinos, this was a small part of their business; they sold mostly milk, bread, lunch meat, and other necessities, "and everyone came." But not everyone came without comment. Doña Juanita noted that one day a woman she had known for a long time came into the store and told her, "I tell all of my neighbors that they can buy here because you are very clean." Doña Juanita explained, "for me, that was no compliment." Another woman assumed that they did not own their store. Doña Juanita recounted the story: "She said to me, 'Imagine if the building was yours, you wouldn't have to pay rent and it would be much better.' Imagine, everything they assumed, you know, well I didn't respond to her, because, yes, the building was mine, but I didn't have to tell her that. . . . There wasn't much of it, but they were rude, you know."

While it was hard work, it helped Don David and Doña Juanita to achieve their goals. Doing most of the work themselves, she recalled, "we had, well, a lot of work, a lot of work." She made sandwiches for people who worked for a nearby trucking company. "It was tremendous, I made *hoagies,* all kinds of *sandwiches* and sometimes the store filled up and I didn't have enough supplies." She added, "I cleaned and I cleaned two houses, I cleaned my house and I cleaned the store." Their children helped a little bit at the beginning, and some of the neighborhood boys did odd cleaning jobs after school for $3. Financially they were better off. "It was very good to us for a long time, not for getting rich or anything like that, but for sending my children to school and to live a little better." She considered it a blessing because of the opportunities it provided for their children. "That same year, [my daughter] was already getting ready to go to college and we saw everything as a blessing, you know, a blessing from God and I thanked God every night because I knew that my children were going to be able to study."

Most Puerto Ricans, however, had become concentrated in the lower levels of the city's economy. For many migrants, wages were low, benefits were rare, and jobs were seasonal. As a result, many Puerto Ricans found themselves poor, even when they had jobs. In 1954, 69 percent of Puerto Ricans were employed, about a fifth were looking for work, and only 1 percent were on relief, according to the Commission on Human Relations' study. More than half of those not working cited "seasonal cutdowns" as the reason; women also cited their need to care for children. Three quarters of those employed worked between 40 and 43 hours a week and only 3 percent worked less than 40 hours. Yet Puerto Ricans earned less than their neighbors. For Puerto Rican men, the median take-home pay was $57 per week, compared to $61 for their neighbors. The gap for women was more pronounced: Puerto Rican women took home $37 and their female neighbors took home $56. Similarly, in December 1953, the average salary for production workers was $74.68. Union representatives estimated that 900 Puerto Rican men averaged $47 per week in the restaurant and hotel trades and $60 in other industries. Not surprisingly, the largest proportion of Puerto Ricans surveyed, 38 percent, identified their major problems as economic, including seasonal work, unemployment, and low pay.[50]

Even with women working, Puerto Rican households remained poorer than others. Puerto Rican women were as likely to work as their counterparts citywide. In 1960, 36 percent of Puerto Rican women were in the labor force, compared to 37 percent of white and 47 percent of African American women. These working Puerto Rican women were more likely than their counterparts to be married with their husband present and to have young children. Sixty-two percent of the Puerto Rican women were working "wives," compared to 43 and 41 percent of white and African American women, respectively. Likewise, more than a third of these working Puerto Rican women had children under six years of age, compared to 13 and 25 percent of white and African American women, respectively. Nonetheless, Puerto Ricans remained poor, with a median family income of $3,435, as compared to $6,269 for white and $4,248 for African American households. Only 8 percent of Puerto Rican households earned $7,000 or more, in contrast to 41 percent of white and 18 percent of African American households.[51]

Though some managed to purchase homes, most Puerto Ricans remained in overcrowded apartments. In 1954, 78 percent of the 209 Puerto Rican households surveyed were overcrowded, with more than one person per room, in contrast to 22 percent of the non-Puerto Ricans in the same neighborhoods. While most Puerto Rican households had their own kitchens, almost a third shared communal bathrooms. More than half of the Puerto Rican households had moved in the previous year, and the Commission on Human Relations concluded, "this mobility is partly attributable to the low quality of the housing generally open to Puerto Ricans in the dilapidated center of the city." In 1960 Puerto Ricans' homes were still more overcrowded and more dilapidated than others in the city. Meanwhile, in the "City of Homes," only 18 percent of Puerto Ricans owned their homes, in contrast to 68 percent of whites and 43 percent of African Americans.[52]

As labor migrants, Puerto Ricans filled specific gaps in the city's economy. The city's jobs were segmented by race and gender, and in the postwar era those available to Puerto Ricans were in manufacturing, and for men, in the service industries too. Informal networks then functioned to funnel even more Puerto Rican workers into those areas of the economy where jobs were readily available to Puerto Ricans. Puerto Rican migrants, furthermore, did not reflect the full spectrum of Puerto Rican society, but only that portion that had been displaced and recruited. Reflecting their rural origins and the farm labor program, migrants' backgrounds contributed to their concentration in particular jobs. Despite working hard and having more than one wage earner, Puerto Rican families in the city were poor. Jobs were available, but in manufacturing jobs, especially in light industries producing nondurable goods, workers faced seasonality, high turnover, and underemployment. Men in service jobs and in construction did not fare much better. Worse yet, even these jobs were about to disappear or deteriorate, as the city neared an era of fundamental economic restructuring. Hence, in addition to low incomes and poor housing conditions, Puerto Ricans' concentration in certain sectors of the city's economy and in certain occupations meant that subsequent shifts in the economy would have a major impact on their employment status and economic well-being.

Conclusion

Puerto Ricans continued coming to the region and the city as labor migrants. In 1963 the *Bulletin* emphasized the continued importance of migrant laborers to the region's economy: "Migrant Worker Army 'Invades' South Jersey to Keep Crops Moving from Fields to Markets." Seasonal farmworkers were brought in with contracts from Puerto Rico and the British West Indies, without contracts from Florida and the southern states, and locally from Camden and Philadelphia. Many of the local workers were Puerto Rican. "It is an invasion," the article commented, "an invasion that happens every day, welcomed by South Jersey farmers with open arms." The "invaders" were credited with saving the crops, by taking jobs others did not want because of "hard work and low wages." While the "invasion" to the farms was welcomed, the settlement of Puerto Ricans in Philadelphia was perceived as a less welcome "invasion." Even as they were recruited to the area as laborers and incorporated into the city's economy as low-wage workers, Puerto Rican migrants were not always welcomed as community members.[53]

This central paradox of labor migration was illustrated in 1957 in the *Bulletin*'s description of Edward R. Murrow's "See It Now" episode on "the influx of Puerto Ricans to this country . . . another explosive subject." Although the "situation" was "less acute" in Philadelphia than the "grave problems" in other cities, the reporter considered it a "universal" and "ages-old problem." He explained: "A host of outsiders descend on a city. They are poverty-stricken, and foreign (not necessarily alien but strange). . . . At best they are not liked by the residents of their new city. At worst they are hated and feared." He was sympathetic to an "obviously decent woman" who "with the utmost reluctance" admitted "that she didn't want Puerto Ricans as her next-door neighbors; they were noisy, unclean and—much as she hated to say it—dangerous." The reporter was concerned: "From bigots, you expect this sort of talk, but when decent people get to feeling this way . . . then you have a problem indeed." The reporter nonetheless acknowledged the contributions of Puerto Rican workers. Murrow noted that "the people who talk about sending them back don't realize that if it were not for the Puerto Rican jobholders parts of our economy would be paralyzed." There were, after all, jobs that "no one but the Puerto Ricans will take," especially seasonal farm work. The reporter added, "on the credit side of the ledger was the stout defense of the Puerto Ricans by a couple of employers in the hotel and garment industry, who declared that Puerto Ricans are very good and reliable employees." While Puerto Ricans were at the very least "not liked by the residents of their new city," social service workers and policy makers shared the reporter's sense of Puerto Ricans as "outsiders" and as "foreign" and "strange." They too defined the "problem" not as racism or the attitudes of "decent people," but rather as inherent in Puerto Ricans and their culture.[54]

Row houses line Spring Garden Street, October 29, 1959. Though Philadelphia's row houses were sometimes converted into cramped apartments, they also provided some Puerto Ricans with an opportunity for home ownership. (Photo by Pasquarella, *Philadelphia Bulletin*. Source: Urban Archives, Temple University, Philadelphia, Pennsylvania.)

Justino and Ana Luisa Navarro, from San Lorenzo, lived in a three-story row house that had been converted into six apartments, when they settled in the Spring Garden area in 1956. A two-bedroom apartment, their home was the site for their *entronización*. The "Consecration of the Family to the Sacred Heart," signed by them and dated March 9, 1958, hangs on the wall and reads in part, "We consecrate to Thee, O Jesus of Love, the trials and joys and all the happiness of our family life, and we beseech Thee to pour out Thy best blessings on all its members." With Justino and Ana Luisa are the first six of their ten children, Justino's brother, and Justino's nephew. (Courtesy of Justino and Ana Luisa Navarro.)

The Navarros purchased a three-story row house at 1819 North Street, and their youngest daughter, Lydia, is sitting on top of their car in front of their house, ca. 1968. (Courtesy of Justino and Ana Luisa Navarro.)

Gloria Roldán from San Lorenzo and Hipolito Amaro from Salinas are in their first rented apartment. Gloria is pregnant with their first child, ca. 1958. (Courtesy of Gloria Roldán Amaro.)

Gloria and Hipolito purchased this row house at 2230 North 4th Street around 1962. Here the first seven of their eight children pose for a Christmas portrait, with the couple's wedding picture on the wall behind them, ca. 1967. (Courtesy of Gloria Roldán Amaro.)

On July 25, 1953, just a couple of days after street fighting in Spring Garden ended, the first Puerto Rican Day was celebrated. In this formal representation of the Puerto Rican community Joseph Monserrat of the Migration Division; F. J. Perez Almiroty, representing Governor Muñoz Marín; and Dr. José DeCelis, chairman of the Day's Sponsoring Committee are pictured giving the Puerto Rican flag to Councilman-at-Large Victor Blanc, who represented Mayor Clark. (Photo by Culross, *Philadelphia Inquirer*. Source: Urban Archives, Temple University, Philadelphia, Pennsylvania.)

Playing music was part of Florencio Sánchez's reason for coming to Philadelphia in 1960. Music was a source of supplemental income and a social outlet, as he played in the Puerto Rican Day Parade, and local clubs. Local bars, a site of conflict in neighborhoods undergoing racial change, were also part of the early Puerto Rican community. Florencio, second from the right, is with Sensación Ocheinta y Cuatro at La Preciosa Lounge, 2111–15 Germantown Avenue, January 25, 1985. (Photo by Ina Rothman. Source: Ina Rothman Collection, Balch Institute for Ethnic Studies Library, Philadelphia.)

For many, community remained a home-centered affair. Nilda and Julio Quiñones are dancing in their neighbors' home on North 7th Street, where Nilda and Julio owned a two-story row house. It is a baptism celebration for their neighbors' child, ca. 1967. (Courtesy of Nilda Sánchez Quiñones.)

At the same celebration, Nilda enjoys some food with four of her five daughters and friends, ca. 1967. (Courtesy of Nilda Sánchez Quiñones.)

Reflecting economic conditions for Puerto Ricans, these Young Lords posters are on abandoned housing, 1400 North 7th Street, May 15, 1971. The Young Lords' demands for Health, Food, Housing, and Education are stated on guns on the poster at the far left. (Photo by Wasko, *Philadelphia Bulletin*. Source: Urban Archives, Temple University, Philadelphia, Pennsylvania.)

The Philadelphia Young Lords advocated grassroots, community-based services and independence for Puerto Rico. Here, at the age of nineteen, Young Lord Wilfredo "Hawkeye" Rojas is serving breakfast to children at the Lighthouse Settlement on Lehigh Avenue, January 26, 1971. (Photo by Gottlieb, *Philadelphia Bulletin.* Source: Urban Archives, Temple University, Philadelphia, Pennsylvania.)

Carmen Aponte, a lifelong advocate for Puerto Ricans and the Director of the Norris Square Senior Citizens' Center for two decades, is watching the Puerto Rican Day Parade from the Concilio de Organizaciones Hispanas float, September 30, 1973. (Photo by DiMarco, *Philadelphia Bulletin.* Source: Urban Archives, Temple University, Philadelphia, Pennsylvania.)

Singing, Philadelphia's Puerto Rican senior citizens march from their old center in the basement of a church to their new Norris Square Senior Citizens' Center in Kensington, December 19, 1983. (Photo by Gralish, *Philadelphia Inquirer*. Source: Urban Archives, Temple University, Philadelphia, Pennsylvania.)

Chapter Six

Formulating the "Culture of Poverty": Philadelphia's Response to Puerto Rican Migration

On the night of July 17, 1953, violence erupted in the Spring Garden neighborhood of Philadelphia between Puerto Ricans and their white neighbors. An incident at a bar on the corner of Mount Vernon and 16th Streets sparked the street fighting. Charles Brooks was stabbed by an unidentified assailant, presumably Puerto Rican. Philadelphia's Commission on Human Relations described the events that followed: "After an altercation in a local bar, a group of white men invaded the homes of two Puerto Rican families and a general melee broke out." The *Bulletin* reported that "shortly after midnight the police quelled disorder in a house on the north side of Mt. Vernon near 16th. A gang of about 15 men invaded the house and began beating the occupants." When police approached Harry Winters, identified by a woman as the man who had entered her home through a back window, Winters "began punching, and kicked out a patrol car window," and "the general free-for-all in the street began." Rioters used knives and hurled bricks and bottles. "Into it, swinging their clubs, waded the police reinforcements," who considered using tear gas but decided against it. The *Philadelphia Inquirer* considered the riot "the worst in recent years here." The fighting continued for two hours, stretched across two blocks, and involved anywhere from three hundred to a thousand people, with forty to seventy-five police responding. Additional fights broke out later that night and early the next morning. Three policemen and four "young men" were injured, and fifteen people were arrested. During the week, there were four more nights of fighting in a five-block area.[1]

The street fighting revealed the tensions surrounding Puerto Rican settlement and forced the city's policy makers and social service agencies to address the Puerto Rican migrants in their midst. Recruited to the area as laborers, Puerto Ricans, as U.S. citizens, could and did stay, finding apartments with the help of family and friends. The rioting reflected white residents' fears of racial change, racism against Puerto Ricans, and perceived competition for housing and jobs. White residents moved out and sometimes reacted with violence. Puerto Rican migrants, in turn, faced the racial hostility that came with racial change in northern urban areas in the postwar era. As they responded to the incident, policy makers and social service workers transformed the riots from a racial incident against Puerto Ricans into an indication of "the Puerto Rican problem." They defined the "problem" not as racism, but rather as Puerto Ricans and their culture. Social service workers and policy makers in Philadelphia interpreted Puerto Ricans through the emerging "culture of poverty" paradigm, a set of widely shared ideas that evolved into a racial ideology with significant gender dimensions.

Street Fighting in Spring Garden

Puerto Ricans settled in Philadelphia at a time of racial change. Within this larger context, neighbors, policy makers, and social service workers could perceive relatively small numbers of Puerto Ricans as an "invasion," a "threat," or a "problem." Puerto Ricans' in-migration was rapid and their settlement was concentrated in just a few Philadelphia neighborhoods (see Map 6.1).[2] Between 1950 and 1954 the Puerto Rican population grew from less than 2,000 to 7,300, with an estimated 2,600 migrants coming in 1953, the year of the street fighting. The violence occurred in the only area of Puerto Rican settlement that had not been significantly affected by African American migration during the 1940s. Here, in the Spring Garden neighborhood, also known as Mount Vernon, white neighbors responded to Puerto Rican settlement with violence.[3]

Puerto Rican migration occurred within the larger context of white emigration and African American in-migration. During the 1940s an estimated 92,000 whites left and 90,000 African American migrants made their way to the city. Philadelphia's population peaked in 1950 with 2,071,605 residents and then started to decline. During the 1950s, the white population decreased by 13 percent as another 340,000 whites left, while the African American population increased by 41 percent, as an additional 65,000 migrants arrived. The African American population increased from 18 to 23 percent of the total population between 1950 and 1960. As African American migrants settled in North Philadelphia, West Philadelphia and Germantown, there was a "pronounced increase in the concentration of non-white population." The proportion of African Americans living in areas where 80 percent or more of their neighbors were also African Americans increased from 27 to 58 percent between 1950 and 1960.[4]

Puerto Ricans settled in three areas of Philadelphia, north of the city center, and their concentration in these areas increased. By 1954, 65 percent of Puerto Ricans lived in these neighborhoods, and by 1960 that had increased to 85 percent. The Spring Garden neighborhood was the only area of Puerto Rican settlement that had remained predominantly white—83 percent in 1950 (see Table 6.1). In the other areas of Puerto

MAP 6.1.　Philadelphia's Puerto Rican Community, 1954

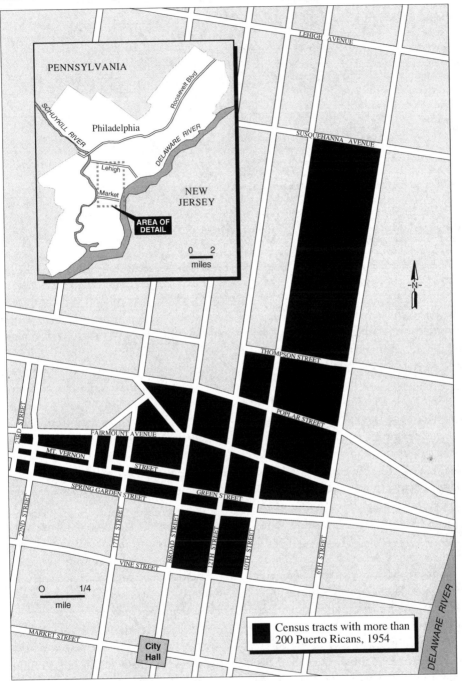

Sources: Philadelphia Commission on Human Relations, *Puerto Ricans in Philadelphia: A Study of Their Demographic Characteristics, Problems and Attitudes,* by Arthur Siegel, Harold Orlans, and Loyal Greer (April 1954; reprint, New York: Arno Press, 1975), 16.

TABLE 6.1.   Racial and Ethnic Change, Spring Garden, 1950–1970

	1950	1960	1970
Total Population	16,737	15,472	12,017
% White	83.3	39.6	45.8
% of Color	16.7	60.4	54.2
Total Percent	100.0	100.0	100.0
% Native-born White	74.7	28.9	29.1
% Foreign-born White	8.6	10.7	16.7
% Black	15.2	34.0	31.1
% Puerto Rican	1.2	25.6	23.1
% Other	0.3	0.8	—

Sources: U.S. Bureau of the Census as compiled in Philadelphia Commission on Human Relations, *Puerto Ricans in Philadelphia: A Study of Their Demographic Characteristics, Problems and Attitudes* (April 1954; reprint, New York City: Arno Press, 1975), 134; U.S. Bureau of the Census, *Census of the Population: 1950,* vol. 3, *Census Tract Statistics,* pt. 42, Philadelphia (Washington, D.C., 1952), 10; U.S. Bureau of the Census, *Census of Population and Housing: 1960, Census Tracts,* Philadelphia, PA–NJ (Washington, D.C., 1962), 26; and U.S. Bureau of the Census, *Census of the Population and Housing: 1970, Census Tracts,* Philadelphia, PA–NJ SMSA (Washington, D.C., 1972), P-139.
Note: Data are for census tract 15A in 1950, tracts 15A and 15E in 1960, and tracts 133 and 134 in 1970. "Of color" includes Puerto Rican, African American, and the census category "other races." For 1950, the Puerto Rican population is based on an estimate of 199 Puerto Ricans living in the census tract.

Rican settlement, 29 and 53 percent of the populations were white. Spring Garden was not an area of settlement for southern African American migrants. African Americans living in the neighborhood were relatively established: 15 percent owned their homes, nearly 80 percent had lived in the same house in 1949, and newcomers came from within the city, not from out of state. During the 1950s, however, racial change came to Spring Garden. The Puerto Rican population grew from 1 to 26 percent of the population, more rapidly than in the other areas of settlement. At the same time, the African American population more than doubled, to 34 percent, and the immigrant population increased slightly to 11 percent, with Irish accounting for 26 percent of the foreign-born population. Native-born whites, on the other hand, plummeted from 75 to 29 percent of the population in the neighborhood.[5]

The incident at the local bar on Mount Vernon Street sparked tensions that stemmed from this racial change. One newspaper explained the cause of the disturbances by paraphrasing Detective Albert Myers: "There has been long-standing dissension between residents of the south side of Mt. Vernon St. and those living on the north side. The tension has spread along Green, Wallace and Mt. Vernon sts., between 15th and 19th sts." Philadelphia's major newspapers did not cover these as explicitly "racial" incidents. Settlement patterns were alluded to only by mentioning the boundary, Mount Vernon Street, and by contrasting the "residents" on one side to "those living" on the other side. Puerto Ricans were "those" who had moved into the area north of Mount Vernon Street. Journalists assumed that Philadelphians were aware of Puerto Ricans' settlement patterns and of the nature of the "long-standing dissension." They did, however, list those arrested by names and addresses. In the week-long reporting, only one article explicitly mentioned ethnicity: "A window on an American store on the corner was broken, but no one seemed to know how it happened." The use of the term "American" implied that Puerto Ricans were not Americans and that Puerto Ricans were responsible for the vandalism.[6]

Beyond revenge for the incident at the bar, the riots became a battle over public terrain, first a community bar and then the neighborhood's streets. Most of the clashes during the week occurred along the contested line of Mount Vernon Street. On July 18, police broke up a crowd of fifty people at the corner of 16th and Mount Vernon streets. Three police were injured and four more people were arrested. After two days of apparent calm, perhaps the result of thunderstorms, two additional clashes occurred on Tuesday night, July 21, on Green Street near 21st. The first incident involved two groups of five men each, and resulted in one person being arrested. The second involved about thirty people, throwing bottles and stones. Three people were arrested, including a sixteen-year-old, who was the only female and the only minor arrested. During the first night of rioting, however, "a number of women were believed to have entered the fray." Additional "arguments" were broken up between Mount Vernon and Wood streets from 2 to 4 A.M. The next night, a fight between two men drew a crowd of 250 people at 18th and Wallace. Two police officers were injured as they arrested one of the fight participants, while the other escaped into the crowd. The following night seven more were arrested in several fights along Mount Vernon street, near 18th. For the white rioters, revenge provided the impetus for "protecting" the neighborhood. During one hearing, a prosecutor asked the defendant if he knew Brooks, the stabbing victim. Although the answer was not permitted by the judge, the prosecutor considered revenge a motive. The defendant's friend, however, described their conversation: "He just said the spiks were getting in there . . . getting in the neighborhood." When asked if that was what caused the riots, he simply replied, "Yes."[7]

The police, prosecutors, and judges viewed white youth as the instigators. Of the thirty-five people arrested, only five were Puerto Rican. These Puerto Ricans were arrested on the first night and three lived at the same address, perhaps one of the "invaded" homes. On subsequent nights, only white rioters were arrested, and almost half lived outside the immediate neighborhood. Identified as "one of the instigators of the fight last Saturday morning," one rioter was arrested for a second time because "he had been warned to stay out of the neighborhood." Another had a reputation as a "neighborhood troublemaker and tough guy," even though he had no Philadelphia address. Testimony in one case centered on whether or not the defendant had a legitimate reason for being in the neighborhood. In another the judge, sentencing the defendant to two years probation for carrying a switchblade, warned, "that means you have to behave yourself and keep out of that neighborhood, and keep away from trouble when it's brewing." When he was reminded that the defendant "lives there," the judge corrected himself: "Well, he has to keep away from those companions."[8]

Yet arrests were made more to stem the violence than to punish the perpetrators. Eight police had been injured during the week, some by punches or kicks and others by hurled bricks or stones. In court, one officer justified an arrest: "There was a bunch of fellows and that is why we grabbed him." He saw the suspect "drop something and kick it with his foot." In searching the area, he found three penknives and a blackjack. Another officer explained the circumstances surrounding an arrest: "They were just standing on the corner . . . he and about ten others . . . I went over and told them to move off the corner . . . the rest of them seemed to go, but he seemed a little lax in moving; so I went over and placed him under arrest." The officer searched him and found a switchblade in his pocket. For the most part judges did not admit testimony on the atmosphere surrounding the riots, and all charges of inciting to riot and disorderly conduct were dismissed. The only two convictions were for carrying a concealed weapon and for resisting arrest. The seven arrested on the night of July 23 were not indicted.[9]

In the aftermath of the violence, the city's Commission on Human Relations conducted its first study of Puerto Ricans and their neighbors. Their findings revealed that white neighbors shared some of the rioters' attitudes. Most neighbors defined Puerto Ricans as "outsiders" and did not want them as neighbors. Three-quarters of all respondents thought that Puerto Ricans were "different," which "to almost all of the respondents meant some unfavorable characteristic." Less than half of the respondents knew that Puerto Ricans were citizens of the United States. Using a biracial system of classification, the study also asked if Puerto Ricans were "white or colored." About one third responded that they were "colored" and another third that they were "some white and some colored." Seven percent thought that Puerto Ricans "have their own color," were "mixed" or "in between," and 7 percent considered Puerto Ricans "white." The remaining 25 percent either did not know or did not respond. When asked, "do you think that Americans willingly admit Puerto Ricans to their streets as neighbors?" 78 percent of the Spring Garden neighbors responded that "Americans" did not. Similarly, when asked, "do you think that Americans would like to exclude Puerto Ricans from this country?" 61 percent thought that "Americans" would like to exclude Puerto Ricans from "this country." The study concluded: "All neighbors seemed to indicate some prejudice against Puerto Ricans. The greatest prejudice was indicated by the neighbors in the core area . . . where, in July, 1953, there had been an outbreak of violence between Puerto Ricans and other residents of the area." This finding of "some prejudice" understated the fact that the majority of those surveyed did not want Puerto Ricans as neighbors and wanted to exclude Puerto Ricans from "this country."[10]

As Puerto Ricans settled in areas where housing was overcrowded, "deteriorated," and mostly rented apartments, they were blamed for the poor conditions found in those areas. Puerto Ricans' neighbors thought the neighborhood was not as clean as it had been, tensions had increased, white families were moving away, and the area was more crowded than it had been before the Puerto Ricans came. In the Spring Garden area, overcrowding, residential mobility, and the disparity in housing conditions may have created the perception of competition for decent housing. The percentage of residents who owned their homes there was half the city-wide average (see Table 6.2). More than 20 percent of all homes were overcrowded compared to less than 10 percent citywide. With half of all homes classified as "deteriorated" or "dilapidated," almost twice as many African American homes were deteriorated compared to white homes. Household incomes were also lower than the city's average, and the area was more transient, with more residents having moved during the preceding year. Puerto Ricans may have searched constantly for housing, as 78 percent of their homes were overcrowded, with more than one person per room in 1954. White residents may have felt displaced, but few Puerto Ricans were purchasing homes: only 7 percent of Puerto Rican housing was owner-occupied, compared to 12 percent for African Americans and 16 percent for the area in 1960.[11]

Some may also have perceived competition for jobs, as white men's position in the economy more closely resembled that of Puerto Rican and African American men in terms of unemployment rates and occupations than citywide. While 7 percent of men were unemployed city wide, 13 percent of the white men living in Spring Garden were unemployed—closer to the 16 and 20 percent of African American and Puerto Rican men, respectively. During the 1950s, white men's unemployment increased to 15 percent, and more worked in areas of Puerto Rican and African American concentration, as service workers and operatives. White women in the neighborhood, like their counterparts citywide, worked in different occupations than Puerto Rican and African American women, and their economic status remained fairly constant during the decade. Although neighbors were more willing to work with Puerto Ricans than to marry them or have them as friends or neighbors, more than a third of the neighbors thought that "Americans" did not want Puerto Ricans in their occupations.[12]

The men arrested during the rioting, most in their twenties, may have been the most affected by economic shifts in the neighborhood. They were unable to hire lawyers or pay fines. Unfortunately, detailed information is available for only one defendant. This

TABLE 6.2. Housing Conditions, Citywide and Spring Garden by Race, 1950 and 1960

	1950			1960			
	Citywide	Spring Garden Total	Spring Garden Black	Citywide	Spring Garden Total	Spring Garden Black	Spring Garden Puerto Rican
Occupied Units	584,698	5,522	681	615,767	5,203	1,609	762
Percent:							
Owner occupied	56.1	15.8	14.7	61.9	14.7	12.2	6.6
Deteriorated	16.9	36.6	71.7	12.7	42.7	58.1	39.9
Overcrowded	9.8	22.1	23.0	7.3	24.5	29.0	56.4

Sources: U.S. Bureau of the Census, Census of the Population: 1950, vol. 3, Census Tract Statistics, pt. 42, Philadelphia (Washington, D.C., 1952), 154, 155, 218; and U.S. Bureau of the Census, Census of the Population and Housing: 1960, Census Tracts, Philadelphia, PA–NJ (Washington, D.C., 1962), 343, 348, 458, 477.
Note: Spring Garden data are for census tract 15A in 1950 and for tracts 15A and 15E in 1960. No comparable data are available for Puerto Ricans in 1950. "Overcrowded" is defined as 1.01 or more persons per room.

eighteen-year-old was charged with carrying a concealed deadly weapon, a switchblade. He testified that he used the knife at his new job, cutting boxes at a pinball place. Since he had been hired only five days before his arrest by a man who simply told him when to come back, this seemed an informal, part-time job. Previously, he had lived in West Philadelphia and worked as a welder. Just one month after receiving two years probation, he was back in court, charged and convicted of mugging a woman. After serving his minimum sentence of two months, he was released when the court determined that he was unable to pay the cost of prosecution or the one-cent fine.[13]

Puerto Ricans were blamed for deteriorating conditions in this low-income neighborhood. In her 1965 dissertation, anthropologist Joan Koss attributed the riot to the "displacement" of white ethnics and the resentment of "remnants of former groups" as "the presence of Puerto Ricans became synonymous with the increased lack of desirability of these neighborhoods as places in which to live." She also pointed to the role of gangs, describing the riots as "the culmination of a period of extreme intensity in inter-group rivalry, particularly promoted by a gang called the 'Green Street Counts,'" composed of youth of "chiefly Italian and Irish descent," and suggested that "incipient" Puerto Rican gangs responded to the challenge. The youth involved in gangs would have been the same cohort that was affected by economic changes and perhaps the most likely to take to the streets. Yet racial and economic change affected the entire neighborhood, and white neighbors shared many of the rioters' attitudes.[14]

As a result, Puerto Ricans confronted racial tensions as they looked for housing and as they made the city their home. Many limited their spheres of activity to home, work, and church, thereby avoiding the battles over public terrain. While they recalled confrontations with landlords, neighbors, and the police, they also emphasized positive aspects of neighborhood life, particularly the relative absence of crime and drugs. As the population continued to grow and as "urban renewal" pushed many Puerto Ricans out of the Spring Garden neighborhood and toward the north and east, Puerto Ricans repeatedly confronted the dilemmas associated with settlement.

When she arrived in Philadelphia with her four children in 1947, Doña Carmen had trouble finding a place to live:

> Housing was very scarce. There wasn't housing because it was all white, it was white, all of the streets white, the houses. They were white with blue eyes. They didn't want to rent houses to others. So, even me, I didn't get an apartment. I had to take a—a black woman had a house and she rented rooms—so she rented me a room. . . . "No, no, no, no, we don't want no children." It was not the children like they said, it was more the color.

She paid $7.00 a week for the room on Marshall Street, which was furnished with a large bed, a crib for her youngest child, a couch, a small table, and a kitchen with an old stove. She then found an apartment on 7th and Brown Streets, where she lived for many years. Other than the racial tensions and the poverty, Doña Carmen remembered her neighborhood in a positive light: "It was really nice in spite of the poverty. . . . It was good. You had the doors to your house open all the time, even at night. You sat on the steps and even slept in a chair on the steps and nothing happened to you. There was order, there was respect. The milkman came and left the milk at the door and the bread and nobody touched it." Nevertheless, she explained the street fighting in the Spring Garden area in 1953: "Well, we weren't accepted, we weren't accepted, and one can't—you had to fight for yours, I have rights too, to study, to work, to live, my children have rights to the school, to the recreation there is, why not?"[15]

When he arrived in the city in 1947, Don José, like Doña Carmen, had trouble finding a place to live. After staying in a hotel, he went in search of an apartment in the Spring Garden area:

> The people that used to got in the church, they all, some of them they already have apartments in the same neighborhood. . . . But when, I remember when I went there to look for apartments, they throw the door in my face. They didn't want no colored people, you know, my skin is dark. When I send my wife, because you know, [with] her white skin, she could talk with the people. . . . This is why we got an apartment.

They got an apartment at 16th and Mount Vernon Streets, and continued attending the church at 18th and Green Streets. In describing the neighborhood, Don José stressed who was and who was not in "the streets." He noted, "they used to be almost all white people, yeah, you could hardly see the colored guys in the street then." Referring to Puerto Ricans, he explained, "so, nobody stay in the corner, nobody walk in the street. Everybody, you inside your job, if you have a job, and inside your house, or in the church. That's the only three places you could be. And it was like that for, Jesus Christ, for about six or five years." Echoing Doña Carmen, he explained the 1953 street fighting: "Because the white people didn't want, they didn't like Puerto Ricans and so you know, Puerto Ricans always fight with the white people and that's what happened."[16]

Puerto Ricans, interviewed in the late 1970s by Taller Puertorriqueño, a cultural center in Philadelphia, recalled moving into the Spring Garden area in spite of discrimination. One migrant explained, "we saw signs on houses that said APARTMENT FOR RENT where it said whites only." When Puerto Ricans approached, they heard, "'You're Puerto Rican' and . . . 'Well sorry but we don't have any apartments.'" Once in the neighborhood, their problems persisted: "In 1952, when I came here, there were very few Hispanics. . . . We sat on the stairs in front of the house, like we did in Puerto Rico. The people on the second and third floors would throw water with soap on our backs." He continued: "I tried to get the American boys to get along well with the Puerto Ricans that lived in Spring Garden, which was the first Hispanic neighborhood in Philadelphia. There were many fights and the *Irish,* at this time, they lived in Mount Vernon. There was blood." In general, he found, "the Americans always controlled the area. . . . The Americans gave us the name *Spics.*" Tensions surrounding racially changing neighborhoods continued and involved not only youth, but people of all ages.[17]

Doña Ana Luisa remembered the Spring Garden area in the late 1950s as tranquil, despite racial tensions: "The whole world was really calm. I already told you, we slept with the doors open because the heat was awful, and we slept on the first floor." The area was changing. "There weren't many blacks in the Spring Garden area, you could count the black families," Doña Ana Luisa noted; Don Justino added, "there were whites and Puerto Ricans. . . . The Americans kept moving from that area." Staying out of public areas decreased the potential difficulties, as Don Justino suggested: "Thank God we never had trouble with anyone. We went from work to the house, and on Sundays we went to church and came home." Doña Ana Luisa added, "we didn't have the children in the street," but there were still challenges: "You had to deal with people who weren't from the same culture. It was very difficult. I am not better than anyone, but no one is better than me, and maybe others have had the luck of being born white with blue eyes. I didn't have that luck, and with money. But with what I have, well, I try to do the best that I can and that is what I taught my children." For Doña Ana Luisa, "Philadelphia was really nice, despite everything, despite the discrimination and even though we felt the prejudice. . . . Because in Philadelphia they discriminated because you were Hispanic, you were Puerto Rican, you were Latino, whatever."[18]

Nor did racial tensions affect only those settling in Spring Garden or only those arriving during the late 1940s and the 1950s. When the Quiñones came to the city in 1965 and lived first on North 4th and then on North 7th Streets, they too confronted racial attitudes and racial change. Doña Nilda explained: "We found a situation where you had to know where you were going to move, because they didn't want Puerto Ricans. . . . In certain parts of Philadelphia, like there in Kensington, they were all whites. . . . They didn't accept the Puerto Ricans." Initially, "there were almost all white Americans," according to Don Julio, and two African American families, but as Doña Nilda added, "then more Puerto Ricans started to arrive and the whites left, the blacks stayed." Reminiscent of Don Justino, Don Julio remarked of New York and Philadelphia, "it wasn't a problem in either of the two places. I pretty much went to work and came home, I didn't go out to drink or anything. I came home. . . . I didn't have any problems." Arriving in 1960 and living first at 11th and Green Streets and then at 7th and Girard, Don Florencio encountered racial tensions as well. "There was always discord between the races, because everywhere you go there is always discord between them, I don't know why." While he thought some tensions stemmed from youth, he held the parents responsible. "A lot of parents don't believe that their children do things wrong sometimes or don't respect their elders. That kid has to be scolded and sometimes the parents don't do it. They don't do it, when they come to see that the kid is lost, they can't control him, that's when the discord between families comes."[19]

In addition to landlords and neighbors, Puerto Ricans also confronted tensions with the police. As with their neighbors, Puerto Ricans clashed with police over the public territory of the streets. While difficulties with the police were perhaps most pronounced for youth, they affected the entire community. Doña Carmen thought that part of the problem stemmed from language barriers and found herself in court interpreting for those who ended up there:

The police were abusive, even today they are abusive, but at that time since we didn't know English, they were more abusive. One day, someone was standing on the corner and the police told him to move, and as he didn't understand, the police took his arm and ripped his shirt with the way they pulled him, and took him to court. I told the judge that the man didn't speak English, I showed the shirt to the judge and explained.

Another Puerto Rican reminisced about growing up in the Mount Vernon area:

A lot of times I was on the streets. I was 14–15 years old. The police would see us in the streets and arrest us. Then they would take us to the police station and hit us with a rubber hose. . . . Afterwards, we had to put a dollar in a basket that they had. There were times, listen, in one week they arrested me three times. That was three dollars that my brother had to pay.

When Puerto Rican nationalists attacked President Truman's residence in 1950, he feared the repercussions. "The Americans remembered this and they said 'You were the ones that tried to kill President Truman'. . . . We waited for a reaction from the police against us."[20]

Similarly, Don José recalled that confrontations with the police were part of the reason migrants limited their spheres of activity:

We used to go to that church all the time, that's why, because it wasn't too far. Because we didn't, we didn't leave the area because I remember, then, the policemen in Philadelphia, they were using red cars and you couldn't stay in the corners. . . . You don't have no chance to hang in the corner because the police come, they say they give you three minutes, and they come back. You might as well not be there, they put you in a car and bring you over. . . . And when they see the Puerto Ricans, they could hardly speak any English, or whatever, oh boy, they grab you by the shirt and put you inside the car and take you to the station for no reason and that's it. That was rough.

Don Justino revealed that problems with the police occurred even though he only went between work, home, and church:

I remember when I was working in construction, we went six in a truck to work. One afternoon, coming back from construction work, all these police made us stop and made us get down from the truck and put our hands like that—that probably we weren't workers. . . . The police abused like that sometimes at the beginning. Another day, coming from work, they did the same thing.

In their 1954 study, the Commission on Human Relations found that one-third of Puerto Ricans felt the police treated them worse than other Americans. Problems persisted between the police and the Puerto Rican community. Identifying "police mistreatment" as a problem in their 1962 study, the Migration Division recommended that the police department develop contacts with leaders of Puerto Rican organizations and make efforts to understand Puerto Ricans and their culture, and that the Police Advisory Board have Puerto Rican representation and work to expedite their review of complaints of police abuse.[21]

Puerto Ricans felt more welcomed in the city as workers than as neighbors, according to the Commission on Human Relations' 1954 study, which asked Puerto Ricans and their neighbors the same "social distance" questions. Fully 80 percent of Puerto Ricans thought that "Continental Americans willingly admit Puerto Ricans to employment in their occupations." In contrast, 48 percent of Puerto Ricans did not feel welcomed "to their clubs as personal friends," 38 percent did not feel welcomed "to their streets as neighbors," and 44 percent thought that "Continental Americans would like to exclude Puerto Ricans from this country." On all questions, however, the neighbors' responses were less welcoming than Puerto Ricans indicated. The largest gap concerned whether Puerto Ricans were willingly admitted to jobs—80 percent of Puerto Ricans thought so, but only 42 percent of their neighbors agreed. The study concluded, "it appears that there is a moderate amount of prejudice, as expressed by the degree of social distance, directed against Puerto Ricans by continental Americans, and that Puerto Ricans perceive the existence of such prejudice. However, the Puerto Rican seems to feel that there is less prejudice than their 'American' neighbors report exist." Puerto Ricans may have felt recruited by their employers, while their potential coworkers were less welcoming.[22]

Defining the "Puerto Rican Problem"

As they responded to the street fighting, policy makers and social service workers transformed the violence from a racially motivated reaction against Puerto Ricans into a manifestation of Puerto Ricans' "problems of adjustment." The Commission on Human Relations' study was a first step in this transformation. Sharing some of Puerto Ricans' neighbors' concerns about racial change, policy makers and social service workers dismissed whites' prejudice and defined the "problem" as Puerto Ricans' culture, their lack of assimilation, and their failure to make use of social services. They responded to the "problem" by forming committees of public and private agencies to explore Puerto Ricans' problems and to foster a solution, which they defined as Puerto Ricans' increased use of existing social service agencies and "assimilation." In Spring Garden, they also supported Puerto Ricans' neighbors in forming a civic association to "improve the neighborhood." This civic association revealed both neighbors' continuing desires to protect "their" neighborhood and social service workers' equating Puerto Ricans with community problems.

Staff at the local branch of the Young Women's Christian Association first identified Puerto Rican settlement as a "problem" in 1947, when a staff person wrote to the International Institute: "With all the problems that this Puerto Rican group will bring to us, it is good to know that we have a person with your experience to call on." The International Institute was founded as a component of the YWCA to work with the foreign-born. Initially, the Institute did not serve Puerto Ricans because they were U.S. citizens. They did "not get the lists from the Immigration and Naturalization Service" and did not receive United Fund monies, as "Puerto Ricans were technically eligible for all existing services." Instead they focused on relocation and translation services for Displaced Persons and continued their traditional Folk Fairs. Because of its location in the Spring Garden neighborhood, however, the Institute's staff became concerned about Puerto Ricans settling in the neighborhood and contacted the Migration Division and large farmers in New Jersey who used Puerto Rican labor.[23]

The city's study of Puerto Ricans and their neighbors, conducted in the aftermath of the street fights, was instrumental in transforming the riots from a racial incident against Puerto Ricans into an indication of Puerto Ricans' "problems." The riots confirmed their worst fears of a developing Puerto Rican "problem." Responsibility first fell to the Commission on Human Relations, a city agency charged with promoting "equal rights and equal opportunity for all people" and "cooperation, understanding and mutual respect among all citizens." Expressing concern over "the recent incidents and the accompanying publicity involving Puerto Ricans and the native white community," the Commission convened a meeting of representatives of interested city and private agencies and decided to conduct a study of Puerto Ricans and their neighbors. Sharing some of the neighbors' fears, the Commission conducted its study with the sense that an "unknown number of Spanish-speaking American citizens of Puerto Rican ancestry had appeared almost overnight on an unknown number of city streets" and considered the neighbors' "anxiety . . . about the possibility of future recurrence" of violence as "naturally aroused." The goal of their study was to determine the "principal needs and problems" of the Puerto Ricans and to develop "immediate and long-range programs to improve the situation and assist the peaceful integration into the community of the new immigrants." In these references to Puerto Ricans as "new immigrants," the emphasis had already shifted to Puerto Ricans' "problems of adjustment" and the solution had already been defined as "assimilation."[24]

The study reinforced neighbors' perceptions of Puerto Ricans as "other." In asking "do you think that Americans would like to exclude Puerto Ricans from this country?" the study supported the view of Puerto Ricans as foreigners. The use of the terms "American" and "this country" and references to Puerto Ricans as "immigrants" suggested that Puerto Ricans were something other than "Americans." While most neighbors considered Puerto Ricans "colored," the Commission, like the U.S. census, considered the majority of Puerto Ricans "white." In essence, white neighbors defined Puerto Ricans as "colored foreigners," while policy makers and social service workers defined Puerto Ricans as "white citizens." Yet both the Commission and the neighbors positioned Puerto Ricans as outsiders, and the study reaffirmed neighbors' stereotypes of Puerto Ricans by focusing on "the behavior of Puerto Ricans," their "social habits," their "language deficiency," and their "clannish" social interactions.[25]

The Commission also downplayed the neighbors' prejudice. While the majority of Spring Garden neighbors wanted to exclude Puerto Ricans from "this country," the study found only "some prejudice" and attributed it to a "lack of factual knowledge." Puerto Ricans' assessments of prejudice were dismissed. One Puerto Rican was quoted as saying: "Not all Americans hate Puerto Ricans; some are good." Trivializing this as how one migrant "charmingly perceived the situation," the study reminded readers that "'attitudes' towards a group are probably not formed as a result of contact with that group, but by contact with the prevalent attitude towards that group." In dismissing prejudice against Puerto Ricans, the Commission deemed Puerto Ricans' perception of prejudice against them as erroneous. Puerto Ricans' mistaken perception of prejudice then became one of Puerto Ricans' major problems, hindering their "social adjustment." The study concluded that the Puerto Rican migrant "perceives this Philadelphia milieu as somewhat distant and unfriendly" and that "it is difficult to adjust to a social world that is so perceived."[26]

Like the Commission, the *Inquirer* and the *Bulletin* emphasized Puerto Ricans' "problems" and dismissed whites' prejudice in their coverage of the study. The articles did not mention the riots or link the study to the riots, but rather stressed Puerto Ricans' "problems of adjustment," including the phrase in their titles. Noting that the study "indicated 'some prejudice' on the part of all of them . . . and little factual knowledge," one article questioned the finding of "some prejudice" by printing it in quotations. The article's use of the term "Philadelphians" excluded Puerto Ricans from the Philadelphia community, setting them apart as "outsiders." The most inflammatory article exclaimed, "Puerto Ricans Here Consider Philadelphians Unfriendly." This account continued: "The study concluded they find it difficult to adjust to life in the city because they believe Philadelphians are unfriendly and prejudiced against them." Whites' prejudice against Puerto Ricans had been dismissed, while Puerto Ricans' perception of prejudice was presented as an obstacle to their adjustment. An editorial revealed the shifting definition of the "Puerto Rican problem": "A number of American cities have lately become more or less acutely aware of a Puerto Rican problem. . . . Perhaps the biggest surprise is that Philadelphia now has only about 7,300 Puerto Ricans. This means that the problem, while not simple, is not at the moment of overwhelming consequence." Puerto Ricans "problems" no longer included or referred to the problems Puerto Ricans encountered, but rather to the "problems" Puerto Ricans caused the city.[27]

The *Philadelphia Independent*, an African American weekly, provided a striking contrast to Philadelphia's major white newspapers. The *Philadelphia Independent* linked the study to the riots, noting that "the Commission became actively interested in obtaining information about the size, location and characteristics of the Puerto Rican population following a clash between Puerto Ricans and other Philadelphians in the summer of 1953." Hence, the riots sparked the Commission's "active interest." This journalist did not dismiss prejudice against Puerto Ricans: "The Philadelphia Puerto Rican likes best the economic advantages of city life but voiced dislike of the discrimination here." The existence of discrimination in Philadelphia was neither quoted nor challenged. Indeed, the article expressed surprise that Puerto Ricans were unaware of the extent of prejudice against them, concluding, "an interesting point brought out by the interviews with the neighbors was that the neighbors are even more prejudiced against the Puerto Ricans than the Puerto Ricans think they are." Finally, this account included Puerto Ricans within the Philadelphia community by referring to "Puerto Ricans and other Philadelphians" and to "Philadelphia Puerto Ricans."[28]

As the riots were increasingly attributed to Puerto Ricans' "problems of adjustment," city and private agencies sought to increase Puerto Ricans' use of existing social services. The International Institute increased their work with Puerto Ricans. The Institute's Puerto Rican Planning Committee, formed in 1953 as a self-education and networking endeavor, worked with the Commission on Human Relations on its 1954 study. After the riots, the Planning Committee became the Committee on Puerto Rican Affairs under the auspices of the city's Health and Welfare Council. The Committee focused on Puerto Ricans' "problems," seeking "to acquaint . . . the community in general with the problems of Puerto Ricans" and "to consider any problems of the Puerto Rican community and refer them to the right place for solution." Their objective was "to facilitate the assimilation of Philadelphia's Puerto Rican population in the community [and] to acquaint them with the health and welfare resources available to them." These goals implied that existing services were adequate and that the "problem" was Puerto Ricans' failure to use available services.[29]

Policy makers and social service workers also assisted Puerto Ricans' neighbors in forming the Spring Garden Civic Association. The riots, referred to here as "the Puerto Rican incident," had "brought to the fore the necessity of community organization in this neighborhood." Elfriede Friese, director of community services at the Institute, noted that the Civic Association "grew out of the recommendations of our Puerto Rican Planning Committee and the Puerto Rican Study." She explained: "We all agreed that the problems of the Puerto Ricans cannot be isolated from the problems of the whole community in which they live." The International Institute, the city's Health and Welfare Council, the Commission on Human Relations, and the YWCA were instrumental in establishing the group. Agency representatives attended meetings of the Civic Association and both the Mid-City Branch of the YWCA and the Health and Welfare Council provided staff support.[30]

While focusing their efforts on preventing juvenile delinquency through increased recreation, the Civic Association drew its impetus from fears of racial change in the neighborhood. Those who joined the Association were the "many people concerned with our shifting neighborhoods." Beginning with "Dear Neighbor," a 1956 flier read, in part:

> Do you realize what it costs you in taxes, community services, and public safety to live in a neighborhood where nearly six out of 100 children are juvenile delinquents? Since the higher than average rate has existed from the time four story dwellings were converted to multi-family units, while the racial makeup of the population changed several times, the blame does not rest on white families, Puerto Ricans, or Negroes. The blame rests on poverty and bad associates.

Ostensibly the flier asserted that Puerto Ricans and "Negroes" were not to blame. Concerns with "public safety," the changing "racial makeup of the population," and the possibility that readers would link "poverty" and "bad associates" with Puerto Ricans and African Americans all indicated remnants of the attitudes and tensions surrounding the riot. Neighbors responded to the Spring Garden Civic Association's appeals with as many as thirty to forty people attending some meetings. A YWCA worker observed that "leadership stems from the concerns of a few people who are property owners in the community."[31]

Although identified as a "neighborhood project," the Spring Garden Civic Association failed to include the Puerto Rican community. Agencies nonetheless continued to support the Association. In 1956 the YWCA recommended that "no encouragement, however small, should be denied if possible to such a struggling group." Specifically, the worker suggested making the YWCA's recreational facilities available, cosponsoring a "teen age canteen," and assisting with the publicity for meetings and special events. Yet she also advocated a full-time worker for the area, noting that "feeling in this area is often high among the various racial groups of which there is a large Puerto Rican element." This social service worker linked the "Puerto Rican element" with racial tensions. The International Institute noted "some tension between the Spring Garden Civic Group which is mostly composed of Americans . . . and the planning committee whose President . . . is a Puerto Rican." When these two neighborhood groups merged in 1964, tensions persisted, as members of the planning committee were not incorporated into the Civic Association. By 1965, the Commission on Human Relations conceded "that the Spring Garden Community Association was not truly Puerto Rican."[32]

Concerned with racial change, most policy makers and social service workers remained focused on the potential "problems" Puerto Ricans might cause the city. Asking "Does Philadelphia Have a 'Puerto Rican Problem?'" a 1958 study answered ambivalently that "a 'Puerto Rican problem' has not yet arisen" but that "the situation could easily change for the worse." The study concluded that "Puerto Ricans have not been involved in a disproportionate amount of crime, delinquency, or other anti-social behavior" and that their participation in antisocial behavior "may indeed be less than that of the general population in the neighborhoods where the Puerto Ricans live." Nor were Puerto Ricans "a disproportionate burden upon either state or county public-assistance services and funds," as they came "with the firm intention of finding work—*not* to get on relief—and that they resort to public assistance only when they are out of a job." Nevertheless, "because of the currency of these stereotypes," the study deemed it "advisable to examine the extent to which Philadelphia has experienced such difficulties at the hands of its citizens of Puerto Rican birth or parentage." A year later, the Commission on Human Relations noted, "concern was expressed for problems which might arise from the rapid in-migration of a low income group with a language handicap and a culture unfamiliar with urban life in the United States. The difficulties involving New York City's mushrooming population was uppermost in the minds of social agency administrators, school authorities and the City departments." One social service worker, however, offered a different interpretation in a 1961 report: "The American White population are the oldest inhabitants of the area. . . . They enjoy the better homes and are quite resistive to the changing pattern of the community. As a result, there is an ever present possibility of racial tension with an occasional flare up." He acknowledged that for Puerto Ricans, "ignorance and prejudice are barriers to opportunity." Yet this attention to whites' "prejudice" and to the "barriers" Puerto Ricans confronted was an anomaly.[33]

Formulating the "Culture of Poverty"

Most policy makers and social service workers interpreted the experiences of Puerto Ricans in Philadelphia through emerging "culture of poverty" perspectives. Appearing in agencies' studies, culture of poverty perspectives were often formulated by those most interested in assisting Puerto Ricans. The local discourse mirrored the national discourse on the "culture of poverty" in its focus on Puerto Ricans' "problems," the cultural roots of those problems, the lack of a work ethic, and the lack of community organizations. Defining Puerto Ricans' perceived problems as stemming from their culture, they defined the solution as "assimilation." It was a social services approach aimed at modifying Puerto Ricans' behavior. Women were at the nexus of the "culture of poverty." With its emphasis on culture, family, and generations, the "culture of poverty" implied that women, traditionally held responsible for these domains, were to blame for the "problems" affecting their families and their communities. For the most part, women's productive labor was ignored and they were depicted as "submissive wives." Contradictions emerged, however, as some acknowledged women's participation in the labor force and portrayed them as "submissive wives" who worked. While white, middle-class women were exalted as "happy housewives" and African American women were portrayed as "black matriarchs," Puerto Rican women were criticized as "submissive" wives who threatened their families with paid employment.

In the national discourse, scholars writing between 1950 and 1971 expressed key elements of the "culture of poverty" ideology.[34] The "culture of poverty deemed the Puerto Rican family "defective" in comparison to both European peasant families and perceived U.S. norms. For Nathan Glazer and Daniel Patrick Moynihan, poverty was often mitigated by "the existence of a network of culture, religion, art, custom that gives strength and grace and meaning to a life of hardship; and . . . the existence of a strong family system that again enhances life." This was not the case for Puerto Rico, they concluded: "In both these aspects Puerto Rico was sadly defective." In short, Puerto Ricans lacked a "network of culture" and "a strong family system," and as a result they lacked "the basis for an improvement in life." Similarly, Joseph Fitzpatrick attributed Puerto Ricans' "problems" to "traditional weaknesses in Puerto Rican families" and to "traditional features of Puerto Rican culture (machismo, the practice of the mistress, consensual unions, the culture of poverty)." Fitzpatrick blamed culture and weak families for Puerto Ricans' problems and equated traditional culture with the culture of poverty.[35]

"Culture of poverty" perspectives linked these defective families with welfare dependency. For Glazer and Moynihan the problem of dependency was tied to the "population problem" and a cultural tendency to have too many children. They included welfare among the causes of Puerto Rican migration: "One must not underestimate another set of material advantages: the schools, hospitals, and welfare services." According to Glazer and Moynihan, welfare then supplanted their ethnic or national culture: "The culture of public welfare . . . is as relevant for the future of Puerto Ricans in the city as the culture of Puerto Rico." Yet the tendency to have too many children persisted: "But old attitudes exist alongside new ones, old-style families alongside new ones, and meanwhile there is a very heavy Puerto Rican birth rate in the city." Hence, "the population problem has been transferred rather than transformed." They concluded: "The special misfortune that consigns so many Puerto Ricans to the relief rolls is their large number of children." This became a "circle of dependency."[36]

Within these "defective" families, Puerto Rican women were portrayed as "submissive" wives and bad mothers. In 1950 C. Wright Mills, Clarence Senior, and Rose Kohn Goldsen summarized the place of Puerto Rican women: "The woman is supposed to be submissive, and her submissiveness is guaranteed by a network of manners and politenesses which confines her major sphere of activities to the home, circumscribes her social contacts, and places her under constant surveillance." They contrasted this with their perception of the U.S. norm: "Compared with the continental American family types, however, the despotic father-husband relationship is the dominant island pattern." Similarly, Fitzpatrick maintained, "in contrast to the characteristics of cooperation and companionship of American families, the woman in Puerto Rico has a subordinate role," and added that the wife's "role is culturally defined and ordinarily maintained as subordinate to the authority of the husband." When they asked "what kind of care the children get from these mothers," Glazer and Moynihan answered that the main "problem" was "overprotection," a tendency they contrasted with the "native American mother who, in her desire to see her child become independent," was "disciplined" enough not to worry too much. This "overprotection" was considered particularly damaging to Puerto Rican boys. Here they found the foundations for the "circle of dependency."[37]

For Oscar Lewis, women were pivotal in the "culture of poverty." His emphasis on culture and generations implied that women were responsible for the perpetuation of the "culture of poverty." He argued, referring to the culture of poverty,

> Once it comes into existence it tends to perpetuate itself from generation to generation because of its effect on the children. By the time slum children are age six or seven they have usually absorbed the basic values and attitudes of their subculture and are not psychologically geared to take full advantage of changing conditions or increased opportunities which may occur in their lifetime.

Presumably it was the mothers who passed "the basic values and attitudes" on to their children. Hence, the "culture of poverty" was "a tenacious cultural pattern," and Lewis found, in his study of one family, "remarkable stability in some of the behavior patterns of the Ríos family over four generations."[38]

In addition to this implication, Lewis explicitly blamed women for family problems: "The failure of the women in the Ríos family to accept the traditionally submissive role of women in Puerto Rican society creates tensions and problems in their marital relations." According to Lewis, women had "a deep ambivalence about their role as women," which explained "the bizarre ways in which they express their independence." He pointed to "their occupational history," "their experience as heads of matrifocal households," and "the greater freedom and independence of women which has accompanied the increasing urbanization, industrialization and Americanization of Puerto Rico." For Lewis this constituted a "role reversal," as the women showed "more aggressiveness and a greater violence of language and behavior than the men," and "the men seem to be more passive, dependent and depressed than the women." Migration to New York increased "marital conflict" and "the number of abandonments, separations, consensual unions and matrifocal families." For Lewis, women were the main cause; increased problems were "the result of wives working." He continued: "Employment outside of the home made the women more demanding of their husbands and gave them a new sense of independence." At the same time, "the position of the male was further weakened in New York by the stricter enforcement of laws against wife- and child-beating and by a more adequate family relief and child-aid program." Here Lewis portrayed Puerto Rican women in ways that paralleled the portrayal of African American women as "black matriarchs."[39]

In Philadelphia, social service and community agencies shared the concern with dependency and pointed to the cultural roots of the lack of a work ethic. The Friends Neighborhood Guild's 1958 survey asserted:

> The Puerto Ricans just do not want to work in many cases and they really need the jobs. The excuses they invent as to why they didn't need that particular job all cover up the underlying fact that they are very lazy and would prefer to think of ways to collect relief money for not doing anything than look for jobs. . . . It all has to do with the greatest factor of all we must cope with in dealing with the Puerto Rican, the Latin mentality and the Latin tradition which is against work and which sees fit to have the women of the lower class bring in the pay while the man sits home.

The survey offered a cultural explanation, "the Latin mentality and the Latin tradition," for men's unemployment and for women's employment. The jobs in question were farm work. The Guild had let the Pennsylvania Farm Association use their auditorium "for an appeal to unemployed Puerto Ricans to come and work on farms in upstate Pennsylvania." Although noting that there had been "horrible experiences with the farms in New Jersey" and that it was "one example of the way these people are pushed around," the survey blamed Puerto Ricans for not taking the jobs and expressed frustration: "There was quite a turnout to hear the speakers. But very few took advantage of the opportunity to take the jobs, and many more showed up days later with wonderful excuses as to why they had missed the meeting."[40]

The Guild was not alone in their view that Puerto Ricans did not want to work. At a Nationalities Services Committee meeting, information provided by the director of Puerto Rico's Migration Division sparked a revelation: "It was also found that those workers who had the closest contacts with the Puerto Rican migrants, even though in the beginning they felt them strange and to be so very different, they eventually gained the most positive attitudes about them. They discovered that Puerto Ricans had a long tradition of hard, diligent labor." This "discovery" seemed to challenge their preconceived notions. Similarly, those attending the meeting were surprised to learn that "mainlanders have often misconceptions about family constellation in Puerto Rico. It was brought out that women are not completely subordinate to their husbands, but in meetings it was observed that they make as much of a contribution as do their husbands."[41]

For the most part, assessments of Puerto Rican women in Philadelphia echoed the descriptions of "submissive" wives and bad mothers. The Guild's survey explained: "If he works during the day, his wife is to stay home where she belongs and not go running around. He is basically very jealous and arbitrary and any Latin woman knows better than to cross him." Despite being relegated to the home, Puerto Rican women were not considered good mothers. The Guild's survey expressed frustration in recruiting Puerto Rican children for summer camp: "But I ran into the Latin traditions again as a stopping block . . . no mother is willing to take the responsibility of saying that her child can go to camp for fear that something might happen to him and then she could expect the firing squad from her husband. The father is still the boss." Here, the submissive wife and the Puerto Rican mother failed to "take responsibility" for her own children. The Health and Welfare Council complained about a Puerto Rican and African American neighborhood: "School nurses see great neglect on the part of most parents in caring for their children's health problems." Although poverty was mentioned as a contributing factor, the study offered "neglect" and a cultural explanation instead: "Health superstitions and folkways still prevail with many residents." Like the national discourse, observations on Puerto Rican women were often couched as contrasts to perceived U.S. norms. The Commission on Human Relations emphasized the change between Puerto Rico and the States: "The Puerto Rican woman, subservient to the male of the island finds the United States offering a different and vastly improved role in society." The States offered "a multitude of social contacts and diversions outside the home."[42]

Contradictions emerged, however, as social service workers in the city sometimes acknowledged Puerto Rican women's roles as workers. The Guild's survey suggested that women worked because they were "submissive wives" and because of their husbands' culture-of-poverty traits:

> There is a tendency because of old Latin traditions to let the wife work among the lower classes while the husband watches television,—which he rarely understands, but he likes the noise and pictures! . . . In one house I actually found three very healthy men in their mid-twenties sitting around while the wife of one and her cousin worked in a factory.

Again, the explanation offered was a cultural one—"old Latin traditions." Yet social service workers also assumed that women's employment was new and that it constituted a threat to men's masculinity and to the already "defective" family. Stressing the impact of migration, the Commission on Human Relations noted that "the Puerto Rican woman finds . . . it easy to get a job, the pay is far better than on the island and the new wage-earning ability raises her status in the family to the point where she is equal, and sometimes superior, to the male." This employment and women's new ideas about "freedom" caused concern, and the Commission cautioned that "they may affect the husband's role as undisputed head of the family. And if the wives are employed outside the household, the husbands find that their authority over their wives is seriously threatened." Similarly, the Nationalities Services Center concluded, "the fact that a woman might have an easier time to earn higher pay than her husband is a threat to the family constellation."[43]

Defining Puerto Ricans' problems as cultural, the Pennsylvania Economy League warned that these cultural problems could be passed on to children and advocated "assimilation." In their 1962 study of Puerto Rican and African American migrants, the League attributed some problems to in-migration and migrants' "rural or slum background," but also noted "those which arise from poverty, ignorance, or color, and which are common to both in-migrants and natives in the 'underprivileged' class." Emphasizing the "cultural" origins of problems rather than the disruptive influence of adapting to a new environment, the League asserted, "some of the problems of assimilation which confront the underprivileged in-migrants are, in our opinion, identical to the problems of underprivileged native Philadelphians." Concerned with dependency, criminal behavior, and disorganized communities, the League defined the solution as "assimilation." They stressed, however, that they did not want migrants to assimilate to "the standards which appear to prevail or do prevail in the neighborhood where he resides," neighborhoods marked by "high degrees of social disorganization and consequent lawlessness and dependency." Instead, they defined assimilation as "living in accordance with the standards that are generally accepted in Philadelphia, [which] requires that the person is self-supporting and law-abiding," and as accepting "the social mores generally accepted by the majority of Philadelphians." As cultural problems could be passed on to children, the League warned, "failure to solve the problems in this category places great obstacles in the path of assimilation of the underprivileged adult and his children, whether born in Philadelphia or elsewhere." This emphasis on "assimilation" suggested that the migrants' "problems" stemmed from their own cultures and could be remedied by modifying individual and group behavior.[44]

These perceptions of Puerto Ricans' cultural deficiencies—dependency, lack of a work ethic, defective families—were extended to the Puerto Rican community. The assumption was that Puerto Ricans lacked community and lacked the willingness or the ability to improve their communities. In the national discourse, Mills had concluded, "in the metropolis the migrant has no community, even in the clusters of Puerto Rican settlement." Puerto Ricans again fell short when compared to European immigrants. Glazer and Moynihan pointed to "the relative weakness of community organization and community leadership among them." Similarly, Oscar Handlin argued that it was "in the character of their communal life" that "Negroes and Puerto Ricans are the farthest removed from the experiences of earlier immigrant groups."[45]

Similarly, the Guild worried about fostering dependency at the same time that it doubted Puerto Ricans' ability to improve their communities. The survey urged the Guild to "take part in helping them," but warned: "Let it be known as a place that one does not just come to when one needs a handout. . . . The Guild should tell those with whom it deals that they can do it all themselves and that they should want to, furthermore. Otherwise, we are just breeding a generation of outstretched hands." Again, the lack of community was perceived as having cultural roots: "The crux of the problem lies not in the lack of material, or at least on men with an underlying potential to be the focal point of the neighborhood, but rather in another of the factors that make up the Latin mentality—a complete lack of any social responsibility." In addition to assuming that community leaders had to be men, the Guild equated "community" with organizations: "There is no real sense of community spirit and unity as there may be with other nationality groups where you find clubs and all sorts of organizations." Revealing the shortcomings of their narrow definition, the survey conceded: "There may not be any community unity among the Puerto Ricans, but there is definitely a warmth within the neighborhood itself and those who like it, really like it." Contradicting itself, the survey concluded:

> In the process of becoming Americanized, suggestions are always welcome and the way is made easier just by wanting to help. There are groups doing just that at the moment. One is a group of Puerto Rican women who . . . work their heads off just going around within the community instructing the Puerto Rican women on the ways of making life easier for themselves in the United States.

Social service workers' culture of poverty perspectives had rendered these women's and others' community work invisible or incomprehensible.[46]

As the Puerto Rican population continued to grow and as gentrification pushed Puerto Ricans out of some of the earliest settlements, Puerto Ricans repeatedly confronted the tensions surrounding racial change. In their 1960 study, Philadelphia's Health and Welfare Council found:

> In recent years Negro and Puerto Rican families have been moving eastward. . . . Nearby white residents are moving out. Residents east of Front Street fear possible racial change more than they do redevelopment and reportedly would rather have their houses torn down than to sell it to Negroes or Puerto Ricans—and anticipate "real trouble" should such a move-in occur.

As in 1953, white neighbors responded to Puerto Rican and African American settlement by moving out, threatening violence, and redefining their western boundary, "which coincides with the drifting color and Spanish language line." The city responded by conducting another study, which mirrored the Commission's 1954 study in its sympathy to white neighbors and its equating of Puerto Ricans with community problems.[47]

The Health and Welfare Council attributed the differences in two neighborhoods to the characteristics of their inhabitants, and proposed different solutions for community problems as a result. Praising Kensington, a white ethnic area, for its "strong community pride," "parochialism," and "stability," the Council considered these positive traits, even though the community's neighborhood council maintained "boundaries" that "serve not only to confine the Council's efforts geographically but deter communication with adjoining communities or with minority groups within its boundaries." For Kensington, the study recommended a "neighborhood conservation program" and "above all, community organization techniques to bring residents into full participation in the program" with "block organizations and community councils." The summer after the study was conducted residents of the Fishtown section of Kensington, according to journalist Peter Binzen, "successfully routed from houses or apartments two Negro families, two Puerto Rican families, one dark-skinned Portuguese family, and a Cherokee Indian from North Carolina." In autumn 1966, five days of rioting ensued against an African American family who had rented a house in Kensington.[48]

In contrast, the study described East of Ninth, an area of first settlement "for Philadelphia bound southern Negro families and for new Puerto Ricans," as an area that "never seemed to have had any distinctive neighborhood identity." The "Negro and Puerto Rican families" were portrayed as having no commitment to the area, preferring to buy homes and participate in social and civic organizations outside the neighborhood. For the Council, community "problems" came with the migrants and stemmed from racial change. East of Ninth's problems were caused, in part, by "rapid changes—and inevitable social disorganization." The "problems" were "fortified by the high proportion of people not yet accustomed to family and community life in Philadelphia and who have a minimum of the community-social skills that are required for fruitful life here." The Council assumed that the methods recommended for Kensington would fail in East of Ninth. Instead of residents' "full participation," they advocated intervention by those thought more capable—"community 'trouble-shooters,'" a youth worker, social workers better trained in human relations, and business owners who no longer lived in the neighborhood. The Council concluded: "This lack of connection and the resulting lack of aspiration was labeled by many informants as 'apathy'—a word so often used in the past to express hopelessness that any service will do any good, but which time after time is disproved when the right kind of service is offered." They defined "the right kind of service" as a focus on "immediate goals" rather than a "long-range effort." Hence, social service workers lacked faith in the abilities of "Negro and Puerto Rican" newcomers but retained faith in social programs.[49]

Conclusion

As "culture of poverty" perspectives emerged and took hold, Puerto Ricans were not considered as labor migrants. Instead of being economically displaced and migrating in search of work, Puerto Ricans gained the dubious distinction of being among the first to be cast as migrating in search of welfare benefits. From this perspective, Puerto Ricans could not be labor migrants because they lacked a work ethic and desired welfare dependency. The obstacles that confronted Puerto Ricans stemmed not from a new urban environment, a tight job market, or discrimination, but rather from their own cultural deficiencies. Puerto Ricans were defined as "lazy," dependent, and lacking "any sense of social responsibility." Puerto Rican women's work—their paid employment in Puerto Rico and Philadelphia, their unpaid subsistence labor within their households, and their community work—was rendered invisible by the culture of poverty. In Philadelphia, the portrayal of Puerto Rican women as "submissive wives" coexisted in a contradictory fashion with some awareness of their roles as workers. Yet, for the most part, any tension between recruiting Puerto Ricans as laborers and not wanting them as community members dissipated, as Puerto Ricans were depicted as welfare dependent.

This reception shaped the context within which Puerto Ricans strove to meet their immediate needs and to recreate their communities in the city. Puerto Ricans confronted the attitudes of landlords, neighbors, policy makers, and social service workers. As they struggled to meet their economic, housing, and social service needs, Puerto Ricans challenged existing agencies and created their own. Within two decades of their arrival, Puerto Ricans also confronted economic restructuring, with the loss of manufacturing jobs within the city and the growth of a service economy. Puerto Ricans became displaced labor migrants. While economic conditions changed, the "culture of poverty" perspectives formulated during the peak period of Puerto Rican migration proved resilient, as policy makers and social service workers continued to attribute the causes of Puerto Rican poverty to Puerto Ricans' culture and their behavior.

Chapter Seven

From Labor Migrants to the "Underclass": Interpreting Puerto Rican Poverty

On July 25, 1953, the *Bulletin* declared, "Puerto Ricans Here Celebrate." Just two days after the last night of street fighting in the Spring Garden neighborhood, Philadelphia celebrated its first Puerto Rican Day. Although planning had been underway prior to the outbreak of violence, in its wake the event took on added significance. The government of Puerto Rico had initiated celebrations of Puerto Rico's first anniversary as a Commonwealth throughout Puerto Rico and in Puerto Rican communities in the States. In Philadelphia, the Friends Neighborhood Guild organized the event, with the support of social service and city agencies, community organizations, and segments of the local Puerto Rican community. As a result, the event revealed the interactions between the agencies and churches most involved with the Puerto Rican community and a few prominent Puerto Ricans. Despite the efforts of those involved to portray positive aspects of Puerto Rican migration, Puerto Rican Day highlighted not only aspects of the early Puerto Rican community, but also the ambiguities surrounding Puerto Rico's and the migrants' status. While the street fighting and the Puerto Rican Day celebration were very different responses to Puerto Rican migration, both events illustrated the city's attempts to define Puerto Rican migrants and their place in "the City of Brotherly Love."[1]

Puerto Ricans settled in Philadelphia and strove to recreate their community at a time when the city was undergoing fundamental economic restructuring. In addition to hostility in their neighborhoods, emerging "culture of poverty" perspectives, and the status ambiguities reflected in Puerto Rican Day, Puerto Ricans were facing declining economic opportunities and increasing residential segregation. The city's economy was shifting from manufacturing to professional services, and the 1960s, 1970s, and 1980s witnessed plant closings and the loss of jobs. Puerto Ricans, especially women, were displaced from the labor market. The impact of economic change was intensified by residential segregation, and Puerto Ricans found themselves living in areas of concentrated poverty. Nonetheless, they continued their efforts to improve the conditions affecting their lives. Striving to meet their needs, Puerto Ricans worked with and challenged existing social service and city agencies to respond to and include them. In time, Puerto Ricans developed their own organizations and became increasingly involved in city politics. By the 1980s, economic restructuring had affected Puerto Ricans in other areas of settlement, and a national discourse had emerged defining Puerto Ricans as "the other underclass," echoing earlier "culture of poverty" perspectives. Continuing racial ideologies and changing economic conditions transformed Puerto Rican labor migrants into the "underclass."[2]

Recreating Community

As they settled in the city, Puerto Ricans focused on adjusting to urban life and meeting their immediate needs. The "community" was family, friend, and church centered. Migrants helped each other find work and housing as they confronted the racial dynamics in their neighborhoods. They learned to negotiate the city and social service agencies they needed, and increasingly insisted that those agencies be more responsive to them. Puerto Ricans went from advocacy for decent treatment from existing agencies to developing their own social service organizations. Puerto Rican Day revealed those institutions serving Puerto Ricans and Puerto Ricans' own earliest organizations. The Concilio de Organizaciones Hispanas reflected the continuing evolution of Puerto Ricans' community organizations. Begun as a social club, Concilio became an umbrella organization in 1962, bringing together Puerto Rican organizations in the city. In 1968 Concilio became a social service agency funded by the Philadelphia Anti-Poverty Action Commission. Although often unrecognized by their contemporaries, Puerto Ricans developed a variety of strategies for improving the conditions affecting their lives—strategies that were shaped by time and place.

The Puerto Rican Day celebration revealed the complex emergence of the Puerto Rican "community," as those involved included the government of Puerto Rico's Migration Division; city, social service, and community agencies; churches; and some members of the Puerto Rican community. It was not, in other words, a community-based event emerging from Philadelphia's Puerto Rican community. The government of Puerto Rico initiated the celebrations of the Commonwealth's first anniversary. Governor Luis Muñoz Marín prepared a speech to honor the first anniversary, while Clarence Senior and the Migration Division took responsibility for plans in the States. Senior arranged to have Governor Muñoz Marín's speech broadcast in New York and was looking for similar possibilities in Philadelphia. As the Friends Neighborhood Guild organized the city's ceremony, Senior "was most enthusiastic about the plan." The Migration Division printed 10,000 programs and provided information on the Puerto Rican migration to interested radio stations and newspapers. Governor Muñoz Marín wrote a letter to Mayor Joseph S. Clark praising his "fine" and "thoughtful" actions in proclaiming Puerto Rican Day.[3]

The Friends Neighborhood Guild, a Quaker settlement house established in the 1890s, organized the Philadelphia event. The Guild had approached Puerto Rican migrants settling in the neighborhood, encouraging their participation and fostering Puerto Rican groups. Indeed, anthropologist Joan Koss described the Guild as "the only agency that took any extensive early interest in this growing group of migrants." As early as 1948, the Guild had identified twenty-one Puerto Rican families living in the neighborhood, and more than 450 Puerto Ricans participated in the Guild's clubs, classes, activities, and individual services over a two-week period in 1950. The Guild concluded, "Puerto Ricans have settled in our neighborhood and have made themselves at home with us. They join in all the group activities and have some groups of their own." The Spanish American Circle, composed almost entirely of Puerto Ricans, was their largest social club, and by 1952 fifty-six Puerto Ricans had become members of the Guild. In the same year, the Guild sponsored Boy Scout Troop #310, with a Puerto Rican Scoutmaster and a Scout Committee of seven Puerto Rican men. Two years after its inception, it received recognition as the largest Troop in Philadelphia, with forty-two boys participating. In addition to programs, the Guild wanted to improve interethnic relations through favorable publicity for Puerto Rican migrants. To this end Bosworth planned not just a rebroadcast of Muñoz Marín's speech, but a full ceremony. The end product exceeded New York's celebration despite the much larger Puerto Rican community there.[4]

The Sponsoring Committee for Puerto Rican Day included two of the earliest churches serving Puerto Ricans: Our Lady of the Miraculous Medal (known as the Spanish Chapel or La Milagrosa) and the First Spanish Baptist Church. Both were established before World War II and both played instrumental roles in the early Puerto Rican community. La Milagrosa's origins date back to 1909, when Spanish-language services were offered in the schoolhouse of Old St. Mary's Church. In 1912, La Milagrosa moved to its own building at 1903 Spring Garden Street and became a nucleus for the city's diverse Spanish-speaking population. The First Spanish Baptist Church started in 1929 as a Bible study group, organized as a mission in 1934, and then became the First Spanish Baptist Church, affiliated with the Philadelphia Baptist Association, in 1946. Reverend Enrique Rodríguez, a student at the Eastern Baptist Theological Seminary, became the pastor in 1944 and served until his retirement in 1971, except for a few years when he was living in Puerto Rico. The Church held religious services at the Fifth Baptist Church at 18th and Spring Garden Streets, had a Bible school operating out of a home, and provided religious services for migrant workers at the Campbell Soup Company and at farm labor camps in New Jersey and Pennsylvania during and after World War II. When migrants came to the city, they sometimes settled nearby. In 1956, the Church acquired its own building at 1218 Wallace Street.[5]

Others supported the Guild's work as well. Although focusing on the foreign-born, the International Institute had become involved with the Puerto Rican domestic workers and aware of Puerto Rican farmworkers in the late 1940s. In 1948, however, the Institute had concluded that "the majority of Puerto Ricans in Philadelphia were being served by the Friends Neighborhood Guild." By 1952, with more Puerto Ricans settling nearby and asking for meeting space, the Institute established the Puerto Rican

Planning Committee. In the aftermath of the street fighting, the Institute worked with the Commission on Human Relations on their study and with the Spring Garden Civic Association. The Institute joined the Sponsoring Committee for Puerto Rican Day. The City of Philadelphia was also "very anxious to participate in any way that will show that they value the good citizenship of the Puerto Ricans who have come to Philadelphia." The Recreation Department facilitated the use of Reyburn Plaza, across from City Hall, while the Police and Fireman's Band provided music and the Police Commissioner arranged patrols. The city's Commission on Human Relations joined the Sponsoring Committee, and Mayor Clark became its honorary chair and issued a proclamation declaring July 25, 1953 Puerto Rican Day.[6]

Consistent with their goal of encouraging Puerto Rican leadership, Francis Bosworth, the Guild's executive director, involved Puerto Ricans in planning the celebration. Several Puerto Ricans, recognized by Philadelphia's organizations as leaders of the Puerto Rican community, attended an early planning meeting and were listed among the Day's sponsors. Dr. José DeCelis, a dentist who had migrated to Philadelphia in the 1920s, became chairman of the Planning Committee. Dr. DeCelis was "considered a 'Philadelphian' even though he is of Puerto Rican extraction, compared to some less Americanized people from Puerto Rico." Sharing Bosworth's goals, DeCelis expressed concern that this be "a dignified program." Four members of Latin American Legion Post 840 were listed among the sponsors, including Diego Meléndez Jr., the post's Commander, who worked with the Pennsylvania State Employment Office. The Latin American Legion Post had been established by Meléndez and fourteen other Puerto Rican U.S. veterans who solicited funding from the American Legion. When they received their permanent title in February 1954, they had thirty-five members and held their meetings at the Guild. The active participation of the Latin American Legion Post assured attention to ritual, show, and American patriotism. Also on the Sponsoring Committee were the Logia Fidelidad, the Pan American Association, the Sociedad Hispanos Unidos, the Latin American Association, the Spanish-American Civic Club of Camden, New Jersey, two teachers, and three representatives from Spanish-language radio programs.[7]

The ceremony revealed the ambiguities of Puerto Rico's and the migrants' status, as well as the ambivalent reception of Puerto Ricans in Philadelphia. Bosworth emphasized Puerto Ricans living in Philadelphia and their status as United States citizens. Writing to the Police Commissioner, Bosworth suggested "one small thing that . . . would mean a great deal to our own Puerto Ricans as well as to the Government of Puerto Rico"— he asked the Commissioner to "write a letter . . . making some mention of the fact that Philadelphia welcomed them to our city and that they are making fine citizens." In a sample proclamation he sent to Mayor Clark, Bosworth referred to the "American Commonwealth of Puerto Rico" and wrote, "We rejoice with the American citizens of the Island of Puerto Rico and here in the Continental United States." He continued: "They have proven their value to our city and their loyalty to our country." Despite his emphasis on Puerto Ricans' citizenship and his reference to "our own Puerto Ricans," other references to "our city" and "our country" made Puerto Ricans outsiders and perhaps implied that their "value" and "loyalty" had to be "proven."[8]

Mayor Clark's proclamation set a more distancing tone for the ceremony. In contrast to Bosworth's emphasis on local Puerto Rican "citizens," Clark stressed the "voluntary" relationship between the United States and Puerto Rico. He noted that Puerto Rico's constitution was "overwhelmingly approved in the elections" and described Puerto Rico as a "wholly autonomous community in all matters regarding its local government, [that] is voluntarily associated with the United States." He referred twice to the Commonwealth of Puerto Rico, adding "American" to the "Commonwealth" only on the third reference. While Bosworth had suggested welcoming local Puerto Ricans— "We of Philadelphia are grateful that so many Puerto Ricans have [come] to live and work and rear their families in our city"—Clark merely mentioned that "hundreds of Puerto Ricans now reside in the City of Philadelphia where many of them are employed and where they are raising their families." He downplayed the local Puerto Rican community, which numbered not in the hundreds but in the thousands, and he did not refer to them as "citizens." In contrast to Bosworth, Clark did not "rejoice" and he was not "grateful." Clark's proclamation hinted that the Mayor was delicately balancing his constituents—the Puerto Rican migrants and their neighbors.[9]

The ceremony symbolized the friendly relations between the United States and Puerto Rico. The program cover announced "Puerto Rican Day" in bold letters at the top. The program was selectively bilingual; this heading appeared only in English. Competing with this was the image of a U.S. flag, larger than the print and centered in the middle of the program cover. The Puerto Rican flag did not appear on the program. The words "Celebrating the First Anniversary of the Commonwealth of Puerto Rico" appeared under the U.S. flag in smaller print. The ceremony opened with a concert by the Police and Firemen's Band, the Presentation of Colors by the Latin American Legion Post, and the audience's rendition of the Star-Spangled Banner, which was identified as the national anthem only in the Spanish translation. The heart of the live program was the Welcome by Councilman Victor Blanc, who represented the Mayor, and the Reply by Joseph Monserrat of the Migration Division, who represented Governor Muñoz Marín. Their speeches praised the relationship between the United States and Puerto Rico, and Philadelphia's reception of the Puerto Rican migrants. The Puerto Rican flag was then presented to the City of Philadelphia—it was handed to the Councilman by Monserrat and members of the Latin American Legion Post. Finally, Governor Muñoz Marín's address was broadcast in English and Spanish.[10]

In covering the event, newspapers portrayed a positive relationship between local Puerto Ricans and the city, while holding out the hope of decreased migration in the future. Combined with the street fighting, this was the most press coverage Philadelphia Puerto Ricans had ever received. The two episodes were not linked, however, even as the July 19 edition of the *Bulletin* covered the second night of "clashes" and announced, "Puerto Rico Day Ceremonies Set: To Mark 1st Birthday of Commonwealth." Instead, migration was presented as potentially temporary and the city was presented as welcoming. In his letter to Mayor Clark, Governor Muñoz Marín had written: "We are not happy that some of our citizens feel that they must seek a better livelihood elsewhere but we are exerting every effort through 'Operation Bootstrap' to improve our economy so that fewer will feel the urge to migrate." The *Inquirer* reassured their readers, paraphrasing the Governor. In the meantime, "Monserrat declared that Puerto Ricans had been made to feel at home in Philadelphia, where true independence was born." Furthermore, the migrants were assimilating: "The governor said the people of his country want to be and are rapidly becoming 'as American as the people of Pennsylvania.'" The Puerto Rican flag given to the city was depicted as "a gift from the 5000-odd Puerto Ricans living here," and newspapers estimated that local Puerto Ricans were among the 350 to 400 people who attended the ceremony. This image of Puerto Ricans celebrating and giving their flag to the city as a gift was a marked contrast to the violence of the previous week.[11]

Despite efforts to present the ceremony and the relationship it symbolized in a positive light, newspaper accounts also revealed confusions over Puerto Rico's political status that shaped the definition of local Puerto Ricans. Most articles referred to Puerto Rico as a "nation" and a "country." When addressing the end of colonialism, however, the articles used "state." In accepting the Puerto Rican flag, Councilman Blanc asserted that "both countries" could look with pride on the "peaceful changes" of a year ago, and continued, "In these days of aggression, the cooperation shown by the United States and Puerto Rico may well set an example for other nations to follow." A July 22 editorial highlighted the contradictions: "The first anniversary of complete self-rule for Puerto Rico, which occurs this week, shows that the legislation putting the island entirely on its own was one of the wisest acts this Government ever performed." The reference to "complete self-rule" contradicted the implication that "this Government" was responsible for the decision. Explaining that Puerto Rico's rights were the same as "any State in the Union"—election of the Governor and legislature, and a Constitution—this editorial overlooked the Commonwealth's lack of voting representation in Congress. At the same time, it was "special privileges by acts of Congress" that were responsible for the island's "progress"—progress evident in new factories, a great irrigation scheme, and the existence of more housing projects in Puerto Rico than in any state except Texas. Apparently, the contradictions and the language problem could be resolved later, provided that "colony" was avoided.[12]

The connection between Puerto Rico's status and migrants in Philadelphia was implicit throughout the ceremony and the press coverage. The ceremony and the press acknowledged Puerto Rican migrants in the city, while honoring the political ties that made their migration easy and unrestricted. One article summarized the Governor's speech: "The good relationship which exists between the United States and Puerto Rico was lauded . . . as a 'permanent affiliation.'" Although the relationship between Puerto Rico and the United States was portrayed as "voluntary" and "permanent," migration was portrayed as a temporary phenomenon linked to Puerto Rico's "progress." Hence, the ceremony also addressed some Philadelphians' reservations about the Puerto Rican migration to the city. Puerto Ricans were depicted as "American" as much as possible—the ceremony emphasized their patriotism and their desire to be "as American as the people of Pennsylvania." In the aftermath of the riots, this emphasis on "celebration" and "peace" may have reflected deeper tensions. The event was a "celebration" of Puerto Rico as "other" and implicitly as subordinate to the United States. Making similar connections between status and migration, as early as 1945 one editorial writer feared, "if they choose statehood, we shall be stuck with them forever." Similarly, after Puerto Rican nationalists attacked the U.S. House of Representatives in 1954, a journalist responded that "the demand for control of the inflow of Puerto Ricans has become rampant, and nobody has suggested a way to do it short of a grant of complete independence." The colonial relationship continued to shape definitions of Puerto Rican migrants in Philadelphia.[13]

While some Puerto Ricans participated in Puerto Rican Day, most focused their efforts on meeting their immediate needs. Nevertheless, all had to deal with the attitudes behind the street violence, the "culture of poverty," and Puerto Rican Day. As they approached social service agencies, these challenges were particularly acute for women in their childbearing years. Both Doña Ana Luisa and Doña Nilda confronted the health care system. Doña Ana Luisa remarked, "we suffered when we first arrived because we didn't know English. I went with four children and six months pregnant to look for medical care there right away and without knowing English or anything." For Doña Nilda, "it was difficult at first in that I didn't know English and he didn't know English, so you have a lot of trouble with the hospitals. . . . I would say it gave me a lot of work."[14]

Having learned some English in school in Puerto Rico, Doña Carmen translated for people at the hospitals and welfare offices, where she encountered firsthand the attitudes of social service workers:

> One time, I was taking a woman to *Pennsylvania Hospital* and I told them to come early because I had to go to work, before 8:00, and we went to the hospital. When we arrived, there was a line of pregnant women and I had to go. When we got to the white American woman, she told me, "*What do you want?*" I responded, "*I am an interpreter, I have to go back to work.*" [She said], "*We cannot waste time here; no, no you have to go to the back, to the end of the line* until I finish with all these people."

Unwilling to return to the end of the line, Doña Carmen went in search of the director of the hospital and explained the situation. This time, when they approached the receptionist, "she took care of them immediately because it was getting late, but the most important thing was her attitude, her attitude that she didn't want to assist them because it was through an interpreter." Similarly, while volunteering to translate at a welfare office, Doña Carmen was asked, "*Why don't you go back to where you came from, why?*" Her response—"I said, 'Why do we have to go? We came here like anybody else.' I used to say, 'I don't know where you came from, but I know we are citizens of the United States.'" On another occasion, "*I took some people for taxes or something, I don't know. Anyway, some man hollered at me! . . . 'Yeah, you should go back if you don't speak English.' I said, 'That's not the problem, English or no English. They have a right for this, whatever service you give.*" Asserting Puerto Ricans' rights to be in the States and their rights to existing social services, Doña Carmen became an early advocate for the Puerto Rican community.[15]

Within this context, Puerto Rican organizations emerged to help arriving migrants and to confront city and social service agencies. The Committee of Puerto Rican Women was a more formal approach to the work Doña Carmen and others had already been doing to help the growing Puerto Rican community: "There were a lot of Puerto Ricans arriving, okay, so they didn't know what to do, they didn't know where to get money, they didn't know where to find housing, they didn't know that you had to give a deposit on a house, they didn't know where to go to look for work, they didn't know anything." Made up of teachers, social workers, and housewives, Doña Carmen noted, "We [the Committee] worked a lot." Their activities included fund raising, children's contests, banquets and guest speakers, voter registration drives, and various committees: "It formed a committee to help the Latinos, when they arrived here in Philadelphia. . . . It was one of our goals, to be able to do something for the community, always looking toward the community." A few year later, another committee was formed to confront social service agencies, as Doña Carmen explained: "*You find a sign on the door, if you don't bring an interpreter, you won't be helped. The welfare used to do that. That's when we formed a committee to take care of that. They had everything in English, English. Then we formed a committee to demand that the welfare have bilingual workers.*"

In addition to paid employment and domestic responsibilities, then, Puerto Rican women in Philadelphia included "community work" in their definitions of "work" and minimized the distinctions between paid and unpaid community work. In recalling leaving the shoe factory and beginning her long career in human services, Doña Carmen stressed the continuity in helping the community rather than the change in jobs. "I am always trying to help Hispanics, with housing, with family, with school, with problems, the students, always. Now with the seniors, seventeen years." Her community activism started before she was employed at the 5th Street Methodist Church's community center and continued after. In the early 1970s she became the director of the Norris Square Senior Citizens' Center, where she worked for more than twenty years. Seeing continuity in her advocacy work for Puerto Ricans, whether paid or unpaid, Doña Carmen reminisced in 1992, "*I've been a fighter since the first days—for my Puerto Rico. . . . I'm still fighting.*"[16]

Similarly, Doña María, who was born in Philadelphia in 1930, added community work to the already challenging demands of paid employment and domestic responsibilities. Before she married, she had worked in a dry cleaner's and in an umbrella factory. After she was married, she worked at a baking factory, decorating and packing cakes, and had five children, one of whom died. Her mother or her aunt took care of the children while she was at work. As for the rest of her household duties, she recalled, referring to her husband, "in a way everything was convenient because I was able to get back before he came back and do all the cooking and this and that, and it was done so he didn't have to worry about it. It didn't interfere with the children or with our relationship as long as everything was in place." Clearly, domestic responsibilities remained hers. In addition, as a Merchant Marine, her husband was away from home often, and they separated when their youngest daughter was about five years old. She assumed more community work, but did not view this work as a conflict with her responsibilities to her children. Instead, she explained, "all of the things I did together with my kids. I enjoyed doing it together, also, with my kids so that they were able to see things and understand." She took her children, and often their friends, to community events, such as the Puerto Rican Day Parade, which she helped to organize.[17]

Like Doña Carmen, Doña María blurred the distinctions between her unpaid and paid work for the community. When I asked her how she came to work for the Board of Education, she emphasized her earlier involvement with community-based school associations and told me the story of a young boy who came to the doctor's office where she was the receptionist. He had been placed in a bilingual Spanish class even though he did not speak Spanish. Doña María concluded her story: "So I said, 'don't worry about it, I'll take care of that for you.' So even when I wasn't working, I was working and explaining to them the schools." Here, Doña María implied that even though her paid job was as a receptionist, her real "work" was helping this young person mediate the school system. Similarly, as she described her job with the Board of Education, she emphasized its community dimensions, recalling, "I started the program with four other ladies and myself. . . . The most important part was communication with the parents, going to their houses and giving them information in Spanish. . . . I got to know people in my block, you know, it wasn't like the whole area was strangers." Doña María merged paid and unpaid community work in her narrative and in her life as she continued doing both.

Puerto Ricans also turned to churches and extended family for social activities and for assistance. By the late 1950s, other churches had joined the Spanish Chapel and the Spanish Baptist Church. Puerto Ricans attended St. Peters and the Cathedral, and the Archdiocese of Philadelphia had established Casa del Carmen in the mid-1950s to provide health programs, job referrals, recreation, education, and other services. Protestant churches and services had proliferated as well, including the Methodist Memorial Temple, the Fifth Street Community Center, the Methodist Social Service Center, and at least eight Pentecostal churches. For the Navarros, having the church close by was one of the benefits of life in Philadelphia, because they could attend mass every day. Doña Ana Luisa remarked:

> I don't know if in the community there was help for everyone, but yeah the Cathedral, the Cathedral helped us a lot. The Cathedral had a priest that helped us, a lot, a lot, a lot. He helped us, not so much monetarily, but with his advice. He gave us support. He told us, which I always remember, he said the children should study, that they should study. He said, "President Kennedy wasn't an American native, he was Irish and look, he got to be President of the United States, why can't a Puerto Rican get to be president?" and he was always giving us good advice. Even more, he was one of the first people during the first winter that we spent in Philadelphia which was the winter of 1956, this priest came to the house with groceries and winter clothes.

Acknowledging the churches, Doña Nilda emphasized extended family instead. "When I arrived in Philadelphia, yeah, there were already a lot of organizations, different things, churches, we knew the churches, they had things for people who wanted to go and spend the day there, but not us, you know—to work and to go to church, and mostly it was to visit our family in New York. When we moved to Philadelphia, well,

we spent time in New York." For Don Florencio, playing music provided social interaction, as well as additional income. He played in local bars, in churches, and in Puerto
Rican Day parades. He also went to the Latin American Legion Post 840, which he
described as "a social club, they had dances, activities. . . . Especially on Sundays, since
the bars were closed, they opened. So everyone that liked beer went."[18]

Though town clubs also offered social activities and mutual aid, their roles in Philadelphia seem to have been limited. While they did not participate, Doña Nilda recalled that
there was a town club for those from Salinas. "We knew that it was there and we knew
a lot of people that went, because it wasn't only for dancing and things, it was also for
certain things that you didn't have." In the mid-1960s Koss found only four town clubs,
representing Salinas, Vieques, Añasco, and Cabo Rojo. Likewise, in encouraging community organizations in 1966, Concilio's president Otilio Maldonado wondered "why
town organizations had not been able to put down roots in this city while they flourished
in other communities." For Doña María, it was the limited scope of town clubs that fostered the emergence of Concilio. She explained, "you never heard what these town clubs
were doing except to have parties on Fridays. They didn't have an agenda, they didn't
have a program or a plan, even something for the organization." Concilio emerged,
according to Doña María, as "something bigger, for the whole, the whole city really."[19]

Concilio, like the town clubs, started as a social club and then became an umbrella
organization for Puerto Rican clubs and organizations in 1962. Revealing the range of
community organizations, Doña Carmen described the beginnings of Concilio:

> It was called the Council of Hispanic Organizations because if you had a woman's organi-
> zation, you joined there. The other had an association of teachers, it joined there; the other
> had an association of mechanics, it joined there; the other had an association of whatever.
> So that's why it was called the Council of Hispanic Organizations. And, yeah, it formed a
> club first, it formed first as a small, social club. Then, it was a little house where on Sundays,
> the husbands went with the wives and the youth and we all met there from noon until what-
> ever hour. There was music, they made *pasteles*, they made rice with chicken and *we had a*
> *good time that way too*. Then we got to a certain point where we said, well that's good
> enough for the socials, let's see if we can do something now for the community. Then we
> organized as an organization.

As community organizations increased, Concilio's role expanded. In 1959 the Commission on Human Relations listed only four Puerto Rican organizations: Comité de
Mujeres Puertorriqueñas de Filadelfia, Unión Cívica Puertorriqueña, Logia Hispana
Fidelidad, and Club Caribe. In 1964 the Commission listed these four organizations and
eleven more, adding: "Many of these clubs and organizations have organized themselves
into the Council of Spanish Organizations. . . . Through this organization, it is hoped
that the Spanish-speaking community can present a unified voice in relation to the
affairs of the Spanish-speaking community in Philadelphia." In 1968 Concilio was
described as "a loose federation of 13 social and fraternal groups."[20]

Concilio sponsored the first Puerto Rican Day Parade in 1964; unlike Puerto Rican
Day in 1953, this event emanated from the Puerto Rican community itself. The Parade

became an annual event and grew into a week-long festival of activities. Wanting her children to have a sense of where their father came from, Doña María took her children to the first event, which she remembered as a series of performances put on by the different clubs, and to the first Parade the following year. While resonating for individuals, the Parade also served to define the Puerto Rican community both internally and to the larger Philadelphia community. In planning the third Parade and encouraging the community to participate, the Parade's president noted that "the parade is the best vehicle that Puerto Ricans of Philadelphia have to show their strength, culture, patriotism, civics, and their unity and therefore a strong weapon against the tribulations that they suffer far away from their homeland." By 1971 the event had grown into a week-long celebration that opened with the raising of the Puerto Rican flag next to the U.S. flag at City Hall, included performances, food, and dances, and culminated with the Parade to Independence Hall. The three-hour parade had marchers, two Puerto Rican beauty queens, floats representing the member organizations of Concilio and city schools with bilingual programs, and bands from the U.S. Armed Services and the Greater Kensington String Band. Concilio's president, Ramon Velázquez, asserted: "It is a symbol of our pride in our background." The director of the Governor's Council on Spanish Speaking Affairs, Bolivar Rivera, served as the Parade Grand Marshal, and the parade was also attended by mayors of Puerto Rican towns. The banquet the previous night was attended by both mayoral candidates, Republican Thacher Longstreth and Democrat Frank L. Rizzo. Beyond "pride," the Parade was a public relations event.[21]

Concilio viewed itself as an advocate for the Puerto Rican community and increasingly as a provider of social services. In its first newsletter, Concilio asserted: "Our voice of protest when it becomes necessary, each year's parade, our employment office and now this medium of communication is only the beginning of what we are planning to contribute." As early as 1966, Concilio housed an employment service that was staffed by personnel from Puerto Rico's Department of Labor. Concilio's president, Carlos Morales, explained the need to provide services: "Puerto Ricans have been taken advantage of because of the language barrier and their low economic level. . . . And the local authorities haven't had the vision to recruit enough Puerto Ricans to help in critical areas." At the same time, he noted, "Puerto Ricans are not used to this type of society where you have to unite and fight for your rights. . . . We're hoping to develop enough leadership in the community so it can take care of itself." Ramon Velázquez, a restaurant owner who later became Concilio's president, was more adamant: "The city has done nothing for the Puerto Rican. . . . They've opened up their hand a little by putting in a few Spanish police, but they must do much more. . . . I think the Mayor is starting to wake up. . . . We need somebody to make sure he doesn't cool off." Yet Morales conceded Concilio's limitations: "We're all volunteers and we do what we can . . . but we can't set up the necessary programs. We just don't have the time." A study found that "many Puerto Ricans in the lower strata have never even heard of the Concilio—especially in the Spring Garden area."[22]

Receiving funding from the Office of Economic Opportunity through the Philadelphia Anti-Poverty Action Commission, Concilio became a social service agency. By

1968 the employment program interviewed a hundred job seekers per week at their building on 2023 North Front Street, and the Philadelphia Anti-Poverty Action Committee had offices in the building, with a staff of four including a job developer and a social worker. Mayor James H. J. Tate supported their efforts: "We will continue in every meaningful way we can the fine and exemplary work which is being done by the Council of Spanish-Speaking Organizations in the improvement of the community." At Concilio's request, the Mayor had appointed Spanish-speaking representatives to the Philadelphia Urban Coalition's four task forces on housing, economic opportunities, education, and employment. Initially, Concilio received $31,000 for a three-month pilot program to provide community organization, training programs, consumer education, and leadership development. By 1971, Concilio was described as "the most official group" in the Puerto Rican community. It received $90,000, had a staff of ten, and operated during standard business hours, nine to five. They offered free services such as help finding jobs, community orientation, translating, and notarizing documents. Concilio's transformation from a social club to an umbrella organization to a social service agency was complete. Nevertheless, despite this increase in Puerto Rican organizations and the emergence of a Puerto Rican social service agency, the economic restructuring that followed on the heels of Puerto Rican settlement limited the ability of these organizations to improve conditions for Puerto Ricans in Philadelphia.[23]

Displaced Labor Migrants

Though Puerto Ricans came to Philadelphia when unskilled jobs were readily available, the city's economy was on the verge of a major change. Because of their concentration in certain sectors and in certain occupations, Puerto Ricans were profoundly affected by these economic shifts, in terms of employment status and economic well-being. With economic restructuring, many unskilled jobs disappeared, and Puerto Ricans were unable to enter the new areas of job growth. Manufacturing plants relocated in search of lower wages, leaving only a downgraded manufacturing sector in the city. Farms on the city's periphery became larger and more mechanized, requiring fewer seasonal agricultural workers. Meanwhile, within the city limits, jobs in professional and related services increased. Yet, as historian Michael Katz writes, "the mix of novelty, complexity, and danger within inner cities signified by underclass did not just happen; its emergence was not inevitable; like the postindustrial city of which it is a part, it is the product of actions and decisions over a very long span of time." Government policies fostered not only labor recruitment, but also Philadelphia's shift to a postindustrial economy and residential segregation. As a result of economic restructuring and government policies, Puerto Ricans became displaced labor migrants.[24]

Once its strength, Philadelphia's diverse manufacturing economy made the city particularly vulnerable to deindustrialization. Writing in 1976, geographer Peter Muller and colleagues observed that "since Philadelphia was perhaps the most overindustrialized of the nation's large old cities, it is suffering more than others as its manufacturing plants continue to die or emigrate." Similarly, anthropologist Judith Goode suggested that "Philadelphia has been harder hit by decline than other rustbelt cities because of the nature of its manufacturing, the degree of suburbanization and the degree of fiscal dependence on state and federal resources." The city's manufacturing sector produced more nondurable than durable goods in comparison to the nationwide average. These were labor-intensive industries that relied on cheap labor and were able to relocate easily. Factories left the city for the suburbs, for other regions of the United States, and for overseas. The federal government's procurement policies during World War II shifted the growth of industry from the northeastern to the southern and western United States. Meanwhile, the Highway Acts of 1944 and 1956 created more than 160 miles of federally funded highway in the Delaware Valley Region between 1950 and 1973, facilitating the suburbanization of industry and people. State, county, and municipal governments issued tax-free bonds to fund the acquisition of land and its development by industry. In 1960, the city claimed 61 percent of the metropolitan area's jobs; by 1972 this had fallen to only 48 percent.[25]

While multinational firms left the city, a downgraded manufacturing sector remained. In their study of 173 firms that closed between 1976 and 1979, Arthur Hochner and Daniel Zibman found that multinational and conglomerate firms "were responsible for the overwhelming majority of jobs lost among the 173 firms." These were the largest and most successful firms, and they relocated in search of higher corporate growth rates. Hochner and Zibman concluded that "the decisions are the outcome not of the free market but of economic and political concentration which gives these enterprises great power and of federal and state government policies on taxes, subsidies, loans, defense spending, labor law, and economic development which favor the multinational and conglomerate firms." On the other hand, those industries that remained in the city were older industries that "because of long term plant investments and the need for cheap unskilled labor not available in the suburbs would simply find it too costly to move."[26]

The garment industry was among the hardest hit by plant closings in Philadelphia. As early as 1961, the *Bulletin* announced, "Union, Employers Join to Bolster Sagging Garment Industry Here," and reported: "The ladies garment industry in Philadelphia employs 9,500 workers in about 150 shops. It has been losing ground to competition from the low-wage South and foreign imports." As a labor-intensive industry facing increased competition from clothing imports, the U.S. garment industry continued its efforts to reduce labor costs by employing two strategies. First, the industry continued earlier patterns of relocation to lower-wage areas. In addition to Puerto Rico (the industrialization of which was discussed in Chapter 2), the industry relocated within the northeast, then to the southern and western states, and increasingly overseas. The second strategy used by the garment industry was an increasing reliance on contractors, which fostered the growth of a downgraded manufacturing sector and sweatshops in cities where union shops had prevailed in the past. In short, the industry relied on the low-wage labor of women, both in their countries of origin and as immigrant workers in the States. These strategies to reduce labor costs were facilitated by the growth of conglomerates and by consumers' shift to less formal and more standardized clothing.

Between 1950 and 1979, the number of textile workers in the Philadelphia area decreased from 42,000 to 1,800, and the number of clothing workers in the union decreased from 20,000 to 8,000. While quality jobs disappeared, as Goode notes, "a somewhat clandestine garment industry has developed based on Korean and Chinese capital and using newcomer Asian labor. . . . They often are subcontractors for Sears, Bloomingdales, the U.S. military, and New York City garment firms."[27]

At the same time, the demand for seasonal agricultural workers decreased, and new groups of workers replaced Puerto Ricans. As farms surrounding the city became larger and more mechanized, Pennsylvania's seasonal work force declined from 45,000 to just 18,000 between 1958 and 1966. Mechanization was "an important factor in reducing the State's peak seasonal agricultural hired work force," affecting potato, bean, pea, spinach, cherry, root, and sweet corn crops and all regions of the state. The trend toward fewer and larger farms facilitated mechanization. Local labor made up less of the seasonal work force, finding jobs elsewhere or becoming year-round agricultural workers; the Farm Placement Program had instituted "farm hiring days" in 1959 to "bring together potential year-round farmworkers and farm employers at one central and convenient location for the sole objective of discussing and completing hiring arrangements." Meanwhile, the number of Puerto Rican farmworkers coming under contract reached its highest point in 1968 when close to 23,000 came, and then dropped to 11,900 by 1972 and to fewer than 3,000 by 1987. The decrease was, in part, a result of growers turning to "the growing supply of more vulnerable, less vocal, and less protected Mexican and other immigrant workers." Some Mexicans and Central Americans joined the migratory stream along the eastern seaboard, and others, along with Southeast Asians, were organized by crew leaders in Philadelphia. As David Griffith and Ed Kissam note, "the tendency in these settings is for the least empowered workers (those without legal documents, who have no access to government programs, and who are isolated) to set the standard against which other workers are judged."[28]

Within the city limits, manufacturing employment decreased, while employment in professional and related services increased (see Figure 7.1). Between 1940 and 1950 employment patterns remained steady, with about a third of those employed working in manufacturing and just 12 percent in professional services. Though the 1950s witnessed a slight decrease in manufacturing and a slight increase in professional and related services, this trend was pronounced during the 1960s, 1970s, and 1980s. By 1990 employment patterns had essentially reversed. More than a third of the labor force was now in professional and related services and just 14 percent still worked in manufacturing.

The city's redevelopment programs facilitated the creation of more professional service jobs, determined their downtown location, and continued the trend toward increasingly polarized incomes at the top and bottom of the pay scale. City officials formed public-private partnerships with business leaders in the expanding services sector. One such alliance, the Greater Philadelphia Movement, established in 1949, challenged the earlier dominance of the Chamber of Commerce, which represented manufacturing interests. The 1950s became known as "the reform era," as civic and business leaders forged links with city government and began downtown renewal programs that shaped Philadelphia's economic development. Reformers formed an electoral coalition comprising the city's business

FIGURE 7.1.   Employment in Manufacturing and Professional
Services, Philadelphia, 1940–1990

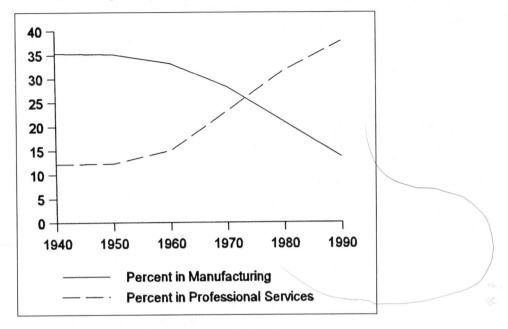

Sources: U.S. Bureau of the Census, *Sixteenth Census of the United States: 1940 Population,*
vol. 3, *The Labor Force,* pt. 5, Pennsylvania–Wyoming (Washington, D.C., 1943), 94; U.S.
Bureau of the Census, *Census of the Population: 1950,* vol. 2, *Characteristics of the
Population,* pt. 38, Pennsylvania (Washington, D.C., 1952), 441–442; U.S. Bureau of the
Census, *Census of the Population: 1960,* vol. 1, *Characteristics of the Population,* pt. 40,
Pennsylvania (Washington, D.C., 1963), 392; U.S. Bureau of the Census, *Census of the
Population: 1970,* vol. 1, *Characteristics of the Population,* pt. 40, Pennsylvania
(Washington, D.C., 1973), 404; U.S. Bureau of the Census, *Census of the Population: 1980,*
vol. 1, *Characteristics of the Population,* pt. 40, Pennsylvania (Washington, D.C., 1983),
288; and U.S. Bureau of the Census, *Census of the Population: 1990, Social and Economic
Characteristics,* Pennsylvania (Washington, D.C., 1993), 837.
Note: Labor force participation is for those fourteen and older in 1940, 1950, and 1960,
and for those sixteen and older in 1970, 1980, and 1990. Professional and related services
include health, education, legal, finance, insurance, and real estate.

leaders, trade unionists, African American leaders, and Democratic Party ward leaders,
and defeated the entrenched Republican machine in the mayoral elections of 1951. Political reforms coincided with federal urban renewal programs. Projects sought to stimulate
growth by recruiting private investment. Tax policies favored real estate developers and
large service firms. Channeling resources to the city's Central Business District at the
expense of its neighborhoods, redevelopment programs improved transportation, refur-
bished the historic district, gentrified selected neighborhoods, and built retail space and a
convention center. Rather than mitigating the negative consequences of economic shifts,
as Carolyn Adams and colleagues argue, "redevelopment can be seen to have helped to
reinforce the existing dichotomy between the haves and the have-nots in Philadelphia."[29]

As in the postwar era, policy makers failed to consider the segmentation of the city's labor market along race and gender lines or the differential impact of economic change on people of color and women. In 1968 the Pennsylvania Bureau of Employment Security claimed that despite the loss of manufacturing jobs, "the area managed to recoup its position because of heavy representation in the fast-growing services sector." The new professional services did not, however, employ those most affected by the decline in manufacturing. Instead, professional jobs were filled by the new suburbanites, while manufacturing jobs in the suburbs were out of reach for Puerto Ricans and African Americans who continued to live in the city. For African Americans, the suburbanization of industry continued earlier patterns of exclusion. For Puerto Ricans, manufacturing provided a brief period of employment followed by the loss of jobs.[30]

Unable to gain a foothold in the expanding sectors of the economy, Puerto Ricans remained concentrated in the declining sectors (Table 7.1). Between 1970 and 1990, Puerto Ricans' employment in manufacturing decreased considerably, but they were still more likely than their counterparts to work in this declining sector—27 percent compared to 14 percent. Similarly, while their numbers in professional and related services increased, they remained underrepresented in this expanding sector—27 percent compared to 38 percent citywide. Few Puerto Ricans worked in public administration or in transportation and utilities, sectors of the economy that provided jobs for African Americans. However, Puerto Ricans were still more likely than their counterparts citywide to work in agriculture, and the proportion of Puerto Ricans in agriculture had increased since 1970. In addition to being concentrated in declining sectors of the economy, Puerto Ricans remained in lower-level occupations, in jobs that were low-paid and

TABLE 7.1.   Industry of Those Employed by Race, Philadelphia, 1970 and 1990

	1970			1990		
	Puerto Rican	Black	Total	Puerto Rican	Black	Total
Number Employed	6,270	232,192	763,520	16,106	230,414	651,621
Percent in:						
Manufacturing	49.3	26.0	28.2	27.4	11.5	13.6
Professional, Related Services	10.0	22.6	23.2	26.6	39.7	37.7
Other Services	9.4	13.4	8.9	7.4	10.3	9.0
Public Administration	2.4	9.9	8.0	5.4	9.5	7.5
Trade	17.9	15.2	20.1	21.1	15.6	19.7
Transportation, Utilities	4.3	6.6	6.5	5.3	9.6	7.5
Construction, Mining	5.3	5.6	4.7	4.1	3.5	4.5
Agriculture, Forestry	1.4	0.7	0.4	2.7	0.3	0.5

Sources: U.S. Bureau of the Census, Census of the Population: 1970, vol. 1, Characteristics of the Population, pt. 40, Pennsylvania (Washington, D.C., 1973), 508, 460, 404; and U.S. Bureau of the Census, Census of the Population: 1990, Social and Economic Characteristics, Pennsylvania (Washington, D.C., 1993), 1136, 994, 837.

Note: Professional and related services include health, education, legal, finance, insurance, and real estate. "Other services" include personal, private household, business, repair, and entertainment. Not all columns total exactly 100 percent due to rounding.

had little room for advancement. Puerto Rican men and women were more likely to work as operatives and laborers and less likely to work as professionals than their counterparts citywide in 1970 and in 1990.[31]

As industry declined, Puerto Ricans suffered from the "last hired, first fired" syndrome. One lighting fixture plant revealed the differential impact of deindustrialization. Although the plant had previously provided stable employment and jobs for newcomers, including Puerto Ricans, total employment there had declined from more than 1,500 in 1985 to 972 in 1989. Some of the factory's labor-intensive operations had been moved to South Carolina, Montreal, and Mexico. The work force was 70 percent white, 20 percent African American, and 10 percent Puerto Rican; 27 percent of the workers were women. During a two-year period of layoffs in the late 1980s, however, 35 percent of Puerto Rican jobs, 28 percent of African American jobs, and just under 20 percent of white jobs were terminated. Working conditions deteriorated as workers were "bumped down" to other sections and workers with less seniority were then laid off.[32]

The impact of deindustrialization was most evident among those workers who had been most concentrated in the manufacturing sector—Puerto Rican women. As manufacturing declined, Puerto Rican women left the work force. Between 1950 and 1970 Puerto Rican women's labor force participation decreased, while other women's increased significantly (Table 7.2). By 1990 Puerto Rican women's labor force participation had returned to its 1950 level, but far fewer Puerto Rican women now worked compared to all women citywide. Meanwhile, Puerto Rican men's labor force participation, which in 1970 was comparable to other men's citywide, had by 1990 decreased faster than labor force participation for men generally, so that fewer Puerto Rican men in the labor force than men citywide (Table 7.3). Hence, understanding Puerto Rican women as labor migrants is crucial not only in migration patterns and the reconstitution of household economies, but also in understanding contemporary Puerto Rican poverty.

Puerto Ricans were poor as a result of economic displacement and of the low wages they received when they were employed. Finding that by the 1980 census "less than half

TABLE 7.2.   Female Labor Force Participation by Race, Philadelphia, 1950–1990

	1950	1970	1990
Percent in Labor Force:			
Puerto Rican	36.3	30.8	36.4
Black	40.3	48.6	54.2
Total	33.8	43.3	51.5

Sources: U.S. Bureau of the Census as compiled in Philadelphia Commission on Human Relations, *Puerto Ricans in Philadelphia: A Study of Their Demographic Characteristics, Problems and Attitudes* (April 1954; reprint, New York: Arno Press, 1975), 124; U.S. Bureau of the Census, *Census of the Population: 1950*, vol. 2, *Characteristics of the Population*, pt. 38, Pennsylvania (Washington, D.C., 1952), 293; U.S. Bureau of the Census, *Census of the Population: 1970*, vol. 1, *Characteristics of the Population*, pt. 40, Pennsylvania (Washington, D.C., 1973), 492, 444, 388; and U.S. Bureau of the Census, *Census of the Population: 1990, Social and Economic Characteristics*, Pennsylvania (Washington, D.C., 1993), 1136, 1014, 789.

Note: Labor force participation is for those age fourteen and older in 1950, and for those sixteen and older in 1970 and 1990.

TABLE 7.3.   Male Labor Force Participation by Race, Philadelphia, 1950–1990

	1950	1970	1990
Percent in Labor Force:			
Puerto Rican	74.0	73.8	62.2
Black	72.8	72.2	63.1
Total	77.8	74.1	66.7

Sources: See Table 7.1.

Note: Labor force participation is for those age fourteen and older in 1950, and for those sixteen and older in 1970 and 1990.

of Puerto Rican men and a quarter of Puerto Rican women were categorized as employed," a 1985 study concluded that this was "indicative of a long term situation in which large percentages of adult Puerto Ricans are not formally connected to the labor force" and that "Puerto Ricans have been less successful than Blacks or Whites in finding work and this difference cannot be accounted for by their sex and age distributions." When employed, Puerto Ricans remained "heavily concentrated in low wage, low skill occupations in competitive sector industries." Puerto Ricans' per capita income was only 40 percent of that of whites and 63 percent of that of African Americans. Indicative of the negative impact low wages had on Puerto Ricans' economic well-being, the gap between Puerto Ricans' and whites' incomes widened for those employed full-time. Half of Philadelphia's Puerto Ricans lived in families with incomes below the poverty level, in contrast to 21 percent of all Philadelphians. Puerto Rican children fared even worse, with 60 percent living in families with incomes below the poverty level.[33]

Because they settled predominantly in areas of the Northeast and the Midwest that were affected by economic restructuring, Puerto Ricans became displaced labor migrants in other areas as well. New York's economy shifted in similar ways, as sociologist Clara Rodríguez concluded: "Even in 1970, the majority of Puerto Ricans were to be found in declining sectors while the growth sectors employed few Puerto Ricans." The impact on the much larger Puerto Rican community there was just as devastating. Similarly, Chicago experienced economic restructuring that displaced and trapped Puerto Ricans in low-wage jobs. Women were often the most affected. Puerto Rican women's labor force participation dropped dramatically in New York between 1950 and 1970. According to sociologists Rosemary Santana Cooney and Alice Colón, "unfavorable labor-market conditions and large declines in central-city industries in which Puerto Ricans are concentrated" were to blame. This was a regional phenomenon, as women's labor force participation increased in Illinois, California, and to a lesser degree in New Jersey in the same period during which it dropped in New York. In short, Puerto Rican women's decreasing labor force participation and Puerto Ricans' poverty were caused by structural economic changes.[34]

For Puerto Ricans in Philadelphia, the negative impact of economic shifts was intensified by residential segregation and government housing policies. Government policies and the actions of private investors fostered residential segregation. Postwar federal housing policies focused on home ownership, public housing, and urban renewal. The

Federal Housing Administration promoted home ownership through mortgage programs, but limited mortgage loans to new housing, creating a housing boom in the suburbs while denying mortgages in the city. In addition, the FHA relied on the 1930s appraisals of the Home Owners' Loan Corporation, which appraised housing in racial and ethnic terms and had restrictions against providing loans to African Americans seeking houses in white neighborhoods. Mortgages were denied in the city's older industrial and streetcar suburb neighborhoods, which were "redlined" based on explicitly anti-black and anti-ethnic criteria. According to David Bartelt, these policies "ensured that the FHA subsidized segregation." Similarly, public housing policies, both the construction of large projects and "scattered site" (or Section 8) placements in properties leased by the city, increased segregation as African Americans were placed in "black areas." Summarizing the impact of federal policies, Bartelt concludes, "housing policies prior to the 1970s supported a predominantly white movement to the suburbs and a disproportionate allocation of home-ownership options to white families. At the same time, urban renewal and public housing policies hurt predominantly black communities by displacing their residents and reinforcing de facto segregation."[35]

Rather than improving low-income housing in the cities, urban renewal programs sought to attract private investment and led to gentrification and the redevelopment of commercial and business centers. According to Adams and colleagues, for Philadelphia's redevelopment officials, "making the transition to a corporate service economy implied remaking the city to attract and retain the professional white-collar classes as residents and to downplay the presence of the poor and working classes." Policy makers focused on housing for white middle-class professionals with the 1960 Plan for Center City. Gentrification was facilitated by federal tax policies, including the 1976 historic-preservation tax credits and the 1986 tax reform, which reduced interest deductions except for those on mortgages and home equity loans. Other neighborhoods were crippled by disinvestment. As federal agencies disinvested, so did banks and individual owners, who abandoned buildings or let them deteriorate. African Americans became concentrated in the city's older industrial neighborhoods and streetcar suburbs, areas north and west of Center City. Puerto Ricans lived in a narrow strip running north and south between black and white Philadelphia. It was a settlement pattern shaped by racial discrimination, "white flight," and government policies.[36]

Government policies had a similar impact on Puerto Ricans in the city. A 1985 study found that for the Puerto Rican community, "housing is among the poorest in the city, it has large rental stock, is old, with a higher degree of structural problems, and is more crowded than other communities." Puerto Rican neighborhoods were plagued by housing abandonment, loss by demolition, tax delinquency, and aging structures. Although of poor quality, housing was relatively expensive and the total number of units decreased during the 1970s in comparison to the rest of the city. These same areas had lower levels of private investment, via mortgages, and higher levels of public subsidies, via public assistance and the activities of Housing and Urban Development. Fewer Puerto Rican households had telephones and automobiles, which the authors considered "real limitations, not just inconveniences, given that the traditional route out of neighborhoods with poor housing conditions has been through access to jobs via a labor market external to those areas." Only 39 percent of Puerto Ricans were in owner-occupied units, in contrast to 68 percent of whites and 55 percent of African Americans. The authors concluded that "Philadelphia's tradition of being a 'city of home owners' is nowhere so contradicted as it is in the Puerto Rican community" and that "the Puerto Rican community in Philadelphia is carrying the burden of too many years' neglect of its housing stock and of its neighborhoods."[37]

Segregation within the city intensified, even as racial and ethnic diversity increased. By 1990 the city's population was 52 percent white, 39 percent African American, 6 percent Hispanic, and 3 percent Asian and Pacific Islander. Puerto Ricans were 4 percent of the total population and 76 percent of the Hispanic population. During the 1980s, the Asian population increased by 145 percent and the Spanish-speaking population increased by 40 percent, reflecting the impact of the 1965 immigration reforms, which eliminated restrictive national origins quotas. Yet as the fifth largest city, Philadelphia ranked only sixteenth among destinations of new immigrants. By 1990 72 percent of African Americans resided in census tracts that were 90 percent or more African American. Similarly, 80 percent of Puerto Ricans resided in 15 of the city's 364 census tracts. In short, African Americans and Puerto Ricans were concentrated in areas of the city that experienced the loss of manufacturing jobs and that were not aided by public redevelopment monies.[38]

The combined impact of economic change, residential segregation, and government policies was evident. During the 1980s, "the region's income distribution became more unequal" and "the metropolitan area's poor became increasingly concentrated in the city," according to economists Janice Fanning Madden and William J. Stull. In 1988 the poverty rate was 8 percent for the metropolitan area and 16 percent for the city. While the decade saw increases in average family incomes and per capita incomes, significant gaps remained not only between the suburbs and the city, but also among racial groups. African Americans' average annual household income was 61 percent, and Hispanics 53 percent, of that of white households. Similarly, employment increased for all groups during the second half of the decade, but remained lower for African Americans and Hispanics. In short, the gap between the rich and the poor increased, and as Madden and Stull conclude, "the most prosperous residents of the metropolitan area became increasingly isolated, both physically and economically, from the least prosperous over the decade." As of 1989 almost half of all Puerto Rican families in the city lived below the poverty level (defined as $12,674 for a family of four)—48 percent, compared to 25 percent of African American families and 8 percent of white families. Furthermore, while fewer white families were living below the poverty level than in 1970, for African Americans and even more so for Puerto Ricans, conditions had deteriorated and more families found themselves living in poverty. By 1990, Philadelphia was ranked the worst of the fifty largest cities in terms of the number of census tracts with high concentrations of the very poor.[39]

While Puerto Ricans' status as U.S. citizens fostered labor recruitment in the aftermath of World War II, citizenship may have made Puerto Ricans a more costly source of labor in the long run. Sociologists Alejandro Portes and Cynthia Truelove suggest that Puerto Ricans' citizenship and their migration to areas with unionized labor markets combined "to make Puerto Rican workers a less pliable, more costly, and better organized source of labor." As a result, "employer preferences in the Northeast thus shifted gradually toward other immigrant groups." Similarly, David Griffith indicates that U.S. apple and sugar growers "prefer alien to domestic labor" and have "refused to hire" Puerto Rican laborers. Reminiscent of the World War II era, growers, according to Griffith, prefer West Indians because they "constitute a willing, reliable, and highly docile . . . [and] captive labor force." New immigrants have not pushed Puerto Rican migrants up the job ladder; instead, Puerto Ricans have increasingly been pushed out of the labor force altogether. Unlike earlier European immigrants who moved up the economic ladder, and unlike Mexican workers who were brutally deported when their labor was no longer needed, Puerto Ricans, like African Americans, remained in the inner cities and continued to face the adverse conditions.[40]

In the postwar era, government policies on the federal, state, and local levels contributed to the conditions of concentrated poverty that affected the lives of Puerto Ricans in Philadelphia. As recent arrivals to urban areas in the Northeast who were concentrated at the bottom rungs of the economic structure, Puerto Ricans, along with African Americans, bore the brunt of the transition to a postindustrial economy. As historian Theodore Hershberg and colleagues write, "today's blacks inherit the oldest stock of deteriorated housing once inhabited by two earlier waves of immigrants, but the jobs that once were located nearby and that provided previous newcomers with avenues for upward mobility are gone." African Americans and Puerto Ricans also bore the brunt of residential segregation and "white flight," which transformed the racial composition and eroded the economic foundations of urban areas. As sociologist Douglas Massey notes of African Americans and Puerto Ricans, "in the nation's largest urban areas, these groups are the only ones that have *simultaneously* experienced high levels of residential segregation and sharp increases in poverty." These migrants-turned-residents became concentrated in urban areas that were devoid of economic opportunities. It was the combined impact of economic change and residential segregation that created conditions of concentrated poverty.[41]

Interpreting Puerto Rican Poverty

Economic restructuring affected not only Puerto Ricans' economic well-being, but also their community-building efforts and the ways in which they were perceived. Puerto Ricans, who came to Philadelphia in the postwar era looking for *mejor ambiente* or a better life, encountered declining economic opportunities, deteriorating neighborhoods, and racial ideologies that held them responsible for causing and incapable of improving those conditions. Nevertheless, Puerto Ricans continued their efforts to improve their lives, their children's lives, and their communities, confronting deteriorating economic and neighborhood conditions in a variety of ways. The social service

approach of Concilio and other agencies was challenged by a younger generation's radical and confrontational politics, and Puerto Rican politics shifted. Meanwhile, as economic restructuring affected Puerto Ricans in other areas of settlement, a national
discourse emerged that defined Puerto Ricans as "the other underclass." The "underclass" echoed the "culture of poverty" in its emphasis on behavior and culture in interpreting the causes of Puerto Rican poverty, ignoring structural conditions and blaming
the victim. Philadelphia Puerto Ricans and those with "underclass" perspectives
offered widely divergent interpretations of the causes of Puerto Rican poverty and of
possible solutions.

Migrants contrasted the earlier availability of jobs with decreasing opportunities, as
their factories closed, the quality of jobs declined, and they were surrounded by abandoned factory buildings. Doña Genara suggested that there were fewer jobs of lower
quality in the garment industry: "Men's overcoats, it was good work. I would say that
before, I liked the jobs before. Since the factories were better to work in, I think because
now I don't work. But you could get a job anywhere. That's true. That was good before.
. . . All those lots that are vacant over there, those were factories." Food processing
plants were closing or relocating too. Doña Juanita's donut factory had closed; and
Doña Nilda's candy factory as well. "It seems to me that it was in '89 or '90, around
there, that they shut it completely. It went, the factory went, bankrupt or I don't know
what happened. They took everything out. They sold the machines, everything, everything." Similarly, Doña Juanita described the impact of a plant closing on her husband's
jobs in metal plating: "He worked twenty-five years and they let him go. . . . They let
him go and other people because they were downsizing things. Already a lot of factories were disappearing from Philadelphia, they were all those empty buildings there. So
they gave him what they told him *lay off* and then he went to collect unemployment."
Although he was able to get another job, the conditions had worsened:

> Well, he got another job, more or less the same, but earning a lot less. And he took it. . . .
> And we didn't have the same benefits that we had with the other. Well, when they let him
> go, well, for a year we could still use the insurance for hospitals, we still had young children.
> And well, then, he went to the place where his brother worked. . . . And he went, you know
> to work—already five or six months passed—for Thanksgiving day, and he wanted to have
> a lot of food like we always had for the children.

Job opportunities had decreased for Puerto Rican women and men, and fewer jobs were
the good ones with the decent pay and benefits that migrants had coveted.[42]

For Don José, Puerto Ricans were without work because of continuing discrimination and because Puerto Ricans were being replaced by immigrants who were paid lower
wages. Don José explained:

> The Puerto Ricans, they try to make a living, so they go, you know, sometimes they get lucky,
> they get a job. But even so, they were getting less pay than the other people. And it's still on.
> Like I said, discrimination never stops, it keeps on going. You don't see it like we used to
> see it then, but it's still on. That's why so many Puerto Ricans are still not working.

While discrimination continued, the availability of jobs had decreased: "There were jobs to find then. No, there are no jobs today, you know." Pointing to employers' continuing search for cheap labor, he suggested that unions had pushed wages up:

> The union is good and the union is bad. It's good because it protects the people, and it's bad because it destroys the corporation. . . . Comes to the point that the companies, they don't have no more to give. So they have to do something. What they do? They move out. So what happens with the people? They ain't got no job.

Meanwhile, employers had another choice, as Don José noted referring to the increased immigration of other Latinos:

> So, they come over here, like now, they're working for peanuts. Now the farms, and all this, they're full of these people. Because when the Puerto Rican [is] gonna work in a farm now, they need like a house, they need, you know, to [be] treated like a person, not like an animal, and so they want good wages. So the farmers, especially, they don't wanna pay that. So, if the Mexican is working for fifty cents an hour and the Puerto Rican working, he wants five dollars an hour, so they're gonna give the Mexican [the job]. And a lot of companies that are also, they got all these kinds of people. That's why you see so many Puerto Ricans on the street without work. Because they ain't gonna work for free. . . . The same thing with the garment, the clothes, all the same things happened. It happens now. That's why so many Puerto Ricans [are] without work.

For Don José, the displacement of Puerto Ricans in the labor force stemmed from continued discrimination and from employers' continued search for cheap labor, as companies closed, relocated, or hired those compelled to accept low wages and poor working conditions.[43]

As economic opportunities declined, living conditions in their neighborhoods deteriorated as well. Migrants again contrasted the earlier era with the present. Doña Genara reminisced:

> The neighborhood here, you didn't see trash, you didn't see houses falling down. You could walk through Philadelphia. I remember that we had milk delivered to the house, they brought us milk, they brought eggs, they brought everything. They left it on the stairs, and nobody stole it. People didn't throw trash in the streets, they didn't mess up anything. Everything was good here. I remember that it was much better before.

For Doña Genara, the change was sudden and drugs were to blame. "That neighborhood was ruined overnight. For me, this neighborhood was destroyed by drugs. So many drugs, drugs on the corners. And when a person falls to drugs, they don't care." Linking drugs to immigration, she continued: "I'm Hispanic but the immigration from all the countries has ruined this. . . . I would say that what ruined this country was drugs. Of course the immigrants bring them, but also among them are the whites."[44]

Doña Ana Luisa emphasized the impact of deteriorating neighborhoods on the families that lived there. She described the change: "The neighborhood had started to deteriorate. We had gone to a really good neighborhood in '56, we returned, everything was really calm, really nice. Already by, before 1970, everything started to change. But in 1973 when they diagnosed me with a brain tumor, the neighborhood was pretty bad, gangs and a lot of things." She was struck by the impact on the "good families" she knew:

> Before when we were in Philadelphia in 1956, I don't remember hearing the word drugs. That appeared later, that was like a plague that came later . . . and then, I don't know if it was because of the drugs or because the gangs came, but those families that we knew there, that were all such good families, and everyone later, we had come and we returned to visit, they told us that they killed this one and that one—good families.

Relieved that her own children were grown, she concluded, "I don't regret it. Sometimes they say that I was too strict, and I tell them thank God that you weren't born now because if they were born now, well, even stricter, since life has changed. Oh, I am so happy that I don't have small children now."45

As some neighborhoods deteriorated, gentrification pushed Puerto Ricans out of others. The Spring Garden neighborhood was one of the earlier Puerto Rican neighborhoods to undergo gentrification, pushing Puerto Ricans northward and eastward. Doña Ana Luisa explained:

> [Puerto Ricans] kept buying houses, yeah, it was a block of family homes, not apartments. . . . Now they have a garden in the whole block. . . . They demolished all of those houses. . . . The area had a lot of Puerto Ricans and then they kept moving and moving and today very few remain. Today you can count the Puerto Ricans, the Hispanics that are there, because now the rents there are, my God.

Though she and her husband had paid $14 a week for a two-bedroom apartment, she thought rents had climbed to $400 a month for a studio and were far out of reach of most Puerto Ricans. Similarly, Don José remarked, "Now they don't want Puerto Ricans in those areas, like 17, 18, Wallace, Mount Vernon, Green, all these streets. They don't want Puerto Ricans, that's why they build all them houses, they renew all them houses and then they rent the apartments for six, seven, eight hundred dollars. Puerto Ricans don't have that much money to pay for apartments. So this is the way they take them out."46

Despite deteriorating conditions, migrants continued their struggles to provide for themselves and their families, to instill a work ethic in their children, and to provide them with an education. Doña Ana Luisa attempted to counter prejudice and discrimination:

> I taught my children, never, never, never think that you are better than anyone, but don't think that anyone is better than you either—because when a person earns without having to go through what you have to do to survive, so they are better than you—but it isn't so. Where others can get there through their color, through their money, you can get there through your tenacity, through your drive, and thank God they listened to me, and they all got there. They haven't gotten that far, but they got there enough that they all work. It's important to me that they work, that they were good men and women that could earn the bread for their children and every day with the sweat from their brows.

Similarly, Doña Genara took pride in her children's work and emphasized her own work ethic. Although she had pointed to the vacant factories, Doña Genara criticized those who did not work: "I taught three daughters and two sons to work. None of them live off *welfare*. People say, 'I can't get work.' Look, that's not true. . . . The five work. They don't live off *welfare*. And imagine that, there are thirteen grandchildren and none get *welfare*. That's why I say that you can work if you want." While conceding that some might need welfare, she dismissed the changed economic conditions in comparing her work history with mothers today: "My opinion is that they should give it to the people that need it, but to try to have people work, because if I worked with five children, why can't a mother with her five children work?"[47]

Some migrants returned to Puerto Rico, with their children's well-being and education having factored into their decisions to migrate and their decisions to return to Puerto Rico. The Quiñones had hoped to return, as Doña Nilda commented: "The nostalgia for one's own country. He always told me that after his daughters were married and they would be fine and set, he was going to Puerto Rico." Because of a disability, Don Julio relinquished his job at the naval base, and after fifteen years in New York and sixteen in Philadelphia, the Quiñones returned to Salinas, Puerto Rico in 1981. Similarly, the Navarros had always hoped to return to San Lorenzo. Their return in 1973, after seventeen years in Philadelphia, was earlier than they anticipated, as Doña Ana Luisa was diagnosed with a serious medical condition and wanted to return to San Lorenzo because she felt Don Justino would have more help with the children there. They considered their children's education in both decisions, as Doña Ana Luisa explained: "We were thinking of giving the children an education. We were thinking that when the kids graduated from school, at least from high school, that we were going to return to Puerto Rico because we always thought that we were going to return to Puerto Rico." While she lamented that she could not be close to all of her children—"We have six in Philadelphia and four in Puerto Rico, we're divided, it makes me sad"—she still concluded, "it was the only thing we could do to give them a better education . . . for their well-being, we would do it again."[48]

Some Puerto Rican youth responded to the poverty and racial discrimination that affected themselves, their families, and their communities by establishing a branch of the Young Lords in 1970. The Young Lords provided grassroots, community-based services and advocated the independence of Puerto Rico. Philadelphia youth had already formed Aspira clubs and a political group called the Young Revolutionaries for Independence. They then adopted the Young Lords' national platform because it addressed their concerns for the issues affecting their communities and for the independence of Puerto Rico. The Young Lords' *Palante* newsletter announced the new branch: "The brothers and sisters in Philly realized months ago that a revolutionary party was needed to improve the conditions there and started acting to meet the needs of our people." Anticipating the accusation that the Philadelphia Lords were "just trying to copy the LORDS in New York," Juan Ramos, a Philadelphia Young Lord, wrote, "These people must realize that the oppression of Puerto Ricans in Philly is the same as the oppression in New York. The conditions in both of these colonies are the same. . . . The struggle is the same." Although it lasted only a couple of years as an organization, the Young Lords fostered a renewed sense of ethnic pride, challenged the established Puerto Rican leadership, and realigned Puerto Rican politics in the city.[49]

In reminiscing about the origins of his political activism, Young Lord Wilfredo Rojas was struck by the fact that his parents worked hard and remained poor. "I became very political because I saw that something was not right. . . . My father cut sugar cane, came from Yauco, Puerto Rico. Here, he went through years of discrimination." The contrasts were stark and the place of Puerto Rican men was clear. "The Ambassador Hotel was the best, classiest Jewish restaurant in the city, right across the street from my house, and all the cooks were Puerto Ricans, in the back." Rojas also felt that his neighborhood was deteriorating: "I saw my neighborhood go from being a Ukrainian, German, Irish, stable neighborhood to being a ghetto. Those things begin to weigh on you. Why is it that when we get here it becomes a ghetto and all the other Europeans move away?" Similarly, Rafaela Colón, a Young Lords supporter, reflected: "I think being in the middle, and having to use hand-me-downs, and the little ones got the milk, and I was one of the older ones so I didn't get any milk, because we were poor, dirt poor." She explained the impact: "One of the things that I would always look at, since I was little, I knew we were poor. . . . So, I knew I wanted it to be different, and I knew something was wrong with the picture, because my father worked, we were church-going, God-loving people." Colón's father migrated as a seasonal agricultural laborer and her mother cooked and washed for the workers in camp. When they moved to the city, her father worked in a factory and her mother stayed home to care for their nine children. By the age of fourteen, Colón had to work. "Every weekend I was either babysitting for somebody's kids, for rich people, or cleaning some lady's house. I ironed and washed for her every weekend and she paid me five dollars. So I was exploited."[50]

The Young Lords emerged through community organizations, even as they came to challenge them. Aspira, a community organization dedicated to promoting the education of Puerto Rican youth, had come to Philadelphia in 1969. Although Aspira fostered their sense of identity and provided role models and organizing experience, these activists came into conflict with the agency's approach. In announcing "Drive Started to Develop Puerto Rican Leaders," the *Inquirer* revealed a tension over what constituted Puerto Rican leadership. Aspira's national director, Louis Nunez, advocated an individualistic model of professionals escaping from "the slums." Instead of students feeling "despair over their dismal atmosphere," he wanted Puerto Rican professionals "to serve as role models, so that the students will see there are some people making it." In contrast, the Pennsylvania director, Rafael Villafane, stated: "Our goal is the development of community leadership. . . . We want to guide students into higher education, but we also must make sure they commit themselves to returning to the community." His approach was collective; students would "come back and help the Puerto Rican community solve its problems." For Colón there were limitations and benefits: "Aspira was very conservative then, but you had progressive counselors, who allowed students to meet and discuss things. . . . They had this young person. He would teach us about capitalism, about Puerto Rico, about the culture, the relation with the Americans, et cetera." Rojas agreed: "Aspira was too conservative. . . . They didn't want to send them to college to come back and give something to the community but more let's send them to college so they can make something and get out of the ghetto. That's not what I wanted to further my education for." Rojas and others split from their Aspira clubs, formed the Young Revolutionaries for Independence, and then became the Young Lords.[51]

Combined with their sense of injustice was a sense of collective responsibility, rooted in their families and their religion. The Philadelphia Lords retained their ties to both. At Casa del Carmen, a Catholic social service agency, they saw their parents volunteering their time. For Rojas, who had wanted to be a priest, "being involved in the Young Lords was an extension of us wanting to do things" for the community. By focusing on their community programs and dismissing their political ideology, some clergy supported the Young Lords. For Father Thomas P. Craven, director of Casa del Carmen, there was a personal dimension: "Just because young people whom I've known for a long time—and whose families I know—have been radicalized by a different ideology, I see no reason to stop being their friend or to break off communications with them." Casa del Carmen provided office space, while the Lords ran a clothing drive, provided interpreters for the health clinic, and joined in a street procession against drugs. Rojas acknowledged, "we were very Catholic. So the thing was that there are these Catholic kids that grew up in the neighborhood, that were always tied to the Casa del Carmen, that are now asking us to take them in and get them an office for them to promote the breakfast program. Because we weren't really talking about revolution, we were talking about a free breakfast program." As a result, Young Lord branches retained a distinctive stamp, according to Rojas: "If we can put labels on the different chapters, you would say that Chicago were like street Lords because they came out of being a gang. New York were like college students who brought in some street people. . . . And in Philadelphia you had a bunch of Catholics—Catholics who got together, brought in some junkies along the way, and dragged in a few students." Nevertheless, on November 5, 1970, the Lords took over the Kingsway Lutheran Church. Ramos reported in *Palante*, "It is becoming apparent that the church, like all other institutions in our community, is not there to serve the people and that the only way they can be made to serve the people is if the people start doing it themselves." They provided a legal information center, an interpreting program, and drug rehabilitation.[52]

The Young Lords were also supported by their families. Colón believed "there were some people, some older people, that were supportive, who came around and understood. And mostly, it was family related, like my parents. They were supportive of me, you know, because I was a good kid. They figured just 'she's very patriotic.'" Rojas felt he had several "families": "When I needed a good Puerto Rican meal, I'd go back home, but my family was the Young Lords because we always hung out together. And we always respected each other's families, so that I can go to Juan's parents' house and they would feed me, or he could come to my house." The support, for Rojas, rested on family ties and the issues: "Our parents would support us because we were their kids, so whenever an event happened they would come to meetings, they would come to protests. They would be there because they were supporting their kids, and a lot of the things we were saying was true—we were talking about an end to discrimination."[53]

The Young Lords provided grassroots, community-based services and demanded that existing agencies meet the needs of the community. Rojas insisted in a 1971 interview:

"Brothers and sisters who prefer to sit around the office and not talk to the people, you know, get out there and help them where they're at in the streets . . . those brothers and sisters can't be Lords." They ran two free breakfast programs, one at the Lighthouse for more than a hundred children, and the other at St. Edwards Parochial School for more than eighty children. They had a continuous clothing drive. They arranged testing for tuberculosis and volunteered at Casa del Carmen's health clinic, as Young Lord Freddy Rosario asserted, "making it possible for our people to get what is rightfully theirs." They approached gangs through political education. Rojas recounted, "Our whole thing was political—we're brothers, we're Puerto Ricans, we're blacks—we shouldn't fight each other. The enemy is the system. We have to beat the system. These young guys weren't trying to hear that. They were about turf."[54]

In October 1970 the Young Lords called a press conference to "declare war on dope pushers." Rosario explained their approach to drug dealers: "They do not understand that they are killing their brothers when they sell them dope. We will educate them." He was convinced that "the big racketeers will keep sending their poison until all of our people are politicized and know that capitalism wants us to be junkies and mindless pawns." Challenging the association of Puerto Ricans with drugs, he continued, "drugs were here long before any Puerto Ricans thought to live in this racist society." Ramos agreed: "The root of the problem isn't the small user in the ghetto. This heroin is coming from outside the ghetto, from white people. Why don't the police track that down?" While mounting this critique of "the system," the Lords rehabilitated addicts, some of whom became Young Lords. At the same time, Rosario charged, "the Anglos' government and hospital system does not see fit to support us in this struggle," and so the Lords vowed to be "a constant reminder to City Hall that we Puerto Ricans are through begging!"[55]

For the Young Lords, these community-based services were a vehicle for criticizing the "system" and for political education. Their platform called for "a Socialist Society . . . where the needs of the people come first" and for "control of our communities by our people and programs to guarantee that all institutions serve the needs of our people." Juan González, a Young Lord in New York City and later a political activist in Philadelphia, described the difference between the Young Lords and the social service agencies. "While those agencies sought assistance from the government for Puerto Ricans, the Young Lords *demanded* that assistance as a right." In doing so, they "broke with the more mainstream, less confrontational approach of earlier agencies." The Young Lords, according to one reporter, served breakfast with "a lesson about why the kids' parents can't afford the food boys and girls need in order to do well in school." The reporter continued: "The Lords believe this is the patent difference between their breakfast program and a bread line. The latter is a handout, the former is a vehicle for instilling political consciousness."[56]

While their community activities generated support from some, the Young Lords faced the wrath of the city administration and the police. In August 1970, the Young Lords were, as one article proclaimed, "Blamed by Police for Unrest." They were "blamed" for spreading "rumors" of police attacking Puerto Ricans during a "disturbance" at a local bar. Police Captain Malcolm Kachigian stated: "They (the reports) are nothing I can base a criminal charge on . . . but I believe them because this is an anti-establishment group." Ramos instead blamed "police harassment" and Councilman Harry P. Jannotti: "He's trying to destroy the Young Lords because we believe in self-determination for Puerto Ricans." Jannotti responded, "he's lying, as far as I am concerned they were causing trouble. . . . We haven't harassed them at all. . . . But we are going to go after them." The *Inquirer* offered another explanation for the "unrest" at the bar: "Police report the disturbance was touched off last Friday night when white patrons . . . beat and ejected a Puerto Rican patron." Racial incidents had occurred at the bar, which was located in a neighborhood undergoing racial change and which regularly hosted the meetings of the Roofers' Union, whose members were mostly white. The Puerto Rican community responded, including María Lina Bonet, the president of the Puerto Rican Fraternity: "The Lords were in it, the Bonets and their tape recorder were in it, nearly everyone living within a three-block radius of the intersection was in it." What the newspapers called a "weekend disturbance" Rojas recalled as "a rising up of the people." When it was over, six people were injured including four police, eight were arrested, and the bar was firebombed. The roofers moved their union meetings to another part of the city, and the bar's owner hired a Puerto Rican staff.[57]

Though she agreed with Ramos about the police brutality, Bonet advocated a conciliatory approach and objected to the Young Lords' politics. She concluded: "There's no question that on Friday there was a lot of police abuse and brutality." Residents charged that police had broken into several homes, used police dogs, and beaten a pregnant woman and several youth. Bonet held a meeting in her home to address police brutality and invited Police Captain Kachigian and Councilman Jannotti. Her solution was to request a meeting with Police Commissioner Frank Rizzo and to circulate a petition to have the bar closed. Highlighting their political differences, Bonet evicted the Young Lords from the Fraternity's building, exclaiming, "and those posters! I don't mind the Puerto Rican patriots, but *no one's* putting Castro and Guevara on *those* walls. . . . If the Lords ever really hurt this community, that's the day I'll go after them." For the Young Lords, this confrontation with the police was not an isolated incident, and the national branch concluded, "they have undergone practically the heaviest attacks of any branch; there have been numerous beatings, false arrests, and several firebombs which have wrecked their offices."[58]

Along with their political differences and their divergent approaches, the issue of police brutality further divided the Young Lords from the established Puerto Rican leadership, especially Concilio. In 1971, Ramon Velázquez, the new president of Concilio, explained his support for the Democratic candidate: "Rizzo is a second generation Italian who worked his way up the hard way, he understands us." Frank Rizzo was the city's police commissioner and then mayor from 1972 to 1980. While he credited Velázquez for helping to bring Aspira to Philadelphia and for permitting the club to meet in his restaurant, Rojas explained, "our break with him was the fact that he supported Rizzo, and Frank Rizzo at that time used to beat folk with his billy stick, and he had a bad reputation in terms of dealing with the black and Puerto Rican community, of police brutality." Angel Ortiz, in a recent interview, described Concilio as "a hat in hand type of leadership," explaining, "They would come into the mayor's office and deal with Frank Rizzo, they were very much pro–Frank Rizzo at that point. They were beholden, he gave them a few anti-poverty grants and so on." Concilio was also criticized for factionalism and for not providing adequate services. Even though she worked in social services, Colón retorted in 1971, "work with Concilio—I wouldn't even bother. They're too established. They don't meet human needs."[59]

The Young Lords contributed to a redefinition of Puerto Rican identity and Puerto Rican politics. Making the connection between identity and politics, Rojas considered it a short step from "ethnic pride" to "respect": "A lot of folks thought that we were crazy for challenging the system, but it wasn't a question of being crazy. It was a question of gaining respect." In June 1971 the *Bulletin* captured the shift: "A wave of ethnic pride has been sweeping the Puerto Rican community here recently. . . . Its exponents reject the attitude that because their culture is different, it is inferior." For one reporter, the presence of the Young Lords "indicates in no uncertain terms that Puerto Ricans do not intend to be victimized for long." Differences remained, however, as the *Bulletin* depicted competing views of "The American Dream," with photographs and quotes from two older and two younger Puerto Rican men. Candelario Lamboy, a furniture store owner, espoused a traditional view of equal opportunity: "The opportunity is here. But we have learned to work and save and do it on our own. We don't get any help." Another businessman, Domingo Martínez, observed a shift: "Before, people who made it didn't want to be called Puerto Rican, now they are proud of it. One of the things we won't sell at any price is our culture." For Temple University recruiter and counselor Epifanio de Jesus, "there is no American dream for us and never was one. Besides who wants to wait four generations to get it?" Finally, Young Lord Caspar Martínez asserted, "our people spend their whole lives picking berries, washing plates and waiting for the crumbs from the table of capitalist society." Yet by 1972 the bridging of independence and local issues, which had given the Young Lords their impetus, became divisive. As the national branch opened offices in Puerto Rico in 1971 "to unite our people on the island and the mainland with a common goal: liberation," repression against them increased, tensions with independence movements in Puerto Rico emerged, and internal divisions over whether to focus their efforts on promoting independence for Puerto Rico or on improving conditions for Puerto Ricans in the States fractured the Young Lords.[60]

Meanwhile, Concilio and Aspira continued their efforts, and other organizations emerged. Although differences persisted within the Puerto Rican community, at times the lines between social service and more radical approaches blurred. In 1972 the Norris Square Senior Citizens Center was established, and Doña Carmen became its director. While the Center provided seniors a hot lunch, a friendly atmosphere for social interaction, and social services and referrals, Doña Carmen and the seniors also kept working to improve conditions for Puerto Ricans in the city. Doña Carmen recalled: "The same thing, that never ends, and when an organization here in the city, for example Aspira, had problems, I took a group of seniors and we picketed. We went to Washington around funding. We get involved, always. . . . I take the seniors, we are always involved for the well-being of other people, the family." Also in 1972, Taller Puertorriqueño was founded with a grant from the Pennsylvania Council of Arts and help from Aspira. Taller taught traditional Puerto Rican arts and crafts to children and adults in Aspira's basement. Over the years, Taller expanded its arts program to include graphic arts and a photo lab, conducted an oral history project, and established a bilingual bookstore, an art gallery, and a cultural resource center.[61]

In city politics, the Young Lords' confrontation with the police and the city administration caused a rift in the longstanding affiliation of Puerto Rican leaders and Frank Rizzo. Although the Young Lords dissolved, former members remained active in politics. Colón held a meeting in her home to study the Puerto Rican Socialist Party, and activists decided to form a chapter in Philadelphia. When Angel Ortiz came to Philadelphia from New York in 1976 as an attorney with Community Legal Services, the PSP began meeting out of his home and the offices of Community Legal Services. Initially focused on independence, the PSP increasingly incorporated local issues, organizing marches and demonstrations, starting housing groups that opposed gentrification, and confronting police brutality and the police killing of Puerto Rican youth José Reyes. Rizzo created a political opportunity, as Ortiz recalled: "We were a small group of PSP individuals and we had a lot of people that were affiliated and associated but we needed to broaden it in terms of the struggles that we were having here. A lot of Puerto Ricans are very much afraid of the word socialist. So we were looking for a mechanism to do that. Frank Rizzo offered us another." During his second term as mayor, in 1978, Rizzo tried to alter the city's charter so that he could run for a third term. Forging a coalition, Puerto Ricans United Against Rizzo, and working with white liberals and African Americans, activists mounted a voter registration campaign. Although a majority of Puerto Ricans had voted for Rizzo in both of his mayoral campaigns, more than 60 percent voted against him in the referendum. Ortiz explained: "The leadership broke down very clearly, the traditional leadership went with the mayor and those of us that were Left, we went to make an alliance with the African American community." Rizzo was defeated.[62]

After the defeat of Rizzo, Puerto Ricans held a convention and formed the Puerto Rican Alliance. Again, former Young Lords and PSP activists were involved, and Juan Ramos became the first president. Like the Young Lords, the Alliance addressed homeland and local issues. Ortiz recalled, "It was known as a socialist, pro-independence, political grouping. . . . It was a very clear, clear Left organization that was dealing with the democratic rights of Puerto Ricans, here in the island, here in the city." The Alliance mobilized the community around housing, workers' rights, education, and police brutality, while protesting the U.S. Navy's presence on Vieques. They continued the confrontational style of politics, organizing squatters to occupy vacant housing owned by Housing and Urban Development, holding a spontaneous sit-in at Independence Hall and raising the Puerto Rican flag, and taking over Jimmy Carter's campaign headquarters in 1980. Unlike the Young Lords, the Alliance entered electoral politics and succeeded. By the mid-1980s, Angel Ortiz was elected to an at-large seat on the City Council and Ralph Acosta was elected to the State House, where he was succeeded by Benjamin Ramos. Though this political representation was consistent with the 4 percent of the city's population that was Latino, issues of electoral districting remained.

Nonetheless, Ortiz explained the importance of the Alliance: "We didn't control jobs, we didn't have community organizations, we didn't hire anybody, but at that point the people—that was the leadership that the community out there trusted, because we were fighting the establishment." In contrast, Ortiz stressed, "none of the other folks who came through traditional leadership have ever been able to get elected." Puerto Rican politics in the city had been realigned.[63]

This shift in Puerto Rican leadership in Philadelphia was the result of Puerto Rican activism from the early 1970s to the 1980s. Despite the changing organizations, many of the activists, the issues, and the confrontational style of politics continued. Writing in the late 1980s, González made the connection: "We have two of the most committed and politically progressive elected officials of any Puerto Rican colonia in the nation. . . . This is no accident. It is a direct result of the struggles of the past fifteen years." Similarly, Colón concluded, "the Young Lords were critical to any progressive movement in Philadelphia." This was a second generation that came of age during an era of political activism and ethnic revitalization, and it was a community shaped not only by its "minority" status, but also, as activist and journalist Pablo "Yoruba" Guzmán noted, by "our overwhelming preponderance in the working class." Concerns with homeland and barrio issues were not mutually exclusive—attention to homeland issues did not prevent activism on issues affecting Puerto Ricans' daily lives in the States. Instead, the continuing colonial relationship made both particularly salient for Puerto Ricans in the States.[64]

As Puerto Ricans in Philadelphia and other areas confronted and responded to changing conditions, they were perceived and defined as "the other underclass" in the national discourse. Some scholars and policy makers, as Katz observes, use the term "underclass" to refer to conditions of concentrated poverty, while others use it to posit cultural and behavioral causes for poverty.[65] Like Lewis's criteria for the "culture of poverty," this latter definition includes pathological behavior and a lack of integration with the larger society or social isolation. In addition, the "culture of poverty's" concern with welfare and dependency and the gendered dimensions that held women responsible for many "problems" have been reasserted in the "underclass" ideology. Whereas Puerto Ricans had failed in earlier comparisons to European immigrants at the turn of the century, they now failed in comparison to other "Hispanics" and new immigrants. In returning to cultural explanations for Puerto Rican poverty and in its lack of historical perspectives, the "underclass" resuscitated the "culture of poverty."

Because of a nearly exclusive focus on African Americans, Puerto Ricans emerged as the "other underclass." Political economist Andrés Torres has noted the "common tendency to classify poverty as an exclusively African American dilemma" despite the greater poverty of Puerto Ricans and the "scant, usually patronizing attention in the general scheme of policy discussions" that is given to Puerto Rican poverty. As a result, Puerto Ricans have suffered from both invisibility and the stigmas embedded in the "underclass." In his article "The Other Underclass," Nicholas Lemann underscored both the invisibility and the stigma: "'Underclass' is a supposedly nonracial term, but by most definitions the underclass is mostly black and discussions of it are full of racial undercurrents." Although "Puerto Ricans are the worst-off ethnic group in the United

States," he added, "after a brief flurry of publicity back in *West Side Story* days, [they] have become invisible." Implying that Puerto Ricans were somehow exempt from racial ideologies or that adding another group somehow diminished racial dimensions, Lemann hoped that a discussion of Puerto Rican poverty "may make possible a truly deracialized grasp of what most experts agree is a non-race specific problem." Lemann, however, offered cultural explanations for Puerto Rican poverty that continued the racialization characteristic of "the culture of poverty."[66]

According to Lemann, "the underclass" was "the result of a one-two punch of economic factors, such as unemployment and welfare, and cultural ones, such as neighborhood ambience and ethnic history." Like proponents of the "culture of poverty," Lemann pointed to family dissolution and the lack of a work ethic and suggested a generational impact: "The statistics show Puerto Ricans to be much more severely afflicted than Mexican-Americans by what might be called the secondary effects of poverty, such as family breakups, and not trying to find employment—which work to ensure that poverty will continue beyond one generation." Citing low labor force participation rates and "the availability of government checks," he endorsed the view that women and welfare were the culprits. Unemployment was "exacerbated by the nature of Puerto Rican sex roles and family life," including "the island ethic that women shouldn't work." For Lemann, Puerto Ricans failed in comparison to African Americans, lacking the "black institutional network of colleges, churches, and civil rights organizations" and suffering from isolation "even more pronounced than the isolation of the black poor." Similarly, contrasting Puerto Ricans with more recent immigrants, Lemann concluded, "Social critics commonly complain that Puerto Ricans lack a true immigrant mentality—they aren't fully committed to making it on the mainland, so they don't put down deep neighborhood and associational roots, as other immigrants do, and they are constantly moving back and forth from Puerto Rico." Here, Puerto Ricans again lacked community and a "mentality" that could enable them to succeed.[67]

In *Out of the Barrio*, Linda Chavez's cultural interpretation of Puerto Rican poverty went farther than Lemann's in blaming the victim. She contrasted Puerto Ricans' experience to what she depicted as the "real progress" of other Hispanics and defined the "Puerto Rican exception": "Puerto Ricans appear to be the one Hispanic group that truly fits the model of a permanently disadvantaged group, indeed one that is developing a sizable underclass." In criticizing "Hispanic leaders," she revealed her views of the causes of Puerto Rican poverty: "Not one of the leaders mentioned family dissolution or low work effort as chiefly responsible for the burgeoning Puerto Rican poverty, or suggested that too much reliance on government—not too little government help—might be the problem in the first place." For Chavez, the causes of Puerto Rican poverty were high rates of "social dysfunction," which included female-headed households, out-of-wedlock births, and welfare dependency, as well as the failure or refusal of Puerto Ricans to assimilate fully.[68]

The gender dimensions of Chavez's argument emerged in her emphasis on the "relationship between the breakdown of the family and diminished Puerto Rican achievement." Echoing the portrayal of "submissive wives," she pointed to women's "surprisingly strong family attachment and traditional family values," and argued, "what they lacked was a strong work ethic, at least with regard to work outside the home." Portrayals of defective families and concerns with welfare dependency took center stage: "What should be an advantage for Puerto Ricans—namely, citizenship—has turned into a liability in the welfare state." Puerto Ricans had been "smothered by entitlements" and "welfare has supplanted the family network of support." In her final analysis, "the solution to these problems will not be found in more government programs. Indeed, government has been an accomplice in enabling fathers to abandon their responsibility. Only the Puerto Rican community can save itself, but the healing cannot begin until the community recognizes that many of its deadliest wounds are self-inflicted." With its wounds "self-inflicted," the Puerto Rican community was called upon to eliminate poverty by behaving properly and by pulling itself up by its proverbial "bootstraps."[69]

In his discussion of Philadelphia's "underclass," historian Roger Lane links the "underclass" with the "culture of poverty," referring to "the behavior associated with an underclass 'culture of poverty.'" Focusing on African Americans, he defines "culture" as "a widely shared set not only of formal values but of attitudes, habits, and priorities," and argues: "In addition to poverty itself . . . the African-American experience has created a large number of people who are easily discouraged, unrealistic about the relation of ends to means, lacking pride in themselves and trust in others." Devoting some attention to economic restructuring and the role of racism in excluding urban blacks "in Philadelphia and elsewhere from the urban-industrial revolution," Lane concludes that the "underclass" is the result of both "structural conditions which simply deny its members the chance to work" and "other 'cultural' factors within the group, which make its members unable or unwilling to take advantage of opportunities even when offered." For possible solutions he does not turn to those he describes as "the great pool of 300,000 undereducated, sometimes hostile, poor Philadelphians who constitute the underclass," but rather to the black middle class. As part of the problem, middle-class African Americans moved out of the poorest areas, leaving "no 'old heads,' no role models, no one to help in any way." For the solution, Lane suggests "formal voluntary action" to replace "the old neighborhoods and natural networks" and provide "role modeling," and advocates the involvement of all levels of government and the corporate business community to increase jobs and improve education. As with the "culture of poverty," the definition of the "problem" shapes the recommended solutions.[70]

Even though most "culture of poverty" proponents called for social programs and most "underclass" proponents are calling for their elimination, both have assumed the need to transform individual and group behaviors, and have paid little attention to the larger forces, often state-initiated or market-driven, that shape and impinge on those behaviors. At the same time, with their focus on "deficient" cultures and "pathological" behaviors, the negative perceptions of poor people of color embedded in the "culture of poverty" and "underclass" paradigms have influenced ideas about who is capable of addressing the issues confronting the urban poor. Historian Thomas Jackson suggests that there has been historical continuity, as "reformist experts and policy makers debate and design programs that can be sold to the overwhelmingly middle-class electorate, without seeking to redress the class bias in the electorate itself, and without more directly involving the poor in transforming the conditions of their own lives." Both the "culture of poverty" and the "underclass" consider their subjects, African Americans and Puerto Ricans, incapable of intelligently shaping their own futures. As a result, these groups confront structural conditions of concentrated poverty and racial ideologies that render them responsible for and incapable of improving those conditions.[71]

Conclusion

While economic and living conditions in the inner cities have changed considerably, racial ideologies have been marked by continuities. The continuities between the "culture of poverty" and the "underclass" paradigms lie in the targets of these labels— World War II migrants of color who were never considered labor migrants—and in their focus on the presumed "problems" of these groups. From the postwar era to the present, Puerto Ricans have been perceived not as labor migrants or as displaced labor migrants but as people with "problems" who create "problems" for the community. The national discourse interpreting Puerto Rican poverty shifted from the "culture of poverty" to "the underclass." Yet both the "culture of poverty" and "the underclass" are racial ideologies that point to particular groups of people, emphasize their "problems," and hold them culpable for their own poverty. They focus on the assumed behaviors of individuals, while downplaying the active decisions Puerto Ricans made to improve their circumstances, and the roles of economic change and residential segregation. Assessments of government policies have centered on welfare and whether or not it creates "dependency," ignoring policies that fostered labor recruitment, deindustrialization, and residential segregation. In short, government policies, structural inequalities, and racism are not viewed as central to the challenges confronting Puerto Ricans. Perhaps these paradigms reflect the demise of biological racism in the postwar era, while operating as more "culturally" based ideologies in marginalizing those who were wanted as laborers but not as community members. Meanwhile, negative perceptions of poor people of color embedded in the "culture of poverty" and "underclass" paradigms have rendered Puerto Ricans' motivations in migrating and their community-building efforts invisible, while shaping ideas about who is capable of addressing conditions of poverty and the proposed solutions. The transformation of Puerto Rican labor migrants into "the other underclass" has obscured not only the historical causes and contours of Puerto Rican migration, but also critical dimensions of the postwar era and the causes of contemporary urban poverty.

Epilogue

Few historical works have addressed the post–World War II Puerto Rican migration or the evolution of racial ideologies from the "culture of poverty" to the "underclass." This lack of historical attention obscures the complexity of the causes and dynamics of Puerto Rican migration. Literature written during the peak period of migration ignored the colonial relationship, thereby missing the impact of U.S. investment in causing displacement, as well as the roles of labor recruitment and state policies. More recently, some scholars have continued to invoke "overpopulation," while others have added a cultural tendency to wander aimlessly as the cause of circular migration. Prevailing explanations of Puerto Rican poverty offer inaccurate portrayals of Puerto Rican culture, rather than analyzing the transition from postwar economic growth to economic restructuring and the impact of residential segregation. Both the continuing reliance on works written during the postwar era and the more recent reliance on "underclass" perspectives have fostered the notion that there was and is no Puerto Rican "community." Instead of a narrow definition based on community organizations and comparisons to earlier European immigrants, "community" requires a broader definition and historical perspectives that take into account economic conditions, the welfare state, racism, and politics, as well as the diversity and dynamics internal to the Puerto Rican community.

Hopefully, this study of Puerto Rican migration contributes to the emerging social histories of the postwar era and provides a foundation for comparative migration studies. The work of immigration historians, as Donna Gabaccia has noted critically, is most often incorporated into U.S. history when it addresses assimilation and Americanization, and there has been a resurgence of interest in these topics.[1] Yet migration scholars ask a broad range of questions, which shed light on topics such as economic change, racial ideologies, gender constructions, foreign policy, and globalization. Meanwhile, the basis for comparative migration studies is emerging, along with scholarship on the post–World War II era.[2] As a colonial migration organized in large measure by state policy, Puerto Rican migration is unique in some ways. Nevertheless, it shares key elements with the postwar migrations of African Americans and Mexicans, as well as the post-1965 immigrations from Caribbean, Latin American, and Asian countries.

As postwar migrants, Puerto Ricans and African Americans encountered a Philadelphia that differed significantly from that encountered by earlier European immigrants.
According to historian Theodore Hershberg and colleagues, for the British, German,
and Irish immigrants arriving during the 1840s and 1850s the city offered an expanding economy and "a context of widening occupational opportunity for whites." With
jobs concentrated in the city's center, being close to particular industries shaped residential patterns more than ethnicity, and neighborhoods were integrated. As work
became more differentiated by wages and status, residential areas became more
homogenous, shaping the context for the Italians, Poles, and Russian Jews between
1885 and 1914. As a result, "the availability of cheap, old housing concentrated in close
proximity to plentiful manufacturing jobs contributed to the considerably higher levels
of residential segregation of the Italians, Poles, and Russian Jews." The economy was
still diversified and manufacturing jobs increased. Despite some shift to outlying areas,
most manufacturing and retail jobs remained concentrated in the city's center, and
workers lived nearby. Housing was predominantly row houses, not tenements, making
Philadelphia the "City of Homes." In contrast, the next wave of migrants, African
Americans arriving after 1945, confronted a "declining opportunity structure" and
institutional racism. Though they lived close to manufacturing jobs in earlier eras,
African Americans had not been hired for those jobs, becoming the exception to the patterns for European immigrants. Now, those manufacturing jobs decreased and decen-
tralized, relocating to the suburbs. Meanwhile, African Americans' residential
segregation, which had always surpassed that of European immigrants, increased during the postwar era. For Hershberg and colleagues, these markedly differing historical
contexts constituted "A Tale of Three Cities."[3]

Beyond the Philadelphia context, there are important parallels in the histories of Puerto
Ricans, African Americans, and Mexicans who were labor migrants in the post–World
War II era, even though regional variations remain significant. These postwar migrants
experienced labor recruitment for low-wage jobs and the expanded role of the state in
shaping that labor recruitment. Men were recruited for seasonal agricultural work and
found work in the expanding low-wage service sector in urban areas. For farmworkers,
the state intervened during World War II and after, not to eliminate contract labor but to
regulate and promote it. Bridging indentured servitude and free labor, labor contracts
demonstrate the different options facing citizens and noncitizens, as well as the limited
employment options available to certain citizens.[4] Women were recruited as domestics. A
contract labor program for one-year "Bracero Maids" was proposed by Anglo housewives
in El Paso, Texas in 1953, mirroring that for Mexican agricultural workers. Although the
program was rejected by the Department of Justice, Mexican women continued a long history of domestic service as commuters with work permits and as undocumented workers.
African American women's concentration in paid reproductive work continued in the
postwar era, even as reproductive work shifted "from the household to the market."[5]

Despite similarities, Puerto Rican migration to Philadelphia also reveals the importance of examining the intersections of race and gender in analyzing labor force participation. In Philadelphia, Puerto Rican men and women encountered different labor
markets segmented by gender, while the employment patterns of Puerto Rican, African

American, and white women differed significantly. Beyond Philadelphia, Puerto Rican and Mexican women were increasingly incorporated into the garment and other labor-intensive industries, while African American women continued to be excluded from industry altogether. Like separating migrants and immigrants, focusing on either race or gender distorts the workings of the labor market and the complexity of employment patterns, as well as their impact on peoples' well-being.[6]

Puerto Rican migration also illustrates the reformulation and continuing significance of racial ideologies and their gender dimensions in the postwar era. Puerto Ricans came to the States as a colonized group that was racially heterogenous and racially mixed. In the post–World War II era the U.S. mainstream sought to define Puerto Rican migrants at a time when biological racism had been challenged. New racialist constructions of marginalization emerged, based in part on notions of inferior "cultures." The "culture of poverty" emerged as a national discourse and a racial ideology with important local and gender dimensions. While responses to culture of poverty perspectives shaped the scholarship in Puerto Rican, Chicano, and African American Studies, the black-white racial binary still defines and in some cases limits the U.S. historiography, even in discussions of the "culture of poverty" and the "underclass."[7] And while Puerto Ricans, African Americans, and Mexican Americans were characterized as having cultures of poverty and pathological behaviors, how these ideologies took shape in particular contexts and their gender dimensions still need to be interrogated. For example, with Puerto Rican women portrayed as submissive and African American women as matriarchs, these similarities and differences highlight the gender dimensions of racial ideologies, as well as the racial dimensions of gender ideologies.[8]

Puerto Ricans, African Americans, and Mexicans who settled in cities in the postwar era confronted the changing nature of urban economies and urban life, the continuing significance of racial ideologies and discrimination, and the increased impact of the state through economic, housing, and welfare policies. The relative lack of historical work, combined with the failure to treat these groups as labor migrants and to address the racial ideologies that have defined them, render most assessments of the contemporary plight of inner-city Puerto Ricans, African Americans, and Mexican Americans ahistorical. As emerging social histories suggest, the roots of today's concentrated poverty in the inner cities are lodged in the postwar era's segregation, suburbanization, and economic restructuring. These postwar migrants bore the brunt of the transition to a postindustrial economy.[9] As Carl Husemoller Nightingale observes, however, "scholars have tended to ignore the relationship between changes in global history and the experience of African Americans, particularly the experience of poor urban black people," while those concerned with economic restructuring have not focused on its impact on "U.S.-born black people or persistent urban poverty and joblessness." Only a few social scientists studying Latinos in the inner cities have addressed these issues. Yet, experiencing the economic consequences of the global economy, especially the continued flight and downgrading of manufacturing jobs and the growth of low-wage service sector jobs, these postwar migrants reveal the changed environments that many post-1965 immigrants encountered as the global economy continues to bring immigrants to urban areas.[10]

Finally, Puerto Rican migration highlights crucial dynamics of the post-1965 immigrations. The colonial ties between the United States and Puerto Rico defined Puerto Rico's insertion into the global economy, giving a particular slant to the global aspects of Puerto Rico's economic development and migration. At the same time, however, these colonial ties foreground the unequal relations between countries in the global economy and the roles U.S. economic and political interventions play in shaping economic development and migration in other countries. In other words, the colonial ties to Puerto Rico and the conquest of Mexico are stark examples, but other migration streams are also influenced by the United States' impact in countries of origin. The post-1965 immigrants have come predominantly from countries in Latin America, the Caribbean, and Asia where the United States has exerted political influence or intervened militarily.[11]

U.S. economic intervention has continued as well; Puerto Rico was only the first of many export processing zones. U.S. capital, especially in labor-intensive industries like the garment industry, has continued its search for ever cheaper labor, relying on women of color as a source of cheap labor in their countries of origin and in the States. Export-oriented industrialization and global divisions of labor dislocate economies and people, fostering migrations. Meanwhile, employers in the United States continue to rely on the most vulnerable sources of labor, through the employment of undocumented workers and the rise of sweatshops. Puerto Rican women were forerunners in the labor migrations of women, sparked by the globalization of labor-intensive industries and by the resurgence of a downgraded manufacturing sector in the United States. Their experiences reveal the ironies and hardships wrought by labor recruitment followed by displacement in both the country of origin and urban areas in the States.

Nor have the tensions between wanting cheap laborers and not wanting community members abated. As immigration from Latin America and the Caribbean increased, policy makers and social scientists defined the newcomers, as well as Mexicans and Puerto Ricans who had been in the States for generations, as "Hispanics." The use of the term obfuscated the complexities of racial and ethnic identities that policy makers, social service workers, and others had been unable or unwilling to resolve in the postwar era, leaving in place many stereotypes and misconceptions. This umbrella term also denied Latino groups their national origins and their particular migration histories, thereby increasing the chances that they would be rendered invisible in U.S. history. Meanwhile, debates over immigration policy and the reception of formerly colonized peoples of color in U.S. society continue.[12] Nevertheless, like Doña Epifania, whose story started this book, and the other Puerto Ricans whose stories fill its pages, immigrants come to the United States displaced from their local communities and looking for work and a better life in the global economy. Like Puerto Rican migrants, many form transnational links between home and migrant communities. While some hope to return to their country of origin, they too work to recreate household economies and communities in the States. In documenting the history of Puerto Rican migration to Philadelphia, this study underlines the inadequacy of the cultural paradigms, situates these migrants at a particular moment in the history of migration to the United States, and illuminates their shared experiences and their differences from other labor migrants.

Appendix I

Additional Data

TABLE A.I. Residence in Puerto Rico of People Born in San Lorenzo and Salinas, 1950–1960

	1950 San Lorenzo	1960 San Lorenzo	1950 Salinas	1960 Salinas
Total Number	34,654	33,400	20,592	21,796
Percent in:				
Municipio of Birth	76.7	75.3	78.6	76.9
Other Municipios	23.3	25.1	21.4	23.1
Number in				
Other Municipios	8,063	8,392	4,414	5,044
Percent in:				
Tobacco	29.7	25.1	21.4	16.7
Coffee	0.2	0.3	0.7	0.3
Southeast	34.5	27.0	35.9	30.8
Southwest	1.2	1.1	21.5	19.6
North	1.2	1.0	1.5	3.0
S.J. Metro	33.2	39.1	23.3	29.6

Sources: U.S. Bureau of the Census, *U.S. Census of Population: 1950*, vol. 2, *Characteristics of the Population*, pt. 53, Puerto Rico (Washington, D.C., 1953), 94–98; and U.S. Bureau of the Census, *U.S. Census of Population: 1960*, vol. 1, *Characteristics of the Population*, pt. 53, Puerto Rico (Washington, D.C., 1963), 161–177.

TABLE A.2.   Migrants' Occupations, According to Philadelphia Marriage Licenses, 1945–1965

	Puerto Rico		San Lorenzo		Salinas	
	Male	Female	Male	Female	Male	Female
Number Employed	587	568	95	105	42	40
Percent:						
Professional	0.2	0.7	—	—	—	—
Manager	0.9	—	2.1	—	—	—
Sales/Clerical	2.7	3.7	1.1	3.8	2.4	2.5
Crafts	3.7	0.5	2.1	—	4.8	—
Service	17.9	6.5	20.0	1.9	9.5	7.5
Operatives	39.2	40.5	46.3	41.0	40.5	32.5
Laborers	26.6	0.2	22.1	—	31.0	—
Farm work	2.4	0.2	1.1	—	—	—
None or Housewives	2.4	44.2	4.2	50.5	7.1	57.5
Other	4.1	3.5	1.1	2.9	4.8	—

Sources: Marriage Licenses, 1945–1965, Court of Orphan Pleas, City Hall, Philadelphia, Pa.

TABLE A.3.   Migrants' Parents' Occupations in Philadelphia, 1945–1965

	Puerto Rico		San Lorenzo		Salinas	
	Male	Female	Male	Female	Male	Female
Number in Philadelphia	217	309	52	69	21	27
Percent:						
Professionals	—	—	—	—	—	—
Managers	4.6	0.3	3.8	—	—	—
Clerical/ Sales	3.2	0.3	—	—	—	—
Crafts	4.1	1.0	3.8	2.9	4.8	3.7
Operatives	18.4	12.9	34.6	10.1	4.8	14.8
Laborers	28.1	0.3	38.5	—	28.6	—
Service	9.2	4.9	1.9	5.8	9.5	7.4
Farmers	5.1	—	1.9	—	23.8	—
Housewives	—	75.7	—	78.3	—	66.7
Retired/None	27.2	4.5	15.4	2.9	28.6	7.4

Sources: Marriage Licenses, 1945–1965, Court of Orphan Pleas, City Hall, Philadelphia, Pa.
Note: Not all columns total exactly 100 percent due to rounding.

Appendix II

A Word on Sources

Puerto Rico's status and Puerto Ricans' U.S. citizenship creates both opportunities and obstacles in terms of the sources available to study migration. I wanted to know where Philadelphia's Puerto Rican migrants had come from. Yet Puerto Rican Studies scholars have long decried the absence of reliable sources on the magnitude and timing of the migration. Airport surveys, conducted by the government of Puerto Rico, are limited in scope and do not distinguish well between migrants and visitors. Scholars concerned with island-wide out-migration use these surveys and demographic data. The absence of naturalization records, so often put to good use by immigration historians, sent me in search of other ways to determine towns of origin and migration patterns. Marriage licenses at Philadelphia's City Hall, unfortunately, listed migrants' place of birth as "Puerto Rico" without reference to a specific municipio in most instances. Catholic Churches in Philadelphia, however, listed the place of baptism by municipio when confirming baptism prior to marriage. Limited mobility in Puerto Rico in the years preceding World War II suggests that migrants may have come from these municipios. Protestant Churches were much less likely to identify migrants' place of birth. Returning to city marriage licenses, I identified the birthplace for some of the migrants married in Protestant churches and gathered information for all Puerto Rican migrants married in 1954 and 1955. In the end, I determined the place of baptism or birth for 2,853 Puerto Ricans married in Philadelphia between 1945 and 1965: 1,634 from St. Peter the Apostle Church; 1,142 from the Chapel of Our Lady of the Miraculous Medal (La Milagrosa); 22 from the Spanish Baptist Church; 13 from the Methodist Memorial Temple; and 42 from city marriage licenses without a church affiliation. This approach provides the most detailed assessment of the origins of Puerto Rican migrants to date.

To explore out-migration, I turned to Catholic church records in San Lorenzo and

Salinas. Migrants requested confirmation of their baptisms in order to get married in Catholic churches. In some instances, the place and date of marriage was recorded in the baptism register. These records enabled me to decipher broad trends in out-migration and destinations in Puerto Rico and the States. I determined the place of marriage for 2,578 of San Lorenzo's migrants who married beyond the municipio's boundaries between 1945 and 1965, and for 1,043 of Salinas's migrants. I supplemented this data with U.S. census materials and demographic studies.

This book supports many scholars' contention that migration must be studied from the vantage points of both sending and receiving societies. Here, Puerto Rico's status provides a wealth of accessible data in the form of published U.S. government documents unavailable to immigration scholars studying other countries. In charting broad economic and population changes, I relied on the U.S. Census for Puerto Rico and Philadelphia. As a federal depository for U.S. government documents, Rutgers University's Alexander Library has an extensive collection of published government documents. Although the census has been criticized for inaccuracy in its treatment of minorities in the States, no other source provides a tool to chart change over time and on such a wide variety of variables. When possible, I supplemented census data with other sources—using Philadelphia marriage licenses as an additional source on Puerto Ricans' occupations, for example. Additional government documents are housed at La Colección Puertorriqueña at the University of Puerto Rico in Río Piedras, along with newspapers and an index for *El Mundo*.

Similarly, unpublished government documents are located in the States and Puerto Rico, although some collections are just beginning to be inventoried. The National Archives in Washington, D.C., and their regional branch in Philadelphia have well-organized documents on Puerto Rican migration and labor recruitment. The Archivo General de Puerto Rico, on the other hand, has an incredible collection of Department of Labor, and specifically Migration Division, documents that are not yet inventoried. Here, through a process of trial and error, I was extremely fortunate to locate farm labor contracts and applications, correspondence, newspaper clippings, sample contracts for the domestic workers program, and other sources. As these documents are organized and inventoried, scholars will be able to pursue a variety of topics. Stateside, when I started my research, Migration Division documents were at the Department of Puerto Rican Community Affairs in the United States (formerly the Migration Division) in New York. This collection has been moved to the Centro de Estudios Puertorriqueños at Hunter College in New York, where it is being organized and inventoried. The collection includes the Migration Division's monthly and annual reports; documents on the farm labor program, the employment service, the identification program, and community organizations; and Puerto Rico government documents. It joins the Centro's already impressive and ever growing collection of sources on Puerto Rican migration and Puerto Ricans in the States.

In Philadelphia, the archival materials at Temple University's Urban Archives proved a valuable source. When I started my research in 1988, the documents of the Urban Archives were not easily accessible and it was not clear what their collections might reveal about Puerto Ricans in Philadelphia. The Archives have since moved to a very user-friendly space and more collections are inventoried. Their holdings of community agencies and organizations, such as the Friends Neighborhood Guild, the Nationalities Services Center, and the YWCA provided not only crucial data but also, as I suggest in Chapter 6, an important lens on the attitudes of the era. The Archive's newspaper clippings, photograph collections, dissertations, and government documents were also extremely useful. Additional government documents were available at the Free Library, and the Balch Institute for Ethnic Studies is collecting documents on Puerto Rican organizations.

Oral histories offered the opportunity to explore migrants' perceptions of changing conditions, their decisions, and their experiences. Between 1991 and 1998 I interviewed twenty-five Puerto Rican migrants in Philadelphia; Camden and Palmyra, New Jersey; and San Lorenzo and Salinas, Puerto Rico. The Norris Square Senior Citizens' Center in North Philadelphia was the site for several of these interviews; I also relied on word of mouth and contacts from long-term Philadelphia residents. Initially I sought people who migrated to the city in the late 1940s and the 1950s. As the project progressed, I focused on people from San Lorenzo and later from Salinas. The stories of thirteen migrants appear in this book, with six from San Lorenzo, three from Salinas, and one each from Santurce, Naguabo, Cayey, and Coamo. There were eight women and five men, including a married couple from San Lorenzo and another from Salinas. These migrants represent a cohort who left Puerto Rico in the postwar era, leaving for the first time between 1947 and 1956. With some going to the farms or New York City first, these migrants arrived in Philadelphia between 1947 and 1965, with eight arriving during the 1950s. Born between 1911 and 1936, seven were in their twenties when they left Puerto Rico; the youngest was sixteen and the oldest was forty-three. Of the women, three were single and had no children, one was a single mother with one child, and four were married or in consensual unions with one to six children when they arrived in Philadelphia. Of the men, one was single with no children, and the others were married or in consensual unions with zero to six children. All continued to live in Philadelphia or nearby areas of New Jersey, except for one couple who returned to San Lorenzo in 1973 and another couple who returned to Salinas in 1981.

The interviews ranged from about an hour and a half to four hours, and most were in two sessions. All but one interview was in Spanish. The interviews were tape recorded, transcribed, and translated. I have used italics to indicate where the original Spanish was left untranslated or where the original word or phrase was in English. I have edited for clarity and readability, eliminating repetition and unclear fragments, and reordering some sentences. I have used ellipsis to indicate a break of more than a few words or where I interjected a question or comment.

For the last chapter, I did five additional interviews with community activists, four of whom were born in Philadelphia or came at an early age, and one who came from New York in the 1970s. These interviews were primarily in English. Throughout the book, I also drew on interviews conducted by Taller Puertorriqueño, a cultural center in Philadelphia. This oral history project, funded between 1976 and 1978 by the National Endowment for the Humanities with a Youthgrant in the Humanities, was a cross-generational project. Fifty-seven people were interviewed by twenty-two Puerto Rican youth, with those involved in the project ranging from sixteen to seventy-seven years of age. The final project report, entitled *Batiendo La Olla ("Stirring the Pot"): A Cross-Generational Comparison and Self-Study by Second Generation Puerto Ricans in Philadelphia,* includes excerpts from these interviews and one longer interview. In addition, transcripts of eleven interviews are at the Pennsylvania Historical and Museum Commission in Harrisburg, Pennsylvania. These interviews offer an important glimpse of the late 1970s, as well as another perspective on the earlier era.

While this combination of sources has been fruitful, a great deal of research on the history of Puerto Rican migration remains to be done. My assessment of Puerto Rico's regions and of out-migration from San Lorenzo and Salinas suggests the complex dynamics of Puerto Rican migration. Yet my definition of regions could be refined, and a full comparative analysis awaits additional studies of other regions and particular communities. Similarly, significant areas of research remain on the roles of contract labor and informal networks in shaping migration and in filling specific niches in the U.S. economy. Meanwhile, comparable historical research on the origins and formation of New York, Chicago, and other Puerto Rican communities in the post–World War II era will provide not only a basis for comparison but also a more thorough understanding of the migration process. Finally, this book begins the work of historicizing Puerto Ricans' place in and impact on the changing urban landscape of the postwar era. Future work will both enrich and be enriched by the emerging social histories of the era.

Notes

The following abbreviations are used in the notes. Where they refer to a record group, they are followed by the record group and box numbers:

AG — Archivo General de Puerto Rico, San Juan, Puerto Rico, Department of Labor Record Groups 61–55 and 63–37. Box numbers not included, uninventoried collection.

BC — Bulletin Collection, Urban Archives, Temple University, Philadelphia, Pa.

CEP — Centro de Estudios Puertorriqueños, Hunter College, New York, N.Y.

CP — La Colección Puertorriqueña, University of Puerto Rico, Río Piedras, P.R.

FNG — Friends Neighborhood Guild, Record Group 32, Urban Archives, Temple University, Philadelphia, Pa.

NA — Population, Emigration, General. Record Group 126, File 9-8-116, National Archives, Washington, D.C.

NSC — Nationalities Services Center, Record Group 625, Urban Archives, Temple University, Philadelphia, Pa.

PABES — Pennsylvania Bureau of Employment Security.

PAFPP — Pennsylvania Bureau of Employment Security, Farm Placement Program.

PCHR — Philadelphia Commission on Human Relations.

PHMC — Pennsylvania Historical and Museum Commission, Division of Archives and Manuscripts, Harrisburg, Pa.

PHWC — Philadelphia District Health and Welfare Council.

PRAES — Puerto Rico Agricultural Experiment Station.

PREDA — Puerto Rico Economic Development Administration (Fomento).

PRFPD — Puerto Rico Department of Labor, Employment Service, Farm Placement Division.

PRMD — Puerto Rico Department of Labor, Migration Division.

PRPB — Puerto Rico Planning Board.

UA — Urban Archives, Temple University, Philadelphia, Pa.

USBC — U.S. Department of Commerce, Bureau of the Census.

USBES — U.S. Department of Labor, Bureau of Employment Security.

WMC — War Manpower Commission Collection, Record Group 211, National Archives–Mid-Atlantic Region, Philadelphia, Pa.

YWCA — Young Women's Christian Association, Record Group 635, Urban Archives, Temple University, Philadelphia, Pa. Box numbers not included, uninventoried collection.

Chapter I

1. A *cuerda* is equal to 0.97 acre, and *gandules* are pigeon peas. Epifania Velázquez, interview by author, 16 December 1991, Philadelphia, Pa., tape recording, trans. by author. See Appendix II.

2. James L. Dietz, *Economic History of Puerto Rico: Institutional Change and Capitalist Development* (Princeton, N.J.: Princeton University Press, 1986), 259; José Vázquez Calzada, "Demographic Aspects of Migration," in *Labor Migration under Capitalism: The Puerto Rican Experience*, ed. Centro de Estudios Puertorriqueños (New York: Monthly Review Press, 1979), 224; José Vázquez Calzada, "La Población de Puerto Rico y Su Trayectoria Histórica" (University of Puerto Rico, School of Public Health, July 1978), 287, CEP; and USBC, *Census of Population: 1970,*, vol. I, *Characteristics of the Population*, pt. 53, Puerto Rico (Washington, D.C., 1973), 11.

3. U.S. Commission on Civil Rights, *Puerto Ricans in the Continental United States: An Uncertain Future* (Report of the U.S. Commission on Civil Rights, October 1976), 23; and Francisco L. Rivera-Batiz and Carlos E. Santiago, *Island Paradox: Puerto Rico in the 1990s* (New York: Russell Sage Foundation, 1996), 127, 136. For an overview of Puerto Rican migration, see Carmen Teresa Whalen, "Puerto Ricans," in *A Nation of Peoples: A Sourcebook on America's Multicultural Heritage*, ed. Elliott R. Barkan (Westport, Conn.: Greenwood Press, 1999), 446–463.

4. Oscar Handlin, *The Newcomers: Negroes and Puerto Ricans in a Changing Metropolis* (Cambridge: Harvard University Press, 1959).

5. U.S. immigration history is just beginning to examine the post-1965 immigrations. For works that include Puerto Ricans, see Barkan, ed., *A Nation of Peoples*; and Teresa Amott and Julie Matthaei, *Race, Gender, and Work: A Multi-cultural Economic History of Women in the United States* (Boston: South End Press, 1996).

6. Important overviews include Centro de Estudios Puertorriqueños, *Labor Migration under Capitalism;* and Edwin Maldonado, "Contract Labor and the Origins of Puerto Rican Communities in the United States," *International Migration Review* 13 (spring 1979): 103–121. The two historical studies are Virginia Sánchez Korrol, *From Colonia to Community: The History of Puerto Ricans in New York City, 1917–1948* (Berkeley: University of California Press, 1994); and Ruth Glasser, *My Music Is My Flag: Puerto Rican Musicians and Their New York Communities, 1917–1940* (Berkeley: University of California Press, 1995).

7. Epifania Velázquez, interview, trans.

8. Epifania Velázquez, interview, trans. On the portrayal of migrants as men, see Donna Gabaccia, "Immigrant Women: Nowhere at Home?" *Journal of American Ethnic History* (summer 1991): 61–87; and Virginia Yans-McLaughlin, "Introduction," in *Immigration Reconsidered: History, Sociology, and Politics*, ed. Virginia Yans-McLaughlin (New York: Oxford University Press, 1990), 14–16. See also Carmen Teresa Whalen, "Labor Migrants or Submissive Wives: Competing Narratives of Puerto Rican Women in the Post–World War II Era," in *Puerto Rican Women's History: New Perspectives*, ed. Félix V. Matos Rodríguez and Linda Delgado (Armonk, N.Y.: M. E. Sharpe, 1998), 206–226.

9. On women's reproductive work and economic development, see Lourdes Benería and Gita Sen, "Accumulation, Reproduction, and Women's Role in Economic Development: Boserup Revisited," in *Women's Work: Development and the Division of Labor by Gender*, ed. Eleanor Leacock, Helen Safa, and contributors (New York: Bergin and Garvey Publishers, 1986), 141–157. See also Christine E. Bose and Edna Acosta-Belén, eds., *Women in the Latin American Development Process* (Philadelphia: Temple University Press, 1995).

10. On immigrant women, see Donna Gabaccia, *From the Other Side: Women, Gender, and Immigrant Life in the U.S., 1820–1990* (Bloomington: Indiana University Press, 1994). On Puerto Rican women, see Rina Benmayor et al., "Stories to Live By: Continuity and Change in Three Generations of Puerto Rican Women," *Oral History Review* 16 (fall 1988): 1–46; Maura I. Toro-Morn, "Gender, Class, Family, and Migration: Puerto Rican Women in Chicago," *Gender and Society* 9 (December 1995): 712–726; and Altagracia Ortiz, ed., *Puerto Rican Women and Work: Bridges in Transnational Labor* (Philadelphia: Temple University Press, 1996).

11. On Puerto Rican women's use of welfare to fulfill reproductive responsibilities, see Rosa M. Torruellas, Rina Benmayor, and Ana Juarbe, "Negotiating Gender, Work, and Welfare: *Familia* as Productive Labor among Puerto Rican Women in New York City," in *Puerto Rican Women*, ed. Ortiz, 184–208.

12. On Puerto Rican women's displacement, see Alice Colón-Warren, "The Impact of Job Losses on Puerto Rican Women in the Middle Atlantic Region, 1970–1990," in *Puerto Rican Women*, ed. Ortiz, 105–138.

13. Hereafter, I use the term "migrant" to refer to both internal migrants and transnational immigrants, unless the distinction between them is germane to my argument.

14. Artistide R. Zolberg, "Reforming the Back Door: The Immigration Reform and Control Act of 1986 in Historical Perspective," in *Immigration Reconsidered*, ed. Yans- McLaughlin, 317, 318, emphasis in original; and Michael J. Piore, *Birds of Passage: Migrant Labor and Industrial Societies* (Cambridge: Cambridge University Press, 1979), 34, 1–2, 168, 106.

15. Cindy Hahamovitch, *The Fruits of Their Labor: Atlantic Coast Farmworkers and the Making of Migrant Poverty, 1870–1945* (Chapel Hill: University of North Carolina Press, 1997), 203. See also Carmen Teresa Whalen, "Displaced Labor Migrants or the 'Underclass': African Americans and Puerto Ricans in Philadelphia's Economy," in *The Collaborative City: Opportunities and Challenges for Blacks and Latinos in U.S. Cities*, ed. John J. Betancur and Douglas C. Gills (New York: Garland Publishers, 2000). For Mexicans, labor recruitment followed by "repatriation" was a repeating pattern—see Gilbert Paul Carrasco, "Latinos in the United States: Invitation and Exile," in *Immigrants Out! The New Nativism and the Anti-Immigrant Impulse in the United States*, ed. Juan F. Pérez (New York: New York University Press, 1997), 190–204; and Juan Ramón García, *Operation Wetback: The Mass Deportation of Mexican Undocumented Workers in 1954* (Westport, Conn.: Greenwood Press, 1980). On wanted laborers and unwanted community members, see David Montejano, *Anglos and Mexicans in the Making of Texas, 1836–1986* (Austin: University of Texas Press, 1987).

16. U.S. Commission on Civil Rights, *Puerto Ricans in the U.S.*, 145. See also Clara Rodríguez, *Puerto Ricans: Born in the U.S.A.* (Boulder, Colo.: Westview Press, 1991), 49–84.

17. Oscar Lewis, *La Vida: A Puerto Rican Family in the Culture of Poverty* (New York: Random House, 1965), xliii, xxviii, lii, xi, li. See also Oscar Lewis, "The Culture of Poverty," in *Contemporary Cultures and Societies of Latin America*, ed. Dwight B. Heath (New York: Random House, 1973):, 469–479.

18. Lewis, *La Vida*, xxxvii-xxxviii; C. Wright Mills, Clarence Senior, and Rose Kohn Goldsen, *The Puerto Rican Journey: New York's Newest Migrants* (New York: Harper and Row, 1950; reprinted, New York: Russell and Russell, 1967), 21, 53; Handlin, *Newcomers*, 49; and Nathan Glazer and Daniel Patrick Moynihan, *Beyond the Melting Pot: The Negroes, Puerto Ricans, Jews, Italians, and Irish of New York City* (Cambridge: MIT Press, 1963), 99, 117.

19. Oscar Handlin, *The Uprooted: The Epic Story of the Great Migrations that Made the American People* (Boston: Little, Brown, and Co., 1951). For responses, see Rudolf Vecoli, "Contadini

in Chicago: A Critique of *The Uprooted*," *Journal of American History* 51 (December 1964): 404–417; and Virginia Yans-McLaughlin, *Family and Community: Italian Immigrants in Buffalo, 1880–1930* (Urbana: University of Illinois Press, 1982). On nativism, see John Higham, *Strangers in the Land: Patterns of American Nativism, 1860–1925* (New Brunswick, N.J.: Rutgers University Press, 1955); and James M. Berquist, "The Concept of Nativism in Historical Study since *Strangers in the Land*," *American Jewish History* 76 (December 1986): 125–141. On the global economy, contrast John Bodnar, *The Transplanted: A History of Immigrants in Urban America* (Bloomington: Indiana University Press, 1985), with Edna Bonacich and Lucie Cheng, "Introduction: A Theoretical Orientation to International Labor Migration," in *Labor Immigration under Capitalism: Asian Workers in the United States before World War II*, ed. Lucie Cheng and Edna Bonacich (Berkeley: University of California Press, 1984), 1–56.

20. On colonialism and capitalism, see Centro de Estudios Puertorriqueños, *Labor Migration under Capitalism*; Frank Bonilla and Ricardo Campos, "Industrialization and Migration: Some Effects on the Puerto Rican Working Class," trans. Peter L. Crabtree, *Latin American Perspectives* 3 (summer 1976): 66–108; and Frank Bonilla and Ricardo Campos, "Wealth of Poor: Puerto Ricans in the New Economic Order," *Daedalus* 110 (spring 1981): 133–176. On internal colonialism, see Felix Padilla, *Puerto Rican Chicago* (Notre Dame, Ind.: University of Notre Dame Press, 1987). This relative absence of historical work stands in contrast to the historiography on African American migration, where scholars have balanced structural constraints and agency in a more integrated fashion. See Joe Trotter Jr., ed., *The Great Migration in Historical Perspective: New Dimensions of Race, Class and Gender* (Bloomington: Indiana University Press, 1991).

21. While early approaches emphasized either the global economy or social networks as causes of migration, the challenge more recently has been to integrate them. Contrast Frank Thistlethwaite, "Migration from Europe Overseas in the Nineteenth and Twentieth Centuries," in *Population Movements in Modern European History*, ed. Herbert Moller (New York: Macmillan, 1964), 73-92; with John S. MacDonald and Leatrice D. MacDonald, "Chain Migration, Ethnic Neighborhood Formation, and Social Networks," *Millbank Memorial Fund Quarterly* 42 (1964): 82–97. More recently, Alejandro Portes has argued, "There is little doubt that immigration is a network-mediated process . . . but questions remain as to what forces initiate the process, why it originates in certain countries and locations and not in others, and what accounts for the different compositions and patterns of incorporation of various groups." "From South of the Border: Hispanic Minorities in the United States," in *Immigration Reconsidered*, ed. Yans-McLaughlin, 167. On globalization's impact on inner cities, see Rebecca Morales and Frank Bonilla, eds., *Latinos in a Changing U.S. Economy: Comparative Perspectives on Growing Inequality* (Newbury Park, Calif.: Sage Publications, 1993).

22. On status, see Edwin Meléndez and Edgardo Meléndez, eds., *Colonial Dilemma: Critical Perspectives on Contemporary Puerto Rico* (Boston: South End Press, 1993).

23. Harvey S. Perloff, *Puerto Rico's Economic Future: A Study in Planned Development* (Chicago: University of Chicago Press, 1950), 137–139, 144; and Richard Weisskoff, *Factories and Food Stamps: The Puerto Rico Model of Development* (Baltimore: Johns Hopkins University Press, 1985), 2–3, 120.

24. Bonilla, "Wealth of Poor," 135, 149; and Dietz, *Economic History*, 227. See Chapter 2.

25. On the emergence of the PPD, see Emilio Pantojas-García, *Development Strategies as Ideologies: Puerto Rico's Export-Led Industrialization Experience* (Boulder, Colo.: Lynne Rienner Publishers, 1990).

26. Pantojas-García, *Development Strategies,* 24–25; Pedro Cabán, "Industrial Transformation and Labour Relations in Puerto Rico: From 'Operation Bootstrap' to the 1970s," *Journal of Latin American Studies* 21 (October 1989): 563; and Michael Lapp, "Managing Migration: The Migration Division of Puerto Rico and Puerto Ricans in New York City, 1948–1968" (Ph.D. dissertation, Johns Hopkins University, 1989), 5–6, 14.

27. See Sherri L. Baver, *The Political Economy of Colonialism: The State and Industrialization in Puerto Rico* (Westport, Conn.: Praeger Publishers, 1993), 42–44.

28. Social historians have not yet turned their attention to the postwar era.

29. A *municipio* is an administrative unit, encompassing a town and the surrounding rural areas, known as *barrios.*

30. Stanley L. Friedlander, *Labor Migration and Economic Growth: A Case Study of Puerto Rico* (Cambridge: MIT Press, 1965), 7; and Puerto Rico Negociado del Presupuesto, "Encuestra Sobre las Personas que Salieron de Puerto Rico en Noviembre de 1946" (San Juan, 1947), 11, as cited in Clarence Senior, "Migration and Puerto Rico's Population Problem," *The Annals of the American Academy of Political and Social Science* 285 (January 1953): note 1. On the 1965 Immigration Reforms, see David M. Reimers, *Still the Golden Door: The Third World Comes to America* (New York: Columbia University Press, 1992).

31. See Arnold R. Hirsch, "Massive Resistance in the Urban North: Trumbull Park, Chicago, 1953–1966," *Journal of American History* 82 (September 1995): 522–550; and Thomas J. Sugrue, "Crabgrass-Roots Politics: Race, Rights, and Reaction against Liberalism in the Urban North, 1940–1964," *Journal of American History* 82 (September 1995): 551–578.

32. Nicholas Lemann, "The Other Underclass," *Atlantic Monthly* (December 1991): 96–110; and Michael Katz, "The Urban 'Underclass' as a Metaphor of Social Transformation," in *The "Underclass" Debate: Views from History,* ed. Michael Katz (Princeton, N.J.: Princeton University Press, 1993), 5.

Chapter 2

1. Margarita Benítez, interview by author, 11 and 18 August 1996, Philadelphia, Pa., tape recording, trans. by author. See Appendix II.

2. USBC, *Census of Population: 1970,* vol. 1, *Characteristics of the Population,* pt. 53, Puerto Rico (Washington, D.C., 1973), 11.

3. Richard Weisskoff, *Factories and Food Stamps: The Puerto Rico Model of Development* (Baltimore: Johns Hopkins University Press, 1985), 132.

4. C. Wright Mills, Clarence Senior, and Rose Kohn Goldsen, *The Puerto Rican Journey: New York's Newest Migrants* (New York: Harper and Row, 1950; reprint, New York: Russell and Russell, 1967), 38, 32, 23; and Oscar Lewis, *La Vida: A Puerto Rican Family in the Culture of Poverty: San Juan and New York* (New York: Random House, 1965), xliii, xliv, xxxv, xxxviii. Mills's and Lewis's data suggest rural origins. Although Mills found that 91 percent of migrants came from urban areas and only one in five had moved from rural to urban areas before migrating to New York City, 52 percent of the sample migrated between 1920 and 1941 and only a quarter between 1946 and 1948. They noted that "later migrants" had "been recruited more heavily from the island's rural areas." Lewis, observing that in the "slum" he studied more than half of the residents were born in the metropolitan area, in contrast to other "slums" where four out of five adults had migrated from rural areas, concluded: "The majority of migrants in the New York sample had made

a three-step migration—from a rural birthplace in Puerto Rico to a San Juan slum to New York." For other indications of migrants' rural origins, see Stanley Friedlander, *Labor Migration and Economic Growth: A Case Study of Puerto Rico* (Cambridge: MIT Press, 1965), 96, 114; José Vázquez Calzada, "La Población de Puerto Rico y su Trayectoria Histórica" (Unpublished research paper, University of Puerto Rico, School of Public Health, July 1978), 279, CEP; and Julio Morales, *Puerto Rican Poverty and Migration: We Just Had to Try Elsewhere* (New York: Praeger Publishers, 1986).

5. These are loosely defined regions based on geographic location and employment in commercial crops, as determined from USBC, *U.S. Census of Population: 1950*, vol. II, *Characteristics of the Population,* pt. 53, Puerto Rico (Washington, D.C., 1953), 40. I also consulted PRPB, "Puerto Rican Migrants: A Socio-Economic Study" (San Juan, 1972), CEP, which defined regions based on 1950 agricultural production. My regions combine several of their smaller groupings, separate the San Juan metropolitan area from the northern region, and assign their municipios of "mixed cultivation" to other regions. The San Juan metropolitan area reflects the urbanization that took place by 1970. Based on geography or agricultural production alone, many municipios would be divided. In *The Geography of Puerto Rico* (Chicago: Aldine Publishing Company, 1974), Rafael Picó defined eleven geographical regions. As defined, the coffee region accounted for 9 percent of the island's population in 1950, the tobacco region 15 percent, the southeastern 13 percent, the southwestern 20 percent, the northern 19 percent, and the San Juan metropolitan region 24 percent. USBC, *U.S. Census of Population: 1960,* vol. I, *Characteristics of the Population,* pt. 53, Puerto Rico (Washington, D.C., 1963), 13–17.

6. Julian Steward, "Introduction," in *The People of Puerto Rico: A Study in Social Anthropology,* ed. Julian Steward, Robert Manners, Eric Wolf, Elena Padilla Seda, Sidney Mintz, and Raymond Scheele (Urbana: University of Illinois Press, 1956), 3.

7. Julian Steward, Robert Manners, Eric Wolf, Elena Padilla Seda, Sidney Mintz, and Raymond Scheele, "Comparative Analysis of Regional Subcultures," in *People of Puerto Rico,* ed. Steward et al., 465–469.

8. Harvey S. Perloff, *Puerto Rico's Economic Future: A Study in Planned Development* (Chicago: University of Illinois Press, 1950): 94, 136–137.

9. Luther H. Gulick Jr., "Rural Occupance in Utuado and Jayuya Municipios, Puerto Rico," (Ph.D. diss., University of Chicago, 1952), 25, 37.

10. Gulick, "Rural Occupance," 19.

11. PRAES, "Análisis Económico del Cultivo del Tabaco en Puerto Rico, 1951–1952," by Gabriel R. Espinet, *Boletín* 133 (April 1956): 5; and PRAES, "Costos de Producción del Tabaco, Zona Central Este, Puerto Rico, 1948–1949," by Manuel Piñero and Juan Calderón, *Bulletin* 96 (November 1951): 26.

12. Robert A. Manners, "Tabara: Subcultures of a Tobacco and Mixed Crops Municipality," in *People of Puerto Rico,* ed. Steward et al., 117, 111.

13. Manners, "Tabara," 112.

14. Manners, "Tabara," 162; and PRAES, "Análisis Económico," 11–15, trans. by author.

15. PRAES, "Análisis Económico," 16; and Manners, "Tabara," 120, 141.

16. Sidney W. Mintz, "Cañamelar: The Subculture of a Rural Sugar Plantation Proletariat," in *People of Puerto Rico,* ed. Steward et al., 338, 315, 348. See also Sidney W. Mintz, *Worker in the Cane: A Puerto Rican Life History* (New York: W. W. Norton & Co., 1974).

17. Mintz, "Cañamelar," 322; Perloff, *Economic Future,* 74–77; PRAES, "Farm Prices and Price Relationships of Sugar and Sugar Cane in Puerto Rico from 1910 to 1945," by Jorge J. Serralles Jr., *Bulletin* 71 (June 1944): 46–47.

18. Perloff, *Economic Future*, 67–68, 76.

19. Mintz, "Cañamelar," 321, 351–360.

20. Mintz, "Cañamelar," 401; Perloff, *Economic Future*, 67.

21. Elena Padilla Seda, "Nocorá: The Subculture of Workers on a Government-Owned Sugar Plantation," in *People of Puerto Rico*, ed. Steward et al., 266.

22. James L. Dietz, *Economic History of Puerto Rico: Institutional Change and Capitalist Development* (Princeton, N.J.: Princeton University Press, 1986), 194–201.

23. Padilla Seda, "Nocorá," 266, 265, 283; PRAES, "An Economic Study of Family Sized Farms in Puerto Rico: San José Farm Security Administration Project, 1943–44, 1944–45," by Guillermo Serra and Manuel Piñero, *Bulletin* 77 (June 1948): 57; PRAES, "Estudio Sobre la Explotación Económica de 134 Fincas de Caña de Azúcar, Puerto Rico, 1950–51," by Manuel Piñero and Juan R. Calderón, *Boletín* 132 (April 1956): 88–90.

24. Padilla Seda, "Nocorá," 287.

25. Perloff, *Economic Future*, 184, 99; and Lloyd G. Reynolds and Peter Gregory, *Wages, Productivity and Industrialization in Puerto Rico* (Homewood, Ill.: Richard D. Irwin, Inc., 1965): 43.

26. Perloff, *Economic Future*, 100, 56; Eric R. Wolf, "San José: Subcultures of a 'Traditional' Coffee Municipality," in *People of Puerto Rico*, ed. Steward et al., 173.

27. USBC, *U.S. Census of Population: 1950*, vol. II, *Characteristics of the Population*, pt. 53, Puerto Rico (Washington, D.C., 1953), 40.

28. PRPB, "Puerto Rican Migrants," 13; Dietz, *Economic History*, 274; Frank Bonilla and Ricardo Campos, "Wealth of Poor: Puerto Ricans in the New Economic Order," *Daedalus* 110 (spring 1981): 133.

29. Emilio Pantojas-García, "Puerto Rican Populism Revisited: The PPD during the 1940s," *Journal of Latin American Studies* 21 (October 1989): 535–538; and Picó, *Geography*, 352, 388.

30. David Ross, *The Long Uphill Path: A Historical Study of Puerto Rico's Program of Economic Development* (San Juan: Editorial Edil, 1969): 105.

31. U.S. Department of Labor, Wage and Hour and Public Contracts Division, Division of Wage Determinations (December 1953): 5; Ross, *Long Uphill Path*, 98.

32. U.S. Congress, House Committee on Education and Labor, *Investigation of Minimum Wages and Education in Puerto Rico and the Virgin Islands: Hearings before a Special Investigating Subcommittee on Education and Labor*, 81st Cong., 1st sess., November 1949, 23, 3.

33. U.S. House, *Minimum Wages* (1949), 13–14; and Office of Puerto Rico, "Puerto Rico's Potential as a Site for Textile, Apparel and Other Industries," by Donald J. O'Connor (Washington, D.C., 1949), 17, 20, Alexander Library, Rutgers University, New Brunswick, N.J.

34. Ross, *Long Uphill Path*, 131, 165, 103, 101; Dietz, *Economic History*, 211–212, 260.

35. U.S. House, *Minimum Wages* (1949), 6, 9; U.S. Division of Wage Determinations (1953), 3, 8; Dietz, *Economic History*, 226.

36. Dietz, *Economic History*, 226; PREDA, "Social Directions in Industrial Development" (3 January 1957): 7–8, CP; Ross, *Long Uphill Path*, 119.

37. Ross, *Long Uphill Path*, 146; PREDA, "Social Directions," 2–3, 1, 8.

38. Palmira N. Ríos, "Export-Oriented Industrialization and the Demand for Female Labor: Puerto Rican Women in the Manufacturing Sector, 1953–1980," in *Colonial Dilemma: Critical Perspectives on Contemporary Puerto Rico*, ed. Edwin Meléndez and Edgardo Meléndez (Boston: South End Press, 1993), 101; Sherri L. Baver, *The Political Economy of Colonialism: The State and Industrialization in Puerto Rico* (Westport, Conn.: Praeger Publishers, 1993), 51, 54. See also Emilio Pantojas-García, *Development Strategies as Ideology: Puerto Rico's Export-Led Industrialization Experience* (Boulder, Colo.: Lynne Rienner Publishers, 1990).

39. Ríos, "Export-Oriented Industrialization," 95; PREDA, Continental Operations Branch, N.Y., "The Apparel and Related Products Industry" (August 1973), CP.

40. PREDA, "Apparel and Related Products."

41. Ross, *Long Uphill Path*, 157, 163, 156; Fernando Sierra Berdecía, "Puerto Rican Agriculture and Manpower," address to Second Farm Placement Conference, San Juan, Puerto Rico (January 7–8, 1958), 2–10.

42. Sierra Berdecía, "Puerto Rican Agriculture"; Ross, *Long Uphill Path*, 157; Reynolds, *Wages, Productivity*, 34.

43. Ross, *Long Uphill Path*, 159; Perloff, *Economic Future*, 239, 208; Annette B. Ramírez de Arellano and Conrad Seipp, *Colonialism, Catholicism, and Contraception: A History of Birth Control in Puerto Rico* (Chapel Hill: University of North Carolina Press, 1983), 25.

44. Puerto Rico Planning, Urbanizing, and Zoning Board, "The Population Problem in Puerto Rico," by Frederic P. Bartlett and Brandon Howell (Santurce, Puerto Rico, August 1944): 3, 4, 17, 19, 20, Alexander Library, Rutgers University, New Brunswick, N.J.

45. Luis Muñoz Marín, *El Mundo* (San Juan), 27 June 1923, as quoted in Ramírez de Arellano, *Contraception*, 17; Ramírez de Arellano, *Contraception*, 97, 126.

46. Ramírez de Arellano, *Contraception*, 136, 138, 143; Ross, *Long Uphill Path*, 163.

47. Ramírez de Arellano, *Contraception*, 35–36, 80–81. See also A. W. Maldonado, *Teodoro Moscoso and Puerto Rico's Operation Bootstrap* (Gainesville: University of Florida Press, 1997), 144–154.

48. Clarence Senior, *Puerto Rican Emigration* (Rio Piedras, Puerto Rico: Social Science Research Center, University of Puerto Rico, 1947): 119; and Clarence Senior, "Puerto Rico: Migration to the Mainland," *Monthly Labor Review* 78 (December 1955): 1356. See also Michael Lapp, "Managing Migration: The Migration Division of Puerto Rico and Puerto Ricans in New York City, 1948–1968" (Ph.D. diss., Johns Hopkins University, 1989).

49. Puerto Rico, Department of Labor, *Informe Anual del Departamento del Trabajo: 1950–1951*, 45; PRFPD, *Annual Report, 1952*, 7, 9; PRFPD, *Annual Report, 1956*, 6; PRFPD, *Annual Report, 1954*, 12–13; PRFPD, *Annual Report, 1955*, 7–8. See also "Afirma obreros envían $75,000 a Puerto Rico," *El Mundo*, 3 September 1948, 5; and "La Isla Recibe $6,800,000 de Migrantes," *El Mundo*, 28 November 1955, 21.

50. PRFPD, *Annual Report, 1953*, 5; "Alegan Emigración Hacia E.U. Perjudica Industria Azucarera," *El Mundo*, 22 May 1952, 1, trans. by author. See also "Agricultores Pelearán: No Quieren Otra Vez Caña en Pie y Cuota sin Cubrir," *El Mundo*, 17 July 1953, 33; "Informan la Emigración no Causa Falta Brazos," *El Mundo*, 27 April 1956, 19.

51. PRFPD, *Annual Report, 1952*, 6, 14; PRFPD, *Annual Report, 1955*, 6; PRFPD, *Annual Report, 1963*, 10–11; PRFPD, *Annual Report, 1961*, 8–10.

52. PRFPD, *Annual Report, 1952*, 2; PRFPD, *Annual Report, 1953*, 9; PRFPD, *Annual Report, 1956*, 5–6; PRFPD, *Annual Report, 1961*, 9.

53. Senior, "Migration to the Mainland," 1354; PRFPD, *Annual Report, 1953*, 14.

54. John P. Augelli, "San Lorenzo: A Case Study of Recent Migrations in Interior Puerto Rico," *American Journal of Economics and Sociology* 2 (January 1952): 155–156.

55. Vernon W. Brockmann, "Land Types and Land Utilization in the Caguas–San Lorenzo Region," in *Symposium on the Geography of Puerto Rico*, ed. Clarence F. Jones and Rafael Picó (Río Piedras: University of Puerto Rico Press, 1955), 323; Perloff, *Economic Future*, 258, 240.

56. Déborah Berman Santana, "Geographers, Colonialism, and Development Strategies: The Case of Puerto Rico," *Urban Geography* 17, no. 5 (1996): 462, 456.

57. Weisskoff, *Factories and Food Stamps*, 123.

58. Ross, *Long Uphill Path*, 163; PRPB, "Puerto Rican Migrants," 1–2.

59. Picó, *Geography*, 268; Perloff, *Economic Future*, 295. See also Janice Monk and Charles Alexander, "Land Abandonment in Western Puerto Rico," *Caribbean Geography* 2 (1985): 2–15.

60. Wolf, "San José," 173; PRPB, "Puerto Rican Migrants," 47.

61. Perloff, *Economic Future*, 92; PRAES, "Some Effects of Federal and Commonwealth Tobacco Programs on the Tobacco Industry of Puerto Rico," by Marciano Avilés, *Bulletin* 162 (February 1962): 11, 14; Picó, *Geography*, 270–271.

62. Sierra Berdecía, "Puerto Rican Agriculture"; PRPB, "Puerto Rican Migrants," 48, 51; Brockmann, "Land Types," 302.

63. PRPB, "Puerto Rican Migrants," 10; Mintz, "Cañamelar," 321, 348; Padilla Seda, "Nocorá," 267; USBC, *Sixteenth Census of the United States: 1940*, Special Reports, Puerto Rico: Population, Bulletin no. 2, Characteristics of the Population (Washington, D.C., 1943), 49–50; USBC, *U.S. Census of Population: 1950*, 40; PRAES, "Explotación Económica," 87; PRAES, "Some Effects of the Sugar Programs on the Sugar Industry of Puerto Rico," by José B. Candelas, *Bulletin* 151 (October 1959): 8; Picó, *Geography*, 263–264.

64. PRAES, "Estudio Económico Sobre el Arrastre de la Caña de Azúcar en Camiones, Puerto Rico, 1954," by Oscar Rodríguez García and José Mariano Ríos, *Bulletin* 142 (July 1958): 30–31; PRAES, "Sugar Programs," 6–9; Picó, *Geography*, 264–265, 389.

65. PRAES, "Sugar Programs," 6, 38, 9.

66. PRPB, "Puerto Rican Migrants," 23–24.

67. Peter Gregory, "The Labor Market in Puerto Rico," in *Labor Commitment and Social Change in Developing Areas*, ed. Wilbert E. Moore and Arnold S. Feldman (New York: Social Science Research Council, 1960): 140–141, 143–148, 150–151, 167.

68. John Macisco Jr., "Internal Migration in Puerto Rico, 1955–1960" (Ph.D. diss., Brown University, 1966), 105, 118.

69. Puerto Rico, Office of the Governor, Division of Statistics, "Estudio Sobre La Emigración en Puerto Rico: Encuestra en la Semana del 21 al 27 de abril de 1952" (San Juan, 1952): 36, 22, 24, 45, 37, 15, CEP.

70. See Appendix II. PCHR, *Puerto Ricans in Philadelphia: A Study of Their Demographic Characteristics, Problems and Attitudes*, by Arthur Siegel, Harold Orlans, and Loyal Greer (April 1954; reprint, New York: Arno Press, 1975), 31, 27. Vázquez Calzada estimated that 70 percent of all migrants during the 1950s were between fifteen and thirty-nine—Vázquez Calzada "La Población," 225.

71. Manners, "Tabara," 153; Mintz, "Cañamelar," 352.

72. Wolf, "San José," 227, 231, quoting editorial in *Revista de Café* 3, no. 9 (1948). For a 1977 survey of emigration from Maricao and Las Marías, see Janice Monk with the late Charles S. Alexander, "Migration, Development and the Gender Division of Labour: Puerto Rico and Margarita Island, Venezuela," in *Women and Change in the Caribbean*, ed. Janet H. Momsen (Bloomington: Indiana University Press, 1993), 167–178.

73. Padilla Seda, "Nocorá," 312, 284–285.

74. Joan D. Koss, "Puerto Ricans in Philadelphia: Migration and Accommodation" (Ph.D. diss., University of Pennsylvania, 1965), 30–31, 13, 516. Her data indicate 39 percent came from the tobacco region, 36 percent from the southeastern region, 6 percent from the southwestern region, 9 percent from the northern region, 3 percent from the coffee region, and 6 percent from the San Juan metropolitan area, with one migrant from St. Croix. In a 1967 study of 26 Puerto

Rican migrants in Philadelphia, Carmen García Olivero found that half were born in rural areas and six in small towns, mostly in southeastern Puerto Rico. García Olivero, *Study of the Initial Involvement in the Social Services by the Puerto Rican Migrants in Philadelphia* (New York: Vantage Press, 1971), 85–86. Similarly, John H. Stinson Fernández found that only seven of the fifty-eight migrants he interviewed came to Philadelphia from the San Juan metropolitan area—Stinson Fernández, "Hacia una antropología de la emigración planificada: El Negociado de Empleo y Migración y el caso de Filadelfia," *Revista de Ciencias Sociales* (June 1996): 142–143.

75. See Table 4.7 on parents' occupations and Appendix II on marriage records. Taller Puertorriqueño Oral History Project, transcript no. 5, PHMC; PCHR, *Puerto Ricans in Philadelphia* (1954), 35.

76. Reynolds, *Wages, Productivity,* 158; PCHR, *Puerto Ricans in Philadelphia* (1954), 35.

77. PRFPD, *Annual Report,* 1954.

78. Margarita Benítez, interview, trans.

79. Edwin Maldonado, "Contract Labor and the Origins of Puerto Rican Communities in the United States," *International Migration Review* 13 (spring 1979): 120–121.

Chapter 3

1. "Oportunidad Para Trabajadores Agrícolas en Estados Unidos," no date, AG 61–55; PRFPD, *Annual Agricultural Report, 1953,* 9–10; Puerto Rico, Department of Labor, Employment Service, "Migration Plan for 1952–53," AG 61–55.

2. Julio Rosario, interview by author, 28 August and 18 September 1997, Philadelphia, tape recording, trans. by author (see Appendix II); and PCHR, *Puerto Ricans in Philadelphia: A Study of Their Demographic Characteristics, Problems and Attitudes* (April 1954; reprint, New York: Arno Press, 1975), 20.

3. On earlier recruitment, see Edwin Maldonado, "Contract Labor and the Origins of Puerto Rican Communities in the United States," *International Migration Review* 13 (spring 1979): 103–121; and Centro de Estudios Puertorriqueños, *Labor Migration under Capitalism: The Puerto Rican Experience* (New York: Monthly Review Press, 1979).

4. Willard B. Kille, Gloucester County Board of Agriculture, to Rexford G. Tugwell, 27 September 1943, NA 126; and Ruth Hampton, U.S. Department of the Interior, Division of Territories and Island Possessions, to Willard B. Kille, 27 November 1943, NA 126.

5. U.S. Congress, Senate, Senator Langer of North Dakota and Senator Hayden of Arizona speaking on the Supply and Distribution of Farm Labor for 1944, H.J. Res. 208, *Congressional Record* 90, pt. 1 (1944): 864–865.

6. As quoted in President's Commission on Migratory Labor, *Migratory Labor in American Agriculture: Report of the President's Commission on Migratory Labor* (26 March 1951), 39; "Puerto Ricans Recruited," *Washington Post,* 19 April 1944, clipping, NA 126; and Julia Henderson, "Foreign Labour in the United States during the War," *International Labor Review* (December 1945): 609–631.

7. Rexford G. Tugwell to B.W. Thoron, Division of Territories and Island Possessions, 12 January 1944, NA 126; Clarence Senior, *Puerto Rican Emigration* (Río Piedras, Puerto Rico: Social Science Research Center, University of Puerto Rico, 1947), 25; and Mason Barr to Rexford G. Tugwell, memo, 28 April 1944, NA 126.

8. Tugwell to Thoron, 12 January 1944; Barr to Tugwell, 28 April 1944; and Manuel A. Pérez, Commissioner of Labor, to Rexford G. Tugwell, memo, "Letter of Mr. Edwin G. Arnold on the possibility of emigration of Puerto Rican Laborers to Hawaii," 20 November 1945, NA 126.

9. Frank L. McNamee, Regional Director, WMC, to Deputy Chairman and Executive Director, WMC, memo, "Preliminary Draft of 1944 Program for Recruiting Workers for Food Processing Industry," 19 January 1944, WMC 211, Box 2299.

10. "Officials in Florida Charge Labor Piracy," *New York Times,* 1 August 1943, 41; "Jersey Tomatoes Swamp Canneries," *New York Times,* 20 August 1943, 17; McNamee, "Preliminary Draft"; and Frank L. McNamee to Deputy Chairman and Executive Director, WMC, memo, "Shortage of Labor for Food Processors, Region III," 6 April 1944, WMC 211, Box 2299.

11. R. E. Worden, Campbell Soup Co., to McNamee, 13 March 1944, WMC 211, Box 2299; Thomas Costello, State Director (N.J.), to McNamee, memo, "Labor Mobilization Program," 14 January 1944, WMC 211, Box 2299; "El contrato para obreros de Pto. Rico," *El Mundo,* 14 November 1944, 5; "Entrevistas con obreros en Arecibo," *El Mundo,* 15 April 1944, 9; and Floran J. Bowland, State Manpower Director (Pa.), "Special E.S. Bulletin No. 244: Immigration of Puerto Rican Workers," 31 July 1944, WMC 211, Box 2298.

12. Gilbert Ramírez, memo, "Importation of Puerto Rican Workers," 29 April 1944, NA 126; Gilbert Ramírez, "Report on the Arrival of Puerto Rican Workers at Weehawken, New Jersey, 9 May 1944," NA 126; and Press Release, "Puerto Ricans Working for Campbell Soup Co.," 21 June 1944, NA 126.

13. Bowland, "Special E.S. Bulletin No. 244"; and Frank L. McNamee to State Manpower Directors, memo, "Puerto Rican Labor," 21 September 1944, WMC 211, Box 2333.

14. Ramírez, "Report on the Arrival"; Costello to McNamee, "Labor Mobilization"; and WMC as cited in Maldonado, "Contract Labor," 111.

15. Enrique Rodríguez to Jesús T. Piñero, Resident Commissioner, 9 March 1945, NA 126; and B. W. Thoron to Jesús T. Piñero, 10 March 1945, NA 126.

16. Joan D. Koss, "Puerto Ricans in Philadelphia: Migration and Accommodation" (Ph.D. diss., University of Pennsylvania, 1965), 64–65; and Taller Puertorriqueño, Inc., *Batiendo la Olla ("Stirring the Pot"): A Cross-Generational Comparison and Self-Study by Second Generation Puerto Ricans in Philadelphia* (March 1979), 49 trans. by author, 43.

17. "Maid Problem," *New Republic,* 28 April 1947, clipping, AG 61–55; and Senior, *Emigration,* 38, 55.

18. Senior, *Emigration,* 38; Meeting Minutes, Metropolitan Industrial Committee, 18 December 1946, YWCA 635; "Hand of Friendship Helps Puerto Rican Domestics Here to Feel at Home," *Bulletin,* 11 August 1947, clipping, UA; and Elizabeth Reck, International Institute, to Mother Mary Basil, Rosemont College, 9 May 1947, NSC 625, Box 62.

19. Meeting Minutes, Metropolitan Industrial Committee, 20 October 1947, YWCA 635; "Standards for Household Employment," YWCA's Sub-Committee on Household Employment, n.d. [May 1946], YWCA 635; and Meeting Minutes, Metropolitan Industrial Committee, 3 December 1947, YWCA 635.

20. "Hand of Friendship"; Frieda S. Miller, Women's Bureau, to Daisy Reck, Office of the Governor, Puerto Rico, 28 July 1947, NA 126; Daisy Reck to Mason Barr, Division of Territories and Possessions, 17 September 1947, NA 126; Meeting Minutes, Metropolitan Industrial Committee, 19 March 1947, YWCA 635; and Puerto Rico, Office of Puerto Rico, "Puerto Rican Domestics Reach Philadelphia," *Puerto Rico: A Bulletin of the Office of Puerto Rico* 2 (May 1947): 30, NSC 625, Box 61.

21. Mason Barr to G. L. Thrall, 16 September 1947, NA 126; Meeting Minutes, Metropolitan Industrial Committee, 5 November 1947, YWCA 635; Meeting Minutes, Metropolitan Industrial Committee, 3 March 1948, YWCA 635; and Frieda Miller to Marian Lantz, International Institute, 26 June 1948, NSC 625, Box 62. Smaltz is from a handwritten note on a formal letter.

22. Daisy Reck to Rex Lee, Division of Territories and Island Possessions, 22 July 1947, NA 126; and Reck to Barr, 17 September 1947.

23. Senior, *Emigration,* 53–54; and Donald J. O'Connor to Mariano Villaronga, Commissioner of Education, 1 April 1947, NA 126.

24. Donald J. O'Connor to Manuel Pérez, Commissioner of Labor, memo, "More on Job Procurement on the Mainland," 13 May 1947, NA 126; and Donald J. O'Connor to Teodoro Moscoso, Puerto Rico Industrial Development Corporation, 6 June 1947, NA 126.

25. O'Connor, "More on Job Procurement"; "Puerto Rican Girls to Get Jobs Here: Scarsdale to Take First Group Trained on Island for Service as Domestics," *New York Times,* 1 January 1948, clipping, NA 126; and O'Connor to Villaronga, 1 April 1947. On dispersing domestics, see also Maldonado, "Contract Labor," 105.

26. O'Connor to Villaronga, 1 April 1947; and memo, "Suggestions for an Experiment in Placement of Household Workers," 9 June 1947, NA 126.

27. O'Connor to Villaronga, 1 April 1947; Meeting Minutes, Emigration Advisory Committee, 18 August 1947, NA 126; "Es el primero de ocho centros que funcionarán en toda la Isla," *El Mundo,* 25 October 1947, 14; and "ATENCION . . .! Damas de Caguas y Pueblos Limítrofes," flier, AG 61–55.

28. "Employment Contract: Puerto Rican Women as Live-in Houseworkers," AG 63–37.

29. "30 Scarsdale Couples Discuss Hiring of Puerto Rican Girls," clipping, AG 61–55; "Puerto Rican Girls Like Transition after Week on Jobs in Scarsdale," *New York Times,* 5 March 1948, clipping, AG 61–55; and "Only 2 of Scarsdale's 21 Puerto Rican Maids Speak English, None Can Cook or Do Housework, but Employers Are Hopeful," clipping, AG 61–55.

30. "Summary of Minutes: Conference Report of Experimental Project in the Placement of Puerto Rican Workers in Selected Homes in Scarsdale, N.Y.," 22 June 1948, AG 61–55.

31. "12 of 21 Puerto Rican Maids Still Working in Scarsdale," *The Reporter Dispatch* (White Plains, New York), 22 July 1949, clipping, AG 61–55; and Petro América Pagán de Colón to Estella Draper, 3 October 1949, AG 61–55.

32. Pagán de Colón to Draper, 3 October 1949; and Estella Draper to Petro América Pagán de Colón, 15 December 1949, AG 61–55. For examples of letters, see Petro América Pagán de Colón to Mrs. Florence Gibson, 12 December 1949; and Manuel Cabranes to Señorita Ana Iris Cruz Hows, 27 October 1949, AG 61–55.

33. Louise D. Hart, YWCA, to Marian Lantz, International Institute, 18 April 1947, NSC 625, Box 62; Marian Lantz to T. M. Dillon, Beaver College, 23 January 1948, NSC 625, Box 62; and G. L. Thrall to U.S. Department of Interior, 12 September 1947, NA 126.

34. Thrall to Department of Interior, 12 September 1947; "Family Census, 1950," FNG 32, Box 65; and Petro América Pagán de Colón, "Programa de Trabajadores Migratorios de Puerto Rico a Los Estados Unidos" (San Juan, 1956), 7.

35. "Plan para la emigración de 1,000 obreros," *El Mundo,* 11 May 1946, 1; "Esta semana saldrán los primeros trabajadores," *El Mundo,* 14 May 1946, 3; "Otro grupo de 26 trabajadores va a los EE. UU.," *El Mundo,* 24 June 1946, 1; and "Obreros boricuas en el Norte objetan descuentos en sueldo," *El Mundo,* 26 August 1946, 4.

36. "250 obreros de Puerto Rico en Glassboro, N.J.," *El Mundo,* 26 August 1946, 12; "Cien portorriqueños en campamento Pensilvania," *El Mundo,* 28 August 1946, 12; "Obreros boricuas"; and Santiago Ortiz, Report on Farm Labor Camps, 10 September 1946, NA 126.

37. "Están trabajando bien boricuas en Filadelfia," *El Mundo,* 1 June 1946, 4, trans. by author; and "Otro grupo," trans. by author.

38. "Cien portorriqueños," trans. by author; Ortiz, Report on Farm Labor Camps, trans. by author; and "250 obreros," trans. by author.

39. Ortiz, Report on Farm Labor Camps; and "Obreros boricuas," trans. by author.

40. "Obreros boricuas"; Ortiz, Report on Farm Labor Camps; and "Pide Gobierno auspicie una emigración," *El Mundo,* 21 August 1946, 1.

41. "250 obreros," trans.

42. "Piñero afirma hay que llevar emigración a zonas agrícolas," *El Mundo,* 6 October 1947, 1, trans. by author; and Meeting Minutes, Subcommittee on Puerto Rican Labor, Committee on Adjustment to City Living, Health and Welfare Council, 31 October 1949, FNG 32, Box 64.

43. Meeting Minutes, United States Employment Service, Washington, D.C., 6 December 1949, AG 61–55.

44. Meeting Minutes, 6 December 1949; and "Alien Farm Labor Protested amid Political, Racial Rifts," *New York Times,* 4 April 1950, 1.

45. President's Commission, *Migratory Labor,* 19, 16.

46. U.S. Congress, House, Rep. Andresen of Minnesota speaking on Farm -Labor Supply Program, H.R. 124, *Congressional Record* 93, pt. 2 (1947): 1657; U.S. Congress, Senate, Senator Lucas of Illinois speaking on Farm Labor Supply Program, H.R. 2102, *Congressional Record* 93, pt. 3 (1947): 3214; U.S. Congress, House, Clerk reading on Recruitment and Distribution of Farm Labor, S. 2767, *Congressional Record* 94, pt. 7 (1948): 9347; and President's Commission, *Migratory Labor,* 49.

47. "Alien Farm Labor Protested"; "Alien Farm Labor Is Barred in State," *New York Times,* 5 April 1950, 33; U.S. Department of Labor, Employment Service, Farm Placement Service, *Handbook for Farm Placement Service, 1950,* 41; and President's Commission, *Migratory Labor,* 36.

48. Arthur C. Gernes, "Implications of Puerto Rican Migration to the Continent Outside New York City," Address before the Ninth Annual Convention on Social Orientation (Río Piedras, University of Puerto Rico), 10 December 1955, 15, UA; USBES, *Employment Security Review* 19 (March 1952); Don Larin, "Domestic Recruitment—Our Basic Job," *Employment Security Review* 19 (March 1952): 4; and Petro América Pagán de Colón, "Farm Labor Program in Puerto Rico," *Employment Security Review* 19 (March 1952): 23, 24.

49. "U.S., Puerto Rico Map a Labor Pact," *New York Times,* 6 February 1949, 7; and "Agricultural Employment Contract (Northeastern Area)," 1950, AG 61–55. On administrative structures, see Michael Lapp, "Managing Migration: The Migration Division of Puerto Rico and Puerto Ricans in New York City, 1948–1968" (Ph.D. diss., Johns Hopkins University, 1989), 174–179.

50. Michael Lapp, "The Migration Division of Puerto Rico and Puerto Ricans in New York City, 1948–1969," in *Immigration to New York,* ed. William Pencak, Selma Berrol, and Randall M. Miller (Philadelphia: Balch Institute Press, 1991), 200, 204–205.

51. Minutes, Subcommittee on Puerto Rican Labor, 31 October 1949; PRMD, *Monthly Report,* October 1952, February 1957, September 1952, November 1951, October 1951, April 1956; PRMD, *Annual Report, 1954–1955,* 6; and PRMD, *Annual Report, 1955–1956,* 117.

52. Clarence Senior, "Patterns of Puerto Rican Dispersion in the Continental United States," *Social Problems* (October 1954): 95–96; and Clarence Senior, "Migration to the Mainland," *Monthly Labor Review* 78 (December 1955): 1356.

53. President's Commission, *Migratory Labor,* 3; "250 obreros," trans.; E. Farabegoli, "Portoricans [*sic*]brought in for farm labor," 5 July 1946, NSC 625, Box 62; "Otro grupo"; and John G. Sholl quoted in "Jersey Welcomes Migrant Workers," *New York Times,* 6 September 1950, 31.

54. U.S. Congress, House, Rep. Gross of Pennsylvania, *Congressional Record* (1947): 1659; U.S. Congress, House, Committee on Agriculture, *Farm Labor: Hearings before the Committee on Agriculture,* 80th Cong., 2nd sess., 11 June 1948, 10–11; PAFPP, *Annual Report, 1953,* 14–15; and PAFPP, *Annual Reports, 1954–1970.*

55. Julio Rosario, interview, trans.

56. USBES, *Puerto Rican Farm Workers in the Middle Atlantic States* (November 1954), 4, 7; and Morrison Handsaker, "Seasonal Farm Labor in Pennsylvania" (Easton, Pa.: Lafayette College, 1953), 58.

57. On Massachusetts, see Julio Morales, *Puerto Rican Poverty and Migration: We Just Had to Try Elsewhere* (New York: Praeger Publishers, 1986); and on Connecticut, see Ruth Glasser, *Aquí Me Quedo: Puerto Ricans in Connecticut* (Middletown: Connecticut Humanities Council, 1997).

58. Agricultural Employment Contract; Fernando Sierra Berdecía to Clarence Senior, 26 November 1951, AG 61–55; Clarence Senior to Fernando Sierra Berdecía and Petro América Pagán de Colón, 20 November 1951, AG 61–55; and Clarence Senior to Petro América Pagán de Colón, 13 July 1951, AG 61–55.

59. Meeting Minutes, USES in Washington, D.C., 8 December 1949, AG 61–55; Estella Draper to Petro A. Pagán de Colón, memo, "Meeting Held with Max Henderson, of Michigan Field Crops, Inc.," 22 September 1949, AG 61–55; Meeting Minutes, Office of Manuel Cabranes, 12 December 1949, AG 61–55; and "Scheduled Airlines Take Over Puerto Rico Farmlift to U.S.," *Bulletin,* 13 June 1950, clipping, AG 61–55.

60. "'Job' Agent Sentenced, Mulcted Puerto Ricans," *Inquirer,* 22 December 1950, 12.

61. USBC, *Census of Population: 1970,* vol. 1, *Characteristics of the Population,* pt. 40, Pennsylvania (Washington, D.C., 1973), 697; Minutes, Subcommittee on Puerto Rican Labor, 31 October 1949; "Diario Explica Condiciones de Vida de la Colonia Boricua en Lancaster," *El Mundo,* 20 July 1959, 16; "Ciudad Pensilvania: Acoge a una Población de Más de 600 Boricuas," *El Mundo,* 9 July 1954, 5; "En Pensilvania: Organizan la Colonia Boricua de Allentown," *El Mundo,* 7 June 1954, 1; and "Prejudice, Language Barrier Add to Puerto Rican Problem," *Morning Call* (Allentown, Pa.), 2 May 1958, 19.

62. "Labor Rates Make City Major Center of Influx," *Bethlehem Globe,* 7 July 1958, 1; and "Religion, Male Superiority, Baseball Dominate Living," *Bethlehem Globe,* 8 July 1958, 1. See also Peter Antonsen, "A History of the Puerto Rican Community in Bethlehem, Pennsylvania, 1944–1993" (Ph.D. diss., Lehigh University, Lehigh, Pa., 1994).

63. "Labor Rates Make City"; "Prejudice, Language Barrier"; "Auto Troubles Biggest of All; Betting, Narcotics No Problem," *Bethlehem Globe,* 8 June 1958, 1; and PRMD, *Monthly Report,* November 1953.

64. New Jersey, Department of Education, Division against Discrimination, "The Puerto Rican in New Jersey: His Present Status," by Isham Jones (July 1955), 42–43, Special Collections and Archives, Alexander Library, Rutgers University, New Brunswick, N.J.

65. Minutes, Subcommittee on Puerto Rican Labor; and Meeting Minutes, Puerto Rican-American Agricultural Union, 2 October 1949, FNG 32, Box 64.

66. Friese, "Report of Visit to Farm Labor Camp"; "Cien portorriqueños"; and "Churches Help Migrant Labor," *Bulletin,* 24 July 1948, clipping, BC.

67. Minutes, Puerto Rican-American Agricultural Labor Union; Minutes, Subcommittee on Puerto Rican Labor; and William Henry Welsh, consultant to Health and Welfare Council, to Elfriede Friese, 6 December 1948, NSC 625, Box 62.

68. Kal Wagenheim, *A Survey of Puerto Ricans on the U.S. Mainland in the 1970s* (New York: Praeger Publishers, 1975), 55; and PCHR, *Puerto Ricans in Philadelphia* (1954), 18, 21, 22.

69. Taller Puertorriqueño Oral History Project, transcript no. 6, 2; transcript no. 3, 1 trans.; transcript no. 2, 2 trans.; transcript no. 11, 6–7; and transcript no. 9, 1–2; all PHMC.

70. "Pide Gobierno"; Migration Division, "Information for Farmers Facing a Manpower Shortage" [1950–1951], FNG 32, Box 64; Friese, "Report of Visit to Farm Labor Camp"; and Larin, "Domestic Recruitment," 4.

71. PRMD, *Monthly Report,* October 1953; Minutes, Subcommittee on Puerto Rican Labor; and Meeting Minutes, Migration Division Staff Meeting, 10 November 1949, AG 61–55.

72. On the limited success of dispersion, see Lapp, "Managing Migration," 164–165.

Chapter 4

1. Carmen Aponte, interview by author, 12 December 1991 and 6 April 1992, Philadelphia, Pa., tape recording, trans. by author. See Appendix II.

2. Florencio Sánchez, interview by author, 21 August 25 September 1997, Philadelphia, Pa., tape recording, trans.

3. See Table 2.1. The migration to Philadelphia also represented a higher proportion of these municipios' 1950 populations than for other municipios, suggesting the significance of this out-migration for the home communities.

4. Gloria Roldán Amaro, interview by author, 22 and 29 July 1997, San Lorenzo, P.R., tape recording, trans.

5. John Augelli, "Rural Settlement Types of Interior Puerto Rico: Sample Studies from the Upper Loíza Basin," in *Symposium on the Geography of Puerto Rico,* ed. Clarence F. Jones and Rafael Picó (Río Piedras: University of Puerto Rico Press, 1955), 329; and Luis Martínez Fernández, *San Lorenzo: Notas Para su Historia: El Comportamiento Electoral del Municipio Durante la Era de Dominación Popular, 1940–1968* (San Juan: El Comité Historia de los Pueblos, 1986), 7–9, CP.

6. USBC, *U.S. Census of Population: 1950,* vol. II, *Characteristics of the Population,* pt. 53, Puerto Rico (Washington, D.C., 1953), 92; and Augelli, "Rural Settlement," 330.

7. Gloria Roldán Amaro, interview, trans.

8. On the decline of tobacco, see Chapter 2. See Figure 4.1 for census citations. PRAES, "Some Effects of Federal and Commonwealth Tobacco Programs on the Tobacco Industry of Puerto Rico," by Marciano Avilés, *Bulletin* 162 (February 1962), 7; and Herminio R. Rodríguez Morales, *San Lorenzo: Notas para su Historia* (San Juan: El Comité Historia de los Pueblos, 1986), 52–53, CP.

9. Rodríguez Morales, *San Lorenzo: Notas,* 57; Robert A. Manners, "Tabara: Subcultures of a Tobacco and Mixed Crops Municipality," in *The People of Puerto Rico: A Study in Social Anthropology,* ed. Julian Steward et al. (Urbana: University of Illinois Press, 1956), 137; and PRFPD, *Annual Agricultural and Food Processing Report, 1958.*

10. Augelli, "Rural Settlement," 330.

11. USBC, *Census of Manufactures: 1954,* Puerto Rico (Washington, D.C., 1956), 41, 46; and USBC, *Census of Manufactures: 1963,* Puerto Rico (Washington, D.C., 1965), 117, 143.

12. Rafael Picó, *The Geography of Puerto Rico* (Chicago: Aldine Publishing Company, 1974), 307; and PREDA, Continental Operations Branch, New York City, N.Y., "The Apparel and Related Products Industry" (August 1973), CP.

13. See Figure 4.1 for census citations; USBC, *Census of Population: 1970*, 490, 472; USBC, *Census of Population: 1950*, 92; *and USBC*, Census of Population: 1960, 204.

14. "San Lorenzo es Ahora Como una Pequeña Isla de Oposición," *El Mundo* (San Juan), 8 November 1948, 7, trans. by author; and Martínez Fernández, *Comportamiento Electoral*.

15. "En San Lorenzo No Hay Problemas: Un Año Después," *El Mundo*, 22 January 1950, 9; and Martínez Fernández, *Comportamiento Electoral*, 23–24.

16. "En San Lorenzo No Hay Problemas"; and Martínez Fernández, *Comportamiento Electoral*, 19, 21, 29.

17. Gloria Roldán Amaro, interview, trans.

18. Justino Navarro Ramos, interview by author, 25 September 1996 and 24 July 1997, San Lorenzo, P.R., tape recording, trans.; and Ana Luisa Navarro Ramos, interview by author, 25 September 1996 and 24 July 1997, San Lorenzo, P.R., tape recording, trans.

19. José Vázquez Calzada, "La Población de Puerto Rico y Su Trayectoria Histórica" (Río Piedras: University of Puerto Rico, School of Public Health, 1978), 403, CEP.

20. Augelli, "Rural Settlement," 333–334.

21. Augelli, "Rural Settlement," 331, 335.

22. Vázquez Calzada, "Población," 304–305; PRAES, "Tobacco Programs," 12; and USBC, *Census of Manufactures: 1954*, 52–53.

23. Baptism records, Parroquia Nuestra Señora de las Mercedes, San Lorenzo. See Appendix II.

24. PRPB, "Puerto Rican Migrants: A Socio-Economic Study" (San Juan, 1972), 17, CEP.

25. John Augelli, "San Lorenzo: A Case Study of Recent Migrations in Interior Puerto Rico," *American Journal of Economics and Sociology* 2 (January 1952): 158; "Organizarán Club Hijos Ausentes de San Lorenzo," *El Mundo*, 4 December 1959, 17, trans. by author; "Sanlorenceños lo Agasajarán," *El Mundo*, 25 November 1954, 10; and "San Lorenzo Recibirá Hijos Ausentes Mañana," *El Mundo*, 26 November 1964, 24, trans. by author.

26. Augelli, "San Lorenzo," 159; Augelli, "Rural Settlement," 334–335; and Baptism records, Parroquia Nuestra Señora de las Mercedes, San Lorenzo.

27. Florencio Sánchez, interview, trans.

28. George Beishlag, "Trends in Land Use in Southeastern Puerto Rico," in *Symposium*, ed. Jones, 284, 291. See also Déborah Berman Santana, *Kicking Off the Bootstraps: Environment, Development, and Community Power in Puerto Rico* (Tucson: University of Arizona Press, 1996), 27–40.

29. Sidney W. Mintz, "Cañamelar: The Subculture of a Rural Sugar Plantation Proletariat," in *People*, ed. Steward, 315; and Berman Santana, *Kicking Off*, 48–53.

30. Nilda Sánchez Quiñones, interview by author, 20 January and 25 July 1997, Salinas, P.R., tape recording, trans.

31. Salinas had 33,184 cuerdas cultivated and San Lorenzo had 31,077. USBC, *U.S. Census of Agriculture: 1959*, vol. 1, *Municipalities*, pt. 53, Puerto Rico (Washington, D.C., 1961), 58; USBC, *Census of Population: 1950*, 92; USBC, *Census of Manufactures, 1954*, 40, 41, 44; and "Jefes y Empleados Salinas: Revelan las Causas de Desempleo," *El Mundo*, 30 August 1955, 1.

32. PRAES, "Labor Efficiency in Harvesting Sugarcane in Puerto Rico, 1950," by Edmundo Silva and Manuel Piñero (January 1953), 1; Beishlag, "Trends in Land Use," 286; and Central Aguirre Sugar Company, Aguirre, Puerto Rico, "Report, 1949," CP.

33. On the decline of sugar, see Chapter 2. USBC, *Census of Population: 1970*, 472; USBC, *Census of Agriculture: 1959*, 58; and USBC, *Census of Agriculture: 1969*, vol. 1, *Area Reports*, pt. 52, Puerto Rico (Washington, D.C., 1972), 160, 161.

34. The 36 percent is the proportion in food processing, which includes sugar. USBC, *Sixteenth Census: 1940*, 61; and USBC, *Census of Population: 1970*, 490.

35. Berman Santana, *Kicking Off,* 56–61; and "El déficit del ELA terminó con Aguirre," *El Mundo,* 19 December 1989, 12.

36. "Señora Muñoz Hace Donativo a Unión Damas," *El Mundo,* 12 December 1949, 5; and "Salinas Pide la Instalación de Industrias," *El Mundo,* 9 April 1951, 24, trans. by author.

37. "Jefes y Empleados Salinas"; and Betram B. Johansson, "Salinas, Puerto Rico: ¿Quién lleva la merienda . . . papá o mamá?" *Fomento de Puerto Rico* 3 (July 1956): 24–25.

38. "Pueblo 'Quedaría Muerto': Tratan Evitar Fábrica Plumas se Mude de la Zona de Salinas," *El Mundo,* 12 December 1957, 2; "Estudio Sobre Terreno: Fomento Espera Evitar Traslado Fábrica Paper Mate de Salinas," *El Mundo,* 13 December 1957, 1; "Una Fábrica en Salinas," *El Mundo,* 14 December 1957, editorials; and "Cierre de la Paper Mate: Crea Desempleo y Caos Económico en Salinas y los Pueblos Limítrofes," *El Mundo,* 29 January 1960, 16.

39. "Ofrece Incentivo Especial a Nuevas Fábricas Salinas," *El Mundo,* 8 February 1960, 16; and Picó, *Geography,* 307.

40. Berman Santana, *Kicking Off,* 63–65; and PREDA, "Apparel and Related Products." According to Berman Santana, when Fomento firms making pens, boots, and pantyhose closed, 1,000 jobs were lost. In 1980, only Salinas Manufacturing remained, and it closed in 1990, putting 150 workers, mostly women, out of work. See also "Fábrica Dedicada a la Manufactura Pantalones Mujer Cierra en Salinas," *El Mundo,* 24 April 1971, 12-A.

41. Mintz, "Cañamelar," 350–351.

42. Mintz, "Cañamelar," 397–398; and Berman Santana, *Kicking Off,* 55–56.

43. Julio Quiñones Navarro, interview by author, 20 January 1997, Salinas, P.R., tape recording, trans.

44. Vázquez Calzada, "Población," 403.

45. "Discuten Casos de Expropiación de 6,000 Cuerdas en Salinas," *El Mundo,* 25 July 1952, 16; Berman Santana, *Kicking Off,* 39; and Beishlag, "Trends in Land Use," 296.

46. Salinas's baptism records identified significantly fewer baptisms with place of marriage than San Lorenzo's. Baptism records, 1911–1940, Nuestra Señora de Monserrate de Salinas, Salinas, Puerto Rico.

47. John Macisco Jr. found that twice as many migrants settled in metropolitan areas as in nonmetropolitan areas. "Internal Migration in Puerto Rico, 1955–1960" (Ph.D. diss., Brown University, 1966), 135.

48. Vázquez Calzada, "Población," 311–313, 284, 301.

49. PRMD, Applications for Farm Labor Contracts, 1948, "Historial Personal" and "Contrato de Empleo," AG 63–37.

50. PRMD, "Historial Personal."

51. PRMD, "Historial Personal."

52. PRMD, "Historial Personal."

53. Manners, "Tabara," 153.

54. Mintz, "Cañamelar," 397, 352, 354.

55. PRFPD, *Annual Agricultural and Food Processing Report, 1954,* 8; and PRMD, *Annual Report, 1954–1955,* 27.

56. Carmen Aponte, interview, trans.

57. Justino Navarro Ramos, interview, trans.

58. Julio Quiñones Navarro, interview, trans.; and Nilda Sánchez Quiñones, interview, trans.

59. Florencio Sánchez, interview, trans.

60. Gloria Roldán Amaro, interview, trans.

61. Morrison Handsaker, "Seasonal Farm Labor in Pennsylvania" (Easton, Pa.: Lafayette College, 1953), 52, 57; and PCHR, *Puerto Ricans in Philadelphia: A Study of Their Demographic Characteristics, Problems and Attitudes,* by Arthur Siegel, Harold Orlans, and Loyal Greer (April 1954; reprint, New York: Arno Press, 1975), 31, 120–121.

Chapter 5

1. Genara Aponte, interview by author, 9 October, 6 and 20 November 1997, Philadelphia, Pa., tape recording, trans. by author (see Appendix II); and José Lacend, interview by author, 15 June 1997 and 14 February 1998, Camden, N.J., tape recording.

2. USBC data as compiled in PCHR, *Puerto Ricans in Philadelphia: A Study of Their Demographic Characteristics, Problems and Attitudes,* by Arthur Siegel, Harold Orlans, and Loyal Greer (April 1954; reprint, New York: Arno Press, 1975), 124; and PCHR, *Puerto Ricans in Philadelphia* (1954), 33.

3. On Philadelphia's economic history, see Walter Licht, *Getting Work: Philadelphia, 1840–1950* (Cambridge: Harvard University Press, 1992); and Sam Bass Warner, Jr., *The Private City: Philadelphia in Three Periods of Its Growth* (Philadelphia: University of Pennsylvania Press, 1968). For photographic histories, see Fredric M. Miller, Morris J. Vogel, and Allen F. Davis, *Still Philadelphia: A Photographic History, 1890–1940* (Philadelphia: Temple University Press, 1983), and *Philadelphia Stories: A Photographic History, 1920–1960* (Philadelphia: Temple University Press, 1988); and Philip Scranton and Walter Licht, *Work Sights: Industrial Philadelphia, 1890–1950* (Philadelphia: Temple University Press, 1986).

4. "Speed in Changeover Hinges on Flow of Materials, Equipment," *Inquirer,* 28 August 1945, 1; "90,000 New Jobs Available in Area," *Inquirer,* 24 September 1945, 1; "Phila. Least Hit by Job Layoffs," *Inquirer,* 31 August 1945, 11; "16,900 Jobs Go Begging Here Despite War Plant Layoffs," *Inquirer,* 26 August 1945, 1; and " 'Less Essential' Plants Need 52,000 Workers," *Inquirer,* 1 September 1945, 1.

5. "Vast Job Program Launched to Bring New Prosperity Era," *Inquirer,* 27 August 1945, 1; "Textile, Hosiery Boom Will Cut Unemployment," *Inquirer,* 29 August 1945, 1; "Mayor Says City Leads in Post-War Planning," *Inquirer,* 26 August 1945, B1; "Vast Housing Program to Give Thousands Jobs," *Inquirer,* 31 August 1945, 1; and "Construction Spending of Half Billion Planned," *Inquirer,* 30 August 1945, 1.

6. "Speed in Changeover"; "Business Boom in City Forecast,"*Inquirer,* 5 October 1945, 3; "1200 on Strike at Candy Firm," *Inquirer,* 28 September 1945, 1; "Sit-Strike Ended at Campbell's," *Inquirer,* 28 August 1945, 1; "4 Strikes Here Still Deadlocked," *Inquirer,* 19 September 1945, 2; "New Contract Rejected by Hosiery Union Here," *Inquirer,* 26 August 1945, B1; "Strike Is Ended at Ritz-Carlton," *Inquirer,* 26 August 1945, 2; and "A Shameful Betrayal of Veterans," *Inquirer,* 28 September 1945, 16.

7. "Vast Housing Program."

8. "Snyder Foresees 8 Million Idle," *Evening Bulletin,* 1 October 1945; "Jamaicans Riot on Way Home," *Inquirer,* 29 August 1945, 12; and "7647 War Captives Will Lose Jobs," *Inquirer,* 28 September 1945, 2.

9. "90 Pct. of Workers to Stay, Study Hints," *Inquirer,* 22 September 1945, 9; and Allen B. Ballard, *One More Day's Journey: The Story of a Family and a People* (New York: McGraw- Hill

Book Company, 1984), 231. On the exclusion of African Americans from industry in Philadelphia, see also Licht, *Getting Work*, 43–55.

10. "Return to School, Job Experts Ask," *Inquirer*, 28 September 1945, 2; and "305 Who Quit School for War Jobs Return," *Inquirer*, 2 October 1945, 18.

11. "Women and Jobs," *Inquirer*, 23 August 1945, 10; and "Advises Women Job Holders," *Inquirer*, 6 September 1945, 10. See also Elaine Tyler May, *Homeward Bound: American Families in the Cold War Era* (New York: Basic Books, 1988).

12. "Back to the Kitchen," *Inquirer*, 29 August 1945, 18; "Jobs for Women," *Inquirer*, 10 September 1945, 8; "For Child Care Centers," *Inquirer*, 8 September 1945, 6; "Seats for Ladies," *Inquirer*, 2 September 1945, 6; and "Despite the Heartache," *Inquirer*, 30 August 1945, 10.

13. "Keep Job Pledge to G.I. Joe," *Inquirer*, 25 September 1945, 12; "War Veteran Employment Problem Minimized in Philadelphia," *Inquirer*, 2 September 1945, 11; PABES, *Labor Market Letter* (March 1947); "90,000 New Jobs Available"; and "5200 Lose Jobs Here in Week as Layoffs Decline," *Inquirer*, 8 September 1945, 1.

14. Alice Kessler-Harris, *Out to Work: A History of Wage-Earning Women in the United States* (New York: Oxford University Press, 1982), 286; "Women Leading in Job Aid Claims," *Inquirer*, 13 September 1945, 6; and PABES, *Labor Market Letter* (June 1947).

15. PABES, *Labor Market Letter* (March 1947); and Jacqueline Jones, *Labor of Love, Labor of Sorrow: Black Women, Work and the Family, from Slavery to the Present* (New York: Vintage Books, 1985), 257, 259.

16. PCHR, *Puerto Ricans in Philadelphia* (1954), 20.

17. Licht, *Getting Work*, 12; and Joseph Oberman and Stephen Kozakowski, *History of Development in the Delaware Valley Region* (Philadelphia: Delaware Valley Regional Planning Commission, September 1976), 78–79.

18. Puerto Rico, Office of the Governor, "Estudio Sobre la Emigración" (San Juan, 1952), 37, CEP; and PCHR, *Puerto Ricans in Philadelphia* (1954), 35.

19. Clarence Senior, *Puerto Rican Emigration* (Río Piedras: Social Science Research Center, University of Puerto Rico, 1947), 51, 55, 49; U.S. Department of Labor, Employment Service, *The Labor Market* (April 1947), as quoted in Senior, *Emigration*, 55; Donald J. O'Connor, "Memorandum: Mainland Labor Force Needs in 1948–1949 and Puerto Rico's Opportunities to Exploit Them," 10 August 1948, NA 126; and Clarence Senior, "Puerto Rico: Migration to the Mainland," *Monthly Labor Review* (December 1955): 1356. On the Migration Division's concern with hostile reactions and limited economic opportunities in New York, see Michael Lapp, "The Migration Division of Puerto Rico and Puerto Ricans in New York City, 1948–1969," in *Immigration to New York*, ed. William Pencak, Selma Berrol, and Randall M. Miller (Philadelphia: Balch Institute Press, 1991).

20. Genara Aponte, interview, trans.

21. Juanita Rodríguez, interview by author, 18 June 1997, Palmyra, N.J., tape recording, trans.

22. Nilda Quiñones Sánchez, interview by author, 20 January and 25 July 1997, Salinas, P.R., tape recording, trans.

23. Taller Puertorriqueño, transcript no. 6, 5; and transcript no. 4, 2–3; Taller Puertorriqueño Oral History Project, PHMC.

24. Carmen Aponte, interview by author, 7 and 12 December 1991, Philadelphia, Pa., tape recording, trans.

25. Friends Neighborhood Guild, "Family Census, 1950," FNG 32, Box 65; and PCHR, *Puerto Ricans in Philadelphia* (1954), 34–35. The 21 percent of Puerto Rican women identified as professionals in the 1950 census data seems erroneously high, as the PCHR study in 1954

found less than 2 percent employed as professionals and less than 2 percent as managers. The 1950 census data were based on a very small sample.

26. While the U.S. census identifies women as operatives, neither it nor other sources specifically identify women as garment workers. See Altagracia Ortiz's discussion in "'*En la aguja y el pedal eché la hiel*': Puerto Rican Women in the Garment Industry of New York City, 1920–1980," in *Puerto Rican Women and Work: Bridges of Transnational Labor,* ed. Altagracia Ortiz (Philadelphia: Temple University Press, 1996), 55–81.

27. PAFPP, *Annual Reports, 1954–1960*; Morrison Handsaker, "Seasonal Farm Labor in Pennsylvania" (Easton, Pa.: Lafayette College, 1953), 83, 100, 42;. USBES, *Puerto Rican Farm Workers in the Middle Atlantic States* (November 1954), 1, 7.

28. Quoted in New Jersey, Department of Education, Division against Discrimination, "The Puerto Rican in New Jersey: His Present Status," by Isham Jones (July 1955), 20, 13; L. J. McConnell to Roberto, 14 March 1955, AG 63–37; and Vic Miller Travel Agency to laborers, 30 July 1955, AG 63–37.

29. Handsaker, "Seasonal Farm Labor," 64–68.

30. Handsaker, "Seasonal Farm Labor," 49–50.

31. Handsaker, "Seasonal Farm Labor," 38, 41.

32. Handsaker, "Seasonal Farm Labor," 78.

33. Handsaker, "Seasonal Farm Labor," 139, 93; and PAFPP, *Annual Report, 1958,* 7.

34. Gloria Roldán Amaro, interview by author, 22 and 29 July 1997, San Lorenzo, P.R., tape recording, trans.

35. Justino Navarro Ramos, interview by author, 25 September 1996 and 24 July 1997, San Lorenzo, P.R., tape recording, trans.; and Ana Luisa Navarro Rodríguez, interview by author, 25 September 1996 and 24 July 1997, San Lorenzo, P.R., tape recording, trans.

36. José Lacend, interview.

37. Florencio Sánchez, interview by author, 21 August and 25 September 1997, Philadelphia, Pa., tape recording, trans.

38. Julio Quiñones Navarro, interview by author, 20 January 1997, Salinas, P.R., tape recording, trans.; and Nilda Quiñones Sánchez, interview, trans.

39. Carmen Aponte, interview, trans.

40. Justino Navarro Ramos, interview, trans.

41. Gloria Roldán Amaro, interview, trans.

42. PCHR, *Puerto Ricans in Philadelphia* (1954), 35; and Henry Wells, "The Puerto Rican Community in Philadelphia: A Report for Mayor Richard Dilworth with Recommendations" (24 February 1958), 7, photocopy in author's possession.

43. PCHR, *Puerto Ricans in Philadelphia* (1954), 37.

44. John Kapralick, Subcommittee on Puerto Rican Labor, 31 October 1949, FNG 32, Box 64; Handsaker, "Seasonal Farm Labor," 10; PAFPP, *Annual Report, 1958,* 7; Margarita Benítez, interview by author, 11 and 18 August 1996, Philadelphia, Pa., tape recording, trans.; and "Job Picture Is Bleak for Puerto Ricans Here," *Bulletin,* 18 June 1971, BC.

45. Justino Navarro Ramos, interview, trans.; and Ana Luisa Navarro Rodríguez, interview, trans.

46. Julio Quiñones Navarro, interview, trans.; and Nilda Quiñones Sánchez, interview, trans.

47. Genara Aponte, interview, trans.

48. Taller Puertorriqueño, transcript no. 3, 4, trans. by author, PMHC; Taller Puertorriqueño, transcript no. 6, 3, PMHC; Friends Neighborhood Guild, "A Confidential Survey, 1958," FNG 32, Box 64; PCHR, *Puerto Ricans in Philadelphia,* by Raymond Metauten (April 1959), 35; and

PCHR, *Philadelphia's Puerto Rican Population: A Descriptive Summary Including 1960 Census Data* (March 1964), 23.

49. Juanita Rodríguez, interview, trans.

50. PCHR, *Puerto Ricans in Philadelphia* (1954), 33–36, 49.

51. PCHR, *Philadelphia's Puerto Rican Population* (1964), 10.

52. PCHR, *Puerto Ricans in Philadelphia* (1954), 25, 54, 24; and PCHR, *Philadelphia's Puerto Rican Population* (1964), 10.

53. "Migrant Worker Army 'Invades' South Jersey to Keep Crops Moving from Fields to Markets," *Bulletin,* 18 August 1963, BC.

54. "Murrow to Examine Puerto Rican Influx," *Bulletin,* 12 June 1957, BC; and "Around the Dials: 'See It Now' Dramatizes Puerto Rican Problem," *Bulletin,* 13 June 1957, BC.

Chapter 6

1. PCHR, *Puerto Ricans in Philadelphia: A Study of Their Demographic Characteristics, Problems and Attitudes,* by Arthur Siegel, Harold Orlans, and Loyal Greer (April 1954; reprint, New York: Arno Press, 1975), 8; "7 Hurt in Fight of 300 at 15th and Mt. Vernon," *Bulletin,* 18 July 1953, 3; and "7 Hurt as 1000 Clash in Riot," *Inquirer,* 18 July 1953, 5.

2. These three contiguous areas were: (1) the Spring Garden/Mount Vernon area west of Broad Street, bordered on the western edge by 23rd Street, between Poplar Street on the north and Spring Garden Street on the south; (2) the area west of Broad Street, bordered by 10th Street on the east, Vine Street on the south, and Thompson Street on the north; and (3) the area between 10th and 6th Streets, from Green Street on the south to Susquehanna Avenue on the north. PCHR, *Puerto Ricans in Philadelphia* (1954), 16.

3. PCHR, *Puerto Ricans in Philadelphia* (1954), 18.

4. Pennsylvania Economy League (Eastern Division) in association with the Bureau of Municipal Research, *Special Assimilation Problems of Underprivileged In-Migrants to Philadelphia* (July 1962), I-6, UA; Peter Muller, Kenneth Meyer, and Roman Cybriwsky, *Metropolitan Philadelphia: A Study of Conflicts and Social Cleavages* (Cambridge, Mass.: Ballinger Publishing Company, 1976), 12–15; and PCHR, *Philadelphia's Non-White Population: Report No. 1, Demographic Data,* prepared by Martha Lavell (November 1961), l-2.

5. In terms of increasing concentration, in 1950, with the Puerto Rican population at 1,910, one census tract had more than 200 Puerto Rican residents, while five bordering tracts had 50 to 199 Puerto Ricans. Thirty-six percent of the Puerto Rican population resided in these tracts, while others resided in another 112 tracts. By 1954, six tracts had more than 200 Puerto Ricans, while an additional ten tracts had 50 to 199. Those tracts with 200 or more Puerto Ricans comprised 49 percent of the Puerto Rican population, and when combined with the bordering tracts, this area contained 65 percent of the total. By 1960, the area of Puerto Rican concentration shifted east and extended north to encompass the area east of Broad between Vine and Lehigh, with one tract lying to the west of Broad. Eighty-four percent of the Puerto Rican population of Philadelphia now resided in this area. In addition, a few areas, previously identified as home to more than 200 hundred Puerto Ricans, now indicated only 1 to 49 Puerto Rican residents. For comparisons to the city and to other areas of Puerto Rican settlement, see Carmen Teresa Whalen, "Puerto Rican Migration to Philadelphia, Pennsylvania, 1945–1970: A Historical Perspective on a Migrant Group" (Ph.D. diss., Rutgers University, 1994), 368–369.

6. "7 Hurt in Fight of 300"; and "3 Police Hurt in Street Clash," *Bulletin,* 19 July 1953, 1.

7. "3 Police Hurt in Street Clash"; "Police Break Up 2 Clashes in New Street Disorders," *Inquirer,* 22 July 1953, 8; "7 Hurt as 1000 Clash in Riot"; "Street Fights Flare Again in Fairmount Area," *Inquirer,* 23 July 1953, 17; "7 More Seized in Street Fights," *Bulletin,* 24 July 1953, 3; and Testimony notes, Case 5307–0718, 6 August 1953, Court of Quarter Sessions, Philadelphia, Pa.

8. "7 More Seized"; "Street Fights Flare"; Testimony notes, Cases 5307–0718; and Testimony notes, Case 5307–0743, 5 August 1953, Court of Quarter Sessions, City Hall, Philadelphia, Pa. Those arrested and their addresses are compiled from newspaper articles—see Whalen, "Puerto Rican Migration," 383.

9. Testimony notes, Case 5307–0718; and Testimony notes, Case 5307–0743.

10. PCHR, *Puerto Ricans in Philadelphia* (1954), 50–53, 60–62, vi. The staff interviewed 102 neighbors of Puerto Ricans, 36 of whom lived in the Spring Garden/Mount Vernon neighborhood. Those interviewed included 44 men and 58 women, and 72 whites and 30 African Americans. All of those interviewed in the Mount Vernon area were white.

11. PCHR, *Puerto Ricans in Philadelphia* (1954), 58. On other areas of Puerto Rican settlement, see Whalen, "Puerto Rican Migration," 372–373.

12. PCHR, *Puerto Ricans in Philadelphia* (1954), 62. For employment patterns in areas of Puerto Rican settlement, see Whalen, "Puerto Rican Migration," 375–376.

13. Testimony notes, Case 5307–0743.

14. Joan D. Koss, "Puerto Ricans in Philadelphia: Migration and Accommodation" (Ph.D. diss., University of Pennsylvania, 1965), 72–74.

15. Carmen Aponte, interview by author, 7 and 12 December 1991, Philadelphia, Pa., tape recording, trans. by author. See Appendix II.

16. José Lacend, interview by author, 15 June 1997 and 14 February 1998, Camden, N.J., tape recording.

17. Taller Puertorriqueño Oral History Project, transcript no. 3, 1, 6, PHMC.

18. Ana Luisa Navarro Rodríguez, interview by author, 25 September 1996 and 24 July 1997, San Lorenzo, P.R., tape recording, trans.; and Justino Navarro Ramos, interview by author, 25 September 1996 and 24 July 1997, San Lorenzo, P.R., tape recording, trans.

19. Nilda Quiñones Sánchez, interview by author, 20 January and 25 July 1997, Salinas, P.R., tape recording, trans.; Julio Quiñones Navarro, interview by author, 20 January 1997, Salinas, P.R., tape recording, trans.; and Florencio Sánchez, interview by author, 21 August and 25 September 1997, Philadelphia, Pa., tape recording, trans.

20. Carmen Aponte, interview, trans.; and Taller Puertorriqueño, transcript no. 3, 5–6, PHMC.

21. José Lacend, interview; Justino Navarro Ramos, interview, trans.; PCHR, *Puerto Ricans in Philadelphia* (1954), 47; and PRMD, "Puerto Ricans in Philadelphia: A Report Prepared by the Migration Division, Department of Labor, Commonwealth of Puerto Rico for the Council of Spanish Speaking Organizations of Philadelphia" (1963), 10, 39–40, UA. See also PCHR, *Bulletin* (February 1961): 3.

22. PCHR, *Puerto Ricans in Philadelphia* (1954), 61–2.

23. Rosalie Allen, YWCA, to Marian Lantz, International Institute, 17 November 1947, NSC 625, Box 62; Marian Lantz to Clarence Senior, 31 July 1947, NSC 625, Box 62; and Inderjit Jaipaul, memo, "Background of Nationalities Services Center's Work with Puerto Ricans," 20 November 1968, NSC 625, Box 62. Displaced Persons settled in the same areas as Puerto Ricans

and were also served by the Friends Neighborhood Guild and the International Institute, later renamed the Nationalities Services Center. An estimated 13,000 Displaced Persons were in Philadelphia by 1952, including Ukrainians, Russians, Poles, Latvians, Lithuanians, Kalmuks, and others. Memo, "Displaced Persons in Phila., 1948–1952," 27 October 1952, NSC 625, Box 30.

24. PCHR, *Puerto Ricans in Philadelphia*, by Raymond Metauten (April 1959), 33; and PCHR, *Puerto Ricans in Philadelphia* (1954), 10, 8.

25. PCHR, *Puerto Ricans in Philadelphia* (1954), 51–52, 45.

26. PCHR, *Puerto Ricans in Philadelphia* (1954), vi, 45.

27. "Puerto Ricans Here Consider Philadelphians Unfriendly," *Bulletin*, 23 May 1954, 12, BC; and "Our Puerto Ricans," *Bulletin*, 12 July 1954, BC. See also "Puerto Rican Unit Faces 'Prejudice': Study of Population of 7,300 in Philadelphia Reveals Problem of Adjustment," *New York Times*, 23 May 1954, 69.

28. "Survey Studies Puerto Rican Problems of Adjustment Here," *Philadelphia Independent*, 29 May 1954, 12. Here and in the PCHR's 1954 study African Americans seem considerably less hostile to Puerto Ricans than do white Philadelphians. Interactions between Puerto Ricans and African Americans have not yet been explored.

29. Elfriede Friese, International Institute, to Marcia Bacchus, Friends Neighborhood Guild, 1 October 1954, FNG 32, Box 64; and PCHR, *Puerto Ricans in Philadelphia* (1959), 26.

30. Elfriede Friese, "Spring Garden Civic Association—A Neighborhood Project," 1 April 1955, NSC 625, Box 62; and Friese to Bacchus, 1 October 1954. On civic associations in postwar Detroit, see Thomas J. Sugrue, "Crabgrass-Roots Politics: Race, Rights, and the Reaction against Liberalism in the Urban North, 1940–1964," *Journal of American History* 82 (September 1995): 551–578.

31. Friese, "A Neighborhood Project"; Spring Garden Civic Association, Flier, "Your Help Is Needed," 24 September 1956, NSC 625, Box 62; and Ben Turner, Mid-City Branch YWCA, report, "The Spring Garden Project" (June 1961), 9, YWCA 635.

32. Janice M. Weir, YWCA, "Outline of Work Done with Spring Garden Civic Association," 17 January 1956, YWCA 635; Nationalities Services Center, "The Puerto Rican Community," December 1964, NSC 625, Box 61; and Inderjit Jaipaul, Nationalities Services Center, memo, 23 July 1965, NSC 625, Box 61.

33. Henry Wells, "The Puerto Rican Community in Philadelphia," a report for Mayor Richardson Dilworth (24 February 1958), 13–15, photocopy in the author's possession; PCHR, *Puerto Ricans in Philadelphia* (1959), i; and Turner, "Spring Garden Project," 2.

34. This period represents the publication of C. Wright Mills, Clarence Senior, and Rose Kohn Goldsen, *The Puerto Rican Journey* (New York: Harper and Row, 1950; reprint 1967) and Joseph Fitzpatrick, *Puerto Rican Americans: The Meaning of Migration to the Mainland* (Englewood Cliffs, N.J.: Prentice-Hall, Inc., 1971).

35. Nathan Glazer and Daniel Patrick Moynihan, *Beyond the Melting Pot: The Negroes, Puerto Ricans, Jews, Italians, and Irish of New York City* (Cambridge, Mass.: MIT Press, 1963), 87–88; and Fitzpatrick, *Puerto Rican Americans*, 159.

36. Glazer and Moynihan, *Beyond the Melting Pot*, 97–99, 122, 118, 120.

37. Mills, Senior, and Goldsen, *Puerto Rican Journey*, 8–9; Fitzpatrick, *Puerto Rican Americans*, 80–81; and Glazer and Moynihan, *Beyond the Melting Pot*, 123, 125.

38. Oscar Lewis, *La Vida: A Puerto Rican Family in the Culture of Poverty: San Juan and New York* (New York: Random House, 1965), xlv, xxvii.

39. Lewis, *La Vida*, xxvi–xxvii, xlii. For a review of the literature on African Americans, see Joe William Trotter Jr., "Black Migration in Historical Perspective: A Review of the Literature,"

in *The Great Migration in Historical Perspective: New Dimensions of Race, Class and Gender,* ed. Joe William Trotter Jr. (Bloomington: Indiana University Press, 1991), 1–21. On the social sciences, see Robin D. G. Kelley, *Yo' Mama's Disfunktional! Fighting the Culture Wars in Urban America* (Boston: Beacon Press, 1997). On women, see Leith Mullings, "Images, Ideology, and Women of Color," in *Women of Color in U.S. Society,* ed. Maxine Baca Zinn and Bonnie Thornton Dill (Philadelphia: Temple University Press, 1994), 265–290.

40. Friends Neighborhood Guild, "A Confidential Survey of the Puerto Rican in the Guild Neighborhood" (September 1958), 2, 11, FNG 32, Box 64. While illustrating "culture of poverty" perspectives, this survey did not necessarily reflect the views of everyone at the Guild. The survey was "confidential" and had this note on the front: "It is the type of survey which can be helpful to us in planning program [*sic*] but could be much misunderstood and harmful to the Puerto Rican people if given wider circulation." On the Guild's work with Puerto Ricans, see Chapter 7.

41. Notes on Annual Meeting, Committee on Puerto Rican Affairs, Health and Welfare Council—Family Division, 8 April 1958, NSC 625, Box 30.

42. Friends Neighborhood Guild, "Survey," 5–6, 10; PHWC, *Community Assessment East of Ninth Street* (January 1960), 13, UA; and PCHR, *Puerto Ricans in Philadelphia* (1959), 20.

43. Friends Neighborhood Guild, "Survey," 7; PCHR, *Puerto Ricans in Philadelphia* (1959), 20; and Notes on Annual Meeting.

44. Pennsylvania Economy League, *Special Assimilation Problems,* II-2, II-1, II-7. The Pennsylvania Economy League sought to promote effective state and local government by monitoring government programs, conducting studies, and serving as a consultant for public officials. For a discussion of social scientists equating culture with behavior, see Robin D. G. Kelley, " 'Check the Technique': Black Urban Culture and the Predicament of Social Science," W.E.B. Du Bois Distinguished Visiting Lecturer Series, City University of New York, 26 April 1994.

45. Mills, Senior, and Goldsen, *Puerto Rican Journey,* 92; Glazer and Moynihan, *Beyond the Melting Pot,* 101; and Oscar Handlin, *The Newcomers: Negroes and Puerto Ricans in a Changing Metropolis* (Cambridge: Harvard University Press, 1959), 105.

46. Friends Neighborhood Guild, "Survey," 11, 4, 6.

47. PHWC, *Community Assessment,* 8, 6. On the continuing attitudes of social serivce workers, see also Carmen García Olivero, *Study of the Initial Involvement in the Social Services by the Puerto Rican Migrants in Philadelphia* (New York: Vantage Press, 1971), esp. chapter 6.

48. PHWC, *Community Assessment,* 6, 8, 5; and Peter Binzen, *Whitetown, U.S.A.: A First-Hand Study of How the 'Silent Majority' Lives, Learns, Works, and Thinks* (New York: Random House, 1970), 86, 112.

49. PHWC, *Community Assessment,* 12, 15, 20, 22.

Chapter 7

1. "Puerto Ricans Here Celebrate," *Bulletin,* 26 July 1953, 23.

2. Nicholas Lemann, "The Other Underclass," *Atlantic Monthly* (December 1991): 96–110.

3. Meeting minutes, "Plans for Celebration of First Anniversary of Commonwealth of Puerto Rico," 23 June 1953, FNG 32, Box 64; and Governor Luis Muñoz Marín to Mayor Joseph Sill Clark Jr., 2 July 1953, FNG 32, Box 64. Compared to New York, the Migration Division's early role in Philadelphia seems limited, with the Camden Office established in 1956 and the Philadelphia Office

in the 1960s. See Michael Lapp, "Managing Migration: The Migration Division of Puerto Rico and Puerto Ricans in New York City, 1948–1968" (Ph.D. diss., Johns Hopkins University, 1989).

4. Joan Koss, "Puerto Ricans in Philadelphia: Migration and Accommodation" (Ph.D. diss., University of Pennsylvania, 1965), 70; "Porto Rican [*sic*] Families in Guild Neighborhood," n.d. (2 November 1948), FNG 32, Box 64; "Agency Study of Interracial Participation by Age Groups and Kinds of Activities," March 1950, FNG 32, Box 26; Francis Bosworth, "The Story of the Friends Neighborhood Guild," in *Friends Neighborhood Guild: Seventieth Anniversary* (1950), 39, FNG 32, Box 64; "Puerto Rican Membership, Jan.-Sept. 1952," FNG 32, Box 64; and Philip How to Francis Bosworth, memo, "Data concerning Pablo Adorno," 7 March 1960, FNG 32, Box 65.

5. "Sponsoring Committee: Puerto Rican Day," n.d. (1953), FNG 32, Box 64; Víctor Vázquez, "Puerto Ricans and Other Spanish-speakers in Philadelphia: A Historical Perspective on the Development of a Community, 1910–1936," paper presented at Puerto Rican Studies Association Third Annual Conference, New York, N.Y., 15–17 October 1998; Edwin David Aponte, "A Philadelphia Story: Oral History and Latino Protestantism," paper presented at Oral History Association Annual Meeting, Philadelphia, Pa., 10–13 October 1996; Koss, "Puerto Ricans in Philadelphia," 65, 91; First Spanish Baptist Church (no author), "Reseña Histórica de la Primera Iglesia Bautista Hispana de Filadelfia," photocopy in author's possession provided by First Spanish Baptist Church, n.d. (late 1960s); and First Spanish Baptist Church Program, "Recognition Dinner and Reception to the Rev. Enrique Rodríguez and his Beloved Wife Mrs. Ramonita Gutiérrez de Rodríguez," 10 June 1971, photocopy in author's possession provided by First Spanish Baptist Church.

6. Nationalities Services Center, "Philadelphia Puerto Rican Community and the International Institute," 19 October 1960, NSC 625, Box 62; and Minutes, "Plans for Celebration."

7. Minutes, "Plans for Celebration"; "Sponsoring Committee"; and "Historia del Puesto #840 Latino-Americano de la Legion Americana," 12 March 1984, photocopy in author's possession, provided by Miguel Santiago, Commander, Latin American Legion Post 840.

8. Francis Bosworth to Thomas J. Gibbons, Commissioner of Police, 10 July 1953, FNG 32, Box 64; and Francis Bosworth, "Suggestions for Proclamation by Mayor Clark," 30 June 1953, FNG 32, Box 64.

9. Mayor Joseph S. Clark, "Proclamation," 15 July 1953, FNG 32, Box 64; and Bosworth, "Suggestions for Proclamation."

10. Program for "Puerto Rican Day," 25 July 1953, FNG 32, Box 64.

11. "3 Police Hurt in Street Clash," *Bulletin*, 19 July 1953, 1; "Puerto Rico Day Ceremonies Set: To Mark 1st Birthday of Commonwealth," *Bulletin*, 19 July 1953, 15; Muñoz Marín to Clark, 2 July 1953; "City Sets Puerto Rico Day," *Inquirer*, 19 July 1953, 14; "Puerto Rico Day Observed Here," *Inquirer*, 26 July 1953, 30; and "Puerto Ricans Here Celebrate."

12. "Puerto Ricans Here Celebrate"; and "Puerto Rico's Progress," *Bulletin*, 22 July 1953, 22. In contrast, "Puerto Rico Hails Progress in Year," *New York Times*, 19 July 1953, 30, notes the lack of voting representation in Congress: "Puerto Rico is virtually like any other state in the union but for one major exception."

13. "Puerto Ricans Here Celebrate"; "Puerto Rican Blackmail," *Inquirer*, 13 September 1945, 10; and "What Happened in 1933: Puerto Rican Case Recalls How Congress Voted to Get Rid of Philippines," *Bulletin*, 4 March 1954, BC.

14. Ana Luisa Navarro Rodríguez, interview by author, 25 September 1996 and 24 July 1997, San Lorenzo, P.R., tape recording, trans. by author. (see Appendix II); and Nilda Quiñones Sánchez, interview by author, 20 January and 25 July 1997, Salinas, P.R., tape recording, trans.

15. Carmen Aponte, interview by author, 7 and 12 December 1991, Philadelphia, Pa., tape recording, trans. except italics.

16. See also Carmen Teresa Whalen, "Labor Migrants or 'Submissive Wives': Competing Narratives of Puerto Rican Women in the Post-World War II Era," in *Puerto Rican Women's History: New Perspectives,* ed. Félix V. Matos Rodríguez and Linda Delgado (Armonk, N.Y.: M. E. Sharpe, 1998), 206–226.

17. María Quiñones, interview by author, 8 and 15 August 1996, Philadelphia, Pa., tape recording.

18. PCHR, *Puerto Ricans in Philadelphia,* by Raymond Metauten (April 1959), 24; Ana Luisa Navarro Rodríguez, interview, trans.; Nilda Quiñones Sánchez, interview, trans.; and Florencio Sánchez, interview by author, 21 August and 25 September 1997, Philadelphia, Pa., tape recording, trans.

19. Nilda Quiñones Sánchez, interview, trans.; Koss, "Puerto Ricans in Philadelphia," 186–187; "Otilio Maldonado Exhorta a la Comunidad a que Formen Organizaciones," *La Voz del Concilio* (September 1966): 4, FNG 32, Box 65, trans. by author; and María Quiñones, interview.

20. Carmen Aponte, interview, trans. except for italics; PCHR, *Puerto Ricans in Philadelphia* (1959), 37; PCHR, *Philadelphia's Puerto Rican Population: A Descriptive Summary Including 1960 Census Data,* (March 1964), 28–29; and "The Puerto Rican: Majority Seeks to Solve Own Problems, but Lacks Leadership," *Inquirer,* 5 June 1968, 34, BC.

21. "Carlos Morales Exhorta a la Comunidad a que Participe en el Desfile," *La Voz del Concilio* (September 1966): 2, trans. by author; "City's Puerto Rican Community Begins Week-Long Festival," *Bulletin,* 19 September 1971, 25, BC; and "Puerto Ricans Parade Today in Center City," *Bulletin,* 26 September 1971, 9, BC. See also Rosa Estades, "Symbolic Unity: The Puerto Rican Day Parade," in *Historical Perspectives on Puerto Rican Survival in the United States,* ed. Clara E. Rodríguez and Virginia Sánchez Korrol (Princeton, N.J.: Markus Weiner Publishers, 1996), 97–106.

22. "El Concilio y la Comunidad," *La Voz del Concilio* (September 1966): 2, trans. by author; "Crece Nuestro Servicio de Empleo," *La Voz del Concilio* (September 1966): 1; and "Majority Seeks to Solve."

23. "Majority Seeks to Solve"; and "Puerto Rican Leadership Split by Bickering and In-Fighting," *Bulletin,* 15 June 1971, BC.

24. Michael Katz, "Reframing the 'Underclass' Debate," in *The "Underclass" Debate: Views from History,* ed. Michael Katz (Princeton, N.J.: Princeton University Press, 1993), 457. See also Carmen Teresa Whalen, "Displaced Labor Migrants or the 'Underclass': African Americans and Puerto Ricans in Philadelphia's Economy," in *The Collaborative City: Opportunities and Challenges for Blacks and Latinos in U.S. Cities,* ed. John J. Betancur and Douglas C. Gills (New York: Garland Publishers, 2000).

25. Peter Muller, Kenneth Meyer, and Roman Cybriwsky, *Metropolitan Philadelphia: A Study of Conflicts and Social Cleavages* (Cambridge, Mass.: Ballinger Publishing Company, 1976), 55; Judith Goode, "Polishing the Rustbelt: Immigrants Enter a Restructuring Philadelphia," in *Newcomers in the Workplace: Immigrants and the Restructuring of the U.S. Economy,* ed. Louise Lamphere, Alex Stepick, and Guillermo Grenier (Philadelphia: Temple University Press, 1994), 200–201; and Joseph Oberman and Stephen Kozakowski, *History of Development in the Delaware Valley Region* (Philadelphia: Delaware Valley Regional Planning Commission, September 1976), 93–94.

26. Arthur Hochner and Daniel Zibman, "Capital Flight and Job Loss: A Statistical Analysis," in *Community and Capital in Conflict: Plant Closings and Job Loss,* ed. John C. Raines, Lenora E. Berson, and David McI. Gracie (Philadelphia: Temple University Press, 1982), 207, 199; and

Muller, *Metropolitan*, 57. On downgraded manufacturing, see Saskia Sassen-Koob, "Changing Composition and Labor Market Location of Hispanic Immigrants in New York City, 1960–1980," in *Hispanics in the U.S. Economy*, ed. George J. Borjas and Marta Tienda (Orlando, Fla.: Academic Press, Inc., 1985), 299–322.

27. "Union, Employers Join to Bolster Sagging Garment Industry Here," *Bulletin*, 29 October 1961, BC; Pamela Haines, "Clothing and Textiles: The Departure of an Industry," in *Community*, ed. Raines, 211; and Goode, "Polishing the Rustbelt," 208. On the garment industry's continuing search for cheap labor, see Helen I. Safa, "Runaway Shops and Female Employment: The Search for Cheap Labor," in *Women's Work: Development and the Division of Labor by Gender*, ed. Eleanor Leacock, Helen I. Safa, and contributors (New York: Bergin and Garvey Publishers, 1986), 58–71.

28. PAFPP, *Pennsylvania Farm Placement Program Annual Report, 1959*, 2, 8; and David Griffith and Ed Kissam, *Working Poor: Farmworkers in the United States* (Philadelphia: Temple University Press, 1995), 162–163, 187.

29. Carolyn Adams, David Bartelt, David Elesh, Ira Goldstein, Nancy Kleniewski, and William Yancey, *Philadelphia: Neighborhoods, Division, and Conflict in a Postindustrial City* (Philadelphia: Temple University Press, 1991), 118. See also Carolyn Teich Adams, "Philadelphia: The Private City in the Post-Industrial Era," in *Snowbelt Cities: Metropolitan Politics in the Northeast and Midwest since World War II*, ed. Richard M. Bernard (Bloomington: Indiana University Press, 1990): 209–226.

30. PABES, "Manpower Planning Report for the Philadelphia, Pennsylvania Area" (June 1968), 4–5.

31. USBC, *Census of the Population: 1970*, vol. 1, *Characteristics of the Population*, pt. 40, Pennsylvania (Washington, D.C., 1973), 396, 452, 500; and USBC, *Census of the Population: 1990, Social and Economic Characteristics*, Pennsylvania (Washington, D.C., 1993), 1136.

32. Carole Cohen, "Facing Job Loss: Changing Relationships in a Multicultural Urban Factory," in *Newcomers*, ed. Lamphere, Stepick, and Grenier, 234.

33. Per capita income is defined as the average annual dollar amount received per person from any source of income, including wages, Social Security and Public Assistance benefits. Eugene P. Ericksen, David Bartelt, Patrick Feeney, Gerald Foeman, Sherri Grasmuck, Maureen Martella, William Rickle, Robert Spencer, and David Webb, *The State of Puerto Rican Philadelphia* (Philadelphia: Institute for Public Policy Studies, Temple University, 1985): 27, 29, 34–37, 41.

34. Clara E. Rodríguez, "Economic Survival in New York City," in *Historical Perspectives*, ed. Rodríguez, 44; and Rosemary Santana Cooney and Alice Colón, "Work and Family: The Recent Struggle of Puerto Rican Females," in *Historical Perspectives*, ed. Rodríguez, 76, 73. On economic restructuring, see also Rebecca Morales and Frank Bonilla, eds., *Latinos in a Changing U.S. Economy: Comparative Perspectives on Growing Inequality* (Newbury Park, Calif.: Sage Publications, 1993). On women, see Alice Colón-Warren, "The Impact of Job Losses on Puerto Rican Women in the Middle Atlantic Region, 1970–1980," in *Puerto Rican Women and Work: Bridges in Transnational Labor*, ed. Altagracia Ortiz (Philadelphia: Temple University Press, 1996), 105–138; and Altagracia Ortiz, "'*En la aguja y el pedal eché la hiel*': Puerto Rican Women in the Garment Industry of New York City, 1920–1980," in *Puerto Rican Women*, ed. Ortiz, 55–81.

35. David W. Bartelt, "Housing the 'Underclass,'" in *"Underclass" Debate*, ed. Katz, 133, 151. See also John F. Bauman, *Public Housing, Race, and Renewal: Urban Planning in Philadelphia, 1920–1974* (Philadelphia: Temple University Press, 1987).

36. Adams, *Philadelphia: Neighborhoods*, 104. See also Neil Smith, *The New Urban Frontier: Gentrification and the Revanchist City* (New York: Routledge, 1996), 119–164.

37. Ericksen et al., *State of Puerto Rican Philadelphia*, 56–59, 70.

38. USBC, *Census of Population and Housing: 1990, Population and Housing Characteristics for Census Tracts and Block Numbering Areas*, Philadelphia, Pa.-N.J. PMSA (Washington, D.C., 1993), 304; Goode, "Polishing the Rustbelt," 213–218; and Judith Goode and Jo Anne Schneider, *Reshaping Ethnic and Racial Relations in Philadelphia: Immigrants in a Divided City* (Philadelphia: Temple University Press, 1994), 4.

39. Janice Fanning Madden and William J. Stull, *Work, Wages, and Poverty: Income Distribution in Post-Industrial Philadelphia* (Philadelphia: University of Pennsylvania Press, 1991), 148, 97, 149; USBC, *Census of the Population: 1990, Social and Economic Characteristics*, Pennsylvania, B-27, 557, 1139; USBC, *Census of the Population: 1970*, vol. 1, *Characteristics of the Population*, pt. 40, Pennsylvania, 428, 468, 516; and Adams, *Philadelphia: Neighborhoods*, 27.

40. Alejandro Portes and Cynthia Truelove, "Making Sense of Diversity: Recent Research on Hispanic Minorities in the United States," *Annual Review of Sociology* 13 (1987): 368; and David Griffith, "Peasants in Reserve: Temporary West Indian Labor in the U.S. Farm Labor Market," *International Migration Review* 20 (winter 1986): 880–881.

41. Theodore Hershberg, Alan Burstein, Eugene Ericksen, Stephanie Greenberg, and William Yancey, "A Tale of Three Cities: Blacks, Immigrants, and Opportunity in Philadelphia, 1850–1880, 1970," in *Philadelphia: Work, Space, Family, and Group in the Nineteenth Century*, ed. Theodore Hershberg (New York: Oxford University Press, 1981), 477; and Douglas S. Massey, "American Apartheid: Segregation and the Making of the Underclass," *American Journal of Sociology* 96 (September 1990): 352.

42. Genara Aponte, interview by author, 9 October, 6 and 20 November 1997, Philadelphia, Pa., tape recording, trans.; Nilda Quiñones Sánchez, interview, trans.; and Juanita Rodríguez, interview by author, 18 June 1997, Palmyra, N.J., tape recording, trans.

43. José Lacend, interview by author, 15 June 1997 and 14 February 1998, Camden, N.J., tape recording.

44. Genara Aponte, interview, trans.

45. Ana Luisa Navarro Rodríguez, interview, trans.

46. Ana Luisa Navarro Rodríguez, interview, trans.; and José Lacend, interview.

47. Ana Luisa Navarro Rodríguez, interview, trans.; and Genara Aponte, interview, trans.

48. Nilda Quiñones Sánchez, interview, trans.; and Ana Luisa Navarro Rodríguez, interview, trans. See also José Hernández Alvarez, *Return Migration to Puerto Rico* (Berkeley: University of California Press, 1967).

49. "Young Lords in Philadelphia," *Palante*, 28 August 1970, 10; and "People's Church in Philadelphia," *Palante*, 20 November 1970, n.p. See also Carmen Teresa Whalen, "Bridging Homeland and Barrio Politics: The Young Lords in Philadelphia," in *The Puerto Rican Movement: Voices from the Diaspora*, ed. Andrés Torres and José Velázquez (Philadelphia: Temple University Press, 1998),107–123; Roberto P. Rodríguez-Morazzani, "Puerto Rican Political Generations in New York: Pioneros, Young Turks and Radicals," *Centro de Estudios Puertorriqueños Bulletin* 4 (winter 1991–1992): 96–116; and Felix Padilla, *Puerto Rican Chicago* (Notre Dame, Ind.: University of Notre Dame Press, 1987).

50. Wilfredo Rojas, interview by author, 3 January 1996, Philadelphia, Pa., tape recording; and Rafaela Colón, interview by author, 3 January 1996, Philadelphia, Pa., tape recording.

51. "Drive Started to Develop Puerto Rican Leaders," *Inquirer*, 21 November 1969, BC; Rafaela Colón, interview; and Wilfredo Rojas, interview.

52. Wilfredo Rojas, interview; Michael Kimmel, "You've Come a Long Way, Bebe!" *Philadelphia Magazine* (August 1971): 180, 88, 174–175; and "People's Church."

53. Rafaela Colón, interview; and Wilfredo Rojas, interview.

54. Kimmel, "You've Come a Long Way," 91, 95; and Wilfredo Rojas, interview.

55. "Young Lords Declare War on Dope Pushers," *Inquirer*, 5 November 1970, BC; and Kimmel, "You've Come a Long Way," 165.

56. "Young Lords Party: Thirteen-Point Program and Platform," in *Palante: Young Lords Party*, ed. The Young Lords Party and Michael Abramson (New York: McGraw-Hill Book Company, 1971), 150; Juan D. González, "The Turbulent Progress of Puerto Ricans in Philadelphia," *Centro de Estudios Puertorriqueños Bulletin* 2 (winter 1987–1988): 37; and Kimmel, "You've Come a Long Way," 91."

57. "Young Lords Blamed by Police for Unrest," *Inquirer*, 13 August 1970, BC; Kimmel, "You've Come a Long Way," 168; and Wilfredo Rojas, interview.

58. "Residents Charge Police Brutality; Captain Describes Rock Barrage," *Inquirer*, 14 August 1970, BC; Kimmel, "You've Come a Long Way," 168; and *Palante: Young Lords Party*, n.p.

59. "Restaurant Is a Strategy Center For New Spanish Council Leader," *Bulletin*, 15 June 1971, BC; Wilfredo Rojas, interview; Angel Ortiz, city councilman, interview by author, 27 December 1995, Philadelphia, Pa., tape recording; and "Puerto Rican Leadership."

60. Wilfredo Rojas, interview; "Puerto Ricans Feel New Wave of Pride," *Bulletin*, 13 June 1971, BC; "Language Is Great Obstacle," *Bulletin*, 19 June 1971, BC; "The American Dream—4 Views," *Bulletin*, 18 June 1971, BC; and *Palante: Young Lords Party*, n.p.

61. Carmen Aponte, interview, trans.; and Cheryl L. Micheau, "Ethnic Identity and Ethnic Maintenance in the Puerto Rican Community of Philadelphia" (Ph.D. diss., University of Pennsylvania, 1990): 501–517.

62. Rafaela Colón, interview; Angel Ortiz, interview; and González, "Turbulent Progress," 38.

63. Angel Ortiz, interview; and González, "Turbulent Progress," 38. On political representation and electoral districting, see Ericksen et al., *State of Puerto Rican Philadelphia*, 102–112.

64. González, "Turbulent Progress," 41; Rafaela Colón, interview; and Pablo "Yoruba" Guzmán, "Puerto Rican Barrio Politics in the United States," in *Historical Perspectives*, ed. Rodríguez, 145.

65. For a review of the literature and competing definitions of the "underclass" as they pertain to African Americans, see Michael Katz, "The Urban 'Underclass' as a Metaphor of Social Transformation," in *"Underclass" Debate*, ed. Katz, 3–23.

66. Torres, *Between Melting Pot*, 5; and Lemann, "The Other Underclass," 96–97.

67. Lemann, "The Other Underclass," 96–97, 102, 104.

68. Linda Chavez, *Out of the Barrio: Toward a New Politics of Hispanic Assimilation* (New York: Basic Books, 1991): 149, 140.

69. Chavez, *Out of the Barrio*, 144–145, 151–152, 159. For a very different interpretation of Puerto Rican women and welfare, see Rosa M. Torruellas, Rina Benmayor, and Ana Juarbe, "Negotiating Gender, Work, and Welfare: *Familia* as Productive Labor among Puerto Rican Women in New York City," in *Puerto Rican Women and Work*, ed. Ortiz, 184–208.

70. Roger Lane, *William Dorsey's Philadelphia and Ours: On the Past and Future of the Black City in America* (New York: Oxford University Press, 1991): 404–405, 378–379. See also Whalen, "Displaced Labor Migrants."

71. Thomas F. Jackson, "The State, the Movement, and the Urban Poor: The War on Poverty and Political Mobilization in the 1960s," in *"Underclass" Debate*, ed. Katz, 403.

Epilogue

1. Donna R. Gabaccia, "Liberty, Coercion, and the Making of Immigration Historians," *Journal of American History* 84 (September 1997): 573–574.

2. Most historical work on Puerto Ricans, African Americans, and Mexican Americans focuses on earlier eras. Despite its strength on migration between the world wars, little of the scholarship on African Americans addresses post–World War II migrations. See Nicholas Lemann, *The Promised Land: The Great Black Migration and How It Changed America* (New York: Alfred A. Knopf, Inc., 1991); Jacqueline Jones, *The Dispossessed: America's Underclasses from the Civil War to the Present* (New York: Basic Books, 1992); Gretchen Lemke-Santangelo, *Abiding Courage: African American Women and the East Bay Community* (Chapel Hill: University of North Carolina Press, 1996); and for a historiographical review, Kenneth L. Kusmer, "African Americans in the City since World War II: From the Industrial to the Post-Industrial Era," *Journal of Urban History* 21 (May 1995): 458–504. The historiography in Chicano Studies has also focused on the earlier eras, but has devoted relatively little attention to immigration. See Alex M. Saragoza, "Recent Chicano Historiography: An Interpretive Essay," *Aztlán* 19 (spring 1988–90): 1–77. By social scientists, the few comparative works include Andrés Torres, *Between Melting Pot and Mosaic: African Americans and Puerto Ricans in the New York Political Economy* (Philadelphia: Temple University Press, 1995); John J. Betancur and Douglas C. Gills, eds., *The Collaborative City: Opportunities and Challenges for Blacks and Latinos in U.S. Cities* (New York: Garland Publishers, 2000); and Alejandro Portes, "From South of the Border: Hispanic Minorities in the United States," in *Immigration Reconsidered: History, Sociology, and Politics,* ed. Virginia Yans-McLaughlin (New York: Oxford University Press, 1990): 160–181.

3. Theodore Hershberg, Alan Burstein, Eugene Ericksen, Stephanie Greenberg, and William Yancey, "A Tale of Three Cities: Blacks, Immigrants, and Opportunity in Philadelphia, 1850–1880, 1930, 1970," in *Philadelphia: Work, Space, Family and Group Experience in the Nineteenth Century,* ed. Theodore Hershberg (New York: Oxford University Press, 1981), 461, 470, 473, 485. On European immigrants, see other essays in Hershberg et al.; and Allen F. Davis and Mark H. Haller, eds., *The Peoples of Philadelphia: A History of Ethnic Groups and Lower-Class Life, 1790–1940* (Philadelphia: Temple University Press, 1973). For examples of the extensive scholarship on African Americans in Philadelphia, see Michael B. Katz and Thomas J. Sugrue, eds., *W.E.B. DuBois, Race, and the City: The Philadelphia Negro and Its Legacy* (Philadelphia: University of Pennsylvania Press, 1998). On migration, see Robert Gregg, *Sparks from the Anvil of Oppression: Philadelphia's African Methodists and Southern Migrants, 1890–1940* (Philadelphia: Temple University Press, 1993); and Allen B. Ballard, *One More Day's Journey: The Story of a Family and a People* (New York: McGraw-Hill, 1984).

4. On earlier contract labor, see Gunther Peck, "Reinventing Free Labor: Immigrant Padrones and Contract Laborers in North America, 1885–1925," *Journal of American History* (December 1996): 848–871; and on the role of the state, see Cindy Hahamovitch, *Fruits of Their Labor: Atlantic Coast Farmworkers and the Making of Migrant Poverty, 1870–1945* (Chapel Hill: University of North Carolina Press, 1997). On farmworkers, see Jones, *Dispossessed*; Erasmo Gamboa, *Mexican Labor and World War II: Braceros in the Pacific Northwest, 1942–1947* (Austin: University of Texas Press, 1990); and Dennis Valdés, *Al Norte: Agricultural Workers in the Great Lakes Region, 1917–1970* (Austin: University of Texas Press, 1990).

5. Vicki L. Ruiz, "By the Day or the Week: Mexicana Domestic Workers in El Paso," in *Women on the U.S. Mexico Border: Responses to Change,* ed. Vicki L. Ruiz and Susan Tiano

(Boston: Allen and Unwin, 1987), 61–76; and Evelyn Nakano Glenn, "From Servitude to Service Work: Historical Continuities in the Racial Division of Paid Reproductive Work," in *Unequal Sisters: A Multicultural Reader in U.S. Women's History,* ed. Vicki L. Ruiz and Ellen Carol Dubois (New York: Routledge, 1994), 406.

6. For example, in *Gender at Work: The Dynamics of Job Segregation by Sex during World War II* (Urbana: University of Illinois Press, 1987), Ruth Milkman focuses on gender and the labeling of jobs as "women's work," arguing that employers reinstated the sexual division of labor in the postwar era despite the lower wages they could pay women. She does not, however, adequately consider the racial dimensions of hiring or racial divisions of labor and their impact on African American men and women. George Lipsitz makes this point in his conclusion to *Rainbow at Midnight: Labor and Culture in the 1940s* (Urbana: University of Illinois Press, 1994), 338. On African American women's exclusion from industry and concentration in domestic work, see Jacqueline Jones, *Labor of Love, Labor of Sorrow: Black Women, Work and the Family, from Slavery to the Present* (New York: Random House, 1985). On Mexican garment workers, see M. Patricia Fernández-Kelly and Anna García, "Hispanic Women and Homework: Women in the Informal Economy of Miami and Los Angeles," in *Homework: Historical and Contemporary Perspectives on Paid Labor at Home,* ed. Eileen Boris and Cynthia R. Daniels (Urbana: University of Illinois Press, 1989), 165–182.

7. On scholarly responses to culture of poverty perspectives, see Tomás Almaguer, "Ideological Distortions in Recent Chicano Historiography: The Internal Model and Chicano Historical Interpretation," *Aztlán* 18 (spring 1987): 7–28; and Joe William Trotter Jr., "Black Migration in Historical Perspective: A Review of the Literature," in *The Great Migration in Historical Perspective: New Dimensions of Race, Class and Gender,* ed. Joe William Trotter Jr. (Bloomington: Indiana University Press, 1991), 1–21. Two books published in the same year highlight the disjuncture between U.S. history and Latino/a Studies. In *The "Underclass" Debate,* Katz omitted Puerto Ricans from his discussions of the culture of poverty and Oscar Lewis, and Latinos/as receive scant attention in the book. In Joan Moore and Raquel Pinderhughes, eds., *In the Barrios: Latinos and the Underclass Debate* (New York: Russell Sage Foundation, 1993), most essays are by social scientists. For Chicano Studies' challenge to the racial binary, see Tomás Almaguer, *Racial Fault Lines: The Historical Origins of White Supremacy in California* (Berkeley: University of California Press, 1994). See also Michael Omi and Howard Winant, *Racial Formation in the United States: From the 1960s to the 1990s* (New York: Routledge, 1994); and Peggy Pascoe, "Miscegenation Law, Court Cases, and Ideologies of 'Race' in Twentieth-Century America," *Journal of American History* 83 (June 1996): 44–69.

8. Two essays in *Not June Cleaver: Women and Gender in Postwar America, 1945–1960,* ed. Joanne Meyerwitz (Philadelphia: Temple University Press, 1994) suggest the importance of the intersections of racial and gender ideologies. Rather than interrogating divergent constructions for white and African American women, Meyerwitz combines most of her data on mass-circulation monthly magazines, marketed to either white or African American women, and argues that "domestic ideals coexisted in ongoing tension with an ethos of individual achievement that celebrated nondomestic activity, individual striving, public service, and public success" ("Beyond the Feminine Mystique: A Reassessment of Postwar Mass Culture, 1946–1958," 231). In contrast, Regina G. Kunzel examines how race and class shaped "discourses of illegitimacy," arguing: "During and after the war, black and white unmarried mothers were cast as very different figures, pregnant for different reasons, and in need of the service of two different sets of experts." (In "White Neurosis, Black Pathology: Constructing Out-of-Wedlock Pregnancy in the Wartime and Postwar United States," 306.)

9. Thomas J. Sugrue, *The Origins of the Urban Crisis: Race and Inequality in Postwar Detroit* (Princeton, N.J.: Princeton University Press, 1996); John T. Cumbler, *A Social History of Economic Decline: Business, Politics, and Work in Trenton* (New Brunswick, N.J.: Rutgers University Press, 1989); and Katz, ed., *"Underclass" Debate.*

10. Carl Husemoller Nightingale, "The Global Inner City: Toward a Historical Analysis," in *W.E.B. Dubois,* ed. Katz, 218, 220. In her discussion of the impact of economic restructuring on Hispanic immigrants, Saskia Sassen-Koob does not adequately address the impact on Puerto Ricans—see her "Changing Composition and Labor Market Location of Hispanic Immigrants in New York City, 1960–1980," in *Hispanics in the U.S. Economy,* ed. George J. Borjas and Marta Tienda (Orlando, Fla.: Academic Press, Inc., 1985), 299–322. For alternatives, see Rebecca Morales and Frank Bonilla, eds., *Latinos in a Changing U.S. Economy: Comparative Perspectives on Growing Inequality* (Newbury Park, Calif.: Sage Publications, 1993); and Moore, ed., *In the Barrios.*

11. For an overview of the post-1965 immigrations, see David Reimers, *Still the Golden Door: The Third World Comes to America* (New York: Columbia University Press, 1992); and on U.S. intervention, see Portes, "From South of the Border."

12. On the use of "Hispanics," see Suzanne Oboler, *Ethnic Labels, Latino Lives: Identity and the Politics of (Re)Presentation in the United States* (Minneapolis: University of Minnesota Press, 1995); and on immigration debates, see Juan F. Perea, ed., *Immigrants Out! The New Nativism and the Anti-Immigrant Impulse in the United States* (New York: New York University Press, 1997).

Selected Bibliography

Church Records, Manuscript Collections, and Government Document Collections

Baptism Records, 1910–1940. Parroquia Nuestra Señora de las Mercedes, San Lorenzo, P.R.; records for 1914–1931 also available through Mormon Church Archives, Family History Center, Cherry Hill, N.J.

Baptism Records, 1911–1940. Nuestra Señora de Monserrate de Salinas, Salinas, P.R.

Marriage Records, 1945–1965. Chapel of Our Lady of the Miraculous Medal, Philadelphia, Pa.

Marriage Records, 1945–1965. Methodist Memorial Temple, Philadelphia, Pa.

Marriage Records, 1945–1965. St. Peters, The Apostle Church, Philadelphia, Pa.

Marriage Records, 1945–1965. Spanish Baptist Church, Philadelphia, Pa.

Alexander Library, Rutgers University, New Brunswick, N.J.
  U.S. Government Documents

Archivo General de Puerto Rico, San Juan, P.R.
  Puerto Rico Department of Labor, Record Groups 61–55 and 63–37
  Migration Division Correspondence, newspaper clippings
  Agricultural Labor Contracts, 1948–1950
  Photographs, Fondo Fotográfico del Departamento de Instrucción Pública

Archivos Históricos y Biblioteca de la Migración Puertorriqueña en los Estados Unidos, Department of Puerto Rican Community Affairs in the United States, New York (documents listed are now located at the Centro de Estudios Puertorriqueños, Hunter College, New York)
  Puerto Rico Migration Division, Monthly and Annual Reports
  Puerto Rico Government Documents

Centro de Estudios Puertorriqueños, Hunter College, New York
  Palante, Young Lords' Newsletter
  Puerto Rico Government Documents

La Colección Puertorriqueña, University of Puerto Rico, Río Piedras, P.R.
  Puerto Rico Government Documents
  El Mundo Index and Newspapers

Division of Archives and Manuscripts, Pennsylvania Historical and Museum Commission, Harrisburg, Pa.
  Taller Puertorriqueño Oral History Project, Manuscript Group 409 Oral History Collection
National Archives, Washington, D.C.
  Population, Emigration, General. Record Group 126, File 9-8-116
National Archives–Mid-Atlantic Region, Philadelphia, Pa.
  War Manpower Commission Collection, Record Group 211
Philadelphia Court of Orphan Pleas, City Hall, Philadelphia, Pa.
  Marriage Licenses, 1945–1965
Philadelphia Court of Quarter Sessions, City Hall, Philadelphia, Pa.
  Cases and Testimony Notes
Philadelphia Free Library, Philadelphia, Pa.
  Philadelphia and Pennsylvania Government Documents
Urban Archives, Temple University, Philadelphia, Pa.
  Bulletin Collection, Newspaper Clippings and Photographs
  Friends Neighborhood Guild, Record Group 32
  Nationalities Services Center, Record Group 625
  Young Women's Christian Association, Record Group 635

Oral Histories and Interviews

Andrade, Irma. Interview by author, 22 August 1996, Philadelphia, Pa. Tape recording.

Aponte, Carmen. Interview by author, 7 and 12 December 1991, Philadelphia, Pa. Tape recording.

Aponte, Genara. Interview by author, 9 October, 6 November, and 20 November 1997, Philadelphia, Pa. Tape recording.

Benítez, Margarita. Interview by author, 11 and 18 August 1996, Philadelphia, Pa. Tape recording.

Carrasquillo, Juan. Interview by author, 13 December 1991, Philadelphia, Pa. Tape recording.

Colón, Rafaela. Interview by author, 3 January 1996, Philadelphia, Pa. Tape recording.

Kensill, Frank, Minister of Methodist Memorial Temple. Interview by author, 31 March 1992, telephone conversation, and 9 April 1992, Methodist Memorial Temple, Philadelphia, Pa. Tape recording.

Lacend, José. Interview by author, 15 June 1997 and 14 February 1998, Camden, N.J. Tape recording.

Monserrat, Joseph. Interview by author, 9 March 1992, Department of Puerto Rican Community Affairs in the United States (formerly the Migration Division), New York, N.Y. Tape recording.

Mora, Natividad. Interview by author, 23 June 1992, Philadelphia, Pa. Tape recording.

Natal, María. Interview by author, 21 August 1997, Philadelphia, Pa. Tape recording.

Navarro Rodríguez, Ana Luisa. Interview by author, 25 September 1996 and 24 July 1997, San Lorenzo, P.R. Tape recording.

Navarro Ramos, Justino. Interview by author, 25 September 1996 and 24 July 1997, San Lorenzo, P.R. Tape recording.

Ortiz, Angel, Philadelphia City Councilman. Interview by author, 27 December 1995, City Hall, Philadelphia, Pa. Tape recording.

Quiñones, María. Interview by author, 8 and 15 August 1996, Philadelphia, Pa. Tape recording.

Quiñones Navarro, Julio. Interview by author, 20 January 1997, Salinas, P.R. Tape recording.

Quiñones Sánchez, Nilda. Interview by author, 20 January and 25 July 1997, Salinas, P.R. Tape recording.

Ramos, Juan. Interview by author, 3 January 1996, Philadelphia, Pa. Tape recording.

Rodríguez, Juanita. Interview by author, 18 June 1997, Palmyra, N.J. Tape recording.

Rodríguez, Julia. Interview by author, 24 January 1997, Salinas, P.R. Tape recording.

Rojas, Wilfredo. Interview by author, 3 January 1996, Philadelphia, Pa. Tape recording.

Roldán Amaro, Gloria. Interview by author, 22 and 29 July 1997, San Lorenzo, P.R. Tape recording.

Roldán Sánchez, Esther. Interview by author, 30 July 1997, Salinas, P.R. Tape recording.

Rosario, Julio. Interview by author, 13 December 1991; 28 August and 18 September 1997, Philadelphia, Pa. Tape recording.

Sánchez, Florencio. Interview by author, 21 August and 25 September 1997, Philadelphia, Pa. Tape recording.

Santiago, Miguel. Interview by author, 25 March 1992, Philadelphia, Pa. Tape recording.

Velázquez, Epifania. Interview by author, 16 December 1991, Philadelphia, Pa. Tape recording.

Government Documents

New Jersey

Department of Education, Division against Discrimination. "The Puerto Rican in New Jersey: His Present Status." By Isham Jones. July 1955.

Pennsylvania

Bureau of Employment Security. *Labor Market Letter*. February 1947–December 1947.
———. *Pennsylvania Farm Placement Program, Annual Reports*. 1954–1970.
———. "Manpower Planning Report for the Philadelphia, Pennsylvania Area." June 1968.

Philadelphia

Commission on Human Relations. *Puerto Ricans in Philadelphia: A Study of Their Demographic Characteristics, Problems and Attitudes*. By Arthur Siegel, Harold Orlans, and Loyal Greer of the Institute for Research in Human Relations. April 1954. Reprint ed., New York City: Arno Press, 1975.
———. *Puerto Ricans in Philadelphia*. Prepared by Raymond Metauten. April 1959.
———. *Philadelphia's Non-White Population: Report No. 1, Demographic Data*. Prepared by Martha Lavell. November 1961.
———. *Philadelphia's Puerto Rican Population: A Descriptive Summary Including 1960 Census Data*. March 1964.
District Health and Welfare Council, Inc. *Community Assessment East of Ninth Street*. January 1960. Urban Archives, Temple University, Philadelphia, Pa.

Puerto Rico

Agricultural Experiment Station. "Farm Prices and Price Relationships of Sugar and Sugar Cane in Puerto Rico from 1910 to 1945." By Jorge J. Serralles Jr. *Bulletin* 71 (June 1944).

―――. "An Economic Study of Family Sized Farms in Puerto Rico: San José Farm Security Administration Project, 1943–44, 1944–45." By Guillermo Serra and Manuel Piñero. *Bulletin* 77 (June 1948).

―――. "Costos de Producción del Tabaco, Zona Central Este, Puerto Rico, 1948–1949." By Manuel Piñero and Juan R. Calderón. *Bulletin* 96 (November 1951).

―――. "Labor Efficiency in Harvesting Sugarcane in Puerto Rico, 1950." By Edmundo Silva and Manuel Piñero. (January 1953).

―――. "Estudio Sobre la Explotación Económica de 134 Fincas de Caña de Azúcar, Puerto Rico, 1950–51." By Manuel Piñero and Juan R. Calderón. *Boletín* 132 (April 1956).

―――. "Análisis Económico del Cultivo del Tabaco en Puerto Rico, 1951–1952." By Gabriel R. Espinet. *Boletín* 133 (April 1956).

―――. "Estudio Económico Sobre el Arrastre de la Caña de Azúcar en Camiones, Puerto Rico, 1954." By Oscar Rodríguez García and José Maríano Ríos. *Bulletin* 142 (July 1958).

―――. "Some Effects of the Sugar Programs on the Sugar Industry of Puerto Rico." By José B. Candelas. *Bulletin* 151 (October 1959).

―――. "Some Effects of Federal and Commonwealth Tobacco Programs on the Tobacco Industry of Puerto Rico." By Marciano Avilés. *Bulletin* 162 (February 1962).

Department of Labor. *Informe Anual del Departamento del Trabajo, 1950–1951.*

Department of Labor, Employment Service, Farm Placement Division. *Annual Agricultural and Foodprocessing Report. 1952–1965.*

Department of Labor, Migration Division. *Annual Report. 1954–1962.*

―――. *Monthly Reports.* January 1951–January 1962.

―――. "Puerto Ricans in Philadelphia: A Report Prepared by the Migration Division, Department of Labor, Commonwealth of Puerto Rico for the Council of Spanish speaking Organizations of Philadelphia." 1963.

Economic Development Administration (Fomento). *Fomento de Puerto Rico 1952–1956.*

―――. "Social Directions in Industrial Development." 3 January 1957.

―――. Continental Operations Branch, New York City, N.Y. "The Apparel and Related Products Industry." August 1973.

Office of Puerto Rico. "Puerto Rican Domestics Reach Philadelphia." *Puerto Rico: A Bulletin of the Office of Puerto Rico* 2 (May 1947).

―――. "Puerto Rico's Potential as a Site for Textile, Apparel and Other Industries." By Donald J. O'Connor. Washington, D.C., 1949.

Office of the Governor, Division of Statistics. "Estudio Sobre La Emigración." San Juan, 1952.

Planning Board. *Municipio de San Lorenzo: Memoria Suplementaria al Mapa de Límites del Municipio y sus Barrios.* 22 (1955).

―――. *Municipio de Salinas: Memoria Suplementaria al Mapa de Límites del Municipio y sus Barrios.* 38 (1955).

―――. "Puerto Rican Migrants: A Socio-Economic Study." San Juan, 1972.

Planning, Urbanizing, and Zoning Board. "The Population Problem in Puerto Rico." By Frederic P. Bartlett and Brandon Howell. Santurce, Puerto Rico. August 1944.

United States

Commission on Civil Rights. *Puerto Ricans in the Continental United States: An Uncertain Future.* Report of the U.S. Commission on Civil Rights. October 1976.

Congress. House of Representatives. *Congressional Record: House of Representatives.* 1943–1948.

Congress. House Committee on Agriculture. *Farm Labor: Hearings before the Committee on Agriculture.* 80th Cong., 2nd sess., 11 June 1948.

Congress. House Committee on Education and Labor. *Investigation of Minimum Wages and Education in Puerto Rico and the Virgin Islands: Hearings before a Special Investigating Subcommittee on Education and Labor.* 81st Cong., 1st sess., November 1949.

Congress. Senate. *Congressional Record: Senate.* 1943–1948.

Department of Commerce, Bureau of the Census. *Sixteenth Census of the United States: 1940.* Special Reports, *Puerto Rico: Population.* Bulletin no. 2, Characteristics of the Population. Washington, D.C., 1943.

———. *Sixteenth Census of the United States: 1940 Population.* Vol. III, *The Labor Force,* Part 5, Pennsylvania–Wyoming. Washington, D.C., 1943.

———. *U.S. Census of Population: 1950.* Vol. II, *Characteristics of the Population,* Part 38, Pennsylvania. Washington, D.C., 1952.

———. *U.S. Census of Population: 1950.* Vol. II, *Characteristics of the Population,* Part 53, Puerto Rico. Washington, D.C., 1953.

———. *U.S. Census of Population: 1950.* Vol. III, *Census Tract Statistics,* Part 42, Philadelphia. Washington, D.C., 1952.

———. *U.S. Census of Manufactures: 1954.* Puerto Rico. Washington, D.C., 1956.

———. *U.S. Census of Agriculture: 1959.* Vol. I, *Municipalities,* Part 53, Puerto Rico. Washington, D.C., 1961.

———. *U.S. Census of Population: 1960.* Vol. I, *Characteristics of the Population,* Part 40, Pennsylvania. Washington, D.C., 1963.

———. *U.S. Census of Population: 1960.* Vol. I, *Characteristics of the Population,* Part 53, Puerto Rico. Washington, D.C., 1963.

———. *U.S. Census of Population and Housing: 1960. Census Tracts,* Philadelphia, Pa.–N.J. Washington, D.C., 1962.

———. *U.S. Census of Manufactures: 1963.* Puerto Rico. Washington, D.C., 1965.

———. *U.S. Census of Agriculture: 1969.* Vol. I, *Area Reports,* Part 52, Puerto Rico. Washington, D.C., 1972.

———. *Census of Population: 1970.* Vol. I, *Characteristics of the Population,* Part 40, Pennsylvania. Washington, D.C., 1973.

———. *Census of Population: 1970.* Vol. I, *Characteristics of the Population,* Part 53, Puerto Rico. Washington, D.C., 1973.

———. *Census of Population and Housing: 1970.* Vol. I, *Census Tracts,* no. 159, Philadelphia, Pa.–N.J. Washington, D.C., 1972.

———. *Census of Population: 1980.* Vol. I, *Characteristics of the Population,* Part 40, Pennsylvania. Washington, D.C., 1983.

———. *Census of Population: 1990. Social and Economic Characteristics,* Pennsylvania. Washington, D.C., 1993.

————. *Census of Population and Housing: 1990. Population and Housing Characteristics for Census Tracts and Block Numbering Areas*, Philadelphia, Pa.–N.J. PMSA. Washington, D.C., 1993.

Department of Labor, Bureau of Employment Security. *Employment Security Review* 19 (March 1952).

————. *Puerto Rican Farm Workers in Florida*, June 1953.

————. *Puerto Rican Farm Workers in the Middle Atlantic States*, November 1954.

Department of Labor, Employment Service, Farm Placement Service. *Handbook for Farm Placement Service*, 1950.

President's Commission on Migratory Labor. *Migratory Labor in American Agriculture: Report of the Presidents's Commission on Migratory Labor.* 26 March 1951.

Dissertations and Unpublished Papers

Aponte, Edwin David. "A Philadelphia Story: Oral History and Latino Protestantism." Paper presented at Oral History Association Annual Meeting, Philadelphia, Pa., 10–13 October 1996.

Antonsen, Peter. "A History of the Puerto Rican Community in Bethlehem, Pennsylvania, 1944–1993. Ph.D. diss., Lehigh University, Lehigh, Pa., 1994.

Ericksen, Eugene P., David Bartelt, Patrick Feeney, Gerald Foeman, Sherri Grasmuck, Maureen Martella, William Rickle, Robert Spencer, and David Webb. "The State of Puerto Rican Philadelphia." Unpublished paper, Philadelphia: Institute for Public Policy Studies, Temple University, 1985.

Gulick, Luther H. Jr. "Rural Occupance in Utuado and Jayuya Municipios Puerto Rico." Ph.D. diss., University of Chicago, 1952.

Kelley, Robin D. G. "'Check the Technique': Black Urban Culture and the Predicament of Social Science." W.E.B. Du Bois Distinguished Visiting Lecturer Series, City University of New York, 26 April 1994.

Koss, Joan D. "Puerto Ricans in Philadelphia: Migration and Accomodative Processes." Ph.D. diss., University of Pennsylvania, 1965.

Lapp, Michael. "Managing Migration: The Migration Division of Puerto Rico and Puerto Ricans in New York City, 1948–1968." Ph.D. diss., Johns Hopkins University, 1989.

Macisco, John Jr. "Internal Migration in Puerto Rico, 1955–1960." Ph.D. diss., Brown University, 1966.

Martínez Fernández, Luis. *San Lorenzo: Notas Para su Historia—El Comportamiento Electoral del Municipio Durante la Era de Dominación Popular, 1940–1968.* San Juan: El Comité Historia de los Pueblos, 1986.

Micheau, Cheryl. "Ethnic Identity and Ethnic Maintenance in the Puerto Rican Community of Philadelphia." Ph.D. diss., University of Pennsylvania, 1990.

Rodríguez Morales, Herminio R. *San Lorenzo: Notas para su Historia.* San Juan: El Comité Historia de los Pueblos, 1986.

Taller Puertorriqueño, Inc. *Batiendo la Olla ("Stirring the Pot"): A Cross-Generational Comparison and Self-Study by Second Generation Puerto Ricans in Philadelphia.* March 1979. Urban Archives, Temple University, Philadelphia, Pa.

Vázquez, Víctor. "Puerto Ricans and Other Spanish-speakers in Philadelphia: A Historical Perspective on the Development of a Community, 1910–1936." Paper presented at Puerto Rican Studies Association Third Annual Conference, New York, N.Y., 15–17 October 1998.

Vázquez Calzada, José. "La Población de Puerto Rico y su Trayectoria Histórica." Unpublished research paper, University of Puerto Rico, School of Public Health, July 1978.

Whalen, Carmen Teresa. "Puerto Rican Migration to Philadelphia, Pennsylvania, 1945–1970: A Historical Perspective on a Migrant Group." Ph.D. diss., Rutgers University, 1994.

Books and Articles

Adams, Carolyn Teich. "Philadelphia: The Private City in the Post-Industrial Era." In *Snowbelt Cities: Metropolitan Politics in the Northeast and Midwest since World War II*, ed. Richard M. Bernard, 209–226. Bloomington: Indiana University Press, 1990.

Adams, Carolyn, David Bartelt, David Elesh, Ira Goldstein, Nancy Kleniewski, and William Yancey. *Philadelphia: Neighborhoods, Division, and Conflict in a Postindustrial City.* Philadelphia: Temple University Press, 1991.

Almaguer, Tomás. "Ideological Distortions in Recent Chicano Historiography: The Internal Model and Chicano Historical Interpretation." *Aztlán* 18 (spring 1987): 7–28.

———. *Racial Fault Lines: The Historical Origins of White Supremacy in California.* Berkeley: University of California Press, 1994.

Amott, Teresa, and Julie Matthaei. *Race, Gender, and Work: A Multi-cultural Economic History of Women in the United States.* Boston: South End Press, 1996.

Augelli, John P. "San Lorenzo: A Case Study of Recent Migrations in Interior Puerto Rico." *American Journal of Economics and Sociology* 2 (January 1952): 155–160.

———. "Rural Settlement Types of Interior Puerto Rico: Sample Studies from the Upper Loíza Basin." In *Symposium on the Geography of Puerto Rico*, ed. Clarence F. Jones and Rafael Picó, 325–336. Río Piedras: University of Puerto Rico Press, 1955.

Ballard, Allen B. *One More Day's Journey: The Story of a Family and a People.* New York: McGraw Hill, 1984.

Barkan, Elliott R., ed. *A Nation of Peoples: A Sourcebook on America's Multicultural Heritage.* Westport, Conn.: Greenwood Press, 1999.

Bartelt, David W. "Housing the 'Underclass.'" In *The "Underclass" Debate: Views from History*, ed. Michael Katz, 118–157. Princeton, N.J.: Princeton University Press, 1993.

Bauman, John F. *Public Housing, Race, and Renewal: Urban Planning in Philadelphia, 1920–1974.* Philadelphia: Temple University Press, 1987.

Baver, Sherri L. *The Political Economy of Colonialism: The State and Industrialization in Puerto Rico.* Westport, Conn.: Praeger Publishers, 1993.

Beishlag, George. "Trends in Land Use in Southeastern Puerto Rico." In *Symposium on the Geography of Puerto Rico*, ed. Clarence F. Jones and Rafael Picó, 269–296. Río Piedras: University of Puerto Rico Press, 1955.

Beneria, Lourdes, and Gita Sen. "Accumulation, Reproduction, and Women's Role in Economic Development: Boserup Revisited." In *Women's Work: Development and the Division of Labor by Gender*, ed. Eleanor Leacock, Helen Safa, and contributors, 141–157. New York: Bergin and Garvey, 1986.

Benmayor, Rina, et al. "Stories to Live By: Continuity and Change in Three Generations of Puerto Rican Women." *Oral History Review* 16 (fall 1988): 1–46.

Berman Santana, Déborah. "Geographers, Colonialism, and Development Strategies: The Case of Puerto Rico." *Urban Geography* 17, no. 5 (1996): 456–474.

———. *Kicking Off the Bootstraps: Environment, Development, and Community Power in Puerto Rico.* Tucson: University of Arizona Press, 1996.

Berquist, James M. "The Concept of Nativism in Historical Study since Strangers in the Land." *American Jewish History* 76 (December 1986): 125–141.

Betancur, John J., and Douglas C. Gills, eds. *The Collaborative City: Opportunities and Struggles for Blacks and Latinos in U.S. Cities.* New York: Garland Publishing, 2000.

Binzen, Peter. *Whitetown, U.S.A.: A First-Hand Study of How the 'Silent Majority' Lives, Learns, Works, and Thinks.* New York: Random House, 1970.

Bodnar, John. *The Transplanted: A History of Immigrants in Urban America.* Bloomington: Indiana University Press, 1985.

Bonacich, Edna, and Lucie Cheng. "Introduction: A Theoretical Orientation to International Labor Migration." In *Labor Immigration under Capitalism: Asian Workers in the United States before World War II,* ed. Lucie Cheng and Edna Bonacich, 1–56. Berkeley: University of California Press, 1984.

Bonilla, Frank, and Ricardo Campos. "Industrialization and Migration: Some Effects on the Puerto Rican Working Class." Translated by Peter L.Crabtree. *Latin American Perspectives* 3 (summer 1976): 66–108.

———. "Wealth of Poor: Puerto Ricans in the New Economic Order." *Daedalus* 110 (spring 1981): 133–176.

Bose, Christine E., and Edna Acosta-Belén, eds. *Women in the Latin American Development Process.* Philadelphia: Temple University Press, 1995.

Brockmann, Vernon W. "Land Types and Land Utilization in the Caguas–San Lorenzo Region." In *Symposium on the Geography of Puerto Rico,* ed. Clarence F. Jones and Rafael Picó, 297–323. Río Piedras: University of Puerto Rico Press, 1955.

Cabán, Pedro. "Industrial Transformation and Labour Relations in Puerto Rico: From 'Operation Bootstrap' to the 1970s." *Journal of Latin American Studies* 21 (October 1989): 559–591.

Carrasco, Gilbert Paul. "Latinos in the United States: Invitation and Exile." In *Immigrants Out! The New Nativism and the Anti-Immigrant Impulse in the United States,* ed. Juan F. Pérez,190–204. New York: New York University Press, 1997.

Centro de Estudios Puertorriqueños. *Labor Migration under Capitalism: The Puerto Rican Experience.* New York: Monthly Review Press, 1979.

Chavez, Linda. *Out of the Barrio: Toward a New Politics of Hispanic Assimilation.* New York: Basic Books, 1991.

Cohen, Carole. "Facing Job Loss: Changing Relationships in a Multicultural Urban Factory." In *Newcomers in the Workplace: Immigrants and the Restructuring of the U.S. Economy,* ed. Louise Lamphere, Alex Stepick, and Guillermo Grenier, 231–250. Philadelphia: Temple University Press, 1994.

Colón-Warren, Alice. "The Impact of Job Losses on Puerto Rican Women in the Middle Atlantic Region, 1970–1980." In *Puerto Rican Women and Work: Bridges in Transnational Labor,* ed. Altagracia Ortiz, 105–138. Philadelphia: Temple University Press, 1996.

Cumbler, John T. *A Social History of Economic Decline: Business, Politics, and Work in Trenton.* New Brunswick, N.J.: Rutgers University Press, 1989.

Davis, Allen F., and Mark H. Haller, eds. *The Peoples of Philadelphia: A History of Ethnic Groups and Lower-Class Life, 1790–1940.* Philadelphia: Temple University Press, 1973.

Dietz, James L. *Economic History of Puerto Rico: Institutional Change and Capitalist Development.* Princeton, N.J.: Princeton University Press, 1986.

Estades, Rosa. "Symbolic Unity: The Puerto Rican Day Parade." In *Historical Perspectives on Puerto Rican Survival in the United States,* ed. Clara E. Rodríguez and Virginia Sánchez Korrol, 97–106. Princeton, N.J.: Markus Weiner Publishers, 1996.

Fernández-Kelly, M. Patricia, and Anna García. "Hispanic Women and Homework: Women in the Informal Economy of Miami and Los Angeles." In *Homework: Historical and Contemporary Perspectives on Paid Labor at Home,* ed. Eileen Boris and Cynthia R. Daniels, 165–182. Urbana: University of Illinois Press, 1989.

Fitzpatrick, Joseph P. *Puerto Rican Americans: The Meaning of Migration to the Mainland.* Englewood Cliffs, N.J.: Prentice-Hall, Inc., 1971.

Friedlander, Stanley L. *Labor Migration and Economic Growth: A Case Study of Puerto Rico.* Cambridge: MIT Press, 1965.

Gabaccia, Donna. "Immigrant Women: Nowhere at Home?" *Journal of American Ethnic History* (summer 1991): 61–87.

———. *From the Other Side: Women, Gender, and Immigrant Life in the U.S., 1820–1990.* Bloomington: Indiana University Press, 1994.

———. "Liberty, Coercion, and the Making of Immigration Historians." *Journal of American History* 84 (September 1997): 570–575.

Gamboa, Erasmo. *Mexican Labor and World War II: Braceros in the Pacific Northwest, 1942–1947.* Austin: University of Texas Press, 1990.

García, Juan Ramón. *Operation Wetback: The Mass Deportation of Mexican Undocumented Workers in 1954.* Westport, Conn.: Greenwood Press, 1980.

García Olivero, Carmen. *Study of the Initial Involvement in the Social Services by the Puerto Rican Migrants in Philadelphia.* New York: Vantage Press, 1971.

Glasser, Ruth. *My Music Is My Flag: Puerto Rican Musicians and Their New York Communities, 1917–1940.* Berkeley: University of California Press, 1995.

———. *Aquí Me Quedo: Puerto Ricans in Connecticut.* Middletown: Connecticut Humanities Council, 1997.

Glazer, Nathan, and Daniel Patrick Moynihan. *Beyond the Melting Pot: The Negroes, Puerto Ricans, Jews, Italians, and Irish of New York City.* Cambridge: MIT Press, 1963.

Glenn, Evelyn Nakano. "From Servitude to Service Work: Historical Continuities in the Racial Division of Paid Reproductive Work." In *Unequal Sisters: A Multicultural Reader in U.S. Women's History,* ed. Vicki L. Ruiz and Ellen Carol Dubois, 404–435. New York: Routledge, 1994.

González, Juan D. "The Turbulent Progress of Puerto Ricans in Philadelphia." *Centro de Estudios Puertorriqueños Bulletin* 2 (winter 1987–1988): 34–41.

Goode, Judith. "Polishing the Rustbelt: Immigrants Enter a Restructuring Philadelphia." In *Newcomers in the Workplace: Immigrants and the Restructuring of the U.S. Economy,* ed. Louise Lamphere, Alex Stepick, and Guillermo Grenier, 199–230. Philadelphia: Temple University Press, 1994.

Goode, Judith, and Jo Anne Schneider. *Reshaping Ethnic and Racial Relations in Philadelphia: Immigrants in a Divided City.* Philadelphia: Temple University Press, 1994.

Gregg, Robert. *Sparks from the Anvil of Oppression: Philadelphia's African Methodists and Southern Migrants, 1890–1940.* Philadelphia: Temple University Press, 1993.

Gregory, Peter. "The Labor Market in Puerto Rico." In *Labor Commitment and Social Change in Developing Areas,* ed. Wilbert E. Moore and Arnold S. Feldman, 136–172. New York: Social Science Research Council, 1960.

Griffith, David. "Peasants in Reserve: Temporary West Indian Labor in the U.S. Farm Labor Market." *International Migration Review* 20 (winter 1986): 875–898.

Griffith, David, and Ed Kissam. *Working Poor: Farmworkers in the United States.* Philadelphia: Temple University Press, 1995.

Guzmán, Pablo "Yoruba." "Puerto Rican Barrio Politics in the United States." In *Historical Perspectives on Puerto Rican Survival in the United States,* ed. Clara E. Rodríguez and Virginia Sánchez Korrol, 143–152. Princeton, N.J.: Markus Weiner Publishers, 1996.

Hahamovitch, Cindy. *The Fruits of Their Labor: Atlantic Coast Farmworkers and the Making of Migrant Poverty, 1870–1945.* Chapel Hill: University of North Carolina Press, 1997.

Haines, Pamela. "Clothing and Textiles: The Departure of an Industry." In *Community and Capital in Conflict: Plant Closings and Job Loss,* ed. John C. Raines, Lenora E. Berson, and David McI. Gracie, 211–219. Philadelphia: Temple University Press, 1982.

Handlin, Oscar. *The Uprooted: The Epic Story of the Great Migrations that Made the American People.* Boston: Little, Brown, and Co., 1951.

———. *The Newcomers: Negroes and Puerto Ricans in a Changing Metropolis.* Cambridge: Harvard University Press, 1959.

Henderson, Julia. "Foreign Labour in the United States during the War." *International Labor Review* (December 1945): 609–631.

Hernández Alvarez, José. *Return Migration to Puerto Rico.* Berkeley: University of California, 1967.

Hershberg, Theodore, Alan Burstein, Eugene Ericksen, Stephanie Greenberg, and William Yancey. "A Tale of Three Cities: Blacks, Immigrants, and Opportunity in Philadelphia, 1850–1880, 1930, 1970." In *Philadelphia: Work, Space, Family and Group Experience in the Nineteenth Century,* ed. Theodore Hershberg, 461–491. New York: Oxford University Press, 1981.

Hirsch, Arnold R. "Massive Resistance in the Urban North: Trumbull Park, Chicago, 1953–1966." *Journal of American History* 82, no. 2 (September 1995): 522–550.

Higham, John. *Strangers in the Land: Patterns of American Nativism, 1860–1925.* New Brunswick, N.J.: Rutgers University Press, 1955.

Hochner, Arthur, and Daniel Zibman. "Capital Flight and Job Loss: A Statistical Analysis." In *Community and Capital in Conflict: Plant Closings and Job Loss,* ed. John C. Raines, Lenora E. Berson, and David McI. Gracie, 198–210. Philadelphia: Temple University Press, 1982.

Jackson, Thomas F. "The State, the Movement, and the Urban Poor: The War on Poverty and Political Mobilization in the 1960s." In *The "Underclass" Debate: Views from History,* ed. Michael Katz, 403–439. Princeton, N.J.: Princeton University Press, 1993.

Jones, Jacqueline. *Labor of Love, Labor of Sorrow: Black Women, Work and the Family, from Slavery to the Present.* New York: Random House, 1985.

———. *The Dispossessed: America's Underclasses from the Civil War to the Present.* New York: Basic Books, 1992.

Katz, Michael. "The Urban 'Underclass' as a Metaphor of Social Transformation." In *The "Underclass" Debate: Views from History,* ed. Michael Katz, 3–26. Princeton, N.J.: Princeton University Press, 1993.

———. "Reframing the 'Underclass' Debate." In *The "Underclass" Debate: Views from History,* ed. Michael Katz, 440–478. Princeton, N.J.: Princeton University Press, 1993.

Katz, Michael B., and Thomas J. Sugrue, eds. *W.E.B. DuBois, Race, and the City: The Philadelphia Negro and Its Legacy.* Philadelphia: University of Pennsylvania Press, 1998.

Kelley, Robin D. G. *Yo' Mama's Disfunktional! Fighting the Culture Wars in Urban America.* Boston: Beacon Press, 1997.

Kessler-Harris, Alice. *Out to Work: A History of Wage-Earning Women in the United States.* New York: Oxford University Press, 1982.

Kunzel, Regina. "White Neurosis, Black Pathology: Constructing Out-of-Wedlock Pregnancy in the Wartime and Postwar United States." In *Not June Cleaver: Women and Gender in Postwar America, 1945–1960,* ed. Joanne Meyerowitz, 304–334. Philadelphia: Temple University Press, 1994.

Kusmer, Kenneth L. "African Americans in the City since World War II: From the Industrial to the Post-Industrial Era." *Journal of Urban History* 21 (May 1995): 458–504.

Lane, Roger. *William Dorsey's Philadelphia and Ours: On the Past and Future of the Black City in America.* New York: Oxford University Press, 1991.

Lapp, Michael. "The Migration Division of Puerto Rico and Puerto Ricans in New York City, 1948–1969." In *Immigration to New York,* ed. William Pencak, Selma Berrol, and Randall M. Miller, 198–214. Philadelphia: Balch Institute Press, 1991.

Larin, Don. "Domestic Recruitment—Our Basic Job." *Employment Security Review* 19 (March 1952): 3–5.

Lemann, Nicholas. "The Other Underclass." *Atlantic Monthly* (December 1991): 96–110.

———. *The Promised Land: The Great Black Migration and How It Changed America.* New York: Alfred A. Knopf, Inc., 1991.

Lemke-Santangelo, Gretchen. *Abiding Courage: African American Women and the East Bay Community.* Chapel Hill: University of North Carolina Press, 1996.

Lewis, Oscar. *La Vida: A Puerto Rican Family in the Culture of Poverty: San Juan and New York.* New York: Random House, 1965.

———. "The Culture of Poverty." In *Contemporary Cultures and Societies of Latin America,* ed. Dwight B. Heath, 469–479. New York: Random House, 1973.

Licht, Walter. *Getting Work: Philadelphia, 1840–1950.* Cambridge: Harvard University Press, 1992.

Lipsitz, George. *Rainbow at Midnight: Labor and Culture in the 1940s.* Urbana: University of Illinois Press, 1994.

MacDonald, John S., and Leatrice D. MacDonald. "Chain Migration, Ethnic Neighborhood Formation, and Social Networks." *Millbank Memorial Fund Quarterly* 42 (1964): 82–97.

Madden, Janice Fanning, and William J. Stull. *Work, Wages, and Poverty: Income Distribution in Post-Industrial Philadelphia.* Philadelphia: University of Pennsylvania Press, 1991.

Maldonado, A. W. *Teodoro Moscoso and Puerto Rico's Operation Bootstrap.* Gainesville: University of Florida Press, 1997.

Maldonado, Edwin. "Contract Labor and the Origins of Puerto Rican Communities in the United States." *International Migration Review* 13 (spring 1979): 103–121.

Manners, Robert A. "Tabara: Subcultures of a Tobacco and Mixed Crops Municipality." In *The People of Puerto Rico: A Study in Social Anthropology,* ed. Julian Steward, Robert Manners, Eric Wolf, Elena Padilla Seda, Sidney Mintz, and Raymond Scheele, 93–170. Urbana: University of Illinois Press, 1956.

Massey, Douglas S. "American Apartheid: Segregation and the Making of the Underclass." *American Journal of Sociology* 96 (September 1990): 329–357.

May, Elaine Tyler. *Homeward Bound: American Families in the Cold War Era.* New York: Basic Books, 1988.

Meléndez, Edwin, and Edgardo Meléndez, eds. *Colonial Dilemma: Critical Perspectives on Contemporary Puerto Rico*. Boston: South End Press, 1993.

Meyerowitz, Joanne. "Beyond the Feminine Mystique: A Reassessment of Postwar Mass Culture, 1946–1958." In *Not June Cleaver: Women and Gender in Postwar America, 1945–1960*, ed. Joanne Meyerowitz, 229–262. Philadelphia: Temple University Press, 1994.

Miller, Fredric M., Morris J. Vogel, and Allen F. Davis. *Still Philadelphia: A Photographic History, 1890–1940*. Philadelphia: Temple University Press, 1983.

———. *Philadelphia Stories: A Photographic History, 1920–1960*. Philadelphia: Temple University Press, 1988.

Milkman, Ruth. *Gender at Work: The Dynamic of Job Segregation by Sex During World War II*. Urbana: University of Illinois Press, 1987.

Mills, C. Wright, Clarence Senior, and Rose Kohn Goldsen. *The Puerto Rican Journey: New York's Newest Migrants*. New York: Harper and Row, 1950. Reprinted., New York: Russell and Russell, 1967.

Mintz, Sidney W. "Cañamelar: The Subculture of a Rural Sugar Plantation Proletariat." In *The People of Puerto Rico: A Study in Social Anthropology*, ed. Julian Steward, Robert Manners, Eric Wolf, Elena Padilla Seda, Sidney Mintz, and Raymond Scheele, 314–417. Urbana: University of Illinois Press, 1956.

———. *Worker in the Cane: A Puerto Rican Life History*. New York: W. W. Norton & Company, 1974.

Monk, Janice, and Charles Alexander. "Land Abandonment in Western Puerto Rico." *Caribbean Geography* 2 (1985): 2–15.

Monk, Janice, and the late Charles S. Alexander. "Migration, Development and the Gender Division of Labour: Puerto Rico and Margarita Island, Venezuela." In *Women and Change in the Caribbean*, ed. Janet H. Momsen, 167–178. Bloomington: Indiana University Press, 1993.

Montejano, David. *Anglos and Mexicans in the Making of Texas, 1836–1986*. Austin: University of Texas Press, 1987.

Moore, Joan, and Raquel Pinderhughes, eds. *In the Barrios: Latinos and the Underclass Debate*. New York: Russell Sage Foundation, 1993.

Morales, Julio. *Puerto Rican Poverty and Migration: We Just Had to Try Elsewhere*. New York: Praeger Publishers, 1986.

Morales, Rebecca, and Frank Bonilla, eds. *Latinos in a Changing U.S. Economy: Comparative Perspectives on Growing Inequality*. Newbury Park, Calif.: Sage Publications, 1993.

Muller, Peter O., Kenneth C. Meyer, and Roman A. Cybriwsky. *Metropolitan Philadelphia: A Study of Conflicts and Social Cleavages*. Cambridge: Ballinger Publishing Company, 1976.

Mullings, Leith. "Images, Ideology, and Women of Color." In *Women of Color in U.S. Society*, ed. Maxine Baca Zinn and Bonnie Thornton Dill, 265–290. Philadelphia: Temple University Press, 1994.

Nightingale, Carl Husemoller. "The Global Inner City: Toward a Historical Analysis." In *W.E.B. DuBois, Race, and the City: The Philadelphia Negro and Its Legacy*, ed. Michael B. Katz and Thomas J. Sugrue, 217–258. Philadelphia: University of Pennsylvania Press, 1998.

Oberman, Joseph, and Stephen Kozakowski. *History of Development in the Delaware Valley Region*. Philadelphia: Delaware Valley Regional Planning Commission, September 1976.

Oboler, Suzanne. *Ethnic Labels, Latino Lives: Identity and the Politics of (Re)Presentation in the United States*. Minneapolis: University of Minnesota Press, 1995.

Omi, Michael, and Howard Winant. *Racial Formation in the United States: From the 1960s to the 1990s*. New York: Routledge, 1994.

Ortiz, Altagracia. "Puerto Ricans in the Garment Industry of New York City, 1920–1960." In *Labor Divided: Race and Ethnicity in United States Labor Struggles, 1835–1960,* ed. Robert Asher and Charles Stephenson, 105–125. Albany: State University of New York Press, 1990.

———. *"'En la aguja y el pedal eché la hiel':* Puerto Rican Women in the Garment Industry of New York City, 1920–1980." In *Puerto Rican Women and Work: Bridges of Transnational Labor,* ed. Altagracia Ortiz, 55–81. Philadelphia: Temple University Press, 1996.

Padilla, Félix. *Puerto Rican Chicago.* Notre Dame, Ind.: University of Notre Dame Press, 1987.

Padilla Seda, Elena. "Nocorá: The Subculture of Workers on a Government-Owned Sugar Plantation." In *The People of Puerto Rico: A Study in Social Anthropology,* ed. Julian Steward, Robert Manners, Eric Wolf, Elena Padilla Seda, Sidney Mintz, and Raymond Scheele. Urbana: University of Illinois Press, 1956.

Pagán de Colón, Petro América. "Farm Labor Program in Puerto Rico." *Employment Security Review* 19 (March 1952): 23–27.

Pantojas-García, Emilio. *Development Strategies as Ideology: Puerto Rico's Export-Led Industrialization Experience.* Boulder, Colo.: Lynne Rienner Publishers, 1990.

———. "Puerto Rican Populism Revisited: The PPD during the 1940s." *Journal of Latin American Studies* 21 (October 1989): 521–557.

Pascoe, Peggy. "Miscegenation Law, Court Cases, and Ideologies of 'Race' in Twentieth-Century America." *Journal of American History* 83 (June 1996): 44–69.

Peck, Gunther. "Reinventing Free Labor: Immigrant Padrones and Contract Laborers in North America, 1885–1925." *Journal of American History* 83 (December 1996): 848–871.

Perea, Juan F., ed. *Immigrants Out! The New Nativism and the Anti-Immigrant Impulse in the United States.* New York: New York University Press, 1997.

Perloff, Harvey S. *Puerto Rico's Economic Future: A Study in Planned Development.* Chicago: University of Chicago Press, 1950.

Piore, Michael J. *Birds of Passage: Migrant Labor and Industrial Societies.* Cambridge: Cambridge University Press, 1979.

Picó, Rafael. *The Geography of Puerto Rico.* Chicago: Aldine Publishing Company, 1974.

Portes, Alejandro. "From South of the Border: Hispanic Minorities in the United States." In *Immigration Reconsidered: History, Sociology, and Politics: History, Sociology, and Politics,* ed. Virginia Yans-McLaughlin, 160–181. New York: Oxford University Press, 1990.

Portes, Alejandro, and Cynthia Truelove. "Making Sense of Diversity: Recent Research in Hispanic Minorities in the United States." *Annual Review of Sociology* 13 (1987): 359–385.

Ramírez de Arellano, Annette B., and Conrad Seipp. *Colonialism, Catholicism, and Contraception: A History of Birth Control in Puerto Rico.* Chapel Hill: University of North Carolina Press, 1983.

Reimers, David M. *Still the Golden Door: The Third World Comes to America.* New York: Columbia University Press, 1992.

Reynolds, Lloyd G., and Peter Gregory. *Wages, Productivity and Industrialization in Puerto Rico.* Homewood, Ill.: Richard D. Irwin, Inc., 1965.

Ríos, Palmira. "Export-Oriented Industrialization and the Demand for Female Labor: Puerto Rican Women in the Manufacturing Sector, 1952–1980." In *Colonial Dilemma: Critical Perspectives on Contemporary Puerto Rico,* ed. Edwin Meléndez and Edgardo Meléndez, 89–101. Boston: South End Press, 1993.

Rivera-Batiz, Francisco L., and Carlos E. Santiago. *Island Paradox: Puerto Rico in the 1990s.* New York: Russell Sage Foundation, 1996.

Rodríguez, Clara. "Economic Survival in New York City." In *Historical Perspectives on Puerto Rican Survival in the United States,* ed. Clara E. Rodríguez and Virginia Sánchez Korrol, 37–54. Princeton, N.J.: Markus Weiner Publishers, 1996.

———. Puerto Ricans: Born in the U.S.A. *Boulder, Colo.: Westview Press, 1991.*

Rodríguez-Morazzani, Roberto P. "Puerto Rican Political Generations in New York: Pioneros, Young Turks and Radicals." *Centro de Estudios Puertorriqueños Bulletin* 4 (winter 1991–1992): 96–116.

Ross, David. *The Long Uphill Path: A Historical Study of Puerto Rico's Program of Economic Development.* San Juan: Editorial Edil, Inc., 1969.

Ruiz, Vicki. "By the Day or the Week: Mexicana Domestic Workers in El Paso." In *Women on the U.S. Mexico Border: Responses to Change,* ed. Vicki L. Ruiz and Susan Tiano, 61–76. Boston: Allen and Unwin, 1987.

Safa, Helen I. "Runaway Shops and Female Employment: The Search for Cheap Labor." In *Women's Work: Development and the Division of Labor by Gender,* ed. Eleanor Leacock, Helen I. Safa, and contributors, 58–71. New York: Bergin and Garvey Publishers, 1986.

Sánchez Korrol, Virginia. *From Colonia to Community: The History of Puerto Ricans in New York City, 1917–1948.* Berkeley: University of California Press, 1994.

Santana Cooney, Rosemary, and Alice Colón. "Work and Family: The Recent Struggle of Puerto Rican Females." In *Historical Perspectives on Puerto Rican Survival in the United States,* ed. Clara E. Rodríguez and Virginia Sánchez Korrol, 69–86. Princeton, N.J.: Markus Weiner Publishers, 1996.

Saragoza, Alex M. "Recent Chicano Historiography: An Interpretive Essay." *Aztlán* 19 (spring 1988–90): 1–77.

Sassen-Koob, Saskia. "Changing Composition and Labor Market Location of Hispanic Immigrants in New York City, 1960–1980." In *Hispanics in the U.S. Economy,* ed. George J. Borjas and Marta Tienda, 299–322. Orlando, Fla.: Academic Press, Inc., 1985.

Scranton, Philip, and Walter Licht. *Work Sights: Industrial Philadelphia, 1890–1950.* Philadelphia: Temple University Press, 1986.

Senior, Clarence. *Puerto Rican Emigration.* Río Piedras: Social Science Research Center, University of Puerto Rico, 1947.

———. "Migration and Puerto Rico's Population Problem." *The Annals of the American Academy of Political and Social Science* 285 (January 1953): 130–136.

———. "Patterns of Puerto Rican Dispersion in the Continental United States." *Social Problems* (October 1954): 93–99.

———. "Puerto Rico: Migration to the Mainland." *Monthly Labor Review* 78 (December 1955): 1354–1358.

Smith, Neil. *The New Urban Frontier: Gentrification and the Revanchist City.* New York: Routledge, 1996.

Steward, Julian H., Robert A. Manners, Eric R. Wolf, Elena Padilla Seda, Sidney W. Mintz, and Raymond L. Scheele. "Comparative Analysis of Regional Subcultures." In *The People of Puerto Rico: A Study in Social Anthropology,* ed. Julian Steward, Robert Manners, Eric Wolf, Elena Padilla Seda, Sidney Mintz, and Raymond Scheele, 465–488. Urbana: University of Illinois Press, 1956.

———. "Introduction." In *The People of Puerto Rico: A Study in Social Anthropology,* ed. Julian Steward, Robert Manners, Eric Wolf, Elena Padilla Seda, Sidney Mintz, and Raymond Scheele, 1–27. Urbana: University of Illinois Press, 1956.

Stinson Fernández, John H. "Hacia una antropología de la emigración planificada: El Negociado de Empleo y Migración y el caso de Filadelfia." *Revista de Ciencias Sociales* 1 (June 1996): 112–155.

Sugrue, Thomas J. "Crabgrass-Roots Politics: Race, Rights, and the Reaction against Liberalism in the Urban North, 1940–1964." *Journal of American History* 82 (September 1995): 551-578.

———. *The Origins of the Urban Crisis: Race and Inequality in Postwar Detroit*. Princeton, N.J.: Princeton University Press, 1996.

Thistlethwaite, Frank. "Migration from Europe Overseas in the Nineteenth and Twentieth Centuries." In *Population Movements in Modern European History*, ed. Herbert Moller, 73–92. New York: Macmillan, 1964.

Toro-Morn, Maura I. "Gender, Class, Family, and Migration: Puerto Rican Women in Chicago." *Gender and Society* 9 (December 1995): 712–726.

Torres, Andrés. *Between Melting Pot and Mosaic: African Americans and Puerto Ricans in the New York Political Economy*. Philadelphia: Temple University Press, 1995.

Torruellas, Rosa M., Rina Benmayor, and Ana Juarbe. "Negotiating Gender, Work, and Welfare: *Familia* as Productive Labor among Puerto Rican Women in New York City." In *Puerto Rican Women and Work: Bridges in Transnational Labor*, ed. Altagracia Ortiz, 184–208. Philadelphia: Temple University Press, 1996.

Trotter, Joe William Jr. " Black Migration in Historical Perspective: A Review of the Literature." In *The Great Migration in Historical Perspective: New Dimensions of Race, Class and Gender*, ed. Joe William Trotter Jr., 1–21. Bloomington: Indiana University Press, 1991.

Valdés, Dennis. *Al Norte: Agricultural Workers in the Great Lakes Region, 1917–1970*. Austin: University of Texas Press, 1990.

Vázquez Calzada, José. "Demographic Aspects of Migration." In *Labor Migration under Capitalism: The Puerto Rican Experience*, ed. Centro de Estudios Puertorriqueños, 223-238. New York: Monthly Review Press, 1979.

Vecoli, Rudolf. "Contadini in Chicago: A Critique of The Uprooted." *Journal of American History* 51 (December 1964): 404–417

Wagenheim, Kal. *A Survey of Puerto Ricans on the U.S. Mainland in the 1970s*. New York: Praeger Publishers, 1975.

Warner, Sam Bass Jr. *The Private City: Philadelphia in Three Periods of Its Growth*. Philadelphia: University of Pennsylvania Press, 1968.

Weisskoff, Richard. *Factories and Food Stamps: The Puerto Rico Model of Development*. Baltimore: The John Hopkins University Press, 1985.

Whalen, Carmen Teresa. "Labor Migrants or 'Submissive Wives': Competing Narratives of Puerto Rican Women in the Post–World War II Era." In *Puerto Rican Women's History: New Perspectives*, ed. Félix V. Matos Rodríguez and Linda Delgado, 206–226. Armonk, N.Y.: M. E. Sharpe, 1998.

———. "Bridging Homeland and Barrio Politics: The Young Lords in Philadelphia." In *The Puerto Rican Movement: Voices from the Diaspora*, ed. Andrés Torres and José Velázquez, 107–123. Philadelphia: Temple University Press, 1998.

———. "Puerto Ricans." In *A Nation of Peoples: A Sourcebook on America's Multicultural Heritage*, ed. Elliott R. Barkan, 446–463. Westport, Conn.: Greenwood Press, 1999.

———. "Displaced Labor Migrants or the 'Underclass': African Americans and Puerto Ricans in Philadelphia's Economy." In *The Collaborative City: Opportunities and Challenges for Blacks and Latinos in U.S. Cities*, ed. John J. Betancur and Douglas C. Gills. New York: Garland Publishers, 2000.

Wolf, Eric. "San José: Subcultures of a 'Traditional' Coffee Municipality." In *The People of Puerto Rico: A Study in Social Anthropology*, ed. Julian Steward, Robert Manners, Eric Wolf, Elena Padilla Seda, Sidney Mintz, and Raymond Scheele, 171–264. Urbana: University of Illinois Press, 1956.

Yans-McLaughlin, Virginia. *Family and Community: Italian Immigrants in Buffalo, 1880–1930*. Urbana: University of Illinois Press, 1982.

———. "Introduction." In *Immigration Reconsidered: History, Sociology, and Politics,* ed. Virginia Yans-McLaughlin. New York: Oxford University Press, 1990: 3–20.

Young Lords Party and Michael Abramson. *Palante: Young Lords Party*. New York: McGraw-Hill Book Company, 1971.

Zolberg, Artistide R. "Reforming the Back Door: The Immigration Reform and Control Act of 1986 in Historical Perspective." In *Immigration Reconsidered: History, Sociology, and Politics*, ed. Virginia Yans-McLaughlin, 315–339. New York: Oxford University Press, 1990.

Index

Spanish words appear in italic and are indexed where first introduced and defined. Page numbers in italic refer to photographs.

citizenship: access to social services and, 194; employment options and, 244; impact on labor recruitment, 50–52, 62–68; of migrant workers, 69; status of migrants, 210–11, 212–13; Puerto Rican patriotism and, 67; status of Puerto Ricans, 10; U.S. migration policy concerns, 66

coffee industry, 19–20, 37, 39; decline of, 40–41, 109; phases of, 20. *See also* farmworkers in Puerto Rico

Colón, Rafaela, 232, 233, 237, 238

colonial people, 245, 246

colonial relationship, 10, 11, 243, 246; contract labor and, 49; migrants' status and, 211–13; political activism and, 238; political status of Puerto Rico and, 39, 212; global economy and ties to, 39; Jones Act (1917), 10, 24, 28. *See also* Commonwealth of Puerto Rico; U.S. Occupation (1898)

colonos, 27

Commission on Civil Rights, United States, 6

Commission on Human Relations, Philadelphia, 188, 193, 194–95, 198

Commonwealth of Puerto Rico, 10, 208, 210–11. *See also* U.S. Occupation (1898)

community: definitions of, 243

community activism, women's, 214

community building in Philadelphia, 208–18

community organizations, 215, 236; ASPIRA, 231–32, 235; Casa del Carmen, 233–34, 215; Concilio de Organizaciones Hispanas, 208, 216–18, 235, 236; and education, 232; Friends Neighborhood Guild, 78, 151, 201–2, 203–4, 207, 209–10; International Institute, 194, 196–97, 198, 201, 209; Latin American Legion Post 840, 210, 211; Norris Square Senior Citizen's Center, 151, 182, 236; Taller Puertorriqueño, 236–37, 251–52; Young Women's Christian Association (YWCA), 57, 58, 62, 194, 197–98. *See also* churches; community organizing

community organizing: electoral politics, 237–38; Puerto Rican Alliance, 237; Puerto Rican Day Parade (1964), 216–17; Puerto Rican Socialist Party, 237; Young Lords, *180, 181,* 231–37. *See also* community organizations

Concilio de Organizaciones Hispanas, 208, 216–18, 235, 236

Confederación General de Trajadores (CGT), 116

contract labor: between indentured servitude and free labor, 244; colonial relationships and, 49; division of labor by gender, 49, 58, 65; division of labor by race, 63; during World War II, 50–55; as economic strategy, 50, 70–80, 156;

farm labor, 56, 153; from Salinas and San Lorenzo, 124, 125; lack of benefits, 66; as population control, 55–56, 58–59, 65; permanent settlement in Philadelphia, 76; and racism, 62; recruitment of, 53–54; and seasonal agricultural workers, 63; and sexism, 62. *See also* domestic workers; farm labor program; farmworkers in Puerto Rico; farmworkers in the United States

cuerdas, 1, 254 n. 1

"cultural deficiencies," 203

"culture of poverty," 6, 15, 198–204, 213, 238; African Americans and, 245; alternative analysis of, 8, 243; compared to "underclass," 240; gender dimensions of, 200, 245; impact on immigration histories, 8; population control and, 199; Puerto Rican Studies' challenge to, 7; as racial ideology, 8; transcending rural/urban differences, 18; and welfare policies, 199

declining employment, 97–102, 113, 114, 115, 218; displaced workers, 218–27; farmworkers, 220; in Philadelphia, 138–39, 142–43, 159; in Salinas, 122; in San Lorenzo, 97–102; of women, 142. *See also* displaced workers

deindustrialization, 218–20, 244; differential impact on Puerto Ricans, 223; and economic displacement, 10; state policies' impact on, 219. *See also* economic change; economic restructuring

discrimination: based on language, 195, 213; by gender in contract labor, 62; and employment decline, 228–29; and housing, 191–92; strategies to counter, 230–33. *See also* division of labor by gender and race; racism; sexism

displaced workers: immigrant, 220; migrant, 218–27; postwar, 142; women as, 142. *See also* declining employment

division of labor by gender, 17, 82, 122, 155, 224; contract labor, 49, 58, 65; displaced women workers and, 142; factory work, 114; Fomento and, 113–15; garment industry, 146–48, 151–52, 153, 160; home needlework industries, 110; labor force participation, 99–100; manufacturing, 115; men's occupations in Philadelphia, 163–65; in Philadelphia, 137, 144, 222, 223; in Salinas, 110, 116, 144, 155; in San Lorenzo, 99–100; service industries, 163; sugar industry, 110; women's occupations in Philadelphia, 151–52. *See also* women's reproductive work

division of labor by race, 143; contract labor, 62; in postwar Philadelphia, 143, 222; service industries, 163